The Iran Primer

The Iran Primer

POWER, POLITICS, AND U.S. POLICY

Robin Wright, editor

UNITED STATES INSTITUTE OF PEACE PRESS
WASHINGTON, D.C.

PUBLISHED IN COLLABORATION WITH

**Woodrow Wilson
International Center
for Scholars**

United States Institute of Peace

1200 17th Street NW

Washington, DC 20036-3011

www.usip.org

First published 2010.

To request permission to photocopy or reprint materials for course use, contact the Copyright Clearance Center at www.copyright.com. For print, electronic media, and all other subsidiary rights, e-mail: permissions@usip.org

Printed in the United States of America

The paper used in this publication meets the minimum requirements of American National Standards for Information Science—Permanence of Paper for Printed Library Materials, ANSI Z39.48-1984.

Library of Congress Cataloging-in-Publication Data

The Iran primer : power, politics, and U.S. policy / Robin Wright, editor.
   p. cm.
ISBN 978-1-60127-084-9 (alk. paper)
1. Iran–Politics and government–1997– 2. Iran–Foreign relations–Middle East.
3. Middle East–Foreign relations–Iran. 4. United States–Foreign relations–Iran.
5. Iran–Foreign relations–United States. I. Wright, Robin B., 1948–

JQ1785.I75 2010
320.955--dc22
                          2010040584

Contents

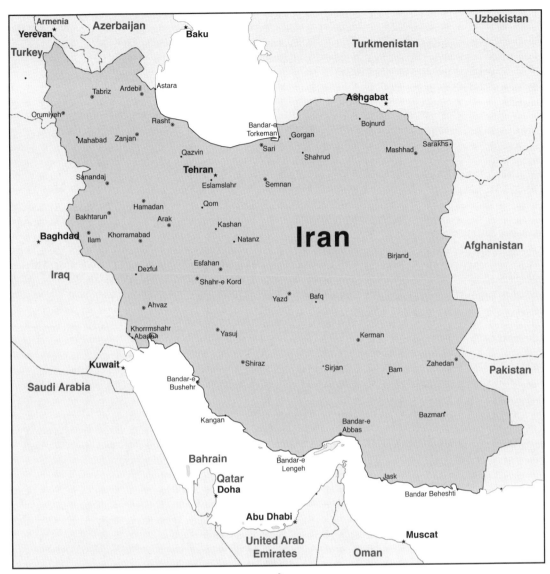

Iran (2010 population: 74.5 million)

Ethnic divisions

Persian – 51 percent
Azeri – 24 percent
Gilaki and Mazandarani – 8 percent
Kurd – 7 percent
Arab – 3 percent
Lur – 2 percent
Baloch – 2 percent
Turkmen – 2 percent
Other – 1 percent

Religious divisions[1]

Muslims – 98 percent
Shiite – 89 percent
Sunni – 9 percent
Other significant minorities—based
  on varying estimates:
Baha'i – 300,000 to 350,000
Jews – 20,000 to 30,000
Christians (mainly Assyrian and
  Armenian churches) – 300,000
Zoroastrians – 35,000 to 60,000

Land borders

Afghanistan – 585 miles
Armenia – 22 miles
Azerbaijan – Naxcivan exclave –
  112 miles
Azerbaijan – 270 miles
Iraq – 911 miles
Pakistan – 568 miles
Turkmenistan – 620 miles
Turkey – 312 miles

Bordering bodies of water

Caspian Sea – 462 miles
Persian Gulf and Gulf of Oman –
  1,525 miles

---

1. According to U.S. State Department's "International Religious Freedom Report 2006."

Editor's Note

Robin Wright

This book is truly the combined effort of 50 seasoned experts on Iran as well as a handful of rising young talent. Each of the authors volunteered time and expertise in a joint effort to provide hard information, thoughtful analysis and historic context about one of the world's most intriguing countries.

The timing is deliberate. Iran has always been an important geo-strategic country. Since its 1979 revolution, the Islamic Republic has been an ever-increasing challenge for the West to understand and to engage. But Tehran's controversial nuclear program, disputed 2009 election, growing violations of basic human rights, and angry rhetoric have generated deeper hostilities with the outside world than at any time since the revolution's early days. The stakes—and consequences—are greater than ever.

This collection explores 50 different aspects of Iranian politics, the economy, the military, the nuclear program and foreign relations. It chronicles U.S.-Iran relations under six American presidents. And it probes the West's five options in dealing with Iran in the future.

The project's goal was to be widely inclusive of the broad range of talent from many think tanks and universities around the world. This volume has no political agenda and no single political perspective. It draws on experts with a wide range of views. It also includes as many Iranian voices as Western authors to ensure the book is sensitive to both sides of the issues.

Many people made this project possible. At the United States Institute of Peace, Board Chairman J. Robinson West and President Richard Solomon were enthusiastic supporters of the concept from the outset. They were also extremely generous in providing the resources to publish this book. At the Woodrow Wilson International Center for Scholars, President Lee Hamilton and Executive Vice President Mike van Dusen eagerly agreed to co-sponsor it.

Two women facilitated this project in so many ways. USIP Executive Vice President Tara Sonenshine's endless energy and enthusiasm made it possible to turn this book around in just three months. And Haleh Esfandiari, director of the WWC Middle East Program, was a font of sage counsel and expertise who checked every chapter. Both mentored this project from the outset.

The United States Institute of Peace managed to break records in getting this book out. The project was conceived in July and put to bed in September—with one editor and two (supposedly) part-time assistants who ended up working around the clock. Rachel Brandenburg deserves enormous credit. She is an extraordinary talent with infinite patience and good cheer who managed 54 writers from around the world, coordinated with production, double-checked editing, and worked late into many nights. Semira Nikou was an outstanding assistant who slaved long hours over Iranian history to assemble four detailed chronologies on Iranian politics, nuclear program, foreign relations and the military history since the 1979 revolution.

Chantal De Jonge Oudraat and Shira Lowinger of the USIP Randolph Jennings Fellowships provided support and constant encouragement. The USIP production team also crashed to get this book out quickly. All credit goes to Valerie Norville, Marie Marr Jackson, Kay Hechler and Christian Feuerstein. Last but far from least, Richard von Zimmer produced this gorgeous cover.

Robin Wright
Washington, D.C.
September 2010

1

The Challenge of Iran

Robin Wright

Iran, proud and passionate, has been a conundrum since its 1979 revolution. It stunned the world by introducing Islam as a form of modern governance, in turn altering the balance of power across the Middle East. It rattled the region by exporting its zealous ideology and siring or sponsoring militant allies elsewhere. And it unnerved both East and West by defiantly challenging international norms and charting its own course. All three factors complicated dealing with the Islamic Republic. But Iran looms even larger today. The confluence of challenges—defiance over its nuclear program, rising repression, support for extremists, and menacing rhetoric—has created a sense of impending crisis both at home and abroad.

Political volatility at home was reflected in six months of tumultuous protests after the disputed 2009 presidential election. For millions of Iranians in many cities, the issue quickly escalated from alleged voter fraud to condemnation of the regime, its leadership and even the Islamic system. The regime, briefly, appeared on a precipice. Tehran eventually restored control. But its tactics indicated the regime's insecurity. It had to militarize to survive.

Tensions with the international community have been reflected in a series of U.N. sanctions since 2006 over Iran's refusal to convince the world it was not building a bomb. In the end, even Russia, which built Iran's first nuclear reactor, voted for a series of punitive sanctions. So did China, which has become Iran's most important big-power trading partner.

Iran now represents a far more complex challenge than other hotspots—Afghanistan, Iraq and North Korea—for several reasons:

- Its revolution was one of the three transformative events in the Middle East in the 20th century. Iran's actions will be pivotal to global events in the early 21st century because of its resources, ideology, weaponry, allies and location.

- Strategically, Iran's frontiers and coastline have for millennia been central to political, military and commercial developments. Today, it spans three of the world's most volatile regions and its most vital shipping lanes for oil. Iran has the potential to help stabilize or destabilize all four.

- Politically, Iran has been the most dynamic and controversial experiment in blending Islam and democracy—and the experiment is far from over. It continues to play out in the domestic political crisis. The outcome could affect the wider Islamic world as profoundly as the revolution.

- Militarily, Iran has the largest armed forces in the Middle East and, with the exception of Israel, Egypt and increasingly Saudi Arabia, the largest arsenal, although much of its weaponry is of low quality, aging or obsolete. It has also armed militant allies from Lebanon to Afghanistan.

- Economically, Iran is one of the world's largest and most valuable properties, rich with oil and natural gas. Its assets in turn give it leverage and political leeway globally.

The revolution

The Islamic Republic still has to prove the long-term viability of its zealous ideology and hybrid political system, the issues at the heart of its domestic crisis. Yet Iran's 1979 revolution was clearly one of the three most innovative revolutions of the Modern Age. Like two other upheavals, it introduced a new ideology and redefined the world's political spectrum.

In toppling the Bourbon monarchy, the French revolution introduced equality and civil liberty as the basis of modern democracy. The Russian revolution overthrew the Romanov dynasty in the name of classless egalitarianism, the foundation of communism. By ousting the last in a string of dynasties dating back more than 2,000 years, the Iranian revolution sought to demonstrate that Islam was an effective idiom of political expression, opposition and governance.

For the Middle East, the revolution was one of the three most important turning points of the 20th century. The collapse of the five-century-old Ottoman Empire after World War I and Israel's creation in 1948 were the other two. In many ways, Iran was a logical place for sweeping political innovation because of its own rich history, religious tenets, two earlier attempts at reform, and struggle to end foreign influence.

Historically, Iran has more independent political experience than virtually any other modern Muslim state. Most were created or gained independence from European colonial powers only in the 20th century. But Iran had a long, if somewhat varied, history of sovereignty. Persia also had long exposure to ideas from the outside world, as a crossroads between East and West and a target of invading armies from ancient Greece to contemporary Britain. And with more than five millennia of civilization, Iranians have a sense of historic importance and a role in shaping the world.

Political Islam

Shiite Islam was also a logical force for change. In Sunni Islam, clerics are advisers; a believer's relationship with God is direct. In Shiite Islam, the clergy is empowered to interpret God's word for the faithful. Their fatwas have absolute authority in telling a believer what is right or wrong, what to do or not do. Shiite clerics also have a leadership hierarchy. And central to the original schism, Shiite Islam demands that the faithful fight against injustice, even if it means certain death. In tapping into strong Shiite traditions, revolutionary leader Ayatollah Ruhollah Khomeini became the most credible authority to mobilize disparate Iranian factions against the last shah.

Islam also provided a framework for an alternative to the monarchy. The new Islamic Republic was the first grand experiment in blending Islam and democracy. Iran's 1979 constitution borrowed heavily from French and Belgian law. It called for separation of powers between the three branches of government. It stipulated that the president and legislature, as well as provincial and local councils, should be popularly elected by men and women, originally as young as 15. It imposed a two-term limit on the presidency. And it continued the monarchy's practice of allocating seats in parliament for Christians, Jews and Zoroastrians—at least token acknowledgement of individual or minority rights.

But the constitution then added a provision that all laws must be compatible with Islamic law, or Sharia. It also established a set of parallel Islamic institutions that mirrored each of the republican branches of government—and often had more power. And on top of it all, the constitution imposed a supreme leader, who had absolute powers. The supreme leader became the equivalent of an infallible political pope.

Revolution within Shiism

The Islamic republic also represented a revolution within Shiism. More than any branch of Islam, Shiites historically were wary of political power. They viewed the state as imperfect, corruptible and a source of persecution. They deliberately distanced themselves from politics. After Iran's revolution, however, they became the political power, changing the role of the clerics as well a central tenet of the "quietist" Shiite faith. Tehran's Shiite theocracy is the only time Muslim clerics have ever ruled a state.

Iran has in turn put Shiism—Islam's so-called second sect, making up between 10 percent and 12 percent of the world's 1.3 billion Muslims—on the political map. In its first three decades, the Islamic Republic fostered a network of Shiite allies in neighboring states stretching from Lebanon to Afghanistan. Sunni governments began to fear the so-called Shiite crescent, anchored by Iran, that stretched west across Iraq, into Syria and Lebanon, and south through Shiite minorities in the oil-rich sheikhdoms.

Political phases

Iran's revolution has passed through at least four phases:

Phase one: The first phase was the Khomeini decade from 1979 until the ayatollah's death in 1989. It was a tumultuous period of revolutionary extremes that included killing off supporters of the *ancien regime,* taking foreigners hostage, and fostering its zealotry across the Islamic world. The turmoil was exacerbated by an eight-year war with Iraq that proved to be the Middle East's bloodiest modern conflict. It produced more than one million casualties.

Phase two: The second phase coincided with the two terms of President Akbar Hashemi Rafsanjani, from 1989 until 1997. The revolution's early passions were replaced by a hard-earned pragmatism, produced in part by excesses that backfired against the clerics and exhausted the population. Under Rafsanjani, arrogance gave way to a conservative realism. The government of God increasingly ceded to secular statecraft.

Phase three: The third phase between 1997 and 2005 coincided with the reformist era of President Mohammad Khatami, a dark horse former cabinet minister who tapped into the groundswell of interest in political openings. The government soon improved relations with its own people as well as the outside world. Iran had, temporarily, a freer press, freer speech, wider debate, relaxed social restrictions and a burgeoning civil society. But parliament failed to legislate reforms. And by the end of Khatami's two terms, a political schism had developed between the regime headed by the supreme leader and the government headed by the president.

Phase four: The fourth phase began in 2005 with the upset election of the little-known mayor of Tehran, Mahmoud Ahmadinejad, over Rafsanjani. The emergence of hardliners reflected three broader shifts: Disillusionment with politics led many, especially young Iranians and women, to boycott the poll. Public anger swelled against the clergy, especially Rafsanjani, for corruption and failing to improve the average Iranian's life in a quarter century. And a second generation of revolutionaries hardened by the Iran-Iraq War, largely laymen, began to challenge the clerics who ended the monarchy.

Domestic crisis

Through each phase, Iranian politics increasingly splintered. In the early 1980s, Iran was a virtual one-party state. The Islamic Republic Party dominated all branches of government. But the infighting quickly became so serious that Khomeini publicly rebuked its officials, "Stop biting one another like scorpions." The divisions became a chasm; the party was dissolved in 1987.

Three decades later, Iran had more than 200 parties, factions and political groups—many of them still squabbling. A common political axiom in Tehran joked: "Where there are five Iranian Shiites, there are six political factions."

The depth of the divide among the original revolutionaries was witnessed after the 2009 presidential election. Mir Hossein Mousavi, the prime minister who led Iran throughout the Iran-Iraq War, charged the regime with massive fraud in his loss to Ahmadinejad. He also warned that it was turning into a dictatorship—the dictator being Supreme Leader Ayatollah Ali Khamenei, who as president had been his colleague in running the government during the 1980s.

The post-election protests were the biggest threat to the regime since the revolution. Beyond the immediate election issue, they reflected the degree of public daring, the diversity of political thought, and the growing unease about the system, even among those inside it. And the internal turmoil did not end with the regime's crackdown. The splintering continued, as conservatives began to turn on Ahmadinejad's core of hardliners for abuse of power.

People power

The more dynamic part of the domestic crisis, however, was the spontaneous display of people power. Since the mid-1990s, the Iranian public—rather than any specific politician—had spurred the movement for political change. It was always an amorphous, leaderless body in search of a head that tapped into the limited number of candidate choices allowed to run after vetting by the Guardian Council. The embryonic reform movement first put Mohammad Khatami into the presidency in 1997 and then turned to Mousavi in 2009. Both men were adopted by the movement; neither was the original inspiration for reform.

The demonstrations were in some ways a logical next step in a longstanding debate over Iran's political system. After the shah's ouster, the revolutionaries were divided between ideologues and realists on the shape of a new government. Ideologues argued that the first modern theocracy should be a "redeemer state" championing the cause of the world's oppressed; restoring Islamic purity and rule in the 57-nation Islamic world; and creating a new Islamic bloc to defy both East and West. Realists argued that Iran should seek legitimacy by creating a capable Islamic state and institutionalizing the revolution. They, too, wanted a new political and social order independent of the outside world, but they also wanted to be realistic about Iran's need to interact economically and diplomatically with the world.

For 30 years, the bottom line issue had been variations on the same theme: whether to give priority to the revolution or to the state. Put another way: whether the Islamic Republic is first and foremost Islamic or a republic. The same theme had played out in the 2009 election. Ahmadinejad championed the revolutionary clerics' original vision of helping the oppressed, while Mousavi campaigned on the need for a viable and practical state. The same issues were also central to the post-election turmoil. Mousavi warned that the alleged vote-rigging was killing the idea that Islam and republicanism were compatible.

In 2009, the public became immersed in the debate too—first by turning out to vote and then in protesting alleged fraud. The newly named Green Movement also launched the most imaginative civil disobedience campaign in the Islamic world. It included a commercial boycott of goods advertised on state-controlled television. It featured anti-regime slogans and caricatures printed on the national currency—from a green V to signify the Green Movement's election victory to a stamped picture of Ahmadinejad with the caption "people's enemy." And it painted imaginative graffiti—usually in green—on public walls, the back of buses, bridge underpasses, university buildings and fences.

The public political energy was admired among reformers in other Muslim countries, including Sunni societies that had disdained the revolution or distanced themselves from Shiite Iran. Despite the government crackdown, the sheer magnitude of participation assured that the debate started shortly after the revolution was still far from over.

Fear of foreigners

Historically, many of Iran's most tumultuous times have been caused by foreign invasions, meddling or influence. From the Persian prism, the showdown with the outside world in the 21st century is only the latest round. Long experience has bred deep suspicion and xenophobia.

Ancient Persia was pivotal to Alexander the Great's drive into India in the 4th century B.C. Its conquest by Arab armies in the 7th century gave the then new Islamic Empire access to central and eastern Asia. Persia was invaded by Turks in the 11th, 16th and 18th centuries. It was conquered by Genghis Khan's Mongol army in the 13th century and by Tamerlane in the 14th century. The Safavid dynasty actually converted to Shiism in the 16th century—some 900 years after Shiism's birth in Islam's great schism—to create a separate identity and prevent the encroachment of Sunnis in the neighboring Ottoman Empire. Persia was then challenged by the Afghans in the 18th century.

In the 20th century, Iran was occupied by Britain and the Soviet Union. The Persian Corridor was also the most viable supply route for U.S. Lend Lease aid to the Soviet Union during World War II. Some 40,000 American soldiers were deployed in Iran to keep the train link open. After the war, Iran was the first crisis of the new United Nations when the Soviets refused to leave. In 1946, the U.N. Security Council passed a resolution calling on Moscow to pull-out its forces from northern Iran. President Harry Truman's ultimatum to Joseph Stalin on Iran spawned a new U.S.-Iran friendship that steadily deepened until the revolution. But the subsequent Cold War arguably also had its origins in this confrontation.

Rejecting encroachment

The fight against foreign influence has also been central to the Iranian campaign for empowerment over the past century. The 1905-1911 Constitutional Revolution erupted after the monarchy doled out political and economic concessions to Britain and Russia. The backlash sparked prolonged instability and forced the Qajar dynasty in 1906 to accept demands for a constitution and parliament, both of which limited the king's powers. Iran had only the second constitution and parliament in Asia, after the Ottoman Empire. The first round of political reforms ended when an army colonel seized power in 1925, crowned himself Persia's new king, took the name Pahlavi, changed the country's name to Iran, and launched rapid modernization. He was forced to abdicate for pro-Nazi sentiments in 1941.

In 1953, Iran went through a second burst of democratic activism. An elected government led by Prime Minister Mohammad Mossadegh challenged the second and last Pahlavi shah, who was also heavily influenced by foreign powers. Mossadegh's four-party coalition advocated constitutional democracy and limited powers for the monarchy. It also wanted to nationalize Iranian oil after the Anglo-Iranian Oil Company refused a 50-50 profit-sharing deal. The shah's attempt to have Mossadegh dismissed backfired; the backlash forced the monarch to flee to Rome. Foreign powers restored the monarchy. The CIA and British intelligence orchestrated riots that forced Mossadegh to resign and allowed the young king to return to the Peacock Throne for another quarter century.

In many ways, the 1979 revolution was an extension of the two earlier challenges. In the 21st century, the struggle against foreign influence still defines Iran's current stand-off with the world. When the outside world today calls for cooperation, many Iranians see it as an attempt to co-opt or coerce them into conformity—to Western ways, morals and influence.

U.S. relations

Since the revolution, Iran's showdown with the world has pivoted most of all on the United States. The shah's ouster transformed a country that for three decades had been one of two pillars —along with Israel—of U.S. policy in the Middle East. After the United States took in the ailing shah, Tehran began to view Washington as the ultimate enemy. The revolutionaries suspected another CIA plot to put the monarch back on the throne.

Defying international law, Iranian students responded by seizing the U.S. Embassy in a drama that dragged out for 444 days. The ordeal of 52 American hostages was largely responsible for ending the presidency of Jimmy Carter after one term. In the mid-1980s, Iran's double-dealing during the covert arms-for-hostage swap—in which Iran helped free three American hostages in Lebanon, only to have three more picked up— was the biggest scandal for the Reagan administration. Iran has been a consistent thorn for all six American presidents who tried to figure out how to deal with Tehran.

The two sides shouted at each other. In 1979, Iran dubbed the United States the "Great Satan." In 2002, the Bush administration called Iran part of an "axis of evil." Both countries occasionally tried outreach, although they were never on the same page at the same time. Their counterparts often suspected that the other would not or could not deliver; opportunities to at least explore rapprochement were missed. The most significant effort by Iran was President Khatami's call to bring down "the wall of mistrust." But it went largely unheeded in Washington until it was too late to salvage the effort.

American presidents also singled out Iran for mention in important speeches. In his 1989 inaugural address, President George H.W. Bush offered "new engagement" to the world, but made a special offer to Iran. "There are today Americans who are held against their will in foreign lands, and Americans who are unaccounted for. Assistance can be shown here, and will be long remembered. Good will begets good will. Good faith can be a spiral that endlessly moves on."

After the announcement of his 2009 Nobel Peace Prize, President Obama said it had to be "shared with every-one who strives for justice and dignity — for the young woman who marches silently in the streets on behalf of her right to be heard even in the face of beatings and bullets." He did not name her, but Iranians knew he was referring to Neda Agha Soltan, the aspiring 26-year-old musician who was shot on a Tehran street during the 2009 election protests. The cell phone video capturing her bloodied death was transmitted around the world.

By the end of 2010, tensions between Washington and Tehran had reached new heights because of suspicions about Iran's long-term nuclear intentions, support for Iraqi and Afghan militias targeting U.S. troops, Ahmadinejad's denial of the Holocaust and Israel's right to exist, and human rights abuses.

Nationalism

Tehran's policies and world perspective today are also rooted in a past rich with accomplishments. Iranians are notoriously proud, as is their right. Persia produced some of history's greatest scientists, physicians, astronomers, mathematicians, philosophers, architects, artists and poets. Iranians believe their contributions are not over—if only the outside world will give them a chance.

Zoroaster founded the first monotheistic religion, which introduced the ideas of good and evil and a day of judgment even before Judaism. Avicenna, or Ibn Sina, was an 11th century philosopher and physician whose medical texts were taught in Europe until the 17th century. A crater on the moon is named after him. In the 11th century, Omar Khayyam was one of the world's leading mathematicians and astronomers as well as a poet famed for more than 1,000 quatrain verses. Rumi, a 13th century philosopher, is the world's most popular poet in the 21st century. Hafez, Saadi, and Ferdowsi were other great medieval poets whose works are still admired today. The list goes on and on.

Iran's intellectual culture has been evident even in the current political infighting. Some of the most modern and democratic ideas in the Islamic world today have emerged among Iranian philosophers, reformers and dissidents. Iranian philosopher Abdulkarim Soroush was the intellectual father of the reform movement. A former revolutionary, he turned on the regime. In the mid-1990s, he began to challenge the theological justification for a supreme leader and called for separation of mosque and state. He also declared that freedom always had precedence over religion, because Muslims could only be true believers if they embraced the faith with their own free will.

Given their past, Iranians see only greatness in their future; they view their current status as only a blip on the screen of history. The quest for nuclear energy, which dates back to the shah, is viewed as a key to modern development. For many ordinary Iranians, the right to enrich uranium to fuel nuclear reactors is first and foremost an issue of sovereignty. As they modernize, they want to avoid any further dependence on the outside world. To understand Iranian nationalism, think of a proud, chauvinistic Texan—then add 5,000 years.

Strategic value

The outside world has always valued Iran because of its location. Today, no nation can afford to ignore Iran, regardless of who is in power, for several reasons:

- It holds some 10 percent of the world's oil reserves. Iran is OPEC's second largest oil producer. It also has the world's second largest reserves of natural gas.

- Iran's vast resources provide enormous leverage in an oil-hungry world. Since World War II, petroleum has been essential to the movement of modern armies and for development of modern industry. Free access to oil has also been essential to both political and economic power.

- Iran's geo-strategic location bridges the world's most volatile blocs of countries—the Middle East to the west, the Asian subcontinent to the east, and the Caucuses and Central Asia to the north. Peaceful relations with Iran are pivotal to the stability of more than one dozen countries.

- Iran's position and the traditions of its Aryan people, the Indo-European race whence Iran gets its name, have long made Iran the crossroads of culture and geography.

- Iran's population is now among the world's top twenty. In the first decade after the revolution, it almost doubled from 34 to 62 million when the clerics called on Iranian women to breed an Islamic generation.

Neighborhood geography

Iran stands apart geographically because of two great mountain ranges, the Alborz and the Zagros, and three great bodies of water, the Capsian Sea, the Persian Gulf and the Indian Ocean. In terms of territory,

- Iran is roughly one-fifth the size of the United States.
- It ranks 18th among the world's nations in geographic mass.
- Neighboring Afghanistan, by comparison, is 41st.
- Neighboring Iraq is 58th.
- Iran is more than twice as large and twice as populated as both countries.

Iran's nine other frontiers are important for more than trade and transit.

Iraq: To the West, Iran's 910-mile border with Iraq is an entry point into the Arab world's Fertile Crescent.

Turkey: To the northwest, Iran shares a 312-mile border with Turkey, a vital member of NATO.

Afghanistan: To the east, Iran shares a 585-mile border with Afghanistan; the two countries share one of the world's most active routes for trafficking narcotics.

Pakistan: To the southeast is the 570-mile border with Pakistan. The father of Pakistan's nuclear bomb provided pivotal equipment to Tehran.

Gulf states: Iran's frontier along the Persian Gulf, through which more than 40 percent of the West's oil passes daily, is the longest of the six countries that rim the strategic waterway. Iran effectively controls the Strait of Hormuz, the so-called chokepoint for Gulf oil exports.

Turkmenistan: To the north, Iran has a 620-mile border with the former Soviet republic, the most autocratic of the Central Asian nations.

Azerbaijan: To the north, Iran shares a 270-mile border with Azerbaijan. About one quarter of Iran's population is ethnic Azeri.

Armenia: To the north, Iran's smallest frontier is the 22-mile border with Armenia. Armenians are among the Christian minorities represented by specially allocated seats for Christians in Iran's parliament.

Azerbaijan-Nakhchivan exclave: To the north, Iran shares a 112-mile border.

Ethnically, Iran is also a geographic crossroad mirroring most of its neighbors. Only 51 percent of Iranians are pure Persians. The rest are Azeris in the northwest and Turkoman in the northeast. Kurds live along the western border with Iraq. Baluchis (or "wanderers") straddle the arid and unruly southeast border with Pakistan. Arabs live on the southern coast. The Lors, an Arab-Persian mix, live mainly in the mountains, while nomadic herding tribes live in the south.

The future

- In the 21st century, Iran's unique version of God's government must prove its viability on earth—and that it can deliver what its people want—or risk the same fate as other utopian ideologies.

- No Islamic country is likely to replicate the Iranian experience. The costs are too high, the results too controversial. The Shiite character of the revolution also makes it unlikely to be repeated among Sunni-dominated societies.

- Yet Iran's Shiite alliance remains a major power bloc capable of heavily influencing the outcome of elections and conflicts—and sparking tensions with Sunni communities.

- Iran's resources create a huge cushion against punitive actions such as economic sanctions. In an oil-hungry world, they also undermine international cooperation.

- Iran's labyrinthine political system—and competing sources of power—complicate all forms of diplomacy. Engagement, especially with the United States, has become a domestic political issue—unrelated to the merits of rapprochement.

Robin Wright, who has visited Iran regularly since 1973, is a joint fellow at the U.S. Institute of Peace and the Woodrow Wilson International Center for Scholars.

Iran's Politics

2

The Supreme Leader

Karim Sadjadpour

- Ayatollah Ali Khamenei is Iran's most powerful official. As supreme leader, he has constitutional authority or substantial influence over the executive, legislative and judicial branches of government as well as the military and media.
- Khamenei lacks the religious credentials and popular support of his predecessor, revolutionary leader Ayatollah Ruhollah Khomeini. As a result, Khamenei has been more insecure and vulnerable to criticism from religious and political circles.
- Khamenei had tried to cultivate the image of a magnanimous guide above the political fray. But his support of President Mahmoud Ahmadinejad in the disputed 2009 elections—amid mass protests and unprecedented political fissures—further undermined his legitimacy and support.
- Khamenei is primarily interested in protecting his power and ensuring the survival of the Islamic theocracy, which he believes is based on justice, independence, self-sufficiency and piety.
- Khamenei's foreign policy is driven by animosity to the United States and Israel. It is unclear whether he could abandon this position without undermining the raison d'etre of the Islamic system.

Overview

There are few leaders in the world more important to current world affairs but less understood than Ayatollah Khamenei, the supreme leader of Iran. He is the single most powerful individual in a highly factionalized, autocratic regime. No major decisions can be taken without his consent, and his top priorities are his own survival and that of the Islamic Republic.

In theory, Iran's constitution was meant to combine theocracy with republicanism. But in practice, Iran's unelected institutions, namely the supreme leader and 12-man Guardian Council, wield far more power than elected institutions like the presidency and parliament. The Guardian Council has the authority to vet all candidates for public office and disqualify any who are not deemed sufficiently loyal to the supreme leader.

Khamenei lacks the popular support, charisma and theological qualifications that Khomeini enjoyed, but his ability to stay out of the limelight contributed to his political resilience—until recently. He has consistently favored conservatives over reformers. His image as the great balancer has been seriously challenged by the disputed 2009 elections, his staunch defense of Ahmadinejad, and the crackdown on protesters.

Khamenei's rise

Khamenei was born in 1939 to a traditional family of humble origins. His father was a cleric, and he began a religious education at a young age. In his early twenties, he studied under Ayatollah Khomeini in Qom; through Khomeini he became involved in the rebellion against the shah. He was arrested numerous times in the 1960s and 1970s, spending several years in prison where he was tortured by the Savak secret police.

After the shah's ouster, Khamenei briefly served as minister of defense and then supervisor of the Revolutionary Guards. In 1981, he survived an assassination attempt that paralyzed his right arm. Later that year, after one president was impeached and a second assassinated, Khamenei was asked by the revolutionary elites to run for president. He served the maximum two terms, from 1981 to 1989. His tenure was dominated by the

Iran-Iraq War, but he played a secondary political role behind Prime Minister Mir Hossein Mousavi, Speaker of the Parliament Akbar Hashemi Rafsanjani, and Revolutionary Guard Commander Mohsen Rezai.

Ayatollah Khomeini died in 1989 just months after firing his heir apparent, leaving no designated replacement. With the help of Rafsanjani, Khamenei emerged as the default choice to become the new supreme leader. His appointment was opposed by some senior clerics who felt he was unqualified, but the Assembly of Experts eventually approved him. Today, his likeness—black turban, oversized glasses, Palestinian *kaffiyeh*, and untrimmed gray beard—is ubiquitous in shops and government offices and on billboards.

The leader's powers

Revolutionary leader Ayatollah Khomeini introduced the concept of *velayat-e faqih,* or guardianship of the jurist. It is derived from Shiite Islam, which believes twelve imams descended from the Prophet Mohammed who inherited his political and religious authority. The twelfth imam went into occultation or hiding in the 9th century, and Twelver Shiites believe he will one day return as a messiah. In the absence of the twelfth imam, Khomeini argued, the missing imam's authority on earth could be exercised by a supreme leader chosen from among the clergy.

As supreme leader, Khamenei has constitutional authority over the judiciary, the regular armed forces and the elite Revolutionary Guards, and the state-controlled media. He also has effective control over Iran's second most powerful institution, the 12-member Guardian Council, which has the authority to vet electoral candidates and veto parliamentary decisions. (Khamenei appoints half its members, as well as the judicial chief who appoints the other half.) The Iranian economy is largely state-controlled, and Khamenei has the most authority over how the country's oil revenue is spent. He also has control over the country's bonyads—charitable foundations with billions of dollars in assets—in addition to the millions more his office receives in charitable donations offered to Iran's holy shrines.

Despite his constitutional powers, Khamenei has often been overshadowed by Iran's presidents. From 1989 to 1997, foreign governments and the international media perceived parliamentary speaker Rafsanjani, not Khamenei, as Iran's most powerful official. From 1997 to 2005, President Mohammad Khatami upstaged Khamenei from the left with his calls for reform at home and a "dialogue of civilizations" with the West. Since 2005, Ahmadinejad has outflanked him from the right with his diatribes against Israel and Holocaust revisionism. Yet Khamenei's views have ultimately prevailed: His domestic vision for Iran is more Islamic than republican. And his foreign policy position is neither outright confrontation nor accommodation.

Several factors have also helped Khamenei gradually consolidate power: He created a vast network of "clerical commissars" in major public institutions who are empowered to intervene in state matters to enforce his authority. Parliament is currently a weak body dominated by conservatives. The Revolutionary Guards, whose leaders he appoints, are increasingly important to both politics and the economy. His most powerful peers, such as Rafsanjani, have at least temporarily been sidelined.

Revolutionary values

For Khamenei, the 1979 revolution was about ridding Iran of two evils—the shah and the United States—and creating a theocratic government imbued with four core values: justice, independence, self-sufficiency and Islamic piety. These revolutionary ideals continue to dominate Khamenei's political discourse, and he interweaves them seamlessly: Islam embodies justice. Independence requires self-sufficiency. And foreign powers are hostile to an independent, Islamic Iran.

Khamenei's vision for a just Islamic society translates as a form of religious socialism. Western governments fail, he argues, because the whims of capitalism and self-interest deny justice to millions. He has championed privatization efforts, yet state subsidies for basic food items and other essentials remain Iran's chief method of providing economic development and social justice.

Four foreign policy themes

The United States: For Khamenei, the Islamic Republic's top four foreign policy priorities include resistance against the United States and Israel, which he sees as two sides of the same coin. Khamenei believes that Washington aspires to go back to the patron-client relationship with Iran that existed during the Pahlavi monarchy. His primary concern is not a U.S. military invasion, but rather a political and cultural campaign to undermine theocratic rule through a "soft" or "velvet" revolution.

The peace process: The Israeli-Palestinian conflict has little impact on the daily lives of Iranians, but Khamenei's contempt for Israel has been remarkably consistent. He has argued that "if Iran stops its support of the Lebanese and Palestinian people [i.e. Hezbollah and Hamas], the United States will also change its hostile attitude toward the Islamic Republic. [But] we consider supporting the Palestinian and Lebanese people one of our major Islamic duties." Arguably, the only way that Khamenei would accept a less strident position toward Israel is when and if the Palestinians themselves accept a peace treaty with Israel.

Nuclear program: For Khamenei, the nuclear program has come to embody the revolution's core themes: the struggle for independence, the injustice of foreign powers, the necessity of self-sufficiency, and Islam's high esteem for the sciences. He wants to ensure that Iran is scientifically and technologically advanced enough to be self-sufficient, self-sufficient enough to be economically independent, and economically independent enough to be politically independent.

Islamic world: Khamenei envisions Iran as the vanguard of the Islamic world. On his official website, he is referred to as the "Supreme Leader of Muslims." Given Iran's political, cultural and religious influence, he believes none of the critical issues facing the Middle East and Muslim world—Iraq, Afghanistan, Lebanon, Persian Gulf security and the Arab-Israeli conflict—can be fully addressed or resolved without Tehran's input.

Challenges

Khamenei has always been notoriously thin-skinned. Until the 2009 election, public criticism of the supreme leader was one of the few red lines in Iranian politics. It is still a virtual guarantee of a prison sentence. His own family is not above reproach. For years, his younger brother, reformist cleric and former Member of Parliament Hadi Khamenei, has criticized the excessive powers of the supreme leader in newspaper columns and lectures at universities and seminaries—at a price. He has been beaten by vigilantes and disqualified from running again for office.

Khamenei's legitimacy was among the many casualties of the tainted 2009 presidential election. Taboos were shattered when hundreds of thousands of Iranians defied his sermon supporting the outcome and calling for calm; they instead took to the streets of cities throughout Iran chanting "death to the dictator" and "death to Khamenei." Among Iran's pious classes, images of government-sanctioned brutality against civilians further undermined his image as a just spiritual leader. Since then, once-respectful subordinates such as Khatami and Mousavi have openly defied him. His chief rival, Rafsanjani, publicly humiliated as a corrupt traitor by Ahmadinejad, waits in the wings for an opportunity to pounce.

Before the presidential elections, Khamenei appeared to have a lifelong lock on the job of supreme leader. But his fate became far less certain after six months of sporadic turmoil. To regain control, he has grown increasingly reliant on Iran's vast intelligence networks, security forces and military. His future rests most of all in the hands of the Revolutionary Guards. With their apparently strong support, Khamenei has refused to cede any political ground since the election, on the grounds that compromise projects weakness and invites further challenges.

Engagement possibilities

The Obama administration has tried harder than any previous administration to engage Iran, and Khamenei in particular. In his first year, President Obama sent two private letters to Khamenei outlining Washington's genuine interesting in overcoming past mistrust and rebuilding relations with Tehran. After the election, Obama also resisted calls to support Tehran's opposition, even as Washington became increasingly critical of Iran's human rights violations.

In response, Khamenei mocked Obama's mantra of change as merely a tactical shift. He said Washington must first change its actions—by lifting sanctions, unfreezing Iranian assets, diluting support for Israel and ceasing criticism of Iran—to show its seriousness. Behind closed doors, however, senior Iranian politicians have conceded that Obama's overtures unsettled Khamenei and put pressure on him to justify Tehran's continued animosity toward the United States.

The future

- Prospects for reconciliation with the United States are low while Khamenei remains in power. At the same time, any engagement policy Iran that aims to ignore or bypass Khamenei is equally unlikely to succeed.

- In both the domestic and international context, Khamenei is averse to compromise under pressure, fearful of projecting weakness and inviting greater pressure.

- Khamenei worries about opposition to his rule among top clerics in Qom, but opposition within the Revolutionary Guards would be far more dangerous for him.

- Khamenei has not appointed an heir apparent and there are no obvious successors, should he die or be removed from power. The supreme leader could be replaced with a *shura* (consultative) council, although the selection of a council could face many problems.

Karim Sadjadpour is an associate at the Carnegie Endowment for International Peace and the author of "Reading Khamenei: The Worldview of Iran's Most Powerful Leader."

3

The Six Presidents

Shaul Bakhash

- Iran's constitution vests ultimate authority in the supreme leader, but the presidency has developed into a powerful office.
- The last three presidents have each stamped his own personality and politics on social and economic life, domestic politics and foreign policy.
- Powerful presidents have also aroused powerful opposition. Presidential administrations have been characterized by factionalism between the president's party and his opponents. They have also been driven by tension over authority between the president and the supreme leader.
- The presidency of Mahmoud Ahmadinejad seems a departure from the past. He is building up a power base among the same constituencies in the military, judiciary and security agencies that are the supreme leader's base of support. This trend, if sustained, has important future implications.

Overview

The Islamic Republic's initial constitution provided for a president with limited powers and a prime minister as head of the cabinet and government. The first president, Abolhassan Bani-Sadr, sought control of the government apparatus. But he faced fierce opposition from the clerical party, even as he dealt with revolutionary turmoil, the American hostage crisis and the Iran-Iraq War. He was impeached during his second year in office. Under Ayatollah Ali Khamenei, the president took a back seat to the prime minister.

Constitutional amendments in 1989 abolished the prime minister's post, creating a presidential system. The three presidents that followed each put his own distinct mark on the country. Akbar Hashemi Rafsanjani moved foreign, economic and social policy in a more pragmatic direction. But in his second term, he lost the initiative to the supreme leader and conservatives. Mohammad Khatami launched a period of unprecedented political liberalization. But he was similarly thwarted by opposition from the hardliners and the leader's office.

Mahmoud Ahmadinejad came to office as a populist and built up a base of support in the security and military services, independent of the supreme leader. A key issue is whether the emergence of the Revolutionary Guards during the Ahmadinejad presidency as powerful political actors will be a passing phenomenon or a permanent feature of the Islamic Republic.

Abolhassan Bani-Sadr (1980–1981)

Abolhassan Bani-Sadr was one of the anti-shah exiles who returned to Iran on the eve of the monarchy's ouster. He was elected the first president of the Islamic Republic and took office in January 1980. He owed his electoral success to close ties to revolutionary leader Ayatollah Ruhollah Khomeini, visibility gained from books and essays on Islamic government and economics, and a prominent role as the architect of the sweeping nationalizations of private industries, banks and insurance companies that immediately followed the revolution.

His presidency was marked by an intense rivalry over policy and power between his camp and the clerical group around Khomeini, led by Ayatollah Mohammad Beheshti and the Islamic Republic Party (IRP). The IRP-dominated Majles, or parliament, frustrated Bani-Sadr's agenda and pushed its own program. The government was paralyzed for months in a stand-off over cabinet appointments between the president and new prime minister, Mohammad Raja'i, a Beheshti protégé. Bani-Sadr wanted to dismantle or at least curb the unruly revolutionary committees and revolutionary courts. The clerical party supported these institutions.

The rivalry was further fueled by the 444-day American hostage crisis and the Iran-Iraq War. Bani-Sadr sought the release of the American diplomats seized when the U.S. Embassy was over-run by militant students in November 1979. His clerical rivals used the embassy seizure to deepen the radical temper of the revolution. In the war with Iraq, Bani-Sadr championed the regular army and conventional military strategy. The clerics championed the Revolutionary Guards and "revolutionary" defense.

Bani-Sadr initially enjoyed strong support from Khomeini, who endorsed the president's call for a return to normalcy and an end to revolutionary turmoil. He allowed Bani-Sadr to name the national broadcasting chief and assume his authority as commander-in-chief. But when Khomeini's attempts to mediate between the president and his IRP rivals failed, he sided with the clerical camp and allowed Bani-Sadr's impeachment. In mid-1981, the Majles voted 177-1 (with 33 absent or abstaining) to oust him. Bani-Sadr, in hiding, escaped into exile.

Raja'i and Khamenei (1981–1989)

Mohammad Ali Raja'i succeeded Bani-Sadr in a hastily-organized and barely-contested election in July 1981. He took the oath of office on August 2, but he was assassinated on August 30. He was succeeded by Ali Khamenei in another largely uncontested ballot held in October. Khamenei's selection reversed an informal Khomeini dictum that clerics should not assume the presidency. One of the founders of the IRP, Khamenei had served briefly as supervisor of the Revolutionary Guards and also as minister of defense.

Khamenei served two four-year terms as president, but was over-shadowed by Prime Minister Mir Hossein Mousavi who steered the country through the difficult years of the Iran-Iraq War. Khomeini even publicly and sharply reprimanded Khamenei in January 1988, when the president dared to suggest that the constitution placed limits on the authority of the state and parliament in the economic sphere.

Khamenei's presidency was marked by the brutal suppression of the radical opposition parties between 1981 and 1983, when thousands of young men and women were jailed and killed, often in the streets; by the marginalization of the centrist opposition parties; and by the murder in prison of over 2,000 members of the radical left-wing groups at the end of the Iran-Iraq War.

In other spheres, Khamenei was indentified with the "moderate," rather than the radical wing of clerics in Khomeini's inner circle. He supported Rafsanjani's controversial proposals to allow more scope for the private sector in the economy. After Khomeini's death in 1989, Khamenei was selected as his successor, with the expectation that he would be a relatively pliant supreme leader.

Akbar Hashemi Rafsanjani (1989–1997)

Rafsanjani was inaugurated in July 1989, at a watershed moment. Khomeini had died in June and his lieutenants were now in charge. The Iran-Iraq War was over, permitting Tehran to begin the post-war reconstruction. After Khomeini's death, the constitution was amended to eliminate the post of prime minister and vest his powers in the president. In the post-Khomeini period, Rafsanjani was the dominant figure in the two-man team of president and supreme leader that ran the Islamic Republic.

Rafsanjani attempted to move the country in a more pragmatic direction by ending Iran's isolation. He launched economic liberalization, opening the state-dominated economy to domestic and foreign private sector investment. He placed technocrats in key posts. And he mollified women, the young and the middle class by easing social and cultural (but not political) controls.

He quietly resumed diplomatic relations with Saudi Arabia, Morocco and Egypt. He in effect sided with the U.S.-led coalition to oust Iraq from Kuwait. And he helped win freedom for American hostages held by Lebanese allies.

He ushered in a controversial five-year development plan that envisaged foreign borrowing and greater private sector involvement. The government reduced exchange rates from seven to three, eased import and foreign currency restrictions, lifted price controls, and reduced state-subsidized goods from 17 to five. Hundreds of state-owned enterprises were slated for privatization.

The easing of social and cultural controls was evident in many spheres. Women could appear in public in brightly-colored scarves and show a bit of hair, nail-polish and lipstick. Young men and women could openly socialize on walks along the foothills of Tehran. The government tolerated a brisk underground trade in video-cassettes of Hollywood films. Previously banned satellite dishes allowed Iranians to tune in to CNN and "Baywatch." Art galleries reopened.

Minister of Culture Mohammad Khatami adopted more liberal policies on film, theater, art, books and journals, such as *Zanan*, which addressed women's issues. In literary and intellectual journals, such as *Kiyan* and *Goftegu*, a guarded but lively debate took place on civil society, the relationship between religion and democracy, and the balance between state authority and individual freedoms. The film industry flourished; Iranians won several international prizes.

Political restrictions remained, however. Several opposition leaders in exile were assassinated by Iranian agents. In 1994-1995, a number of intellectuals in Iran were found mysteriously dead on the streets or died in police custody. Rafsanjani never publicly condemned these killings. The political press remained closely controlled. Even centrist opposition parties, such as the Iran Liberation Front, were barely tolerated. The radical wing of clerics was excluded from 1990 elections for the Assembly of Experts, a body that chooses the supreme leader, and from 1992 parliamentary elections. But with the right-wing dominant, cultural liberalization ran into trouble. A conservative parliament purged Culture Minister Khatami in 1992, and Rafsanjani's brother as the head of state radio and television two years later.

Supreme leader Khamenei, gradually amassing power, campaigned against a Western "cultural onslaught." Officially-sanctioned zealots attacked bookstores, cinemas and lectures by philosopher Abdolkarim Soroush, who argued for a tolerant, pluralistic Islam open to change and free of clerical domination. In 1993-1995, several journalists were sentenced to lashings or jail.

Other parts of Rafsanjani's program also began to unravel. Excessive government spending and the easing of import and currency controls depleted foreign exchange reserves and led to inflation. Iran's foreign debt rose. Severe retrenchment followed. In 1994–1995, imports were cut and private sector credit restricted. Foreign exchange controls, multiple exchange rates and price controls reappeared. Hardship led to riots in several towns in 1992 and again in 1994–1995.

Rafsanjani's attempt to normalize foreign relations was hampered by Iran's opposition to the Arab-Israeli peace process launched in Madrid in 1991 and support for Hezbollah, Lebanon's radical Shiite movement. Iran objected to America's large military presence in the Persian Gulf. Unable to purchase armaments from the West, Iran turned to China and Korea for short- and medium-range missiles and other weaponry. Washington was also disturbed by evidence Iran was pursuing a nuclear weapon. Iranian protégés were implicated in Buenos Aires bombings in 1992 and 1994 at the Israeli Embassy and a Jewish community center.

Rafsanjani tried but failed to limit the damage done to Iran's international relations by a death sentence issued by Ayatollah Khomeini against British writer Salman Rushdie, whose novel *The Satanic Verses* he considered offensive to Islam. In an attempt at an opening to the United States in March 1995, Rafsanjani signed a $1 billion agreement with the American oil company Conoco to develop Iranian offshore fields. But President Clinton killed the deal with an executive order that barred U.S. investment in Iran's oil sector.

By the beginning of his second term, Rafsanjani had lost the initiative to the conservatives, now led by Khamenei. Rafsanjani left behind a legacy of pragmatism in domestic and foreign policy and also a political organization, the Executives of Construction, which would play a significant role in launching the reforms of the Khatami presidency. Launched by 16 of Rafsanjani's cabinet ministers and high officials on the eve of the 1996 parliamentary elections, the group emphasized economic development and private sector entrepreneurship rather than ideology and revolutionary zeal. Along with allies, it won a bloc of 80 seats in the 270-member Majles and subsequently threw its electoral weight and skills behind the election campaign of Mohammad Khatami.

Mohammad Khatami (1997–2005)

Khatami was the dark-horse winner of the 1997 presidential election. He galvanized voters by emphasizing the rule of law, respect for rights, tolerance for diverse views, special attention to the needs of women and youth, and an opening to the outside world. Khatami won 70 percent of the vote—in an 80 percent turnout. He won a second term in 2001 by a similar margin.

The Khatami era ushered in political openings not experienced since the revolution's early months. The culture and interior ministries granted licenses allowing the emergence of a vigorous press and professional, civic and political associations. Khatami forced two intelligence ministers to resign and curbed some of the ministry's excesses. Elections for local councils—promised in the constitution but never held—were conducted for the first time.

Economically, the sharp drop in oil prices that coincided with Khatami's election restricted government spending and investment opportunities. His aides were also initially divided between economic liberalization and state control. But by Khatami's second term, differences had been ironed out in favor of economic liberalization. The government simplified the tax code and import regulations, unified exchange rates, and allowed private banks and insurance companies for the first time since the revolution. A considerable portion of oil revenues was set aside in a reserve fund for investment and as a cushion for difficult times. Privatization of state-owned industries was resumed.

In foreign policy, Khatami adopted language to end Iran's opposition to Israel's existence and the Arab-Israeli peace process. In a CNN interview, he called for a dialogue between the Iranian and American people, a possible prelude to government talks. He boldly nullified Khomeini's death decree against writer Salman Rushdie, removing a major obstacle to economic and diplomatic relations with Europe. He agreed to suspend Iran's nuclear fuel enrichment program to allow negotiations with the Europeans to go forward.

From the beginning, hardliners in the security services, the Revolutionary Guards, the leader's office and parliament sought to undercut Khatami's political liberalization. Several reformist newspapers were closed down. Tehran Mayor Gholam Hossein Karbaschi, who helped engineer Khatami's victory, was tried on trumped-up charges of corruption. He was sentenced to two years in prison and barred from public office for 10 years. Parliament forced Interior Minister Abdollah Nouri out of office, and the judiciary imprisoned him after he started a popular newspaper. Khatami's chief political strategist and adviser, Sa'id Hajjarian, barely survived an assassination attempt that left him disabled. Khamenei undercut Khatami's overture to America and softer tone on Israel.

During Khatami's first term, the reform movement survived attempts to derail it. In 2000, voters gave a loose coalition of parties closely associated with Khatami a working majority in parliamentary elections. But the vote proved to be the turning point. Reformists called for changes hardliners found threatening: a liberal press law, an independent judiciary, a ban on Revolutionary Guards' involvement in the economy, parliamentary oversight of the intelligence ministry and national broadcasting and limits on the supreme leader's wide powers. In a 10-week period, the judiciary closed over 20 publications, virtually shutting down the reformist press. The Guardian Council, a constitutional watch-dog body, barred parliamentary oversight of organizations that came under the supreme leader—the judiciary, military and national radio and television. The supreme leader prevented parliament from passing a more liberal press law.

Journalists and intellectuals were again arrested and jailed. Khatami seemed helpless to protect them. His silence then—and when security forces and thugs beat up protesting students at Tehran University in 1999—were indicators that he had lost the initiative. Control had passed to the hardliners.

Mahmoud Ahmadinejad (2005 –)

Ahmadinejad, the mayor of Tehran and a former provincial governor, was elected president in 2005 after a run-off vote against Rafsanjani. He campaigned as champion of the "little man" against the old establishment. His humble life-style contrasted sharply with Rafsanjani's wealth. Revolutionary Guards and paramilitary forces mobilized voters for Ahmadinejad, while many young and middle class voters, disappointed at the failure of reform, stayed home.

A populist in style and substance, Ahmadinejad distributed largesse to the poor and lower middle class. His presidency coincided with high oil prices. Oil revenue during his first five years equaled the total oil income for the previous 25 years, but was largely wasted on short-term, non-productive programs.

He removed many in the ruling establishment from office and named others from the armed services and bureaucratic middle ranks to the cabinet, ministries, government organizations and even hospitals and universities.

He ignored established procedures, laws and regulations. He drew on the oil reserve fund for pet projects without consulting parliament. The Plan Organization, responsible for Iran's five-year development plans, was abolished, as he considered long-term planning pointless. He stopped attending meetings of the Supreme Defense Council. Later in his two-term presidency, he named personal envoys on the Middle East, Afghanistan and elsewhere, bypassing the foreign ministry.

Ahmadinejad's presidency was marked by a sharp increase in the powers of the Revolutionary Guards and security agencies. He named many former Revolutionary Guard commanders to top posts and favored the Guards with huge, no-bid government contracts. By his second term, the Revolutionary Guards had become

Iran's Politics — The Six Presidents

an economic powerhouse in the energy sector, armament manufacturing, contracting, electronics, automobile assembly and transportation. They also began to interfere in political matters. He named hardliners to head the ministries of culture, interior and intelligence. Press censorship press and harassment of intellectuals sharply rose. In political coverage, state television became an instrument of the intelligence ministry.

In foreign policy, Ahmadinejad adopted a truculent posture towards the international community. He called for the eradication of Israel and denied the Holocaust. He challenged America's international dominance and called for a new world order. His government pushed ahead with its nuclear fuel enrichment program, despite new U.N. and U.S. sanctions between 2006 and 2010.

In June 2009, Ahmadinejad won a second term in a widely disputed election. Peaceful protests by hundreds of thousands in Tehran were put down brutally. Thousands were detained and more than 100 accused in a televised mass show trial. Iran appeared to be edging towards a police state, reflected most by the increasing powers of the Revolutionary Guards in internal security and the propensity of its commanders to comment on political affairs.

The future

- Khamenei outmaneuvered and neutralized both Rafsanjani and Khatami, whose basic policies he did not always embrace. Khamenei initially supported Ahmadinejad, but the distance between the two men has been growing.

- Ahmadinejad has been able to build a base of support among the very constituencies on which Khamenei depends: The Revolutionary Guards, the paramilitary forces, the security agencies and the judiciary.

- The Revolutionary Guards, the security agencies and their branches crushed the Green Movement that emerged to protest the contested 2009 election. They are claiming an increasingly larger role in political affairs.

- Allegations of vote tampering in the 2009 election could impact what happens in the next elections for parliament in 2012 and president in 2013. The key issues are: First, whether those in power—fearing re-emergence of the Green Movement and determined to hold onto power—will try to influence the outcome. Second, whether the Green Movement will put up—or be allowed to—run candidates. Third, how much of the electorate will turn out to vote.

Shaul Bakhash is the Clarence Robinson Professor of History at George Mason University.

4

The Parliament

Farideh Farhi

- Iran's Islamic Consultative Assembly (*Majles-e Shoraye Eslami* or *Majles*, for short) has long been an arena for heated policy debates.
- The 290-member parliament is weak compared with the presidency, as well as with the non-elected institutions such as the 12-member Guardian Council and the supreme leader's office.
- The Majles has been further weakened by the absence of conventional political parties and high turnover of members.
- The Majles has forced a degree of accountability on the executive branch through its powers over the budget, confirmation or impeachment of ministers, and interpellation, or issuing formal questions that the government is required to answer.
- Iran's parliaments have always been diverse, including women and many ethnic minorities. It also designates five seats for religious minorities, including Jews, Christians and Zoroastrians, proportionate to their populations.

Overview

The legislative branch in Iran has had a turbulent history since the first National Consultative Assembly was formed in 1906 during the Constitutional Revolution. The monarch saw the legislature as a way to limit his authority, while clerics were uncomfortable with new laws being passed without their supervision. The 1979 revolution revived this tension. Iran's Islamic constitution created two bodies that reflected the Islamic and republican nature of the new state: It created a popularly elected unicameral Majles, or parliament. It also called for a Guardian Council made up of 12 appointed Islamic jurists to supervise parliament.

But the mix of popular sovereignty and religious supervision has often been fraught with problems. The Guardian Council repeatedly vetoed parliamentary candidates as well as legislation in the name of either Islam or the constitution. And parliament's reluctance to reformulate legislation to accommodate the Guardian Council often produced legislative deadlock.

The impasse led revolutionary leader Ayatollah Ruhollah Khomeini in 1988 to establish a third body to resolve disputes. Its formal name is the Council for the Discernment of the Interest of the Islamic Order, although it is generally referred to as the Expediency Council. The new institution has been headed by former president Akbar Hashemi Rafsanjani since its inception. This three-tier legislative process is designed to overcome any impasse, but often only further slows the passage of new laws.

Outlet for diversity

Despite the authoritarian political setting, Iran's Majles has long served as the one public outlet for political differences. Debates have been feisty. Criticism of government performance has been blunt. Parliaments have rejected or impeached ministers proposed by both Presidents Rafsanjani and Mahmoud Ahmadinejad. By Middle East standards, the persistence and vitality of Iran's Majles has been somewhat remarkable.

Highly contested elections have been held at regular four-year intervals, even if in a flawed and manipulative manner. The Guardian Council controls who runs through its powers to vet candidates' qualifications, which has often led to charges of election engineering. The council has even disqualified incumbents so they cannot run again. Voter participation has varied significantly, yet the (official) turnout has not dropped below 50 percent. More than 71 percent turned out for the highly contested 1996 election.

The unicameral parliament initially had 270 members, but increased to 290 in 2000. Another increase is expected for the 2012 election. Deputies represent 207 districts. Five seats are allocated to religious minorities: two Christian Armenians, one Assyrian-Chaldean Christian, one Jew and one Zoroastrian. Districts with large populations have multiple seats. All eight parliaments have had female members. The largest and most important district is Tehran, which has 30 seats. The original voting age was 15. But in 2008 the voting age was raised to 18, and the minimum age for deputies is now 30.

Eight parliaments

The Islamic Republic has had eight Majles sessions. Except for the eighth Majles, transitions have generally entailed a change in political make-up.

- The **first parliament** (1980-1984) was the most eclectic. It included many deputies from the liberal Freedom Movement, which was later banned, and the Marxist-leaning People's Mujahedin of Iran.
- The **second parliament** (1984-1988) was almost completely taken over by the cleric-dominated Islamic Republic Party (IRP). But divisions within the IRP created a raucous and feisty atmosphere.
- The **third parliament** (1988-1992) was elected after a split among clerical groups and the 1986 disbanding of the IRP, so the new members mostly came from groups on the left of the political spectrum.
- Candidates for the **fourth parliament** (1992-1996) were heavily vetted by the Guardian Council, which paved the way for a takeover by conservative forces.
- The highly contentious election for the **fifth parliament** (1996-2000) created a Majles with relative balance between conservatives and a new political centrist organization called the Servants of Construction.
- This balance gave way to a decisive victory by reformists in the 2000 election for the **sixth parliament** (2000-2004).
- The Guardian Council's wholesale disqualification of reformist candidates set the stage for the return of conservatives to power in the **seventh parliament** (2004-2008).
- The conservative dominance continued in the **eighth parliament** (2008-), again through aggressive vetting of reformist candidates by the Guardian Council.

Membership trends

One of the most notable trends has been the decreasing participation of clerics in the legislative process. The first parliament had 131 clerics, and the second parliament had 148 clerics. The sixth parliament, elected in 2000 and dominated by reformists, had only 35 clerics, the lowest number to date. In 2008, 42 clerics were elected to the eighth parliament, which was dominated by hardliners and conservatives.

The second notable trend is that the decline in the number of clerics has coincided with a rise in the number of deputies with backgrounds in the Islamic Revolutionary Guard Corps (IRGC). But the growing IRGC presence in parliament is still far from the clerical dominance of the 1980s.

Majles powers

On paper, the Majles is endowed with broad prerogatives, including:

- Drafting legislation
- Ratifying international treaties
- Approving state-of-emergency declarations
- Approving foreign loans
- Examining and approving the annual budget
- Investigating all national affairs
- Approving a cabinet request for proclamation of martial law
- Removing cabinet ministers from office
- Recommending to the supreme leader that the president should be removed on the basis of political incompetence.

In practice, the Majles has been particularly active in examining the yearly budget and questioning cabinet ministers. The affiliated Supreme Audit Court supervises governmental spending. Parliament also has investigative powers to deal with the complaints of the public against government organizations.

The Majles' powers have often created conflict with the executive branch, except between 2000 and 2004 when reformers controlled both the presidency and parliament. During those four years, the main political conflict pitted the government's elected branches against its unelected offices.

Institutional rivalries

In practice, however, parliament faces many constraints. The Majles no longer has the power to investigate unelected institutions, such as the Guardian Council. And the investigation of any institution under the control of the supreme leader, such as the state-controlled media, requires his approval. The constitution also limits parliament's power by requiring the Guardian Council to confirm the constitutionality and Islamic nature of any new law, which has not come easily on issues as varied as property rights and foreign investment. The council has also resisted parliamentary attempts at substantive political reform.

Parliament has faced other obstacles. The supreme leader's office has intervened in the legislative process through a mechanism called the "state order." The supreme leader's most controversial intervention was in mid-2000, when he ordered a bill proposing to reform Iran's repressive press laws be removed from the docket.

Two other institutions—the High Council of Cultural Revolution and the Supreme National Security Council—have found ways to get around Majles' exclusive legislative role. On foreign policy, the National Security Council has occasionally acted in direct opposition to explicit legislative mandates. At other times, it has pushed parliament to pass resolutions in favor of its decisions, notably its negotiating positions on nuclear issues.

Political limitations

Parliament has also been weakened by domestic political dynamics, particularly the absence of well-developed parties and the constant change in members. Iran's political parties have been more like elite blocs with limited membership formed as vehicles for particular elections. Once in the Majles, various political cliques or tendencies have operated as factions, which form into fluid majority and minority coalitions. But these coalitions have also been difficult to discipline. And individual members have proven susceptible to outside influence.

The high turnover of deputies is reflected in the low incumbency return rate, which has averaged only 29 percent in parliament's eight elections. The disqualification of sitting members by the Guardian Council has contributed to the high turnover. But voters have also punished deputies who have been unable to bring projects to their districts. In some provinces, clan rivalries also led to a rotation of the local Majles slot from one clan to another.

Disputes over priorities have also played a role. Deputies from larger cities have been mostly concerned with bigger political, economic and cultural issues, while deputies from smaller cities have been more interested in getting government resources to help develop their districts. The executive branch has often played to those differences. Strong presidents, such as Rafsanjani and Ahmadinejad, have often treated parliament as a nuisance and tried to bypass, contain or co-opt its members.

The future

• The Majles will continue to be an arena of raucous interaction and confrontation with both elected and non-elected bodies. But parliament's relevance will ultimately be determined by its ability to challenge the executive branch and implement the laws it passes.

• The elected parliament's reliance on non-elected bodies, such as the office of the supreme leader, to resolve conflicts with the elected president enhances the powers of non-elected bodies.

• Any move towards a more democratic Iran must address parliament's institutional and political weaknesses enshrined in the current constitution.

Farideh Farhi is an independent scholar and affiliate graduate faculty at the University of Hawaii at Mānoa.

5

The Islamic Judiciary

Hadi Ghaemi

- The judiciary plays a vital role in preserving Iran's Islamic system, often by prosecuting critics under vaguely defined national security laws.

- The judiciary falls under the authority of the supreme leader. He appoints its chief for five-year terms. Iran has the traditional criminal and civil courts, but it also has separate Islamic revolutionary courts that can try people on vague charges of being un-Islamic.

- During the Islamic Republic's first three decades, crime rates, drug-related offenses and financial crimes rose significantly. The surge has seriously overstrained the court and prison systems.

- Allegations of corruption and bribery within the judiciary are rife. Judicial officials have regularly acknowledged problems and promised major overhauls to address them, but there are few indications of improvement.

- The judiciary implements the Islamic penal code, including stoning, amputations and flogging, all considered torture under international law. Iran also has the largest number of executions of any country proportional to its population.

Overview

The 1979 revolution erased six decades of modernization of Iran's judicial system. The theocrats moved swiftly to overhaul the legal system to incorporate Islamic Sharia law. Criminal and civil codes were modified; family laws that cover marriage, divorce, child custody and many women's rights faced the biggest changes. The new Islamic penal code included controversial articles, such as the Qisas law of retribution for murder, stoning for adultery, amputations of body parts for theft and certain national security offenses, and flogging for a wide range of offenses.

Many of the new laws were legislated in vague terms, allowing for subjective interpretations as well as diverse and even contradictory rulings by judges. As a result, the judiciary is widely considered one of the Islamic Republic's most dysfunctional institutions. Even judges are critical. When Ayatollah Mahmoud Hashemi Shahroudi was appointed judicial chief in 1999, he said in his inaugural speech that he inherited an institution "in ruins" and in serious need of reforms.

Of the three branches of government, the clerics have the strongest presence in the judiciary. Only clerics who trained in Islamic jurisprudence or have degrees from religious law schools can now become judges. Women are barred from becoming judges altogether. The head of the judiciary, the country's prosecutor general, and all Supreme Court judges have to be mojtahids, or high-ranking clerics.

Political tool

The judiciary plays the paramount role in suppressing dissent and prosecuting dissidents, often on charges of "acting against national security." Working closely with intelligence services, the judiciary has for decades tried a wide range of opponents and critics, from students and street protesters to civil society activists and political reformers.

Trials are often criticized for lack of evidence and not conforming to fundamental standards of due process. Detainees can be held for long periods in solitary confinement. Many are denied access to their lawyers. Verdicts are often based on "confessions" extracted during interrogations. And many are sentenced to lengthy prison terms.

Iran's Revolutionary Courts are primarily in charge of prosecutions involving acts against national security, as well as drug smuggling and espionage. After the disputed 2009 presidential election, the judiciary emerged as a key instrument to intimidate protesters and remove many leading activists and opinion makers, steps that were both critical to the regime's survival.

The Revolutionary Courts conducted a series of show-trials that included televised confessions. Among the more than 250 defendants were protesters, prominent journalists, human rights defenders and reformist politicians. They included former Vice President Mohammad Abtahi and former Member of Parliament Mohsen Mirdamadi, who headed the Islamic Participation Front, the largest reform party in Iran. The sentences ranged from floggings to prison terms of up to 10 years and executions. Much of the evidence was produced in "confessions" by defendants. Since the majority of defendants were held in solitary confinement before the trial and had no access to their lawyers, many confessions appeared to have been coerced.

Executions

- During the 1980s, Revolutionary Courts routinely sentenced political prisoners to death. In 1988, at least 4,000 political prisoners who had already been prosecuted and sentenced to prison terms were summarily retried and executed within a two-month period, according to Amnesty International and Human Rights Watch.

- Iran still carries out more executions proportionate to its population than any other country. Only China executed more people in sheer numbers than Iran. In 2005, the year President Mahmoud Ahmadinejad assumed office, Iran executed 86 individuals. In 2009, Iran executed 388 people.

- A large number of executions are for drug-related offences. Despite tough penalties, drug use and smuggling remain serious problems.

- Iran leads the world in executing juvenile offenders. In 2008 and 2009, it was the only country to carry out executions of minors, in violation of its obligations under the Convention on the Rights of the Child.

- In the 2009 show-trials after the election turmoil, eleven dissidents were sentenced to death for participating in street demonstrations. Between November 2009 and May 2010, Iran executed nine political prisoners.

- Crimes punishable by death under Iranian law include armed resistance against the state (defined as enmity against God), murder, drug trafficking, rape, adultery and homosexuality.

The court system

Iran's legal system has many layers of courts. The constitution calls for civil and criminal courts, as well as military courts. Prosecutions originate in lower courts and can be appealed to higher courts. The Supreme Court reviews cases of capital offenses and rules on death sentences. It is also tasked with ensuring proper implementation of the laws and uniformity of judicial proceedings.

But the Islamic Republic also has Revolutionary Courts and the Special Court for the Clergy. Both sets of tribunals were based on decrees by revolutionary leader Ayatollah Ruhollah Khomeini. They have never been incorporated into the constitutional clauses defining the role and structure of the Judiciary. Legal experts critical of these tribunals have repeatedly challenged their legal standing. The Special Court for the Clergy has also been used as a political tool against clerics who urge reforms, criticize the regime or challenge the role of the supreme leader. It has been compared to the Inquisition courts of the Middle Ages.

The constitution defines the judiciary's general responsibilities as:

- Investigating and passing judgment on grievances, violations of rights and complaints
- Resolving litigation
- Restoring public rights and promoting justice and legitimate freedoms
- Supervising the proper enforcement of laws
- Uncovering crimes
- Prosecuting, punishing and chastising criminals
- Enacting the penalties and provisions of the Islamic penal code
- And taking suitable measures to prevent the occurrence of crime and to reform criminals.

The legal code

Iranian laws reflect a specific interpretation of Shiite jurisprudence, which is not embraced by all Shiites. It has particularly changed family laws, instituted broad discriminatory laws against women, introduced the laws of retribution and toughened the penal code with punishments such as stoning, floggings and amputations.

Among the most controversial laws are those relating to the age at which offenders are held responsible as adults for criminal activity. The Islamic penal code defines this age of responsibility as nine for girls and 15 for boys. This has resulted in large numbers of juvenile executions.

Reformist religious scholars have challenged these interpretations of Sharia law. They claim Islamic jurisprudence does not allow for the implementation of executions in the absence of a divine individual, such as the Prophet Mohammed or his descendents. Reform of the civil and penal codes is a major flashpoint between reformist and conservative factions within Iran's political system.

Impunity and accountability

The accountability of courts and judges, especially in political cases, is hotly debated among the ruling elite. Iran has a court in charge of prosecuting offending judges, but it has not been used as a way to impose accountability. Parliament has undertaken several investigations into judicial practices, but the judiciary has rebuffed their intervention and stonewalled any meaningful investigations. The supreme leader appoints the judiciary chief, and judicial officials contend they are only accountable to the supreme leader.

The impunity of intelligence and judicial officials has been demonstrated in many high profile cases since the revolution. In 1998, intelligence agents allegedly murdered several dissident intellectuals. President Mohammad Khatami acknowledged the role of state agents in these murders, but the judicial process was stifled by the intelligence apparatus derailing a credible and independent investigation. In the end, no information was ever publicly disclosed about how these murders were planned or on whose orders.

After the 2009 uprising, four detainees died after being tortured at Tehran's Kahrizak Detention Center. A parliamentary investigation held Tehran prosecutor general Saeed Mortazavi personally responsible. Mortazavi was also suspected of direct involvement in the murder of Zahra Kazemi, an Iranian-Canadian photojournalist, in Evin prison in 2003. He and other high-ranking officials suspected of serious offenses have never been subjected to a judicial investigations or prosecution.

Attempts at reform and ensuing resistance

Shahroudi, who headed the Judiciary from 1999 to 2009, made the most serious attempts at reforming judicial institutions. But his initiatives were largely stymied by conservative clerics within the judiciary and their allies in influential positions.

Iran's justice system is particularly criticized for two practices that distinguish it on the global stage: death by stoning and execution of juvenile offenders (under the age of 18). Shahroudi tried but failed to put an end to both practices. The powerful 12-man Guardian Council, which can veto legislation, has repeatedly blocked reforms. Shahroudi instead issued several internal directives to judges urging them to refrain from issuing such sentences. But his directives were largely ignored. His successor, Ayatollah Sadegh Larijani, abandoned any attempts at reform on these issues.

Shahroudi also attempted to outlaw harsh interrogation techniques and ill-treatment of detainees. His efforts led to the parliament's adoption of a Citizens Bill of Rights in 2004. In practice, however, these safeguards have not been implemented, and judiciary officials have not shown any willingness to enforce them through courts.

The future

- The role of the judiciary as a key institution in suppressing dissent and implementing politically-motivated prosecutions is likely to continue. But its abuses are also increasingly likely to undermine its independence and legitimacy.

- Despite growing international condemnation, Iran's current regime appears defiantly committed to the extensive use of capital punishment, juvenile executions and cruel and inhumane punishments such as stoning. However, concerted focus on these violations of Iran's obligations under international human rights treaties will empower reform advocates.

- The debate over rival interpretations of Islamic laws—and their incorporation into Iran's legal system—is a major flashpoint in the political struggle between reformist and conservative factions. The outcome of this political struggle will seriously affect the power of the judiciary.

Hadi Ghaemi, a physicist, is the executive director of the International Campaign for Human Rights in Iran.

6

Politics and the Clergy

Mehdi Khalaji

- For several decades, Iran's Shiite clerical establishment has proven extremely effective at mobilizing the Iranian masses.
- The Shiite clergy were historically independent from politics. But especially under Ayatollah Ali Khamenei, the Iranian government seized control of the "sacred" and co-opted the clerical establishment.
- Since 1979, Iran's theocratic regime has deprived the entire clerical class of its autonomy—but also made it rich and powerful.
- Any serious crisis in Iran could jeopardize the clergy's favored position in government. To retain its legitimacy and religious standing, the clergy may have to distance itself from politics.

Overview

Shiite clerics have been able to mobilize the Iranian masses far better than any other socio-political authority. Clerics form the broadest social network in Iran, exerting their influence from the most remote village to the biggest cities. So while most opposition groups participated in the 1979 revolution, the clergy established hegemony over Iran's new political system after the shah's ouster. They emerged from a crowded field for several reasons. First, Islamic revolutionaries ruthlessly eliminated their rivals. Second, the regime tapped into the popularity and legitimacy conferred by its call to Islam, a force rooted in Iran's social history. None of the other revolutionary political factions benefited from the traditional legitimacy and social network provided by the Shiite clerical establishment.

The new Islamic government tapped into the clergy's power to achieve its agenda—not only on religious or political matters. After the Iran-Iraq War, clerics were dispatched throughout the country to encourage families to have fewer children. A soaring birth rate after the revolution had almost doubled the population within a decade from 34 million to 62 million, which threatened to stifle future economic growth. The government's ploy was effective; the Iranian birth rate declined dramatically.

The regime and the clerical establishment now have a symbiotic relationship that shapes both politics and production of the next clerical generation. The alliance no longer tolerates clerics who think or behave outside the framework of the regime's specific Islamic ideology. Prominent clerics such as Ahmad Ghabel, Mohsen Kadivar, Hassan Youssefi Eshkevari and Mohammad Mojtahid Shabestari have been excommunicated for heretical interpretations of Islamic theology.

But relations between the clergy and the government have also had adverse effects on the clerics' social authority. In the 1997 presidential election, the clerical establishment supported the conservative speaker of parliament, while the majority of people voted for the dark-horse reformist candidate Mohammad Khatami. In the 2005 election, Mahmoud Ahmadinejad won in part because of voters' frustration with government clerics, who were increasingly associated with corruption and elitism. He was the first non-cleric to win the presidency since Khomeini had a falling out with early technocrats shortly after the revolution.

The political guardian

Support from Shiite clerics was traditionally one of the monarchy's sources of political legitimacy. But the 1906-1911 Constitutional Revolution ended clerical control over Iran's educational and judicial systems. Reza Shah Pahlavi's forced secularization and modernization campaigns in the early twentieth century further marginalized Iran's religious leaders. His son, Mohammad Reza Shah Pahlavi, initiated land reform that alien-ated both of the monarchy's traditional power bases: the clerics and large landowners.

Feeling abandoned by the state, major landowners formed an alliance with clerics incensed at the gradual decay of their own social and political power. The shah attempted to protect himself from waves of Islamic revolutionary sentiment by using minor clerics, such as Ayatollah Ahmad Khansari and Ayatollah Kazem Shariatmadari. But they lacked sufficient clout to prop up the monarchy.

After the revolution, Ayatollah Ruhollah Khomeini announced the formation of the Islamic Republic of Iran and declared that ultimate political authority would rest in the hands of a senior cleric, the *velayat-e faqih*, or guardianship of the jurist. The idea represented a revolution within Shiism, which had for centuries deliber-ately stayed out of politics and never before ruled a state. A clerical front soon emerged to oppose the specific idea of a *velayat-e faqih* and the broader concept of reinterpreting Shiite theology. Many clerics believed the *velayat-e faqih's* absolute authority was actually non-Islamic.

Khomeini moved swiftly to stifle clerical opposition to his rule. Many opponents were killed, jailed, exiled or marginalized. He labeled his clerical critics "stupid," "ossified," "colonized" and "loyal to American Islam." To widen his influence, the charismatic revolutionary leader also tried to assume control over the international Shiite community. But several grand ayatollahs from the Iranian holy city of Qom and Shiism's theological center in Najaf, Iraq still enjoyed large followings. The stature of these religious figures—including Abul Qassem Khoi, Mohammad Reza Golpayegani and Shahab Al-Din Marashi Najafi—prevented the regime from swallowing the clerical establishment. Eight years of war with Iraq also prevented Khomeini from doing more to eliminate his clerical rivals all at once.

The successor

Khomeini died in 1989, and the Assembly of Experts selected Ayatollah Ali Khamenei as the new supreme leader. Khamenei was not a natural successor of Khomeini. He lacked serious religious and political creden-tials and was noticeably devoid of charisma. Many other figures in his generation were closer to and seen as potential heirs to Khomeini's rule.

Khamenei's chief rival was Ayatollah Ali Montazeri, who had actually been appointed Khomeini's successor years earlier. But Montazeri had been fired after sharp disagreements, particularly after the execution of thousands of political prisoners in 1988. Khamenei's appointment disappointed the traditional Shiite clergy; he was able to assume control only with the help of Iran's security apparatus and state propaganda.

Clerical purge

Khamenei gradually began to consolidate his hold on power. He was aided by the deaths of grand ayatollahs, such as Mohammad Reza Gopayegani and Shahab Al-Din Marashi Najafi, who had fought to guarantee the clergy's independence from government. But the regime also launched a second concerted attack on the clerical establishment. It began with an attempt to monopolize management of the clergy, many of whom ran their own seminaries, had their own followings, and earned their own incomes.

The regime computerized and unified data on the clergy of all ranks to make information on their economic and intellectual lives accessible to the government. It also co-opted the clerical establishment through hefty government stipends as well as other exclusive and profitable privileges. Khamenei increasingly became the ultimate authority over all religious seminaries, as well as supreme leader of the Iranian government. By throwing in with the regime, the clergy also increasingly abdicated their role as the exclusive "managers of the sacred affairs" of Iranian society. The clerical establishment effectively became the central ideological appara-tus of the state. And the government increasingly gained control of defining the "sacred."

The Islamic regime now uses its control over mosque and state to suppress both "popular Islam," Sufism and religious intellectualism, which have all gained ground among the public since the mid-1990s. "Popular Islam" is the faith as lived and practiced by ordinary people and does not necessarily correspond with theological Islam or official Islam imposed by state. Sufism is an interpretation of Islam that focuses on spiritual content of the Prophet Mohammad's message, rather than Islamic law. And religious intellectualism centers on liberal democratic interpretations of Islam. All three extend the borders of the "sacred" far beyond what is acceptable to the Islamic Republic. All three threaten the regime's version of "official Islam."

The regime's expanding power over traditionally independent clerics has stifled religious thought and even forced clerics to disconnect from the establishment. Many do not have the intellectual freedom even outside the seminaries; they are still harassed by intelligence services. Another clerical minority has tried to withdraw from politics and avoid public activities, instead devoting themselves to worship and education. But the majority of clerics prefer the benefits of government financial resources and the political advantages of a close association with the regime.

Important organizations

- **Supreme Council of Qom Seminary:** A group of clerics who are in charge of policy planning in Iran's seminaries. Members of the council are appointed by the supreme leader and can be dismissed by him. The executive director of the clerical establishment is appointed by this council.
- **Center for Management of Seminaries:** The executive management body of the clerical establishment that oversees all educational, administrative and economic activities of the clerics.
- **Association of Teachers of Qom Seminary:** A group of conservative clerics that oversees the Supreme Council of the Qom Seminary under supervision of the supreme leader. This group does not include all important teachers or scholars of the seminaries.
- **Association of Teachers and Scholars of Qom Seminaries:** A group consisting of former officials of the Islamic Republic, as well as a few middle-ranking reformist clerics. This reformist group is marginal and has little support from the grand ayatollahs.
- **Association of Militant Clerics of Tehran:** A group of clerics who participated in the revolution. It includes current and former members of the government. Along with the Bazaar—the traditional market—this group forms a pillar of old conservative establishment in Iran.
- **Al-Mustafa International University:** A university owned and run by Ayatollah Khamenei. It specializes in educating non-Iranian clerics and has branches in several other countries.
- **Special Court of Clerics:** A court that works outside the judiciary system and does not respect the country's juridical codes. The court's head is appointed and dismissed by the supreme leader. The court is one of the government's main tools for controlling clerics.
- **Imam Sadeq 83 Brigade:** A military unit whose members are clerics. This unit was created during the Iran-Iraq War but now serves as the police force of the clerical establishment and works under supervision of Ayatollah Khamenei.

Prominent clerics

Grand Ayatollah Ali Sistani: A grand ayatollah in Najaf, Iraq. Sistani enjoys the most widespread following in the Shiite world. But his followers outside Iraq mostly look to him for answers on private religious matters rather than political issues.

Ayatollah Ali Khamenei: Current leader of Islamic Republic and the de facto head of the Shiite clerical establishment. Khamenei's authority over the Shiite religious network extends beyond Iran and is the richest and most effective Shiite religious network in the world.

Ayatollah Naser Makarem Shirazi: A pro-regime ayatollah who has thousands of followers inside Iran. He is best known for his extra-clerical economic activities and benefits from government, which have made him one of Iran's richest clerics in Iran.

Mohammad Mojtahid Shabestari: A cleric who reads Islamic texts by modern hermeneutics and the methodology of historical criticism. He believes that Sharia or Islamic law is not valid in anything related to the public sphere. He unconditionally defends the universal declaration of human rights. He recently chose to forsake his robe and turban in order to disassociate himself with the pro-regime establishment.

The future

- Compared with the pre-revolutionary era, the quality of seminary education in Iran has declined significantly. Government intervention in all aspects of clerical life, including seminary curriculum, has changed the clergy's traditional way of thinking and living.
- The clerical establishment is now producing mostly missionaries and preachers, rather than true scholars of Islamic law and theology. The symbiotic relationship between the clergy and the country's judicial and political order will continue the qualitative decay of Islamic education. Ironically, as Islamic

scholarship decays, so too will the clergy's ability to provide convincing religious justification for the government's actions.

• Given the mounting power of anti-clerical radicals like Ahmadinejad's faction and the Revolutionary Guards, the relative power of the clergy will deteriorate. It is unlikely that clerics in the Assembly of Experts will even be able to play their traditional role of appointing or removing the supreme leader.

• Iranian reformists such as the pro-democracy, student and women's movements have secular demands: they call for elimination of various forms of discrimination embodied in the constitution. This vision for Iran leaves little room for clerics' leadership. Even if a minority of clerics would like to join civil society movements, it would be as followers rather than leaders.

Mehdi Khalaji, a senior fellow at The Washington Institute for Near East Policy, studied Shiite theology in the Qom seminary of Iran.

7

Iran and Islam

Juan Cole

- Iran is a theocracy that mixes religion and state more thoroughly than any other country in the world.
- Shiite Islam gives a special place to its clerics and demands blind obedience to their rulings on religious law.
- The commemoration of the martyrdom of holy figures is central to Shiite religious sensibilities and plays out in Iran's populist politics.
- Since 1979, the Islamic Republic has imposed a strongly patriarchal order, but pious women have found ways to assert themselves in society and education.
- The contemporary Shiite revival has given Iran influence in the Muslim world and especially among other Shiite communities in the Arab world and South Asia, challenging the Sunni secular nationalists and traditional monarchies.

Overview

The 1979 revolution unseated the last dynasty to rule Iran from the Peacock Throne. But it also represented a revolution within Shiism, which had traditionally shunned direct clerical involvement in politics. Revolutionary leader Ayatollah Ruhollah Khomeini introduced the idea of clerical supervision of a modern republican state that has all three standard branches of government—the executive, legislature and judiciary.

Iran is today the world's only clerically-ruled government. Shiite Islam is not just the religion of state, but also forms the framework for a theocracy. As such, religion and politics are inseparable. The starting point for debates in Iran is not secular law and civil rights, but the tradition of Muslim jurisprudence and practice called the Sharia. Lively debates center on issues such as the nature of a just government, women's rights in Islam, economic justice and the extent of limits on personal liberty. Since the mid-1990s, the Iranian political divide has also played out over the balance of power between the republican and religious nature of the state.

Shiite history

Only 10 percent of the world's Muslims belong to the Shiite branch of Islam; most of the rest are Sunnis. The initial split between Islam's two main branches followed the Prophet Mohammed's death in 632 AD. It was triggered by a dispute over leadership of Islam. Shiites believed that the Prophet should have been succeeded by the relatives or descendants most familiar with his thinking and practices. In contrast, the group that later evolved into the Sunnis believed that the early Muslim community had the right to select elders from the noble tribe of Mecca, even if they had no blood ties to the Prophet.

Many Shiite traditions—which heavily influence practices and policies in Iran today—emerged during that early schism. Shiites hold that the Prophet's son-in-law and first cousin, Ali, should have been his immediate successor. Shiite is the short form of Shi'atu 'Ali, or followers of Ali. Ali did become the fourth caliph for five years, but was murdered in 661 AD. The new Umayyad Dynasty then assumed leadership of the young Islamic empire. Ali's son Hussein and his followers decided to fight against harsh governance, knowing that they were likely to be massacred. But they believed it was better to die fighting for justice than to live with injustice—a concept that today defines Shiite beliefs. Hussein was killed in the battle of Karbala. His tomb is one of Shiism's two holiest shrines and Shiites annually mourn his death in reenactment passion plays. His martyrdom also defines contemporary Shiite beliefs.

Clergy's powers

Twelver Shiites, the branch to which most Iranians belong, hold that the twelfth imam, or divinely-appointed successor of the Prophet, disappeared as a child in 874 AD and will one day become visible again in this world to restore it to justice as the Mahdi, or the promised one. In the absence of the Mahdi, Twelver Shiites believe that clerics trained in seminaries can substitute for his authority on some issues. So clerics in Shiism are powerful in interpreting God's word for their followers. And the faithful are obliged to give blind obedience to clerics' religious rulings. Khomeini transferred this religious power to Iran's new theocracy after the revolution.

At the core of Shiite belief and history is a basic contradiction. Shiites believe in the need for divine authority in this world. But the disappearance of the Twelfth Imam in the ninth century left the community rudderless. Over time, Shiites have tried to answer this power vacuum in their faith in several contradictory ways. They came to hold that, in general, seminary-trained clergymen could substitute themselves for the absent Imam. Thus, they could authorize the state to collect and distribute the poor tax. They could authorize the appointment of Friday prayer leaders. But the trained clergymen only solved half the problem posed by the absence of the Imam, since no one alleged that they had the prerogative actually to rule, as the Imam did. Instead, they uneasily co-existed with lay monarchs, who exercised authority on a customary, common-law, not an Islamic-law, basis.

Sunni clergymen do not have the same prerogatives or powers as Shiite ayatollahs; they are more pastors than priests. The Sunni faithful do not owe blind obedience to their sheikhs. As a result, most Sunni Muslims are today organized, like Europeans, on the basis of the nation-state, and many have chosen a relatively secular national framework. The Sunni world is thus dominated by nationalist republics and by conservative monarchies. As a result, many Sunni governments, whether secular nationalists or monarchs, view Shiite Iran as a dire threat because it offers an alternative vision of the state based on religion and clerical authority. Sunnis are also concerned by the appeal of Khomeini-ism among Shiite communities outside Iran, especially in Bahrain, Saudi Arabia, Iraq and Lebanon, part of the so-called "Shiite crescent."

Khomeini-ism

Khomeini's reform of Shiism proclaimed that there is no place for the monarchy in Islam. He described secular nationalism as a tool of the devil. Under Khomeini-ism, only clerical rule in accordance with Shiite law can create just government in the absence of the Prophet and the imams. But the Islamic Republic he founded in 1979 represented a unique blend, since the supreme cleric or leader presided over a government formed by parliamentary and presidential elections that implied popular sovereignty.

During the revolution's first decade, many popular Shiite themes melded with regime goals. This was the height of Khomeini-ism—and the last decade of his life. During the 1980-1988 Iran-Iraq War, young men who died at the front fighting the secular Arab nationalist regime of Saddam Hussein were commemorated as martyrs. Fountains spewing red water—symbolizing blood—were set up in Tehran's main cemetery. The Iranian Revolutionary Guard Corps was founded as a sort of Shiite national guard to defend theocratic rule. Imbued with the passions of popular religion, it often competed with the regular army for preeminence—and won. Khomeini brought Friday prayer preachers from all over the Muslim world to Iran in hopes of influencing even Sunnis with his theocratic ideals.

The balance between religion and republicanism shifted from the late 1990s during the reform era. President Mohammad Khatami, who served two terms between 1997 and 2005, emphasized popular sovereignty over the clerical authority of the supreme leader. He sought to increase the scope of personal liberties and freedom of speech. Shiite philosophers began debating ideas about Islamic democracy. By the time Khatami left office, however, this second political tendency was crushed by clerical hardliners.

A third tendency emerged after the 2005 election of populist Mahmoud Ahmadinejad as president. He led the so-called "principlists," a faction named for adhering to the strictest interpretation of the revolution. The principlists attacked both the wealthy upper echelon of clergymen as fat cats preying on the people, and the Khatami liberals as traitors to the ideals of the Islamic Republic. Ahmadinejad often invoked the Twelfth Imam and predicted that he would soon return.

The reform tendency reemerged in 2009, when Muslim liberals launched the Green Movement to protest what they saw as the stealing of the presidential election by Ahmadinejad and his clerical allies. They too employed the symbols of Islam to prove legitimacy. Green is associated with the descendants of the Prophet and is considered the color of Islam. And their rallying cry was Allahu Akbar, or "God is great." The Green Movement leaders sought less stringent controls on personal liberties and speech. But they insisted their mission was to defend the ideals of Khomeini's Islamic Revolution, even though they emphasized the sovereignty of the Shiite populace over high clerical authority. The regime effectively curbed this movement, reasserting the joint control of the high clergy and the principlist populists.

Shiism and women

The 1979 Islamic Revolution proved a turning point for women in Iran and in the Muslim world generally. Khomeini, the theocrat-in-chief, and the new regime, imposed veiling on women and forbade them from serving as judges. The regime insisted on segregating beaches, sporting events and universities, on gender lines. Yet the populist character of Iran's revolution also led to the establishment of many new provincial schools and resulted in impressive advances in female literacy.

The Iran-Iraq War also drew large numbers of women into the work force for the first time, so that practical developments often offset patriarchal law-making, and unexpectedly gave women a prominent place in Iranian society. The strongly patriarchal Islamic Republic has paradoxically created an active, literate and idealistic class of women who will increasingly shape its society, to the dismay of many male ayatollahs.

Factoids

- Iran was largely a Sunni area until the 1500s, when the Safavid dynasty began imposing Shiite Islam on the population as the state religion. This era also saw international competition between the Safavids and the Sunni Ottoman Empire.

- The most important religious holiday for Shiites is Ashoura, which commemorates the martyrdom of Imam Hussein, the Prophet's grandson, who Shiites believe was unjustly killed in 680 AD. Shiites recite elegiac poetry, tearfully tell the tales of Hussein and his family and companions, and march in processions with banners. Some practice flagellation, whipping themselves with chains or cutting themselves with knives—folk rituals frowned upon by the educated clergy.

- Twelver Shiite-majority countries include Bahrain, Iraq and Azerbaijan, along with Iran (though Azerbaijanis are mostly secular in outlook). Countries with Shiite minorities include Lebanon, Afghanistan, Pakistan, Kuwait and Saudi Arabia.

Notable players

- The International Center for Islamic Studies is in the theological center of Qom, Iran. This non-governmental institute, backed by Shiite religious authorities, teaches Shiism to non-Iranian students and prepares them to become teachers, sermonizers, researchers, jurisprudents and translators. It seeks to spread worldwide the teachings, sayings and practices of the Twelve Imams, which are studied by Shiite scholars but not by most Sunnis. It has students from 101 countries.

- As an alternative to orthodox Shiism, Sufism has experienced a fresh wave of popularity in Iran in the early twenty-first century, especially among youth. Nur-Ali Tabandeh is a leader of the mystical Nimatul-lahi Sufi order based in Gunabad, northeastern Iran. Sufis believe in a quest for a mystical union with God and organize themselves in orders or *tariqehs*. Their ecstatic chanting, love of poetry, and tendency to believe that God is present in all things makes them hated by orthodox Shiites. Tabandeh has been accused by the regime of a political alliance with the reformists. He was briefly arrested in 2007. In 2010, he was accused of meeting with leaders of the reformist Green Movement, which seeks greater personal liberties.

- Zahra Rahnavard represents the new Islamic feminists. A political scientist and sculptor, she became prominent as an anti-shah Muslim activist in the 1970s. During the monarchy, she argued that attempts to abolish the veil or headscarf were an imperialist imposition of foreign ways on Muslim Iran. But after the revolution, she also became the first female chancellor of Alzahra University. She is from a conservative religious family, but she has emerged as a leading political activist, as wife of Green Movement leader Mir Hossein Mousavi. Through her essays and books she argues for an Islamic feminism that does not challenge the principles of the Khomeini-ist state, but makes a place in Muslim society for dynamic, educated women.

The future

- The central political conflict in the Khomeini-ist system is between clerical authoritarianism and populist aspirations for liberty. This seems likely to play out with potentially momentous consequences in coming years.

- The ideological underpinnings of the clerical state may be undermined in the next generation by either a lack of interest in religion or an enthusiasm for unorthodox forms of Islam such as Sufism, which is now widespread among Iran's youth.

- Iran has influence in the Arab world, but its theocratic form of rule has limited appeal. It has largely been rejected by Iraqi and Lebanese Shiites. And it seems inappropriate for minorities in countries such as Saudi Arabia and Pakistan. Most Sunni activists are hostile to the Islamic Republic.

- Iran is a regional player, but the monolithic Shiite crescent feared by some Sunnis has not materialized.

Juan Cole is professor of history at the University of Michigan and runs the Informed Comment weblog. His latest book is Engaging the Muslim World *(2010).*

8

Iran and Democracy

Daniel Brumberg

- The Islamic Republic of Iran has struggled with its primary political identity since the 1979 revolution: Should the state be based on religious principles mandated by God? Or should it be based on man-made laws about democratic governance and the will of the people?

- Prominent reformists have sought to harness Islam for democratic ends. But hard-line clerics insist that Twelver Shiism vests ultimate power in the Rahbar, or supreme leader, with his allies in the clerical establishment.

- Protests after the disputed 2009 presidential election reflected the intense internal debate over the linkage between Islam and democracy.

- A new generation of ultra-hardliners in the "New Right," led by President Mahmoud Ahmadinejad, has sought to weaken parliament, even as they proclaimed their commitment to the will of the "people."

- The New Right has antagonized well-established lay political groups and the clergy who share a common interest in preventing a new Islamic despotism. But they lack a common vision of the political future and a leader with the populist allure to define such a vision.

Overview

Ayatollah Ruhollah Khomeini, leader of the 1979 Islamic revolution, was also the principal author of the hybrid political system in the Islamic Republic of Iran. Khomeini did not simply advocate for a modern theocracy. He advocated a blended system that tried to both assign ultimate authority to the clerics, but also ensure that their actions were responsive to and expressive of popular will.

The ideological tension is reflected in Iran's constitution as well as its government structure. The constitution borrows heavily from French and Belgian law, yet it also requires that all laws be compatible with Islamic Sharia. And the government has all the pieces of a modern democratic republic—independent executive, legislative and judicial branches—but it also has a set of parallel institutions dominated by the clergy.

Republican institutions	Islamic institutions
*President	*Supreme leader
*290-member parliament	*12-member Guardian Council
*Civil and criminal courts	*Islamic courts
*Regular military	*Revolutionary Guards and Basij

Hybrid politics

Khomeini's efforts stemmed from two social forces that brought about the Islamic revolution:

- The clerical right was a group of radicalized clerics. Backed by the urban lower classes, they perceived Khomeini as a charismatic, even semi-divine, savior. Loyal disciples, they embraced his novel idea of *velayat-e faqih* or the guardianship of the jurist. Khomeini's doctrine called for a supreme leader who would rule with executive and judicial authority inherited through the Prophet Mohammed.

- The Islamic left was a group of lay political intellectuals joined by a new breed of left-leaning clerics. These clerics were based in institutions such as Tehran University and invoked the ideas of a charismatic sociologist, Ali Shariati. Shariati blended Shiite Islam with Marxist notions of popular revolution under an intellectual vanguard speaking for the masses. Shariati held that a dominant lay political party—rather than the clerics—should constitute that vanguard.

In the run-up to the Islamic revolution, many Islamic leftists argued that a clerical body was needed to inspire and mobilize the masses. For the Islamic left, clerical authority was a means to achieve political power rather than a prescription for clerical rule itself.

Iran's 1979 constitution attempted to bring together these two notions of republican governance and religious authority. It mentions the word "democracy" only once—in the preamble. The constitution notes that the Islamic revolution reflects "an attempt, also made by other Islamic and democratic movements, to open the way for the establishment of the unified world community." The guiding assumption of the constitution is that the ultimate purpose of political action—even elections—is to express one common sacred vision of political community.

Revolutionary splits

The ideological tensions reflected in the constitution often bogged down Iranian politics. The elected parliament, or Majles, was often at odds with appointed clerical bodies, especially the Guardian Council. The 12-member council regularly vetoed legislation passed by the 290-member parliament on the vague grounds of being "un-Islamic." Individuals or groups that criticized the system could be charged with being an enemy of the state and face possible imprisonment.

After his return from exile, Khomeini originally returned to the theological center at Qom. He intended to play a behind-the-scenes role as guide. And he initially tried to avoid getting involved in increasingly bitter disputes. But he ultimately had no choice but to return to live in Tehran and try to create order. He publicly reprimanded squabbling politicians and urged greater unity.

Two key decrees

In the late 1980s, Khomeini issued two decrees to help sort out internal tensions. In reality, they also added another whole layer of bureaucracy that complicated governance. His first decree created the Expediency Council. It is made up of 22 to 30 members who try to resolve differences between the Guardian Council and parliament over legislation. Empowered to override the Guardian Council's veto of legislation, the unelected council further undermined Khomeini's claim that the Majles was to be the "house of all the people."

The second complicating factor was a fatwa, or religious opinion, that Khomeini issued in 1988. Standing before a Tehran University audience, he declared: "Government is among the most important divine injunctions and has priority over all peripheral divine orders. The government…which is part of the total (or absolute) vice-regency of the Prophet… can prevent any matter, whether religious or secular, if it is against the interests of Islam."

Decades later, Khomeini's fatwa still provides crucial ammunition in the escalating political battle over his legacy. Politicians who want the elected Majles and president to be the main base of authority cite Khomeini's focus on "government." Others who want to invest ultimate authority in the faqih assert, quoting Khomeini, that government is part of the "absolute" authority of the vice-regency of the Prophet, and thus subservient to the will of the supreme religious authority.

Political battle

Khomeini's charisma and religious credentials were critical to holding the regime together. His death in 1989 set the stage for a broader political struggle over his legacy and the source of political authority. This battle began in the run-up to 1992 parliamentary elections. The new supreme leader, Ayatollah Ali Khamenei, working closely with then President Hashemi Rafsanjani, tried to purge leading members of the Islamic left from the Majles and cabinet.

The effort to banish the Islamic left initially backfired. They offered a spirited defense, citing Khomeini's statements praising the authority of parliament and the role of elections. Ebrahim Asgharzadeh told a Majles session, "In the constitution, there is a whole chapter about the rule of the people, which is something that cannot be split apart…We cannot destroy the people's rights" by banishing "all those people" who had "made such sacrifices for the revolution." Minister of Culture and Islamic Guidance Mohammad Khatami was among those forced out. He argued that, "we should free our society from the old mentality of law evasion," and "replace it with the mentality of the constitution," which provides for "security, justice, freedom and participation."

By the mid-1990s, Islamic leftists were actively pushing radical new ideas about the relationship between mosque and state. Disillusioned Islamic leftists, such as philosopher Abdolkarim Soroush, even questioned the idea of clerical rule. Soroush argued that the Islamic faith would be strengthened, not undermined, by distancing political and religious authority.

Widening power struggle

In the 1997 presidential election, Mohammed Khatami led the Islamic leftists and reformers to power. But the power struggle only deepened over the next eight years, during his two terms in office, as defenders of the clerical establishment used their power over religious institutions to undermine elected offices. Ayatollah Mohammad Reza Mahdavi-Kani lambasted the idea that the rule of a supreme leader should somehow be "based on popular demand." Similarly, Mohsen Azhini asserted that Khomeini's 1988 edict gave the leader "absolute authority." In a speech before parliament, Khatami countered that while the leadership will "guide and assist us," the "legitimacy of government stems from the people's vote."

The deepening struggle was reflected in July 1999, when students at Tehran University protested the regime's efforts to shut down a popular reformist newspaper. Following the regime's bloody repression of the protesters, the leader of the Revolutionary Guards sent Khatami a letter threatening to overthrow him if he did not distance himself from the students. Khatami offered the students only lukewarm support. In return, he was warmly embraced by Khamenei during a Friday sermon attended by thousands of regime loyalists.

Khatami's retreat helped to open the door to a sustained campaign by the judiciary and security apparatus to shut down the reform movement. They were able to silence intellectuals, professors and journalists clamoring for a more democratic Iran. Khatami was reelected in 2001, but by then the clerical right was well on its way to reasserting authority and preventing any form of Shiite reformation. The right's campaign gave almost unlimited power to the security apparatus, particularly the Revolutionary Guards and veterans of the Iran-Iraq War that had become part of a rising counter-elite of political apparatchiks. In 2004 elections, a new generation of radical revolutionaries won a large share of seats in parliament as well as many city and village council elections.

The right wins power

In 2005, Mahmoud Ahmadinejad's election was a stunning upset over former President Akbar Hashemi Rafsanjani. It signified the consolidation of this new force in Iranian politics who took the name "principlists," for their commitment to the original goals of the revolution. The semblance of a democratic vote was a means to an end, but no longer an end in itself. Ahmadinejad's religious mentor Ayatollah Mohammad Mesbah-Yazdi warned his disciples, "Accepting Islam is not compatible with democracy."

Pledging loyalty to the supreme leader, Ahmedinejad and his allies accelerated their campaign to take over key state institutions. In 2006, they even made a bid to put their allies on the Assembly of Experts, an elected body of 86 clerics who select a supreme leader and monitor his work. But the new president and his chief clerical ally on the assembly, ultra hard-line Ayatollah Mesbah Yazdi, overreached. They were soundly defeated by Rafsanjani and his allies.

The defeat of the clerical right in 2006 election intensified their quest for power using a variety of tools. Islamic courts tried clerics for un-Islamic activities. Newspapers were closed after publishing even modest criticism of government actions. The government increasingly warned of plots by foreign governments to carry out a "velvet revolution" similar to the upheavals in Ukraine and Georgia that produced democratic elections. Ahmadinejad and others from the ultra-right even publicly assailed early revolutionaries and longstanding political figures. The wave of repression was a harbinger of the regime's crackdown on the new Green Movement opposition after the disputed June 2009 presidential elections.

The future

- The debate over republic versus religion will be central to Iranian politics for the foreseeable future, even if the Green Movement recedes as an opposition force.

- The new generation of ultra-hardliners will complicate—and possibly preclude—a peaceful resolution to the democracy versus Islam debate.

- For the New Right, electoral procedures now appear useful largely to legitimize their rule.

Daniel Brumberg is a senior adviser to the Center for Conflict Analysis and Prevention at USIP, where he also served as acting director of USIP's Muslim World Initiative.

The Opposition

9

The Green Movement

Abbas Milani

- The Green Movement took its name from a green sash given to Mir Hossein Mousavi by Mohammad Khatami, Iran's two-term president and the reform movement's first standard-bearer.

- The Green Movement reached its height when up to 3 million peaceful demonstrators turned out on Tehran streets to protest official claims that Mahmoud Ahmadinejad had won the 2009 presidential election in a landslide. Their simple slogan was: "Where is my vote?"

- The movement soon embodied the frustrated aspirations of Iran's century-old quest for democracy and desire for peaceful change.

- Mousavi and his wife, Zahra Rahnavard, are the nominal leaders. Mehdi Karroubi has been its most radical and relentless advocate. Former President Akbar Hashemi Rafsanjani embodies politicians who vacillate between supporting the movement and siding with Supreme Leader Ali Khamenei.

- The movement has no hierarchical structure. Its global reach resembles the Internet it uses. But its amorphous structure is both its strength and weakness.

Overview

A new opposition was born after the disputed June 12, 2009, presidential election that changed the face of Iranian politics—and Iran. A nation long maligned—for a regime of corrupt zealots that harbored terrorists and took diplomats hostage—suddenly became a beacon of democratic hope. The movement was widely seen as a new non-violent, non-utopian and populist paradigm of revolution that infused twenty-first century Internet technology with people street power. In turn, the regime's facade as a populist theocracy, led by a divinely sanctioned "guardian" and supported by a deeply pious nation, was torn asunder.

Over the next six months, the Green Movement evolved from a mass group of angry voters to a nation-wide force demanding the democratic rights originally sought in the 1979 revolution, rights that were hijacked by radical clerics. Every few weeks, protesters took to the streets to challenge the regime and its leadership. But by early 2010, the regime had quashed public displays of opposition. The Green Movement retreated into a period of soul-searching and regrouping.

Origins

The Green Movement is, in its composition and genealogy, both old and new. The revolution of 1979 was the result of a historically incongruent alliance between modernizing middle and technocratic classes, the urban poor, women's and students' groups, some disgruntled members of Iran's new industrialist class, members of the bazaar and "de-modernizing" forces led by revolutionary leader Ayatollah Ruhollah Khomeini. The foot-soldiers of the revolution were the new urbanites—culturally religious, conservative and a-modern, if not anti-modern, peasants who had come to the cities in search of their share of petro-dollars.

Since 1941, this class had been assiduously courted by radical Islamist groups. They played an important role in the 1979 revolution. They have since splintered into factions that are today pitted against each other. They were part of the incongruent coalition that overthrew the shah. Included in that coalition were Mir Hossein Mousavi and his activist wife Zahra Rahnavard, who represented the moderate religious elements of the unwieldy anti-shah coalition. At the other end of the coalition were forces today represented by Mahmoud

Ahmadinejad and his allies in the Revolutionary Guards (IRGC) and Basij. They represent the Nietzschean resentments of the new conservative urbanites and their déclassé leaders.

After Ali Khamenei succeeded revolutionary leader Ayatollah Khomeini as supreme leader in 1989, he needed to find a political and social base of his own. He lacked charisma, and his religious credentials were weak. He increasingly relied on and strengthened these forces, particularly the IRGC. Khomeini had banned the IRGC from politics, but Khamenei encouraged both political and economic involvement.

Mousavi emerges

Ahmadinejad's election in 2005 marked the beginning of this group's political rise. The 2009 election was crucial to consolidate its hold on power. But then Mir Hossein Mousavi announced his candidacy for president. He had been prime minister during Iran's war with Iraq between 1980 and 1988. After the constitution was amended to create an executive president and remove the prime minister, Mousavi returned to his roots as an architect and a painter. His eclectic buildings resembled the new style of Italian Renzo Piano.

In 2009, the Guardian Council, responsible for vetting candidates, allowed Mousavi to run. Rejecting his candidacy would have been difficult. The conservative camp apparently calculated that Mousavi's lack of charisma and long absence from politics hurt his election prospects. But Iran's nascent civil society, reformers, the women's movement and student organizations suddenly came to life. Vast networks of supporters appeared all over the country, connected through the Internet and social network sites. Mousavi was often met with large and enthusiastic crowds.

Election turmoil

The day after the June 12 election results were announced, hundreds of thousands of people poured onto Tehran's streets to protest. The regime was caught off guard by the Green Movement's demonstration. Security forces were initially paralyzed by the numbers. But then the regime unleashed security forces, including Revolutionary Guards, units of the Basij paramilitary units, and plain-clothed paramilitary forces called *Lebas Shakhsi*. Thousands of protesters were beaten, hundreds were arrested and dozens were killed by snipers.

On June 18, Khamenei delivered a Friday prayer sermon that dismissed the protesters' complaints and endorsed the election results. It reflected the regime's formal announcement that it would not tolerate the Green Movement—and would do whatever it took to suppress it. The new confrontation was symbolized by the death of 26-year-old Neda Agha Soltan, an aspiring musician, on June 20. She was shot by a sniper, as she stood at the edge of a Green Movement protest. A cell phone video that captured her dying on the pavement was circulated around the world. Neda and pictures of her blood-spattered face became symbols of the Green Movement.

For the next six months, an array of groups under the Green Movement umbrella used public holidays and national commemorations to rally on the streets of several cities. In the past, the government had bussed in people to attend events and used them to claim popular support. In 2009, however, it dispatched security forces to get the people off the streets. With each new round, the government grew more repressive, yet also appeared increasingly vulnerable.

Fall protests

During demonstrations in the fall, the issues shifted from alleged election fraud to challenges of the system and the supreme leader himself. "Death to the dictator" became a common refrain at protests. Others chanted, "Khamenei is a murderer. His rule is null and void." Students were particularly active. The key events included:

- Sept. 18–Qods Day, or Jerusalem Day. In the past, Iranians shouted "Death to Israel" at rallies. In 2009, protesters instead shouted "Death to Russia," because it was the first government to recognize Ahmadinejad's election.

- Nov. 4–Anniversary of the U.S. Embassy takeover. Pupils traditionally get the day off and schools bus them to the old American compound for a rally. In 2009, thousands turned out on the streets to instead protest their own regime, not the United States. Chants of "Death to America" were replaced by cries of "Death to No One." Some even shouted, "A green Iran doesn't need nuclear weapons." More pointedly, others shouted, "Obama, you are either with us—or with them."

- Dec. 7–National Students Day, commemorating the deaths of three students in protests around the time of Vice President Nixon's 1953 visit to Tehran. The turnout was the largest since the summer and spread to campuses across the country, despite increasingly harsh government tactics, including alleged torture, rape and deaths in prison.

- Dec. 19–Montazeri's death. The death of Grand Ayatollah Ali Montazeri, Iran's leading dissident cleric and spiritual father to the Green Movement, sparked more mass demonstrations. Crowds were enormous in the holy city of Qom, earlier off-limits to protests, and elsewhere. Montazeri had been the clerical face of the opposition since 1989, when he was fired as heir apparent to Khomeini, for criticizing the regime's mass executions and failure to live up to its revolutionary promises. The government responded to the outpouring by redistributing the statement about Montazeri's dismissal as supreme leader 20 years earlier.

- Dec. 27–Ashoura, the holiest day of the year for Shiites as they commemorate the seventh century martyrdom of Hussein, the Prophet Mohammed's grandson. Hundreds of thousands turned out in mass protests. In response, government forces opened fire on unarmed civilians in the streets. Turmoil spread to at least 10 major cities. There were several confirmed deaths, scores of injured and hundreds of arrests. The fact that a clerical regime had opened fire on peaceful demonstrators on the day of Ashoura was a serious departure from a long tradition of non-violence on that day.

Show trials

As momentum grew behind the Green Movement, the government response was increasingly tough. In the fall of 2009, more than 100 of the Green Movement's most important leaders, activists and theorists appeared in show trials reminiscent of Joseph Stalin's infamous trials in the 1930s. They included:

- Saeed Hajjarian, architect of the reform movement and senior adviser to former President Khatami.

- Mohammad Abtahi, former vice president under Khatami.

- Moshen Miradamadi, head of the largest reform party, former member of parliament, former head of parliament's foreign affairs and national security committee, and one of three masterminds of the U.S. Embassy takeover.

- Behzad Nabavi, co-founder of a reform party and former deputy speaker of parliament.

The accused were forced to confess on television to several crimes against the nation. But their confessions seemed designed to make a similar point: The Green Movement was a creation of the United States and its goal was to weaken the Islamic regime. Not all the detainees made it to trial. The torture and death of prisoners in the Kahrizak prison became a lingering source of political embarrassment for the regime.

The regime also shut down newspapers, magazines and websites close to the Green Movement. Iran became the country with the most imprisoned journalists. To help fight the reform movement's use of the Internet, the Revolutionary Guards became majority owner of Iran's telecommunications giant.

Soul-searching

In 2010, the Green Movement tried to mobilize demonstrations for the February 11 anniversary of the revolution. But the advance crackdown was so pervasive that leaders of the movement called it off. Public demonstrations were basically over.

The Green Movement moved into a phase of soul-searching. The key question was whether the movement was in temporary retreat, regrouping to develop a new strategy and tactics, or had simply been defeated. A few activists even talked about the need to reconcile with Khamenei and his allies, given signs that the conservative camp had also begun to see Ahmadinejad as a liability.

Some in the Green Movement also talked of a post-Mousavi phase. His unwillingness to criticize Khamenei and his insistence on working within the constitution convinced some Iranians that he no longer reflected the movement's views. Yet another group, led by Mousavi himself, attempted to formulate a more precise platform. A proposed covenant issued in June 2010 was his first step.

A new covenant

One year after the Green Movement's birth, Mousavi published a proposed new covenant. He said the regime represented "institutionalized corruption hiding behind a pretense of piety." He placed the Green Movement in context of Iran's 100-year-old quest for democracy. He was silent on the *velayat-e faqih,* but he clearly stated that a government's legitimacy can be founded only on the will and support of the people. Nothing in the constitution is sacrosanct, he declared, and every article of the law should be the subject to debate and reconsideration.

The current regime, he wrote, disdained, ignored and broke its own laws. In contrast, the Green Movement insisted not only on the rule of law, it also called for laws to reflect international standards on human rights and democracy. Iran's democrats, he added, would insist on equality before the law, irrespective of gender, religion and ideology. Finally, he demanded a "separation of institutions of religion from institutions of the state," although he acknowledged that "religion will certainly have a presence" in Iran's democratic future.

Foreign policy

In foreign policy, Mousavi's covenant differed sharply with the regime. He insisted that Iran should enjoy all the rights afforded law-abiding nations under the Nuclear Non-Proliferation Treaty. But he was emphatic that a new democratic Iran would have full transparency in its relations with other nations and the international organizations—and would not seek a nuclear bomb. Mousavi and other Green Movement leaders have blamed the regime's "adventurism" for U.N. sanctions.

The future

- Short-term, the opposition faces political purgatory. The regime has been willing to use unprecedented brutality to maintain power.

- Long-term, Iran's many challenges are likely to be solved only in a more democratic environment. The pressures include a dominant, Internet-savvy youth, an assertive women's movement, structural economic difficulties (including double-digit unemployment and inflation), badly needed investments in oil and gas industries, and a troubled private sector.

- To survive, the Green Movement must offer a more cohesive leadership and a more cogent platform. It must also find a way to surmount the regime's cyber-jihad, which uses Western, Russian, Chinese and Indian technologies to stifle the opposition's voice.

- The most serious potential problem for Iran's democratic movement is the threat of war. Smart sanctions focused on weakening the regime's ideological and oppressive apparatus can facilitate the maturation of this movement. A military assault could sideline or kill the movement for the foreseeable future.

Abbas Milani, author of The Myth of the Great Satan, *is director of Iranian Studies at Stanford University, where he is also a co-director of the Iran Democracy Project at Hoover Institution.*

10

The Women's Movement

Haleh Esfandiari

- Since the 1979 revolution, women have struggled to regain lost rights and win a larger role in society, despite a regime unfriendly to women's issues.
- The theocracy's suspension of the Family Protection Law enacted under the monarchy once again put women at the mercy of men in the family.
- Women fared modestly in politics. They won positions in parliament, city councils, cabinet and other decision-making jobs, but in small numbers.
- But women made significant gains in education, particularly after obstacles to certain specialized fields were removed.
- After initially pushing for rapid population growth, the government launched a highly successful family planning program. Iran's birth rate went from one of the highest to one of the lowest in the region.

Overview

Iranian women made considerable progress during the Pahlavi era (1925-1979). Education for both girls and boys was free. When Tehran University opened in 1936, Iran's first university admitted both men and women. In 1963, women acquired the right to vote and run for parliament. Under the Family Protection Law, women won the right to petition for divorce and gain child custody. A husband could no longer unilaterally divorce his wife or automatically gain custody of the children. The marriage age for girls was raised from 13 to 18. And men needed the court's permission to take a second wife. By 1978, on the eve of Iran's revolution, 22 women sat in parliament and 333 women served on elected local councils. One-third of university students were female. Two million women were in the work force, more than 146,000 of them in the civil service.

The 1979 revolution politicized the mass of Iranian women. But women's expectations were not realized. The new theocracy systematically rolled back five decades of progress in women's rights. Women were purged from government positions. All females, including girls in first grade, were forced to observe the hejab, or Islamic dress code. Family laws were scraped. For the next three decades, however, the energy Iranian women displayed during the revolution propelled them deeper into the public arena to regain their rights. The result is one of the most dynamic women's movements in the Islamic world, and female activists who have won international recognition in a wide array of professions.

The Khomeini decade (1979–1989)

Under revolutionary leader Ayatollah Ruhollah Khomeni, Iran's new theocracy gave priority to Islamic tradition over modern mores. One of the revolutionary government's first acts was to suspend the Family Protection Law and dismantle Family Courts. Men were once again free to divorce their wives by simple declaration; they also gained exclusive custody of their children. Women could no longer file for divorce unless the right was stipulated in marriage contracts, and they lost the right to child custody. Restrictions on polygamy were also removed. The marriage age for girls was reduced to puberty, which is nine under Islamic law. In 1981, parliament approved the Islamic Law of Retribution, introducing flogging, stoning and payment of blood money for crimes ranging from adultery to violation of Islamic dress codes.

Professionally, women were slowly pushed into traditional female fields, such as teaching and nursing. Women were barred from becoming judges. Government–run day care centers were closed, making it difficult for women to stay in jobs anyway. At universities, the idea of segregating women and men was soon abandoned as impractical, but it took several years before bars were removed on certain fields of education—in turn affecting job prospects.

Politically, women held on to the right to vote and run for parliament. Four women were elected to the first parliament in 1980, and later sat on local councils. But most women in decision-making positions were either dismissed, given early retirement, or demoted. A decade passed before the first woman was named deputy minister, 17 years passed before a woman was appointed vice president, and 30 years passed before the Islamic Republic named its first female minister. The constitution bars women from the position of supreme leader—the highest post in the country—but does not stipulate the gender of the president or cabinet members. Women have tried to run in presidential elections, but they have all been disqualified.

On social issues, the theocracy's initial policies were harsh. Hejab, or Islamic dress and head cover, was forcibly imposed. Showing a bit of hair became punishable, with penalties ranging from heavy monetary fines to 70 lashes. The regime also attempted to segregate men and women in public places, but did not succeed. But the eight-year Iran-Iraq War (1980-1988) had a galvanizing influence on the status of women. Women were drawn into the work force as nurses, doctors and support for soldiers on the war front. In the absence of men, many women became the family bread winners. During the revolution's first decade, women in the work force fell from about 13 percent to 8.6 percent.

The Rafsanjani presidency (1989-1997)

After the war, women became pivotal politically. They voted in substantial numbers for Akbar Hashemi Rafsanjani for president in 1989, and again in 1993 because he was pragmatic on women's issues. Rafsanjani gradually eased social controls. Women were harassed less on the streets. They benefited from minor changes in the personal status law and were able to participate in international sports competitions. The number of girls in schools and universities soared.

Rafsanjani also reversed the Islamic Republic's policy of encouraging large families and launched a family planning program to curb Iran's alarmingly rapid rate of population growth. The success of this program is one of the Islamic Republic's most striking achievements. The total fertility rate (the average number of births per woman) dropped from 5.6 in the early 1980s to 2.0 in 2000, and to 1.9 births per woman in 2006. The decline has been particularly impressive in rural areas, where the average number of births per woman dropped in one generation from 8.1 to 2.1. As a result, the annual rate of natural population increase declined from 3.2 percent in early 1980s to 1.8 percent in 2006.

The Khatami years (1997-2005)

Women fared even better during the presidency of Mohammad Khatami. Riding on a wave of pro-reform sentiment, he appointed a handful of women to prominent posts. Among them: Masoumeh Ebtekar was his vice president for the environment and Zahra Rahnavard became the first woman chancellor of an Iranian university. In 2004, 13 women were elected to parliament—the largest number since the revolution.

Under Khatami, women also scored several legal victories. Pressure from women led the government to reintroduce modified parts of the suspended Family Protection Law. Women judges became special advisers to presiding clerics on special family courts. In 1994, parliament enacted a law awarding a woman monetary compensation when her husband initiated divorce proceedings and she was not at fault. In 2002, parliament raised the age of marriage for girls from nine to 13. The ban on unaccompanied single women studying abroad on government scholarships was also lifted. Khatami's presidency also saw the burgeoning of non-government organizations that laid the foundation for a more vibrant civil society. Many were founded around women's issues.

The Ahmadinejad years (2005-)

Mahmoud Ahmadinejad struggled to balance rival trends at a time women carried growing weight at the ballot box. He faced deepening resolve among hardliners to curb the female quest for full equality; he was also confronted by public pressure from women not to be relegated to second-class status again.

Under hardliners, women generally fared poorly on several fronts. The momentum for change built up over the previous 16 years virtually evaporated. The government closed down *Zanan*, the country's leading feminist magazine. In 2007 elections, only 43 women were elected to local councils out of tens of thousands of seats. In the 2008 parliamentary elections, the only two reformist women in parliament were voted out.

Of 7,168 candidates, 585 were women, but only nine were elected. Police cracked down on women for dress code violations. Ahmadinejad also called on women to have more children.

In the June 2009 presidential campaign, tens of thousands of women from all social classes supported the two reformist candidates who backed greater women's rights. For the first time, candidates had women advising and campaigning for them in public. After the election, Ahmadinejad lost the support of a large number of conservative women because of atrocities committed by the security forces against protesters. He was noticeably silent on the trials and harsh on the sentencing of women, allegations of rape and torture of detainees, and the mistreatment of women protesting the detention of relatives.

After his reelection, Ahmadinejad nominated three women to his cabinet. But only one of his nominees, Marzieh-Vahid Dastjerd as minister of health, was approved by parliament because of objections by a number of leading clerics and conservative politicians.

Factoids

- In 2009 elections, 42 women registered to run for the presidency. All were disqualified by the Guardian Council. But for the first time, the council also indicated that women were not banned from running for the top political job.

- Because of growing pressure from both reformers and conservatives, women's rights became one of the four top issues in the 2009 presidential election. All four candidates developed positions on women's issues.

- In 2010, 65 percent of all university students were female.

Prominent women

Farrokhru Parsa, the minister of education, was the first woman named to a cabinet position in 1968.

Mahnaz Afkhami was named minister of state for women's affairs in 1975.

Simin Behbahani, Iran's greatest living female poet, used her poetry to describe social and cultural deprivations, both before and after the revolution. Born in 1927, she was beaten up by police during a demonstration on International Women's Day in 2006, and in 2010 was prevented from leaving Iran to accept a prize in Paris.

Masoumeh Ebtekar became Iran's first female vice president during the reform era of President Mohammad Khatami. She was also a spokeswoman for the students who seized the U.S. Embassy in 1979.

Shahla Sherkat, editor of *Zanan*, the leading feminist journalist under the Islamic Republic. *Zanan* was shut down in 2008, after 16 years of publication.

Faezeh Hashemi, Rafsanjani's daughter, became a symbol of women's expanding role in the 1990s. She founded the Islamic Countries' Women's Sports Solidarity Council In 1992. She was elected to parliament for one term in 1996. And in 1998, she founded the first women's daily newspaper, *Zan* or "Woman." The paper was closed by the authorities in 1999.

Samira Makhmalbaf, one of several female filmmakers, was the youngest director to show a film at the 1998 Cannes Film Festival—at the age of 18. She won her first prize at Cannes for her second film at the age of 20.

Shirin Ebadi, the first female judge in Iran during the monarchy, and a human rights lawyer, won the Nobel Peace Prize in 2003. The first Iranian and first Muslim woman laureate, she used the prize money to establish the Center for Defense of Human Rights, which was closed by security officials in 2010. Ebadi went into exile.

Under Ahmadinejad, **Nasrine Soltankhah** was vice president for science and technology and Fatemeh Javadi was vice president for the environment.

Zahra Rahnavard was the first female university chancellor and wife of former Prime Minister and 2009 presidential candidate Mir Hossein Mousavi. Appointed by Khatami, she was removed when hardliners took political control. Ahmadinejad questioned her academic credentials during the televised campaign debates, a move that backfired on him among women. She was the first wife to campaign for her husband. She became a spokesperson for the opposition Green Movement after her husband lost.

The One Million Signatures Campaign for Equality is a movement launched in 2006 to secure one million signatures on petitions demanding equal rights for women in all spheres. Under Ahmadinejad, several organizers were arrested, put on trial and sentenced to prison terms. The government tried to crush the campaign, but did not succeed.

The future

- Since 1979, women have persistently emerged as one of the most dynamic political forces in the Islamic Republic. Despite many obstacles, they have won considerable freedom in education, employment, the public sphere and personal dress—all of which will be difficult to completely roll back.

- The struggle for women's rights is central to the larger struggle for individual rights. It has become one of the four top issues in national elections.

- Women's issues are important to both the modern and traditional sectors of society. So the pressure for expanded rights will continue, no matter who is in power.

Haleh Esfandiari is director of the Middle East Program at the Woodrow Wilson International Center for Scholars and the author of Reconstructed Lives: Women and Iran's Islamic Revolution *and* My Prison, My Home: One Woman's Story of Captivity in Iran.

11

The Youth

Omid Memarian and Tara Nesvaderani

- Youth is the largest population bloc in Iran. Over 60 percent of Iran's 73 million people are under 30 years old.

- Iranian youth are among the most politically active in the 57 nations of the Islamic world. As the most restive segment of Iranian society, the young also represent one of the greatest long-term threats to the current form of theocratic rule.

- Young activists have influenced the Islamic Republic's political agenda since 1997. After the 2009 presidential election, youth was the biggest bloc involved in the region's first sustained "people power" movement for democratic change, creating a new political dynamic in the Middle East.

- The Islamic Republic forcibly regained control over the most rebellious sector of society through detentions, expulsions from universities, and expanding the powers of its own young paramilitary forces.

- But youth demands have not changed, and anger seethes deeply beneath the surface. The regime also remains vulnerable because it has failed to address basic socio-economic problems among the young.

Overview

Iran's youth have been politically active since the 1953 ouster of Prime Minister Mohammad Mossadegh. The death of three students in protests against Vice President Nixon's 1953 visit —to support the shah after a CIA-backed coup against the elected government—is still a national holiday. The young were key players in the 1979 revolution. Today, their strength is also in numbers. A baby boom after the revolution almost doubled the population from 34 million to 62 million in the first decade. Iran is now one of the youngest societies in the world, skewing politics, the economy and social pressures. The demographic bulge is one of the biggest threats to the status quo.

The youth bloc has been shaped by political and military crises. In the 1980s, they were the majority of combatants in the eight-year war with Iraq; even pre-teen Basij volunteers became human minesweepers. In the 1990s, Iranian youth demanded their post-war due in politics, the economy and society. By 1997, their growing numbers helped elect reformist President Mohammad Khatami. But as he failed to produce change, the young pulled back. The partial youth boycott of the 2005 presidential election was key to Mahmoud Ahmadinejad's election. Their reentry into politics in the 2009 election seriously altered Iranian politics.

Iran's youth are increasingly pivotal to elections. After the 1979 revolution, the voting age was lowered to 15, but later raised to 16 then 18, as the theocrats recognized the youth's political power. The young constitute nearly 40 percent of the electorate, a number expected to grow over the next decade. Whether they vote, and how, will be a major factor in the 2013 parliamentary elections, the regime's next official test.

Conditions of life

Three decades after the revolution promised opportunity, Iran's youth instead face growing problems:

- The government generates only about 300,000 of the roughly 1 million jobs needed annually to absorb young people entering the labor market.

- Unemployment among youth has almost doubled since 1990. Young people between 15 and 29 make up 35 percent of the population but account for 70 percent of the unemployed. Among males, roughly one in four is unable to find a job. Among women with higher education, unemployment is estimated at around 50 percent.

- In 2010, the government intensified its monitoring of youth activities and issued a list of approved men's hairstyles and women's clothing that affected mainly the young.

- Young Iranians have borne a large share of the regime's retributions for unrest in 2009. Thousands were detained in the tumultuous months following the disputed election. Many student activists were also given failing grades or threatened with expulsion from universities.

Key issues

For Iran's youth, four problems are particularly sensitive. All have contributed to a deep frustration—and political dissent.

Unemployment: Even with a university degree, it takes about three years to find a job. And vast numbers of young people end up chronically underemployed, which has produced a widespread sense that their future prospects are bleak. Employment issues have contributed to other problems, including alcohol and drug abuse, prostitution and runaways, escape into marriages that end in early divorce, social unrest, and the flight of the educated class. Iran has one of the world's highest rates of brain drain, according to the International Monetary Fund.

Independence: Due to chronic job shortages and an even larger housing shortage, the number of unmarried youth in their twenties has doubled over the past generation. Up to three-quarters of Iranians in their twenties still live with their parents, partly because they are not able to afford living on their own.

Sexual crisis: Social interaction among young males and females who are not married is officially prohibited, albeit widely ignored in the privacy of homes. Rigid restrictions have spawned an underground social culture, despite stiff penalties. Drinking or dancing can lead to arrest by the morality police and punishment of 70 lashes. Many young people also face a sexual crisis.

"In the absence of any option for overt political dissent, young people have become part of a self-proclaimed revolution in which they are using their bodies to make social and political statements. Sex has become both a source of freedom and an act of political rebellion," Pardis Mahdavi wrote in her 2009 book, *Passionate Uprisings: Iran's Sexual Revolution.* The government has encouraged "temporary marriage," which is allowed in Shiite Islam, as one solution. The sexual crisis has also contributed to increases in HIV/AIDS, sexually transmitted diseases and abortion. In 2009, the head of Iran's AIDS research association said the highest prevalence of AIDS was among people between 25 and 29 years old.

Drugs: Use of narcotics has become a serious problem among youth. Opium has been used for centuries in Iran, and cultivation of opium poppy was a large part of Persia's gross national product in the 19th century, before oil, according to the U.N. Office on Drugs and Crime. It was outlawed in 1955. But drug use and the variety of drugs used began to grow again after the 1979 revolution, particularly among youth and women.

Statistics vary widely. In 2010, the Islamic Republic had some 1.2 million hardcore drug addicts, with another 800,000 casual users, according to the head of Iran's drug prevention program. The average age for users was in their twenties. Another 130,000 become addicted to drugs annually, according to Iran's police chief. But the U.N. 2010 World Drug Report reported that Iran had one of the world's highest rates of heroin addiction, with some 20 percent of the population aged 15 to 60 involved in illicit drug use, and up to 16 percent in that age group injecting drugs. Iran also consumed the largest amount of the opium not converted into heroin— a staggering 42 percent of the world total. Proximity to Afghanistan facilitated the trend. From 1996 to 2008, Iran accounted for more than two-thirds of all global opium seizures, much of it from across the 600-mile border with Afghanistan, the U.N. report said.

Political actors

After the 2009 presidential election, youth activism played out in three phases. Phase one witnessed a spontaneous uprising for two weeks after the June 12 election. The original issue was alleged election fraud. Iran's youth—including students but also a cross-section of non-students—constituted a large percentage of the opposition that poured out on the streets in several major cities to protest alleged vote rigging in favor of Ahmadinejad. Protesters organized through the Internet and word of mouth. Neda Agha Soltan, a 26-year-old philosophy student gunned down during the June 20 street protests, became the symbol of the uprising.

Phase two played out in protests pegged to national and religious holidays in the fall. Demands grew to include calls for political change and condemnation of Supreme Leader Ali Khamenei. Protesters took to the streets under cover of longstanding commemorations, such as Qods Day on Sept. 18; the anniversary of the U.S. Embassy takeover on Nov. 4; National Student's Day on Dec. 7; and Ashoura, the week-long Shiite holiday in late December. Students were the main organizers and participants. The second phase gained momentum after the abrupt death of dissident cleric Grand Ayatollah Ali Montazeri on Dec. 19, which sparked a huge outpouring in Qom—the first time the Green Movement spread to Iran's center of religious learning.

Phase three began with the crackdown that blocked all major protests in 2010, including demonstrations called for on Feb. 11, the 31st anniversary of Iran's revolution, and during the Iranian New Year in late March. But students kept the opposition movement alive in smaller protests at universities in Tehran, Shiraz, Isfahan, Mazandaran and Kurdistan. On May 1, Labor Day, some 2,000 students reportedly protested an unannounced visit by Ahmadinejad to Tehran University. Students quickly organized a march and chanted slogans urging unity among workers and students. On May 10, some 1,000 students, shouting "freedom" and "resign," protested another unannounced presidential visit at Shahid Beheshti University. Students in Tehran also protested lectures by Mojtaba Samaereh Hashemi, a presidential adviser, on Apr. 14, and Saeid Ghasemi, a Revolutionary Guards commander, on May 10. They used banners, chanted slogans, and demanded freedom for political prisoners. University of Kurdistan students went on a hunger strike to protest the execution of five political activists on May 9. Other demonstrations were held at Amir Kabir University, Iran University of Science and Technology, University of Kurdistan and Babol Noshirvani University of Technology. Tightened security throughout the country prevented protests on the first anniversary of the disputed election.

Youth organizations

The **Office for Consolidating Unity,** or *Daftar-e Tahkim-e Vahdat,* is Iran's largest student movement. It was known as the Students Following the Imam's Line when it was formed in 1979; it has branches in most state and private universities. Its national central council is elected annually. Its original agenda was to support the revolution and combat secular and liberal political trends. The group gained fame for the 1979-1981 U.S. Embassy seizure, an event it still commemorates annually. But its agenda gradually evolved from a focus on Islamic ideology to individual rights under Islamic rule. The group's calls for political and social openings contributed to the reform movement's birth in the late 1990s. Members were involved in 1999 student protests, the largest demonstrations until the 2009 election.

The umbrella movement fragmented over support for President Khatami and reform. In 2002, a minority faction met in Shiraz and elected its own leadership; it is called the **Shiraz faction.** The majority faction met later at Tehran's Allameh Tabatabai University and elected its central council. It is called the **Allameh faction.** Disillusioned with politics, Allameh favored a boycott of the 2005 presidential election; Shiraz supported Ahmadinejad.

Before the 2009 election, Allameh wrote the four presidential candidates with a list of demands, including academic freedom, free speech and release of student prisoners. Only Karroubi responded; he supported their demands, which led Allameh to formally endorse him. After the election, Allameh was at the forefront of Green Movement protests. They called people to the streets through social networks, and organized protests on campuses. Since the election, many members, including four of nine central council members, have been detained. Activists have also reportedly been given failing grades or expelled from universities in Tehran, Shiraz, Tabriz, Isfahan and Babol.

Independent student organizations, such as the **Students for Freedom and Equality,** tried to create a national student network and campaign against government agents on campuses. The left wing student group organized demonstrations in 2007 and participated in the 2009 protests. Several members were arrested. The United Student Front, founded in 1996, is a radical secular group that meets off-campus due to its unofficial status. Officials closed down its website and central office in 2000, forcing the group underground. It called on followers to protest after the 2009 election.

The **Basij,** or "mobilization of the oppressed," is a quasi-volunteer paramilitary organization with branches in most mosques, universities, government offices, and public institutions. Along with the Islamic Revolutionary Guard Corps, the Basij prop up Iran's theocracy. The 'Ashoura' militia is the male wing; the 'Al-Zahra' militia is the female wing. The Basij network includes university Basij and student Basij. Student Basijis, called "seekers," are between the ages of 12 and 14; the "vanguard" are high-school students between 15 and 17 years old.

Ansar-e Hezbollah, or "Followers of the party of God," is a vigilante group that uses force but is not part of official law enforcement. Members wear plain clothes. Ansar-e-Hezbollah is often unleashed against protesters, notably during the 1999 student riots and the 2009 election.

Civil society includes hundreds of youth groups. Iran's youth have been active in the **One Million Signature Campaign** to alter discriminatory laws on women. The **Committee of Human Rights Reporters** was started in 2005 by student and social activists to record human rights violations. Members have been jailed. Founded in 1998 by student activists, the **Committee for Defense of Political Prisoners** advocates for prisoner rights and provides legal aid.

Factoids

- Iran is one of the most tech-savvy societies in the developing world, with an estimated 28 million Internet users, led by youth.

- Iran boasts between 60,000 and 110,000 active blogs, one of the highest numbers in the Middle East, led by youth.

- Despite prohibitions on women's dress and make-up, Iranian women account for almost one-third of all cosmetics bought in the two dozen countries of the Middle East, again led by youth.

The future

- The impact of Iran's baby boomers, born in the 1980s, is only beginning to be felt. Now in their twenties, the boomers will become even more important as they age in defining—and potentially redefining—Iran's political, economic and social agenda over the next quarter century.

- Like the general population, a significant percentage of young Iranians are believed to support Iran's quest for nuclear energy as a key to economic development—and their own futures.

- Despite sanctions, Iran's young are better educated and more worldly than any previous generation. Most are exposed to global media, ideas and culture through satellite television and the Internet. Most young Iranians are believed to want to be part of the international community and globalization.

- But given millennia-old Persian nationalism, even young reform advocates may be reluctant to compromise with the outside world on issues viewed as impinging on national sovereignty.

Omid Memarian is an Iranian-born journalist and blogger who specializes in youth and human rights issues. Tara Nesvaderani is a research assistant at the U.S. Institute of Peace.

12

The New Political Tools

Geneive Abdo

- Internet use in Iran continues to increase at a fast pace. The number of Internet users in Iran has grown from less than 1 million in 2000 to about 28 million, or 38 percent of the population, in 2009.
- The Persian blogosphere is considered one of the most active in the world. The number of active bloggers includes approximately 60,000 routinely updated blogs, according to the Berkman Center for Internet & Society at Harvard University.
- The Islamic Revolutionary Guard Corps is the arm of the state most involved in Internet control and filtering.
- The Iranian filtering system continues to strengthen and deepen. In addition to targeting "immoral" content on the Internet, independent and dissenting voices are filtered across a range of issues, including political reform, criticism of the government, reporting on human rights issues and minority and women's rights.

Overview

Free speech in Iran is severely limited, and the media are predominantly state-controlled. Restrictions on free speech are enshrined in Iran's constitution, which declares, "The media should be used as a forum for healthy encounter of different ideas, but must strictly refrain from diffusion and propagation of destructive and anti-Islamic practices." As a result, communication technology has liberated Iranian society from government restrictions on free speech. Going online has allowed Iranians to express their views. The so-called Green Movement and the broader opposition, in particular, have used new technologies to communicate with their fellow citizens inside as well as outside Iran.

The Internet was particularly critical for civil society in the months before the disputed June 12, 2009, presidential election, and the months shortly thereafter. Opposition activists relied on the Internet to organize activities, express their grievances with the state and expose the state security forces' human rights violations. Civic activism had not been so pervasive since the time of the 1979 Islamic revolution.

Techno-savvy

Of all the countries in the Middle East and Persian Gulf, Iran is the nation with the greatest number of bloggers and an accelerating number of Internet users. Iranian society has become more politicized by adopting Internet-based technology as the primary instrument of dissent. There are tens of thousands of Persian bloggers, which include those inside and outside Iran. More than one-third of the Iranian population, or 28 million people, used the Internet in 2009—compared with less than 1 million in the year 2000, according to reports issued by the International Telecommunications Union.

Access to online media, which includes blogs, Facebook and discussion groups, has created for Iranians an alternative media that shapes public opinion and serves to counter the contrived political narrative advanced by the regime through the state-run media.

In order to deal with the expansive role of the Internet, the state has turned to Internet surveillance as the primary mechanism to maintain control over an increasingly restive society. In fact, aside from China, the Iranian state is deemed to have the most sophisticated technology among authoritarian regimes in blocking and strictly filtering the Internet, controlling social networking and targeting bloggers engaged in civil disobedience. Reporters Without Borders ranked Iran at the bottom of its World Press Freedom Index in 2007, behind repressive countries such as Burma and Cuba.

The state has far more resources to control and manipulate the Internet compared with civil society. Yet Iranian activists' use of new media as a political weapon against the state is among the most sophisticated and savvy in the world. Facebook was one of the main tools for the opposition during the presidential campaign in the spring and summer of 2009 and shortly after the disputed June 2009 election, as were video exchange websites, such as YouTube.com.

Media history

Iranians' widespread use of new communication technologies is the second phase of a media revolution that began with the election of President Mohammad Khatami in 1997. During the early years of his presidency, a relatively free press flourished in Iran. Khatami believed that the media could be a main tool to transform Iran's authoritarian political system. As a former head of the ministry of culture and Islamic guidance, the government agency in charge of the press, Khatami understood the transformative nature of the media. When he was first elected president, hundreds of reformist newspapers and journals began publication, and a free press became the hallmark of his administration—and a way to disseminate his reformist ideas.

By 2000, however, the conservative political elites decided that a free press was too threatening to the Islamic Republic. Supreme Leader Ayatollah Ali Khamenei sounded the warning bell on April 20, 2000, about an end to an independent press. He declared that the press had become "bases for the enemy." With that declaration, Iran's judiciary began closing journals and newspapers and imprisoning journalists. By 2003, the independent press had virtually disappeared.

The emergence of widespread Internet access and use in Iran converged with the end of a brief window of press freedom. For a newer generation of Iranians, freedom of expression through the Internet is less vulnerable to state controls than the press movement of the Khatami era. Thus, telecommunication technologies have ended the regime's monopoly on the media and created more democracy in communication.

Persian blogosphere

Iranians rely on blogs more than any other tool for social networking, particularly blogs used for political discourse. Even in a restrictive country such as Iran, blogs offer a rare opportunity for political discussion.

The widespread use of blogging is often cited as being primarily responsible for communicating grievances against the Iranian regime, but in fact this narrative is only part of the story. Social networking analysts at Harvard's Berkman Center place bloggers in four categories:

- Secular/reformist, which includes famous dissidents usually living outside Iran
- Conservative/religious, which includes bloggers supportive of the regime and the Islamic revolution
- Persian poetry and literature, which contribute to Persian poetry as an important form of cultural expression
- And mixed networks, which include discussions about sports and many other topics.

The secular/reformist bloggers have taken the lead in ongoing discussions about Iranian politics, the separation of religion and state in Iran and current affairs in the world. "The Iranian blogosphere remains a viable arena of political contestation and a forum of viewpoints challenging the ruling ideology of the Islamic Republic," according to the Berkman Center.

The secular oriented bloggers include a high percentage of women. Gender is an interesting and notable feature of the Persian blogosphere, as bloggers in other parts of the world tend to be men.

Another striking characteristic among the secular and reformist bloggers is that they tend to use their real names, which makes them vulnerable to retaliation from Iranian authorities. But an undetermined number of blogs are written outside Iran. Readers inside Iran still have access to those blogs written outside, which is an important way bloggers are able to evade any action from the authorities who block blogs that are critical of the regime.

State censorship

The regime's technical filtering and censorship of the Internet is one of the most extensive in the world. Strategies to gain control of the Internet were well underway in 2001, even though Internet use was still at a minimum. A series of decrees were passed in 2001 by the Supreme Council of the Cultural Revolution that required Internet Service Providers (ISPs) to employ filtering systems. In 2002, a Committee in Charge of Determining Unauthorized Sites was established.

In 2009, Iran required all private ISPs that offer Internet connections to the public to connect through the state-owned Telecommunications Company of Iran. This requirement means that all Internet activity must pass through one gateway, which the government controls. Through this system, the state conducts Internet surveillance. State security services can interrupt and monitor online networks, monitor discussions about planned protests and other forms of civil disobedience, and target the names and locations of activists.

Since the June election in 2009, state authorities have slowed the Internet's speed significantly to 56 KB, according to a report issued in March 2010 by Reporters Without Borders. The slow speed has dramatically hampered the opposition movement's ability to mobilize demonstrators in as large numbers as it did shortly after the June election, when an estimated 3 million Iranians protested on the streets of Tehran.

Iran has produced technology for identifying and blocking web sites considered politically harmful. Like China, Iran is becoming less reliant on Western sources by producing this technology domestically. This achievement has been important for the regime, which considers using Western technology for the Internet a weakness. Domestically produced technology is used for filtering, for searching the Internet for tracking keywords and links to banned websites, and for tracking material considered to be un-Islamic.

Before the events on February 11, 2010, marking the thirty-first anniversary of the Islamic revolution, the Iranian authorities slowed Internet service in Iran, shut down text messaging services and blocked Google and Gmail. Google confirmed a drop in traffic during this period. Blocking Facebook is now a permanent strategy employed before demonstrations.

Revolutionary Guards' role

In September 2009, a firm called the Mobin Trust Consortium, which was partially owned by the Islamic Revolutionary Guards Corps (IRGC), bought 51 percent of shares in the Telecommunications Company of Iran, for an estimated $8 billion. This was considered the largest sale in the history of Iran's stock exchange.

The IRGC then established entire hubs of technology blockades with foreign expertise. In 2009, the Revolutionary Guards established a state-sanctioned Cyber Defense Command, the most significant action by the state to counter online political activism. This institution is responsible for investigating so-called cyber crimes, which are generally allegations against Internet users who are activists or journalists. The IRGC, with its vast political influence, has also managed to get laws passed that make distributing anti-filtering technology, or introducing the public to methods of bypassing censorship, illegal.

In March 2010, the office of Tehran's General and Revolutionary Courts announced that 30 individuals suspected of being involved in organized cyber wars were arrested after a series of complicated intelligence operations in communications technology. This move followed a wave of attacks against anti-government websites and blogs by a group called Iran's Cyber Army, which are renegade pro-regime activists.

Factoids

- All Internet Service Providers in Iran are routed through a central hub owned by a company under the command of the Islamic Revolutionary Guards. This allows the government to monitor, filter, slow or shut off all Internet in the country.

- The IRGC formed a "Cyber Defense Command" in 2009, which is responsible for monitoring potentially subversive Internet activity.

- Monitoring and filtering the Internet is enshrined through law, which mandates that all users' browsing data must be stored for three months.

- Methods of the government's Internet control and monitoring include technical filtering of the Internet to prevent access to specific types of information by identifying specific keywords, domain names and web addresses deemed to be subversive; intercepting email to identify and monitor dissidents; and hacking blogs and websites, which can disrupt and shutdown sites.

The future

- Internet use continues to increase annually in Iran, despite government restrictions.

- Iranian activists outside the country are working to encourage technology firms and governments to make available advanced tools to counter state censorship.

- These tools include a hardened satellite to host Iranian channels. This would enable effective Persian news services, such as the BBC Persian Service and Voice of America, to escape the authorities' routine jamming efforts.

- Activists are also working to facilitate the provision of high-speed Internet. Because the regime deliberately slows the Internet, making alternative satellites available—aside from those used by the regime—could allow Iranians to have access to high-speed Internet.

Geneive Abdo is the director of the Iran program at The Century Foundation and the editor and creator of www. insideiran.org.

The Iranian Military

13

The Revolutionary Guards

Alireza Nader

- The Islamic Revolutionary Guard Corps is Iran's most powerful security and military organization, responsible for the protection and survival of the regime.
- The Guards are also currently Iran's most powerful economic actor, reinforcing their influence over political decisions.
- Supreme Leader Ayatollah Khamenei and the Revolutionary Guards have formed a symbiotic relationship that buttresses the supreme leader's authority and preserves the status quo.
- U.S. and international sanctions against Iran may be strengthening the Guards at the expense of more pragmatic elements.

Overview

The Islamic Revolutionary Guard Corps (IRGC) was created after the 1979 revolution to enforce Ayatollah Ruhollah Khomeini's concept of an Islamic state ruled by a *velayat-e faqih* (guardianship of the jurist). The Guards played a crucial role not only in crushing early opposition to Khomeini's vision, but also in repelling Saddam Hussein's invasion of Iran in 1980. Since then, the Guards have functioned as both the primary internal and external security force. The IRGC has now eclipsed the Artesh, or conventional forces. It operates substantial and independent land, sea and air forces. It commands burgeoning missile forces. It runs asymmetric warfare through the elite Qods Force and proxy groups, such as Hezbollah. And it would most likely command a nuclear arsenal, if the regime chooses to develop a nuclear weapons capability.

Over time, the Guards have also been transformed into a leading economic and political actor. The IRGC and its associated companies are involved in many sectors of Iran's economy, allowing it to amass unprecedented power. The Guards' ascendance could not have happened without the support of Supreme Leader Ayatollah Ali Khamenei and President Mahmoud Ahmadinejad. Khamenei relied on the Guards to buttress his declining authority and to block political reform. As guarantor of the revolution's core principles, the IRGC played a key role in marginalizing reformist and pragmatic conservative factions seen to challenge those principles.

Military and security role

The IRGC has played an important role in suppressing groups that opposed Khomeini's objectives, such as the Mujahedin-e Khalq (MEK) Organization. The MEK, a leftist group founded in the 1960s, backed the revolution but then split from the theocrats; it was the largest Iranian opposition group until the 2009 election spawned the Green Movement. The Guards were also responsible for putting down various leftist and ethnic insurgencies that broke out after the revolution.

Iraq's 1980 invasion of Iran actually proved to be a boon for Khomeini and the Guards, as it helped unite the nation around the new regime and bolstered the Guards as Iran's premier military force. The Artesh was the shah's main prop; they were also trained and supplied by the Unites States, so were viewed with suspicion by the regime. The Guards, loyal to *velayat-e faqih,* took the lead in repelling Iraq, although their involvement may have actually prolonged the conflict because of their ideological commitment and lack of military experience. Nevertheless, the Guards' role in Iran's so-called "holy defense" against Iraq has been used over the years to burnish their credentials as defender of the revolution and the nation.

The Guards forces now number up to 150,000 men divided into land, sea and air forces. The IRGC land forces are estimated to number between 100,000 and 125,000. The IRGC's navy may total as many as 20,000, though some estimates are significantly lower. Another 20,000 are in the IRGC naval forces. And the Qods Force totals around 5,000. The Basij militia, which is subordinate to the Guards, can also mobilize hundreds of thousands of its members to defend Iran against a foreign invasion.

The Guards are also in charge of executing Iran's strategy of asymmetric warfare in the event of a U.S. or Israeli attack. The IRGC's secretive Qods Force has trained and equipped proxy groups, such as Hezbollah, Hamas, Iraqi Shiite insurgents, and even elements of the Taliban. Some surrogates have already been used to target U.S. and other Western forces in Lebanon, Iraq and Afghanistan; they could be used against U.S. targets outside Iran in the event of a future conflict.

The Guards have also developed an asymmetric naval strategy for use against the U.S. Navy, which has a superior conventional force. The Guards have hundreds of fast attack boats, anti-ship cruise missiles, and naval mines. Together they impede U.S. operations in the Gulf, disrupt shipping, and impose a painful cost on U.S. forces in the event of an armed conflict. The Guards also operate hundreds of ballistic missiles that can target U.S. forces stationed in Gulf Cooperation Council countries, in addition to Israel and beyond.

The Guards are also Iran's most powerful internal security force, at times cooperating and competing with the ministry of intelligence and other security organizations. The Guards' intelligence organization appears to have eclipsed the ministry of intelligence in scope and authority, especially after the disputed 2009 presidential election. Other security organizations such as the Basij and the Law Enforcement Forces have become subordinate to the Guards.

Economic giant

The Guards' involvement in the Iranian economy began during Ayatollah Akbar Hashemi Rafsanjani's presidency. Reconstruction of Iran's economy, battered by nearly 10 years of war and revolution, was one of his major priorities. The IRGC had the manpower to engage in reconstruction activities. Rafsanjani may have also hoped to co-opt the Guards by giving them a slice of the economic pie.

Over the next 20 years, however, the Guards became Iran's largest economic force. The Guards currently dominate most sectors of the economy, from energy to construction, telecommunication to auto making, and even banking and finance. Khatam al Anabia (the Seal of the Prophets), the Guards' construction headquarters, is involved in much of the Guards' official economic activities. But the IRGC is also linked to dozens, perhaps even hundreds, of companies that appear to be private in nature but are run by IRGC veterans. So the Guards' economic influence activities encompass a broad network of current and former members rather than a single official or centrally administered organization.

The IRGC has taken advantage of its national security authority to extend its control. The Guards prevented a Turkish company from building the Imam Khomeini international airport in 2004 on national security grounds. The takeover of the Telecommunications Company of Iran by a Guards-affiliated consortium in 2009 may have also been motivated by security concerns, especially after the presidential election and subsequent unrest.

The Guards have arguably benefitted from international sanctions and Iran's isolation, which hurt their domestic and foreign business competitors by increasing business costs. The IRGC's ability to tap into state funds and its relatively vast independent resources have provided a decisive advantage. Under Ahmadinejad, the Guards have been awarded hundreds of no-bid government contracts in addition to billions of dollars in loans for construction, infrastructure and energy projects. The Guards' reported involvement in illicit economic activities may also cushion them from the full effects of sanctions. Ironically, tougher sanctions would undoubtedly further damage Iran's economy, but they may actually strengthen the very force driving national security policies, including the nuclear program.

Political role

One of the key issues dividing reformist and conservative factions has been the role of the Guards in Iranian politics. Reformists and even some conservatives contend that Khomeini explicitly forbid the Guards' involvement in politics. The Guards, they argue, were established only to protect the regime. The Guards' political ascent began during the presidency of Mohammad Khatami between 1997 and 2005. Khatami and his supporters envisioned a series of political, social, and economic reforms to make the Islamic Republic a more "modern" Islamic system. But the reformist agenda threatened the conservative ideology, political power and ideological authority of Supreme Leader Ali Khamenei, who succeeded Khomeini in 1989. Reformist intellectuals questioned Khamenei's leadership, and even the efficacy of having a supreme leader. Khamenei viewed the Guards as an effective bulwark against the reformist agenda.

The Guards' rank and file has historically reflected Iranian society and politics at large. Many Guards members supported Khatami in 1995 and Mir Hussein Mousavi in 2009. Nevertheless, the Guards' top leadership comprises conservatives and "principlists" deeply opposed to political reforms. The IRGC leadership's opposition to Khatami's reforms was manifested in the "chain murder" of reform intellectuals. The Guards also wrote a letter to Khatami threatening a coup d'etat if he did not rein in the 1999 student demonstrations.

The 2005 election of President Mahmoud Ahmadinejad, a former Revolutionary Guard and a "principlist," could not have been possible without the active support of Khamenei and the Guards. Allegations of fraud and ballot-stuffing by the Guards and Basij surrounded Ahmadinejad's victory over Rafsanjani. After the election, Ahmadinejad awarded the IRGC even more government loans and contracts. Guard members also won increasing control of Iran's internal and national security organizations. IRGC ideologues loyal to Ahmadinejad and the political status quo were also appointed to replace reformists, pragmatic conservatives and technocrats in the bureaucracy.

The 2009 presidential election confirmed the Guards' role as Iran's preeminent power broker, after the supreme leader. Senior Guards officials indicated they would not tolerate a reformist such as former Prime Minister Mir Hossein Mousavi, Ahmadinejad's leading opponent. Interior Minister Sadegh Mahsouli, a former Guards officer turned businessman who was responsible for supervising the election, played a crucial role in Ahmadinejad's re-election. And after the disputed poll, the Guards were in charge of crushing the mass protests that flared for six months. The reformist and Green Movement accused the Guards of conducting a coup.

But the Guards are not a united or monolithic force. And not all IRGC members are ideologues. Many respect Mousavi, who was prime minister in the 1980s, for his devotion to the revolution and his conduct during the Iran-Iraq War. Some Guards have also reportedly been disappointed with Ahmadinejad—and even Khamenei—because of the post-election suppression of dissent. Nevertheless, the symbiotic relationship between Khamenei and the top echelon of the Guards is likely to ensure the IRGC's role as enforcer of the status quo and the principles of the revolution.

The future

- The Guards' and so-called principlists' domination of the regime after the 2009 election may result in more belligerent Iranian foreign and domestic policies, especially on the nuclear issue.

- The Guards may be able to maintain the political status quo if they remain a unified force. However, they face internal divisions, which could potentially weaken Khamenei's hand in a moment of crisis.

- The Guards' involvement in the business world may erode its credibility to the extent that it will not be able to function as an effective security or military force in the future.

Alireza Nader, an international policy analyst at the RAND Corporation, is co-author of Mullahs, Guards, and Bonyads: An Exploration of Iranian Leadership Dynamics.

14

The Basij Resistance Force

Ali Alfoneh

- The Basij Resistance Force is a volunteer paramilitary organization operating under the Islamic Revolutionary Guards Corps (IRGC). It is an auxiliary force with many duties, especially internal security, law enforcement, special religious or political events and morals policing. The Basij have branches in virtually every city and town in Iran.

- The Basij have become more important since the disputed 2009 election. Facing domestic demands for reform and anticipating economic hardships from international sanctions, Supreme Leader Ayatollah Ali Khamenei has mobilized the Basij to counter perceived threats to the regime.

- The Basij's growing powers have in turn increased the force's political and economic influence and contributed to the militarization of the Iranian regime.

- Yet the Basij also face problems, reflected in their poor handling of the 2009 protests, limited budget and integration into the IRGC Ground Forces in July 2008. Targeted U.S. and international sanctions against the IRGC could further weaken the Basij.

Overview

On November 25, 1979, revolutionary leader Ayatollah Ruhollah Khomeini called for the creation of a "twenty million man army." Article 151 of the constitution obliges the government to "provide a program of military training, with all requisite facilities, for all its citizens, in accordance with the Islamic criteria, in such a way that all citizens will always be able to engage in the armed defense of the Islamic Republic of Iran." The "people's militia" was established on April 30, 1980. Basij is the name of the force; a *basiji* is an individual member.

The Basij were initially engaged in assisting the Revolutionary Guards and the Revolutionary Committees (disbanded in the early 1990s) to secure law and order in major population centers. The auxiliary military unit also aided the central government in fighting against Baluchi, Kurdish and Turkoman separatists in remote regions. But their role shifted after Iraq's 1980 invasion. As the war took its toll on Iranian forces, the poorly trained Basij were deployed alongside the regular Iranian military. They were often used in "human wave" tactics, in which they were deployed as cannon fodder or minesweepers, against Iraqi forces. Mobilization of Basij for the war-front peaked in December 1986, when some 100,000 volunteers were on the front. The Basij were often criticized for mobilizing child soldiers for the war effort and using children for "martyrdom" operations.

After the war ended in 1988, the Basij became heavily involved in post-war reconstruction. But their role increasingly shifted back to security as a political reform movement flowered in the late 1990s. The Basij became a policing tool for conservatives to check the push for personal freedoms, particularly among students and women. The Basij were mobilized in 1999 to put down anti-government student protests and to further marginalize the reform movement.

Since the 2005 election of President Mahmoud Ahmadinejad, Basij interventions in politics have become more frequent. The Basij were pivotal in suppressing the anti-government protests after the disputed presidential election on June 12, 2009. Various branches of the Basij were mobilized to counter anti-government protests at high schools, universities, factories and on the street. Yet the Basij also performed poorly, as they were unable to suppress demonstrations through their local branches. The Iranian press reported that neighborhood Basij were not willing to beat up neighbors who protested against the election result by chanting "God is great" from their homes. Some Basij members at high schools and universities also reportedly deserted their assignments after commanders tried to mobilize them to intimidate, harass or beat up fellow students engaged in sit-ins and demonstrations against the election results. And many Basij members evaporated in the face of angry demonstrators in major population centers. Basij and IRGC commanders reported transporting Basij members from outside towns to counter dissidents as the local Basij members were not ready to act in their own neighborhoods or place of work.

Mission and command

The Basij statute stipulates that the militia's mission is to "create the necessary capabilities in all individuals believing in the Constitution and the goals of the Islamic Republic to defend the country, the regime of the Islamic Republic, and aid people in cases of disasters and unexpected events."

After an initial rivalry over who would control them, the Basij were formally incorporated in the organizational structure of the Revolutionary Guards in 1981. There was significant rivalry between the Basij and the Revolutionary Guards during the Iran-Iraq War, according to the memoirs of then parliamentary speaker Akbar Hashemi Rafsanjani. Over the years, the Basij managed to carve out some independence within the IRGC. But they came under the formal authority of the IRGC commander in 2007 and were incorporated into IRGC ground forces in 2008. The IRGC seems to have succeeded in suppressing the independent aspirations of the Basij.

The Basij organizational structure divides each city in Iran—depending on its size and population—into "resistance areas." Each resistance area is then divided into resistance zones, each zone into resistance bases, and each base into several groups. The smaller towns and villages have Basij "resistance cells." Sensitive social housing areas, such as housing for members of the regular army, also appear to have a special Basij presence. The Revolutionary Guards and the regular military are effectively rivals for resources, equipment and power.

Branches

The Basij has several branches. There are three main armed wings:

- Ashoura and Al-Zahra Brigades are the security and military branch tasked with "defending the neighborhoods in case of emergencies."
- Imam Hossein Brigades are composed of Basij war veterans who cooperate closely with the IRGC ground forces.
- Imam Ali Brigades deal with security threats.

The force also has multiple branches with specialized functions. They include:

- Basij of the Guilds [*Basij-e Asnaf*]
- Labor Basij [*Basij-e Karegaran*]
- Basij of the Nomads [*Basij-e 'Ashayer*]
- Public Servants' Basij [*Basij-e Edarii*]
- Pupil's Basij [*Basij-e Danesh-Amouzi*]
- Student Basij [*Basij-e Daneshjouyi*]

Each specialized branch of the Basij functions as a counterweight to non-governmental organizations and the perceived threat they pose to the state. Basij of the Guilds, for example, is a counterpart to professional organizations. The Labor Basij provides a counterpart to labor organizations, unions and syndicates. And the Student Basij balances independent student organizations.

Membership

Estimates of the total number of Basij vary widely. In 2002, the Iranian press reported that the Basij had between 5 million to 7 million members, although IRGC commander Gen. Yahya Rahim Safavi claimed the unit had 10 million members. By 2009, IRGC Human Resource chief Masoud Mousavi claimed to have 11.2 million Basij members—just over one-half the number originally called for by Khomeini. But a 2005 study by the Center for Strategic and International Studies, a Washington think-tank, put the number of full-time, uniformed and active members at 90,000, with another 300,000 reservists and some 1 million that could be mobilized when necessary. Persian language open-source material does not provide any information about what percentage of the force is full time, reservists or paid members of the organization.

Members include women as well as men, old as well as young. During the Iran-Iraq War, Basij volunteers were as young as 12 years old, with some of the older members over 60 years old. Most today are believed to be between high school age and the mid-30s. The perks can include university spots, access to government jobs and preferential treatment.

The Basij statute distinguishes between three types of members:

- Regular members, who are mobilized in wartime and engage in developmental activities in peacetime. Regular members are volunteers and are unpaid, unless they engage in war-time duty.

- Active members, who have had extensive ideological and political indoctrination, and who also receive payment for peacetime work.

- Special members, who are paid dual members of the Basij and the IRGC and serve as the IRGC ground forces.

The Basij statute says members are selected or recruited under the supervision of "clergy of the neighborhoods and trusted citizens and legal associations of the neighborhoods." The neighborhood mosques provide background information about each volunteer applicant; the local mosque also functions as the Basij headquarters for the neighborhood. For full-time paid positions, applicants must apply at central offices of the Basij, in provincial headquarters of the Basij.

Budget and business

The Basij's budget is modest. According to the 2009/2010 national budget, the Basij were allocated only $430 million—or less than $40 per member, on the basis of 11.2 million members. But as a corporation, the Basij reportedly accumulated vast sums through so-called interest-free financial institutions that the Basij and the IRGC established in mid-1980s and the early 1990s to provide social housing and general welfare to their members. As subsequent governments began privatization of publicly owned enterprises, Basij financial institutions used their funds to purchase the privatized companies.

By 2010, the Basij were allegedly a major investor in the Tehran Stock Exchange. The largest Basij-owned investors in the Tehran Stock Exchange allegedly include Mehr Finance and Credit Institution, and its subsidiary Mehr-e Eghtesad-e Iranian Investment Company. Iranian critics of the Basij accuse them of distorting the market, marginalizing not only the private sector, but also the revolutionary foundations that have been a large part of Iranian economy since the revolution. The Basij and the IRGC are also accused of widespread corruption.

Political role

Presidential contender Mehdi Karroubi, a former speaker of parliament, accused the Basij and the Revolutionary Guards of helping manipulate the outcome of the 2005 election, when Ahmadinejad defeated former President Rafsanjani. Karroubi and Mir-Hossein Mousavi raised similar allegations against the Basij after the disputed June 12, 2009 presidential election.

The Basij's performance since the June 2009 election has been mixed. It managed to suppress street protests in the provinces with the help of the local police forces, but maintaining order in major urban centers, especially Tehran, was more difficult. And their actions have faced backlash. On June 15, Basij members reportedly shot and killed protesters at Azadi Square who were forcing their way into the local militia station. From June 22 onward, the Basij constituted only a minority of the forces cracking down on protesters. Basij commander Hossein Taeb, a Shiite cleric with the rank of hojatoleslam, claimed that eight Basij had been killed and 300 wounded during the anti-government protests.

The Student Day protests in December 2009 proved equally challenging for the Student Basij, who had mobilized several thousand members but were still unable to suppress dissidents at campuses in Tehran, Shiraz and Tabriz. The Basij were also unable to contain the massive demonstrations three weeks later during Ashoura, the holiest time of the year for Shiite Muslims. Senior military officials admitted that the IRGC had to mobilize militia members from the capital's outskirts and even from other provinces in order to suppress the unrest.

The regime signaled its displeasure with the Basij's performance. In October 2009, Taeb was removed as Basij chief. A few days later, the militia was formally integrated into the Revolutionary Guards ground forces, with Brig. Gen. Mohammad Naghdi as the new chief. In 2010, the Basij focused significant attention on combating perceived threats to the regime from the Internet. Thousands of members were educated in blogging and filtering of dissident websites, Basij officials acknowledged.

The future

- Without a solution to Iran's internal political turmoil, the Basij's role and powers are almost certain to grow.

- But because they receive less training than other Iranian security forces, their tactics are often the toughest against dissidents—and in turn generate more public anger that could weaken rather than strengthen the regime long-term.

- Incorporating the Basij into the Revolutionary Guards ground forces may improve the overall Basij performance in the future, but in the short- and middle-term, the IRGC and not the Basij are likely to remain the main pillar of support for the regime.

Ali Alfoneh is a resident fellow at the American Enterprise Institute for Public Policy Research.

15

The Conventional Military

Anthony H. Cordesman

- Iran's conventional army, navy and air force are severely limited in capability but are strong enough to create major problems for any invasion. They are unlikely to win any major military clash if the United States intervened decisively to defeat them.

- Like the Islamic Revolutionary Guard Corps (IRGC), Iran's conventional forces have significant capabilities for irregular warfare and to threaten, intimidate, and conduct asymmetric operations and wars of attrition.

- Iran can use conventional long-range missiles as terror weapons and has strong influence over non-state actors like Hezbollah, Hamas and Iraq's armed Shiite groups.

- Iran is a declared chemical weapon state in compliance with the Chemical Weapons Convention, may have a biological weapons program, and has acquired the technology and production capabilities necessary to obtain nuclear fission weapons within the next several years.

- These capabilities act as a growing, if limited, deterrent to attacks on Iran, and in some ways compensate for the limits of its conventional forces.

Overview

Iran is sometimes described as the "Hegemon of the Gulf," but it is a comparatively weak conventional military power with limited modernization since the Iran-Iraq War. It depends heavily on weapons acquired by the shah. Most key equipment in its army, navy and air force are obsolete or relatively low quality imports. Iran now makes some weapons, but production rates are limited and Tehran often exaggerates about its weapons designs. Its forces are not organized or trained to project significant power across the Gulf. Its land forces are not structured to project power deep into a neighboring state like Iraq or to deal with U.S. air-to-ground capabilities.

But Iran is proficient at irregular warfare. It has built up a powerful mix of capabilities for both regular and IRGC forces to defend territory, intimidate neighbors, threaten the flow of oil and shipping through the Gulf, and attack Gulf targets. It has a dedicated force to train and equip non-state actors like Hezbollah, Hamas and Shiite extremists in Iraq—potential proxies that give Iran leverage over other states.

Iran's acquisition of long-range missiles from North Korea and development of its own liquid- and solid-fueled missiles has given it a strike capability that partly compensates for the weakness of its air force. It has declared that it is a chemical weapons power and may have a biological weapons program. It has acquired the technology to produce fission nuclear weapons and has enriched uranium to levels where it is clear it can eventually produce fissile material. These capabilities help compensate for the limited capabilities of its conventional forces by increasing deterrence of outside attack and act as a deterrent to attacks on its irregular and asymmetric forces.

Force strength

- Total forces: 500,000 to 525,000, including Revolutionary Guards. Most are poorly trained conscripts.
- Regular army: 350,000
- Regular navy: 18,000, including some 3,000 to 5,000 Marines
- Regular air force: 25,000 to 35,000

- Reserves: An additional 350,000 poorly trained reserves
- Paramilitary: Some 40,000. In theory, it can mobilize up to 1 million more men (3,500 battalions) in the Basij Resistance Force, which has a nominal strength of over 11 million. Only a fraction of that force receives meaningful training, although Iran has created a substantial local mobilization capability and gives Basij core elements some training with the IRGC.
- Virtually all regular military officers are now products of the revolution.

The status of Iran's military

Estimates of Iran's military differ significantly. More reliable sources include the International Institute of Strategic Studies, Jane's publications, declassified U.S. intelligence, and Congressional Research Service reports. These sources indicate that Iran is still heavily dependent on arms acquired by the shah, and relatively low-grade weapons systems imported from China, North Korea and Viet Nam during the eight-year war with Iraq. Iran has been unable to obtain advanced weapons and military technology from the West, and has had limited deliveries from Russia. Its only major weapons imports from Russia have been short-range missiles, three Kilo-class submarines and TOR short-range surface-to-air missiles. Tehran has not obtained modern armor, artillery, aircraft or major combat ships.

Iran's annual defense budget of roughly $10 billion excludes much of its spending on defense industry, missile programs, support of foreign non-state actors, nuclear capability and intelligence activity. The total is likely to be in the range of $12 billion to $14 billion—less than the United Arab Emirates, and only between 25 percent to 33 percent of Saudi defense spending. Iran spends only about 20 percent of the amount allocated by the six sheikhdoms in the Gulf Cooperation Council—a consistent trend since the Iran-Iraq War ended in 1988.

Despite claims of indigenous production of major weapons systems, Iran has actually only deployed some 100 Zulfiqar main battle tanks (roughly equivalent to the T-72), a small number of Townsan light tanks, 140 Boragh armored personnel carriers and small numbers of self-propelled artillery weapons. But it has produced large numbers of towed artillery weapons and short- to long-range rockets. It has updated and modified many of its older weapons systems, and does produce a variety of effective short-range anti-tank, man-portable surface-to-air, anti-ship and other guided weapons. It is also producing unmanned aerial vehicles, some of which have been modified to carry a conventional warhead.

Iran's land forces

Iran's land forces are large by regional standards, with some 350,000 men in the army and 100,000 in the IRGC land forces. Neither is well equipped. They do not have modern tanks or armored vehicles. Their roughly 1,600 tanks are largely locally made Zulfiqars and some 480 aging versions of the Soviet-designed T-72.

Iran has some 3,200 major artillery weapons, but 2,010 tube artillery weapons are towed systems left over from the Iran-Iraq War. Most of its roughly 900 multiple rocket launchers are area fire weapons with limited operational effectiveness. Many army aircraft and attack helicopters are not operational or cannot be sustained for more than limited periods.

Together, the Army and IRGC have the size and capability to defend Iranian territory. But they are neither organized nor trained for power projection or sustained combat outside Iran. Turkey and the southern Gulf states, led by Saudi Arabia, have weapons that are far more modern and effective. Iran's northern neighbors are much weaker, and Iraq and Afghanistan have limited forces. Iran's land forces do have the bases and ability to operate in Iraq's border areas if Iraq does not have U.S. support.

Iran's air and air defense forces

Iran's air force and the IRGC air branch are its weakest military elements. They have 25,000 to 35,000 members. The International Institute of Strategic Studies (IISS) says Iran has an inventory of some 312 combat aircraft. But 40 percent to 60 percent have limited or no mission capability at any given time, and many are so old or poorly supported that they cannot sustain a high sortie rate.

Some 60 percent of Iran's warplanes were purchased by the shah, including (44) F-14s, (20) F-5Bs, (64) F-4Ds and F-4Es, and (over 60) F-5E/Fs, which have had limited, local modernization since 1979. Its other major combat aircraft comprise (30) Su-24MK, (35) MiG-29, (13) Su-25K Russian fighters; (10) F-1E French Mirages; and (24) Chinese F-7Ms. These include Iraqi fighters flown to Iran during the 1991 Gulf War. Their operational status is uncertain. The Su-24s and MiG-29s are early export versions with less capable avionics.

Iran has modified and updated some aircraft, acquired relatively modern Russian air-to-air and surface-to-air missiles, has Chinese anti-ship missiles, and has tried to equip its F-14s with modified I-Hawk missiles for long range air-to-air combat to make up for the fact that they can no longer operate the Phoenix MISSILE. It is producing its own unmanned aerial vehicles. Tehran is also trying to produce its own light Saegheh and Azarakhsh fighters and has apparently introduced some into its active force. Yet, its air force lags behind the technology, readiness, and sustainability of U.S. air units and obsolete compared with the Saudi Air Force and rapidly modernizing U.A.E. Air Force. Iran has reportedly bought large numbers of modern Russian and/or Chinese fighters, but none has been confirmed. Purchases are now sharply restricted by U.N. sanctions.

Iran has even more problems with its land-based surface-to-air missiles. Its only modern systems are short-range man-portable systems and some 30 short-range Russian TOR-Ms suitable only for point defense. Its other systems are 30 short-range Rapier fire units and 15 Tigercats of uncertain operational status. Its longer-range systems include roughly (154) U.S. IHawks, (45) Russian SA-2s, (10) SA-5s and a limited number of CSA-1 Chinese versions of the SA-2. All are obsolete. While Iran has tried to modernize its electronics and integrate them into a modernized command-and-control and radar system, they are highly vulnerable to electronic countermeasures and anti-radiation missiles. This situation could change, however, if Iran can acquire operational versions of a more modern system like the S-300. There are reports it may have obtained four batteries from Belarus.

Iran's entire air defense system remains vulnerable to "stealth" strike fighters, cruise missiles, and air-to-surface missiles fired from ranges outside its effective surface-to-air missile coverage. Tehran would need to acquire large numbers of advanced surface-to-air missile systems with anti-ballistic missile capabilities, like the Russian S300, and advanced radars and command-and-control systems necessary to integrate them into an effective system. Russia had refused to make such sales as of mid-2010.

Iran's navy and the naval branch of the IRGC

Iran's 18,000-man navy and 12,000- to 15,000-man Naval Guards pose the most serious threat to other Gulf states and the U.S. Navy. Iran's Navy oversees operations in the Caspian and the Gulf of Oman. The naval branch of the IRGC oversees Gulf operations. Both have serious limitations. They lack modern surface vessel combat capability and depend on four obsolete frigates and three obsolete corvettes from the shah's era with limited modernization and uncertain combat readiness. Iran is apparently building a prototype Mowaj-class corvette/destroyer, which is not yet operational.

The navy does, however, have three Russian Kilo-class submarines—which some reports indicate can lay smart mines and fire long-range homing torpedoes. The IRGC has four to seven North Korean/Iranian-made Yono and Nahand-class midget submarines, and is producing four more. It also has small, semi-submersible craft. The navy also has an aviation branch with three aging P-3F maritime patrol and airborne command and control aircraft, three Falcon aircraft modified for electronic warfare and intelligence, and anti-submarine and mine warfare helicopters.

The IRGC has a wide range of mine warfare and smaller, more modern missile patrol boats armed with Chinese and Iranian-made anti-ship missiles. It also has land-based anti-ship missile batteries, including HY-2s with ranges of approximately 100 kilometers, which can be directed to a target by an aircraft or unmanned aerial vehicle. (China has anti-ship missiles with 200-280 kilometer ranges, but it is not believed these have been sold to Iran.) U.S. experts note that Iran can attack targeted ships with C-701, C-801, C-802 and Iranian-made anti-ship cruise missiles from its own shores, islands, and oil platforms using relatively small mobile launchers.

The navy and IRGC cannot close the Gulf for an extended period, but they could severely restrict shipping through the Gulf for five to 10 days. IRGC naval forces can operate from bases along the Gulf coast, bases near Strait of Hormuz shipping channels, Gulf islands and in the Gulf of Oman. Its anti-ship missile vessels include 13 Kaman-class and 38-meter Thondor (Hudong)-class vessels with C-802 anti-ship missiles, and 9 C-14 and 10 Mk-13 smaller patrol boats with short range Chinese anti-ship missiles. Iran has made and deployed at least 25 Peykapp II-class missile boats and 15 of its own Peykaap I-class coastal patrol craft. The IRGC also has some 100 other, smaller patrol boats, many of which are small enough to be difficult to detect reliably by radar. A number of Iran's patrol boats are armed with torpedoes and short-range or man-portable anti-air missiles.

The Iranian Navy and IRGC regularly exercise laying mines. The navy can use submarines and five aging mine warfare ships. But all IRGC patrol vessels and many Iranian commercial vessels can lay mines. U.S. Navy intelligence estimates that Iran has the Chinese EM52, a rocket-propelled anti-ship mine, and that the Iranian purchase of three Russian KILO-class submarines probably included modern magnetic, acoustic and pressure-sensitive mines. Iran also produces its own mines, although these may still be limited to less advanced designs. U.S. experts estimate that Iran had at least 2,000 mines by 2004. This is a key threat. The United States normally deploys limited mine warfare capabilities in the Gulf. And Gulf naval capabilities include only five Saudi mine layers and some helicopters with uncertain readiness and training.

The Marines and IRGC could use patrol boats, small craft and commercial vessels to raid key offshore facilities in the Gulf, attack key petroleum facilities on the coast, strike at shipping vessels, or raid shore facilities such as desalination or power plants. Iran could also use marines and specially trained IRGC forces to seize ships and infiltrate land targets. It has amphibious ships, but some exercises include activities that train small craft with teams of IRGC fighters in ways suitable for raids on offshore or coastal targets.

Finding and destroying all of the active elements of the naval branch of the IRGC and Iran's smaller surface craft would be difficult. While Iran's smaller craft have limited ability to stay at sea, they can be remotely located and used in a war of attrition to launch sudden raids with anti-ship missiles, using direct fire weapons, or drop mines. The IRGC and some elements of the Iranian Navy regularly practice the use of small craft, commercial vessels and amphibious vessels in moving forces that can defend and seize targets in the Gulf and on its coast, and support the deployment of medium to long-range, land-based anti-ship missiles and operations of small craft and missile patrol boats outside regular peacetime bases.

The future

- The United States could destroy all key elements of Iranian military power in virtually any scenario in a matter of weeks, if Washington had the support of Iran's neighbors. It could inflict devastating damage in a matter of days.

- Iran's missile and potential nuclear capabilities should be weighed against vast U.S. and Israeli superiority in existing missile and nuclear capabilities. Israel alone could win any nuclear arms race with Iran for at least the next decade.

- Iran could not win any serious confrontation with Turkey and cannot match the rate of modernization and defense spending by Saudi Arabia and the five other Gulf Cooperation Council sheikhdoms.

- But Iran has also already proven its ability to threaten, intimidate and carry out significant low-level or terrorist attacks—directly or through surrogates—against both major and regional powers.

Anthony H. Cordesman holds the Arleigh A. Burke Chair in Strategy at the Center for Strategic and International Studies and also acts as a national security analyst for ABC News.

16

Iran's Military Doctrine

Michael Connell

- The Iran-Iraq War (1980-1988) was a defining moment for the Iranian military, and it continues to underpin many aspects of Iranian military doctrine.

- Iranian military planners are adept at incorporating lessons from other conflicts, such as the U.S.-led invasion of Iraq and the 2006 war between Israel and Hezbollah, to refine their own doctrines and strategies.

- To challenge a technologically superior adversary, such as the United States, Iranian doctrine emphasizes aspects of asymmetric warfare that play to Iran's strengths, including geography, strategic depth and public willingness to accept casualties.

- The Islamic Revolutionary Guard Corps (IRGC), the branch of the Iranian military tasked with protecting the Islamic revolution, is undergoing a major restructuring to enhance its survivability and give regional commanders more flexibility to respond to potential threats.

- These capabilities act as a growing, if limited, deterrent to attacks on Iran, and in some ways compensate for the limits of its conventional forces.

Overview

Iranian military doctrine constitutes a unique hybrid of western (especially U.S.) military concepts coupled with ideological tenets, including martyrdom and revolutionary zeal. Since the 1979 revolution, Iranian military doctrine has continued to evolve and adapt with the regime's shifting threat perceptions and regional political developments.

Iran's armed forces have tailored their war-fighting strategies to counter technologically superior adversaries, such as the United States. Tacitly acknowledging it has little chance of winning a conventional force-on-force conflict, Iran has opted for deterrence-based model of attrition warfare that raises an opponent's risks and costs, rather than reducing its own. The goal is to inflict a psychological defeat that inhibits an enemy's willingness to fight.

Asymmetric warfare plays a central role in Iranian military theory. Iran's armed forces appear to be focusing on the development of niche capabilities that play to Iranian strengths—manpower, strategic depth and a willingness to accept casualties—while exploiting the weaknesses of Iran's adversaries, who are regarded as risk averse, casualty sensitive and heavily dependent on technology and regional basing facilities for access.

Doctrine evolution

The basis of Iranian military doctrine was developed during Iran's long and traumatic war with Iraq (1980-1988). Most senior officers are veterans of the "imposed war," which has had a major influence on Iranian strategic thinking. Concepts such as self-reliance, "holy defense," and export of the revolution first entered the military lexicon during the Iran-Iraq War and were codified as doctrine in the early 1990s. These ideas mingled with concepts from pre-revolutionary doctrine, which was heavily influenced by the United States, to form a unique hybrid that distinguished modern Iranian military doctrine from its largely Soviet-inspired counterparts in the Arab world.

After the war, Tehran gradually scaled back its efforts to export its revolution. As its foreign policy goals shifted, Iran's national security strategy also became more defensive. Iranian military strategists began to pay more attention to the principles of modern maneuver warfare, such as combined and joint operations.

In the mid-1990s, there was even talk about merging the IRGC with the regular military, the Artesh, to alleviate the command and control-related problems of having two parallel military services operating in tandem. Iran's military capabilities still lagged behind its doctrine, but by the end of the decade, its forces were gradually evolving into professional, Western-style militaries.

The 9/11 attacks and U.S. invasions of Iraq and Afghanistan led Tehran to reconsider the trajectory of its armed forces. The regional security environment had changed drastically. Ba'athist Iraq and Taliban Afghanistan—two of Iran's main rivals—were no longer a threat. But the United States suddenly had troops positioned along both its western and eastern flanks. This confluence of events, coupled with rumblings in Washington about opportunities for regime change, led Tehran to reassess its national security strategy. Iran's armed forces began to tailor their strategies specifically to counter the perceived U.S. threat.

Land warfare doctrine

In 2005, the IRGC announced that it was incorporating a flexible, layered defense—referred to as a mosaic defense—into its doctrine. The lead author of this plan was General Mohammad Jafari, then director of the IRGC's Center for Strategy, who was later appointed commander of the IRGC.

As part of the mosaic defense, the IRGC has restructured its command and control architecture into a system of 31 separate commands—one for the city of Tehran and 30 for each of Iran's provinces. The primary goal of restructuring has been to strengthen unit cohesion at the local level and give commanders more latitude to respond to potential threats—both foreign and domestic. But the new structure would also make it difficult for hostile forces to degrade Iranian command and control, a lesson the Iranian military has learned by analyzing U.S. operations in Iraq, Afghanistan and the Balkans.

The mosaic defense plan allows Iran to take advantage of its strategic depth and formidable geography to mount an insurgency against invading forces. Most of Iran's population centers and major lines of communication are spread out within the interior of the country. Iran's borders are ringed by rugged mountain ranges that serve as natural barriers to invasion. As enemy supply lines stretched into Iran's interior, they would be vulnerable to interdiction by special stay-behind cells, which the IRGC has formed to harass enemy rear operations.

The Artesh, a mix of armored, infantry and mechanized units, would constitute Iran's initial line of defense against invading forces. IRGC troops would support this effort, but they would also form the core of popular resistance, the bulk of which would be supplied by the Basij, the IRGC's paramilitary volunteer force. The IRGC has developed a wartime mobilization plan for the Basij, called the Mo'in Plan, according to which Basij personnel would augment regular IRGC units in an invasion scenario.

IRGC and Basij exercises have featured simulated ambushes on enemy armored columns and helicopters. Much of this training has been conducted in an urban environment, suggesting that Iran intends to lure enemy forces into cities where they would be deprived of mobility and close air support. Iran has emphasized passive defense measures—techniques used to enhance the battlefield survivability —including camouflage, concealment and deception.

Naval doctrine

Tehran views maritime combat operations much the same way as it views land-based operations. Iranian naval doctrine is geared toward confronting a technologically superior adversary—often assumed to be the U.S. Navy—with a form of guerrilla warfare at sea. The bases of this doctrine were developed during the Tanker War (1984-1988), during which Iran used aircraft, speedboats, sea mines and land-based anti-ship cruise missiles to attack civilian tanker shipping in the Persian Gulf. After a U.S. frigate, the *Samuel B. Roberts*, was badly damaged by an Iranian mine, the U.S. Navy retaliated with Operation Praying Mantis (1988), destroying two Iranian oil platforms and sinking several Iranian surface vessels, including a corvette, a guided missile patrol craft and smaller gunboats.

After Operation Praying Mantis, Iran apparently determined that its maritime forces would not be as effective in a conventional force-on-force naval conflict with adversaries such as the United States. Incorporating lessons learned from the Tanker War, the IRGC Navy (IRGCN) and, to a lesser degree, the regular Navy (IRIN) developed an asymmetric strategy based on avoiding direct or sustained confrontations at sea. It instead relies on surprise attacks, ambushes and hit-and-run operations. Rather than inflict a decisive defeat, Iran's maritime forces would seek to inflict enough casualities to raise the cost of victory to an unpalatable level.

Iran's naval doctrine relies on a layered defense and massing of firepower, integrating multiple sea, land and air-based weapons simultaneously to overwhelm and confuse adversaries. As Iran's naval doctrine has matured, the Iranians have acquired a large inventory of naval materiel suitable for asymmetric warfare. This includes naval mines, which can be covertly deployed using small boats or commercial vessels; land and sea-based anti-ship cruise missiles; small fast-attack craft, which can engage in swarming operations or suicide attacks; and submarines, including three Russian-supplied KILO-class diesel-electric submarines and numerous North Korean and domestically produced midget submarines, which can be used in the Gulf's shallow areas.

Geography is a key element in Iranian naval planning. The Gulf's confined space, which is less than 100 nautical miles wide in many places, limits the maneuverability of large surface assets, such as aircraft carriers. But it plays to the strengths of Iran's naval forces, especially the IRGCN. The Gulf's northern coast is dotted with rocky coves ideally suited for terrain masking and small boat operations. The Iranians have also fortified numerous islands in the Gulf that sit astride major shipping lanes.

Iran has developed a strategy to deny hostile navies access to the Persian Gulf that focuses on the strategically sensitive Strait of Hormuz. This strategic maritime chokepoint is only 29 nautical miles wide at its narrowest point. Iranian officials have hinted that they might close the strait during a conflict, thereby temporarily cutting off as much as 30 percent of the world's oil supply. But closing the strait would also cause tremendous economic damage for the Iranians, so they are not likely to undertake such a measure lightly. Given the strait's importance, however, disrupting maritime traffic in it or even threatening to do so would be an effective tool for Iran to pressure neighbors and intimidate foes.

Air and air defense doctrine

Iranian air and air defense doctrine is focused on defending Iranian airspace and deterring aggression, although certain Iranian aircraft, such as the Su-24 fighter-bomber, can be used in an offensive capacity. Surface-to-air missiles (SAMs) and interceptor aircraft—most of which belong to the regular Islamic Republic of Iran Air Force (IRIAF)—both play an important role in this effort. Iran's pilots are among the best trained in the region. They continue to use U.S. training manuals and employ U.S. tactics—a legacy of U.S.-Iranian military exchanges during the shah's rule.

The IRIAF and the Air Defense Force, a separate command within the Artesh, face numerous challenges in defending Iranian air space. In this case, geography is a limiting factor, given the size of Iran and its mountainous terrain, which tend to produce gaps in radar coverage. For the IRIAF, aging and outdated equipment remains another problem. Many aircraft in the IRIAF's inventory, including mainstays such as the F-14A and the F-4D, were supplied by the United States before the 1979 revolution. Some of these platforms have been kept running, either by cannibalizing parts from other aircraft or procuring spare parts on the black market, but IRIAF readiness levels are assumed to be low due to maintenance issues.

Iran has managed to acquire several batteries of the advanced Tor-M1 medium altitude SAM system from the Russians, but its air defense capabilities remain limited. As of mid-2010, efforts to buy the advanced long-range SA-300 SAM from the Russians had failed. Iran also lacks an integrated air defense network or the ability to engage air-to-air targets beyond visual range.

As a result of these challenges, Iran's military has opted to use its limited air and air defense assets to protect high-value point targets, including Tehran and the country's nuclear facilities. Iranian pilots have been trained to compensate for the limitations of their aircraft, avionics and weapons systems by using advanced tactics, such as terrain masking, to ambush enemy aircraft without being detected. Iran's air and air defense forces have also attempted to augment the survivability of their units with passive defense measures, including asset dispersion and the use of forward operating bases, hardened shelters and hidden installations.

Ballistic missile doctrine

Iran's ballistic missile program dates back to the middle of the 1980s, during the Iran-Iraq War. For Tehran, Iraq's use of ballistic missiles against Iranian strategic targets highlighted a critical vulnerability in Iran's defenses; it also demoralized Iran's civilian population. To deter Iraq from attacking its population centers and strategic industries, Iran initiated its own ballistic missile program, beginning with the initial shipment of a limited number of SCUD-B missiles from Libya. By the end of the war, Iran had launched over 100 ballistic missiles at Iraqi targets in what would become known as the "War of the Cities."

Iran's strategic missile forces are now key to its deterrence strategy, in part because they are implicitly linked to Iran's weapons of mass destruction programs. In 2010, Iran had the largest inventory of ballistic missiles in the Middle East. The IRGC, which has operational control over Iran's missile forces, continues to extend the range and improve the performance of its ballistic missiles, several classes of which can range Israel and the Gulf countries. Their limited accuracy suggests they would not be useful in a conventional counter-force role. Instead, they are probably intended for strategic targets such as cities, oil production and export facilities, ports and water desalinization plants.

The future

- Iranian military doctrine is primarily defensive in nature and based on deterring perceived adversaries. Iran is therefore unlikely to seek a direct, force-on-force confrontation with the United States.

- However, there is ample room for miscommunication between Iranian and U.S. forces at the tactical and operational levels. The recent push to decentralize command and control within the IRGC could have unintended consequences in terms of escalation, especially in the Persian Gulf.

- For the foreseeable future, lack of coordination between the IRGC and the Artesh is likely to remain a key weak point in terms of Iranian military planning, due to underlying structural issues and institutional rivalries.

Michael Connell is director of Iranian Studies at the Center for Naval Analyses, a non-profit institution that conducts research and analysis in Washington, D.C.

The Nuclear Controversy

17

Iran's Nuclear Program

David Albright and Andrea Stricker

- Since the 1970s, even before the revolution, Iran has sought access to the technology that would give it the option to build a nuclear bomb, should it believe its security situation requires it.
- Iran intensified its drive toward nuclear weapons in the 1980s during the Iran-Iraq War, following reports of an Iraqi clandestine nuclear program.
- Iranian leaders continue to advance Iran's nuclear program and use it as a symbol of national pride. They deny that Iran's nuclear program has a military purpose.
- As a signatory to the Nuclear Non-Proliferation Treaty (NPT), Iran claims its nuclear program is purely for peaceful, energy and medical purposes, despite evidence of possible work on nuclear warheads.

Overview

A majority of the international community is at odds with Iran over its nuclear program because of its history of concealing its nuclear activities, the possible military nature of some of these activities, and its building of facilities in secret. Many of Iran's Arab neighbors, in addition to Israel, fear an Iranian nuclear bomb and could seek their own nuclear deterrent if Iran succeeds in acquiring nuclear weapons.

Iran initially constructed in secret its gas centrifuge uranium enrichment plant at Natanz and a heavy-water production plant at Arak. The existence of these major facilities was revealed in 2002, and they are under International Atomic Energy Agency (IAEA) inspections. In 2006, Iran significantly reduced the inspection rights of the IAEA with its refusal to continue implementing the Additional Protocol to the Nuclear Non-Proliferation Treaty (NPT). This reversal prompted concern that it could conduct significant nuclear activities in secret. The Protocol requires Iran to supply the IAEA more detailed declarations of its nuclear activities and much greater access to nuclear sites than traditional safeguards.

Amplifying worries about Iran's nuclear intentions, in September 2009, the United States, France and Britain revealed the existence of a small, covert uranium enrichment plant being built in Iran near the city of Qom. The United States suspected the facility could be used to quickly produce enough nuclear explosive material, or highly enriched uranium, for a nuclear weapon, in what is commonly called "break out." The IAEA does not have confidence Iran is not building additional clandestine enrichment sites. Iran has refused to answer the IAEA's questions about evidence of past and potentially ongoing work on nuclear weaponization and the development of nuclear warheads for missile delivery systems.

Evolution

Iran's controversial nuclear program has evolved through at least six phases.

Phase one: Beginnings, 1950s-1960s

Iran first established its nuclear program in 1957, under Mohammad Reza Shah Pahlavi, with an agreement on nuclear cooperation with the United States under the Atoms for Peace program. In 1960, it purchased from the United States a small research reactor, which is located at the Tehran Nuclear Research Center. The reactor started in 1967. Iran signed the Nuclear Non-Proliferation Treaty (NPT) in 1968, on the day it opened for signature. The United States provided highly enriched uranium fuel for the first several years of the reactor's operation. In the early 1990s, Argentina took over providing low enriched uranium fuel.

Phase two: Ambitious options, 1970s

The shah established the Atomic Energy Organization of Iran (AEOI) in 1974 and announced plans to build 20 nuclear power reactors for energy production. The United States, France and West Germany subsequently sought lucrative power reactor deals. In 1974, Iran signed a contract with the German firm Kraftwerk Union (a subsidiary of Siemens) to build two reactors at Bushehr. It also purchased nearly 600 tons of uranium yellow-cake from South Africa.

The shah wanted to keep open the option of developing nuclear weapons by seeking access to the full nuclear fuel cycle. The former head of AEOI, Akbar Etemad, revealed to *Le Figaro* in 2003 that he tasked a special research team with "giv[ing] the country access to all technologies, giving the political decision-makers the possibility of making the appropriate decision and doing so while time permitted them to build a bomb if that is what was required."

Iran attempted during the 1970s to develop laser enrichment technology and tried to acquire a plutonium reprocessing capability. Declassified U.S. government documents from 1974 to 1977 indicate that Iran's quest for a reprocessing capability was opposed by the United States during negotiations over sales of U.S. reactors to Iran. The United States also sought to deny the sale of a reprocessing facility from Germany to Iran. Washington eventually secured the right to the return and storage of spent reactor fuel from any reactors it built in Iran in a nuclear agreement concluded in 1978.

Phase three: Revolution, war and secret contacts, 1979–1988

After the 1979 revolution, Iran suspended its nuclear program because of opposition to nuclear power by its new leader, Ayatollah Ruhollah Khomeini. Its nuclear cooperation with the United States ended with their rupture in bilateral relations. Construction on two semi-finished reactors at Bushehr and plans for two reactors to be built by France at Ahvaz were scrapped. In 1982, Iran sought to resume work on the Bushehr reactors, partially due to the regime's recognition of the financial complexity of halting the commercial reactor project.

The devastating 1980-1988 Iran-Iraq War heavily influenced Ayatollah Khomeini's decision to re-start Iran's nuclear program. The war prompted leading political figures to call for Iran's development of a nuclear deterrent, demands that were bolstered by its fear of the United States and growing evidence of a covert Iraqi nuclear weapons program. A 2009 internal IAEA working document reports that in April 1984, then President Ali Khamenei announced to top Iranian officials that Khomeini had decided to reactivate the nuclear program as the only way to secure the Islamic Revolution from the schemes of its enemies, especially the United States and Israel.

Iran began developing an indigenous gas centrifuge program in 1985, according to IAEA reports. Iranians visited potential suppliers abroad in order to acquire and learn how to operate key centrifuge equipment. In 1987, Iran acquired key components from the A.Q. Khan network, a rogue nuclear supply network operating out of Pakistan's state-run nuclear weapons program. The components included:

- A starter kit for a gas centrifuge plant
- A set of technical drawings for a P-1 (Pakistani) centrifuge
- Samples of centrifuge components
- And instructions for enriching uranium to weapon-grade levels.

Weapon-grade uranium is the most desirable highly enriched uranium for fission nuclear weapons and is over 90 percent enriched.

Phase four: Enrichment and procurement, 1988–2002

Iran made deliberate, steady progress in its quest to achieve the full nuclear fuel cycle. It advanced its uranium mining infrastructure, uranium conversion capabilities, indigenous heavy water reactor and associated heavy water production plant, and uranium enrichment programs. In 1990, Iran and China signed a nuclear cooperation agreement. In 1991, Iran secretly imported from China one metric ton of uranium hexafluoride (UF6), which it was obligated under its IAEA safeguards agreement to report to the Agency, but did not. Uranium hexafluoride is the feed gas for gas centrifuges and is difficult to make. Between 1994 and 1996, Iran also purchased from the A.Q. Khan network design drawings and components for 500 P-1 centrifuges, according to the IAEA. It received drawings for the more sophisticated P-2 centrifuge from the network in 1995 but claimed that it did not start work on the P-2 until 2002.

In early 1995, Russia began reconstructing one of the reactors at Bushehr, which had been badly damaged during the Iran-Iraq War. The United States persuaded Russia to halt its negotiations to sell Iran a centrifuge enrichment facility. Russian companies also provided technical assistance in designing a heavy-water reactor that Iran was constructing at Arak, but U.S. pressure succeeded in convincing Russia to halt cooperation on this venture in the late 1990s. After years of delay, the Bushehr reactor was started in 2010 and will be under IAEA safeguards, with Russia providing the fuel and taking it back.

In 1999 and 2002, Iran conducted tests on test centrifuges installed at Kalaye Electric Company, its secret centrifuge R&D facility, using the Chinese-supplied UF6. These tests constituted violations of Iran's safeguards agreements, or violations of Iran's verification requirements under the NPT. In 2001, again in secret, Iran began constructing a vast underground enrichment facility near the city of Natanz. In 2002, the National Council of Resistance of Iran held a press conference in Washington, D.C., to disclose secret nuclear activities taking place at Natanz and Arak and revealed the names of entities and officials involved with the nuclear program. The Institute for Science and International Security (ISIS) located these sites and released satellite imagery of both Natanz and Arak in December 2002. ISIS identified Natanz as a gas centrifuge facility.

Phase five: Investigations, diplomacy and sanctions, 2003–2009

The IAEA visited Iran's newly disclosed nuclear facilities in February 2003 following substantial international pressure for Iran to open its facilities to inspection. The Natanz above-ground pilot enrichment plant could hold 1,000 centrifuges, while its underground halls were equipped to hold 50,000. The agency also inspected the heavy water production facility at Arak.

Britain, France and Germany, referred to as the EU-3, succeeded in the fall of 2003 in persuading Iran to verifiably suspend its uranium enrichment activities and implement the NPT's Additional Protocol. These two measures significantly strengthened the IAEA's ability to inspect Iran's nuclear program and ensure that it did not have secret nuclear sites. In 2004, Iran and the EU-3 signed the Paris Agreement, which extended the temporary suspension of Iran's nuclear activities, pending negotiations of long-term arrangements.

Iran's suspension lasted for three years, and then Iran restarted its gas centrifuge program and the manufacturing of centrifuges. It also resumed operations at the Isfahan uranium conversion facility that makes uranium hexafluoride. It stopped voluntarily implementing the Additional Protocol in 2006, and refused to answer satisfactorily the IAEA's questions about past or ongoing experimentation on nuclear weaponization and the development of nuclear warheads for missile delivery systems.

In mid-2009, the United States joined the EU-3 in diplomatic negotiations with Iran, after years of refusing to do so. These negotiations did not produce a breakthrough. In September 2009, the leaders of the United States, France and Britain publicly revealed the existence of a secret uranium enrichment site being built underground near the holy city of Qom. The facility's revelation prompted concern that Iran intended to construct a potential breakout facility where it could quickly make weapon-grade uranium for a bomb.

Against the backdrop of diplomatic negotiations, the U.N. Security Council passed four rounds of economic sanctions against Iran between 2006 and 2010, for its failure to suspend enrichment and cooperate adequately with the IAEA. The sanctions target entities and officials associated with the nuclear program, and Iran's illicit banking, shipping and trading activities that support its nuclear program.

Phase six: International tensions, 2010–

Iran continues to refuse to halt its enrichment program and has expanded work at Natanz. It has also increased the level of enrichment at the Natanz pilot plant. In 2010, Iran began enriching its 3.5 percent uranium to 20 percent at the Natanz pilot plant, purportedly for use in fueling the Tehran Research Reactor. Suspicions remain that the underlying motivation is to learn to enrich even further, to 90 percent, or weapon-grade. International efforts stalled in 2009 to broker a deal in which Iran would send most of its 3.5 percent enriched uranium out of the country, in return for 20 percent enriched fuel from abroad. This deal would obviate the need for Iran to make 20 percent uranium. The United States proposed this deal as a way to build confidence in negotiations and extend the timeline of Iran acquiring the capability to make enough weapon-grade uranium for a nuclear weapon.

In mid-2010, most estimates put Iran within a year of being able to build a crude nuclear weapon, and longer to make a reliable warhead for a ballistic missile. International discussion about the merits of a strike on Iran's nuclear facilities by Israel, the United States, or some combination of countries continues, at odds with those favoring sanctions or engagement to induce Iran to change its apparent course.

Factoids

- The Natanz Fuel Enrichment Plant has approximately 4,000 P-1 centrifuges enriching and almost 9,000 P-1 centrifuges installed. The Qom site has a few installed centrifuges, but Iran halted work at the site following its discovery.

- Iran has produced approximately 2,400 kg of 3.5 percent low enriched uranium (LEU) as of May 2010, and 17 kg of 19.75 percent uranium as of June 2010 at Natanz. Iran continues to refine its ability to efficiently produce 19.75 percent enriched uranium and to expand its centrifuge efficiency, as well as the numbers in operation.

- Iran has enough low enriched uranium (LEU) to produce about two nuclear weapons, if it decided to enrich the LEU up to weapon-grade.

- Other undeclared enrichment sites may be under construction. Iran announced it will begin construction on the first of 10 new sites in March 2011. But Iran lacks the capability to outfit 10 enrichment sites.

- A parallel nuclear program could be used for breakout. A secret enrichment site using diverted low enriched uranium from Natanz would require approximately 2,000 P-1 centrifuges to produce about 25 to 40 kilograms of weapon-grade uranium in one year. The upper bound would require the P-1 centrifuges to operate better than they currently do at Natanz. However, Iran is working to improve the P-1 centrifuges' operation and in parallel to develop more powerful, reliable centrifuges. Operating with 1,000 centrifuges, a covert enrichment site using P-1s could produce about 40-70 kg of weapon-grade uranium per year, starting with 20 percent enriched uranium. A nuclear weapon test device could require less than 20 kg of weapon-grade uranium. A nuclear warhead for a missile may contain as much as 25 kg of weapon-grade uranium.

- The IAEA believes Iran has sufficient information to design and produce a workable implosion nuclear device based upon highly enriched uranium as the fission fuel. A high-explosive implosion system developed by Iran could be contained within a payload container small enough to fit into the re-entry body chamber of the Shahab-3 missile. The IAEA does not believe that Iran has yet achieved the means to integrate a nuclear payload into the Shahab-3.

Individuals or organizations

Atomic Energy Council (AEC): Iran's general nuclear policy is directed by the AEC, which was created by the same law that created the Atomic Energy Organization of Iran in 1974.

Atomic Energy Organization of Iran (AEOI): The AEOI was established in 1974 to oversee Iran's civil nuclear program. It also oversees Iran's clandestine nuclear activities.

Field for Expansion of Advanced Technologies' Deployment (FEDAT): This is reportedly the current name of the sector working on Iran's clandestine nuclear activities.

Ministry of Defense: The IAEA believes the ministry plays an active role in the development of a nuclear payload for the Shahab-3 missile.

Supreme leader: Ayatollah Ali Khamenei has ultimate say over Iran's nuclear program, and all major decisions on the nuclear issue require his approval.

Supreme National Security Council (SNSC): The SNSC is concerned mainly with defense and national security policies. Key nuclear decisions are dominated by the supreme leader and a relatively small group of senior leaders and advisers, including those in the Supreme National Security Council.

The future

- It is not known whether Iranian leaders intend to break out and build a nuclear weapon. A breakout using facilities under safeguards at Natanz is likely to be detected within weeks, which would likely precipitate a military strike on Iran's nuclear facilities.

- To avoid risking an attack, there are two main ways for Iran to secretly produce highly enriched uranium for a nuclear weapon. One way is to produce it through an entirely secret parallel program, which would duplicate its current capabilities. The other way is to build a secret enrichment facility and divert low-enriched uranium from Natanz to the new facility for further enrichment. Diversion would be detected, but inspectors may not be able to determine the new location of the low-enriched uranium.

• Using a military strike to significantly set back Iran's nuclear program poses immense difficulties. Many of Iran's nuclear facilities are constructed partially or entirely underground. Research and development as well as centrifuge manufacturing facilities—at least those that have been identified—are widely dispersed and often located in major population centers.

• Several of Iran's neighbors are now seeking to build nuclear reactors. And Jordan, Egypt, Turkey and Saudi Arabia have not ruled out enriching uranium or reprocessing plutonium domestically. The spread of advanced nuclear technology in the Middle East, combined with the perceived Iranian threat, raises the potential for significant regional proliferation.

• The Obama administration has stated that it will prevent Iran from acquiring nuclear weapons. Its priority means to achieve this goal is diplomacy, but it has not ruled out use of military force.

David Albright, a physicist and former U.N. weapons inspector, is the president and founder of the Institute for Science and International Security (ISIS) in Washington, D.C. Andrea Stricker is a research analyst at the Institute for Science and International Security (ISIS).

18

The Politics of Iran's Nuclear Program

Shahram Chubin

- Iran's nuclear program, initially cancelled after the 1979 revolution, was revived in the closing phases of the 1980-1988 war with Iraq. Tehran wanted to guard against a future surprise analogous to Iraq's repeated use of chemical weapons.

- Iran has depicted international pressure to suspend its uranium enrichment as a politically motivated attempt to keep it scientifically backward and to deprive its rights under the Nuclear Non-Proliferation Treaty.

- Through appeals to nationalism, Tehran has used the prolonged crisis to revive flagging support for the regime and keep the revolutionary faithful mobilized.

- In a profound sense, the nuclear dispute is now inextricably tied to the political nature of the regime itself.

Overview

One of the central ironies about Iran is that its controversial nuclear program has become a defining political issue, even though many of the program's details remain shrouded in secrecy. Tehran is public about its quest to acquire peaceful nuclear energy to serve a population that has doubled since the 1979 revolution. But the theocracy vehemently denies any interest in developing a nuclear weapon—even as it boasts about its growing ability to enrich uranium, a capability that can be used to generate power or for a weapons program.

Technically, Iran does not yet need to enrich, since Russia is providing the fuel for the new reactor it built in Bushehr. Tehran counters that it has the right to enrich uranium as a signatory to the Nuclear Non-Proliferation Treaty (NPT). It also intends to build additional reactors and says it does not want to be dependent on foreign powers for fuel. But since 2002, international suspicions about Iran's long-term intentions have deepened because of revelations—by other governments or Iranian exile groups—that it has built secret facilities that could be used for a weapons program. The Islamic Republic has only acknowledged them after the fact. And as of mid-2010, Tehran had still not provided full details about its programs to the International Atomic Energy Agency, as it is also required to do under the NPT.

Iran appears to have wanted to start a secret program for several reasons, from its experience during Iran-Iraq War to the fact that five of the world's nine nuclear powers are nearby or on its borders. At the same time, it also appears to have adopted a strategy of nuclear hedging—or maintaining the option of a weapons program, while trying to remain within the nuclear treaty. But the disclosures between 2002 and 2009 about its secret facilities and the subsequent international pressure have turned the program into a major political issue at home. In the already tense environment after disputed 2009 presidential elections, Iran's nuclear program became a political issue that pitted the hardline regime against both conservatives and the Green Movement opposition.

Program's evolution

Iran's nuclear weapons program was part of a broader attempt to become more self-reliant in arms and technology in the 1980s. Increasingly isolated, Tehran struggled to acquire arms to fight Iraq, which used chemical weapons and had a nuclear weapons program. The eight-year war was the Middle East's bloodiest modern conflict. Iran's nuclear program was an outgrowth of this experience.

The program may also have been a byproduct of the troubled revolution's omnipresent need for legitimacy and Iranian nationalism's quest for respect and international status. Tehran has long sought access to nuclear technology generally as a key to development and a means of restoring its former greatness as a center of scientific progress. The theocracy appears to have further dug in its heels because of a perception that the outside world is trying to deny technology and discriminating against a country that—unlike Israel, Pakistan and India—signed the global treaty on non-proliferation. The regime views the international community's dictates as an attack on a founding principle of the revolution, namely Iran's independence from outside influence or intervention.

Nuclear politics

Iran's nuclear program unfolded in context of its overall politics. Since the 1979 revolution, Iran's political elite has long been divided over how the theocracy should evolve and what international role it should pursue. Beyond broad concepts, such as independence, self-reliance and social justice, consensus has proven elusive—even three decades after the Islamic Republic's birth. The most fundament difference is whether Iran should continue as a revolutionary state willing to defy the world, or whether it should settle down and become a normal state that plays by international rules. The nuclear issue is increasingly a reflection of this basic division.

Throughout the program's early stages, there appeared to be a general consensus among the political elite about the need or right to proceed. But by 2005, the consensus appeared to be crumbling. Rival factions in Iran's political labyrinth began to criticize the nuclear program's costs and centrality to Iran's development goals. Iran's nuclear program had become a domestic political football.

For the public, the nuclear program also initially enjoyed broad popular support since it promised energy independence and scientific progress. It was also popular because the regime depicted it as an assertion of Iran's rights against foreign arrogance. But the program has not been subjected to informed debate or public discussion about its ultimate goals, the costs, and the relationship with Iran's other objectives. Consensus ends where specifics begin.

Politics goes nuclear

The nuclear program has evolved through three phases.

Phase one: Period of consensus, 1987-2002

The period of maximum consensus on Iran's nuclear program spanned 15 years. The revival of the shah's nuclear program was initially presented as necessary to diversify energy sources. Nuclear technology was equated as cutting edge for development and indispensable for any self-respecting power.

But the regime only presented a rationale for energy; it did not acknowledge whatever weapons intentions it had. The program progressed slowly during this phase, as Iran encountered problems of organization and getting access to technology that had to be acquired clandestinely abroad. The United States, already wary of Iran's weapons intentions, sought to block its access to any nuclear technology. Ironically, the regime may have received a boost from blanket U.S. opposition, which extended to the construction of a light-water reactor at Bushehr that Washington had approved when the shah was in power. Iran's attempts to evade international opposition—which included purchases from the Pakistan network run by A.Q. Khan—were never discussed domestically.

Phase two: Early controversy, 2003-2005

Throughout this period, the nuclear program was largely a concern of Iran's political elites. The Supreme National Security Council technically acted as the body that reflected all political tendencies. Its decisions therefore allegedly reflected a national consensus.

The 2002 revelation about Iran's construction of an undeclared enrichment facility at Natanz put Tehran on the defensive. The disclosure coincided with U.S. concern about the spread of weapons of mass destruction to rogue regimes and extremist networks. To avoid exacerbating the issue, the reformist government of President Mohammad Khatami won agreement in the Supreme National Security Council to meet international concerns halfway. Iran agreed to apply the NPT's Additional Protocol—without ratifying it—which permitted stricter international inspections. It also agreed to voluntarily suspend enrichment for a limited though unspecified time.

Iran's ensuing negotiations with Britain, France and Germany proved unproductive and added to mutual suspicions. With the U.S. military preoccupied in Iraq, the threat of military action against Iran receded. But hardliners who gained control of Iran's parliament in 2004 began criticizing reformists for being too soft on the United States for compromising Iran's interests. In 2005, newly elected President Mahmoud Ahmadinejad, backed by Iran's supreme leader, began enriching uranium again. The deal with the Europeans was dead.

Phase three: Deep divisions, 2005-2010

Iran's nuclear program became increasingly political during this phase. As of 2005, both the executive branch and parliament were dominated by hardliners and conservatives. Both Ahmadinejad and Supreme Leader Ayatollah Ali Khamenei used the nuclear issue to stigmatize reformists, depicting them as defeatists willing to negotiate away Iran's interests. Their use of the nuclear issue as an instrument of partisan politics ended the phase when the nuclear program was supposed to be a national issue. And debate was actively discouraged.

Yet the nuclear issue gradually slipped from the hands of the elite to the street. Among hardliners, Ahmadinejad's populist rallies included frequently orchestrated chants in favor of Iran's nuclear rights. The president announced that Iran's nuclear program was "like a train without brakes," not susceptible to deflection by outside pressure. Slogans, stamps, banknotes and medals became substitutes for informed discussion.

Two factors spurred intense backlash—and a reaction on the other side of the street. First, the United Nations imposed a series of U.N. resolutions between 2006 and 2010 that included punitive sanctions. The United States and the European Union imposed even tougher unilateral sanctions. For the Iranian public, the costs of continued defiance became increasingly clear—and complicated daily life.

Second, Iran's disputed 2009 election—won by Ahmadinejad amid widespread allegations of fraud—sparked the largest protests against the regime since the 1979 revolution. A new Green Movement opposition was born. Many conservatives also had growing concerns about the populist hardline president, particularly his economic mismanagement. Iran's new political chasm quickly began to play on the nuclear issue. Four months after the election, Ahmadinejad agreed to a U.S.-backed interim agreement designed to ease tensions and open the way for broader negotiations on Iran's long-term program. Leaders of the Green Movement as well as key conservatives publicly criticized the deal—reportedly in large part just to oppose Ahmadinejad and prevent him from taking credit for ending tensions with the outside world. Iran soon walked away from the deal.

By 2010, the divide over Iran's nuclear program had more to do with domestic politics—and very little to do with what many of the key players actually wanted to see happen.

Factoids

- Iran envisages an energy program that encompasses 10 to 12 reactors generating some 24,000 megawatts and several enrichment plants. It is also building a heavy-water plant at Arak, a source of proliferation concern.

- Bushehr's 1,000 megawatt light-water reactor was built by Russia and took 15 years to complete. The deal stipulates that fuel is provided by Russia and the spent fuel rods will return to Russia.

- The average reactor takes at least a decade to construct and a minimum of $1 billion before start-up, with costs likely to increase with inflation and international sanctions.

- Even with its own enrichment capability, Iran may lack sufficient indigenous sources of uranium ore.

Major players

Akbar Hashemi Rafsanjani is a two-time president and veteran political operative who was in charge of Iran's defense when the decision to revive the nuclear program was taken in the 1980s. He has alluded to the need for Iran to be prepared for the unexpected in defense matters, and most likely led the decision to hedge by seeking a weapons option. Known as a leading pragmatist, he is personally opposed to Ahmadinejad, whom he ran against for president in 2005. On the nuclear issue, he is more likely to seek a pragmatic accommodation with the world than to accelerate enrichment.

Mir Hossein Mousavi was prime minister during the Iran-Iraq War. Considered a radical supporter of the revolution at the time, he would have been privy to and may have strongly supported the revival of the nuclear program, including a weapons option. Mousavi reflects the evolution of first generation of revolutionaries. Now more pragmatic, he is also more disillusioned by the tendency toward authoritarianism and praetorianism, the control of society by force or fraud. He leads the Green Movement opposition, and straddles the rift between those who feel the regime can be reformed and those who feel it needs to be replaced. On the nuclear issue, he has suggested a reasonable accommodation with the international community.

Moshen Rezaie was the Revolutionary Guards commander during the Iran-Iraq War and is known to have told Rafsanjani that Iran could not pursue the war with Iraq to victory without a nuclear weapon. He is now considered a "pragmatic conservative" and was a presidential candidate in 2009. He suggested an "international consortium" as a possible compromise solution on the enrichment issue. All three of the opposition presidential candidates—Mousavi, Rezaie and former Parliamentary Speaker Mehdi Karroubi—criticized Ahmadinejad's nuclear policy as provocative and costly for Iran, despite the supreme leader's explicit support of it.

Ali Larijani, parliamentary speaker and formerly chief nuclear negotiator (2005-2007), is ambitious and a political opportunist. Larijani started the factionalization of the nuclear issue by accusing the reformists of selling out Iran's enrichment "pearl" for "candy." He is a conservative but has also had disputes with Ahmadinejad.

Supreme Leader Ali Khamenei, weakened since the disputed 2009 election, has aligned himself with the hardliners. He has rarely pronounced on the nuclear program except in generalities. He insists that there is an unspecified fatwa against the development of nuclear weapons, but has supported polices that make it impossible to verify this fatwa in practice.

The future

- Support for Iran's nuclear program, always vague, is likely to become even more politicized. The weapons component of the program has never been debated or acknowledged, and further revelations or costs associated with it could make it more controversial. Since 2009, factions take positions that do not reflect their real preferences, mainly to thwart political rivals.

- Increased international pressure and sanctions are likely to increase the program's costs, which is also likely to make the program more contentious at home—and potentially exacerbate existing political differences in the leadership.

- Iran's hardline default position—to negotiate only under the most severe pressure—has been reinforced by the change in the domestic balance of power. The Revolutionary Guards are now a principal player in decision-making.

- A wild card is the possibility of an Israeli or U.S. military strike on Iran's nuclear facilities; the repercussions are unpredictable. A reasonable assumption is that initially Iranians may rally around the flag and hardliners will try to further consolidate their position by purging the moderates. The regime will also see its rationale for a weapons option reinforced and may shift to an overt weapons program and even leave the NPT. Once the dust settles, however, the domestic backlash to an attack may discredit the regime for its brinksmanship and intransigence.

- Iran's technical progress is uneven and allows time for more diplomacy. Any compromise agreement will need to find a balance between not rewarding Iran's confrontational policies while also meeting Tehran's minimal political needs in order to win domestic support for an agreement. This may be harder than it sounds.

Shahram Chubin is a Geneva-based specialist on Iranian politics and a nonresident senior associate of the Carnegie Endowment for International Peace.

19

Iran's Ballistic Missile Program

Michael Elleman

- Iran has the largest and most diverse ballistic missile arsenal in the Middle East. (Israel has more capable ballistic missiles, but fewer in number and type.) Most were acquired from foreign sources, notably North Korea. The Islamic Republic is the only country to develop a 2,000-km missile without first having a nuclear weapons capability.

- Iran is still dependent on foreign suppliers for key ingredients, components and equipment, but it should eventually be able to develop long-range missiles over time, including an intercontinental ballistic missile or ICBM.

- The military utility of Iran's current ballistic missiles is limited because of poor accuracy, so missiles are not likely to be decisive if armed with conventional, chemical or biological warheads. But Tehran could use its missiles as a political or psychological weapon to terrorize an adversary's cities and pressure its government.

- Iran should not be able to strike Western Europe before 2014 or the United States before 2020—at the earliest.

- Iran's space program, which includes the successful launch of a small, crude satellite into low Earth orbit using the Safir carrier rocket, proves the country's growing ambitions and technical prowess.

Overview

Iran's pursuit of ballistic missiles pre-dates the Islamic revolution. Ironically, the shah teamed with Israel to develop a short-range system after Washington denied his request for Lance missiles. Known as Project Flower, Iran provided the funds and Israel the technology. The monarchy also pursued nuclear technologies, suggesting an interest in a delivery system for nuclear weapons. Both programs collapsed after the revolution.

Under the shah, Iran had the largest air force in the Gulf, including more than 400 combat aircraft. But Iran's deep-strike capability degraded rapidly after the break in ties with the West limited access to spare parts, maintenance, pilot training and advanced armaments. So Tehran turned to missiles to deal with an immediate war-time need after Iraq's 1980 invasion. Iran acquired Soviet-made Scud-Bs, first from Libya, then from Syria and North Korea. It used these 300-km missiles against Iraq from 1985 until the war ended in 1988.

Since the war, Tehran has steadily expanded its missile arsenal. It has also invested heavily in its own industries and infrastructure to lessen dependence on unreliable foreign sources. It is now able to produce its own missiles, although some key components still need to be imported. Iran has demonstrated that it can also significantly expand the range of acquired missiles, as it has done with Nodong missiles from North Korea, which it then renamed. Iran's missiles can already hit any part of the Middle East, including Israel. Over time, Tehran has established the capacity to create missiles to address a full range of strategic objectives.

Iran's expanding arsenal

The Islamic Republic's arsenal now includes several types of short-range and medium-range missiles. Estimates vary on specifics, and Iran has exaggerated its capabilities in the past. But there is widespread consensus that Tehran has acquired and creatively adapted foreign technology to continuously increase the quality and quantity of its arsenal. It has also launched an ambitious space program that works on some of the same technology. The arsenal includes:

Shahab missiles: Since the late 1980s, Iran has purchased additional short- and medium-range missiles from foreign suppliers and adapted them to its strategic needs. The Shahabs, Persian for "meteors," were long the core of Iran's program. They use liquid fuel, which involves a time-consuming launch. They include:

The Shahab-1 is based on the Scud-B. (The Scud series was originally developed by the Soviet Union). It has a range of about 300 km or 185 miles.

The Shahab-2 is based on the Scud-C. It has a range of about 500 km, or 310 miles. In mid-2010, Iran is widely estimated to have between 200 and 300 Shahab-1 and Shahab-2 missiles capable of reaching targets in neighboring countries.

The Shahab-3 is based on the Nodong, which is a North Korean missile. It has a range of about 900 km or 560 miles. It has a nominal payload of 1,000 kg. A modified version of the Shahab-3, renamed the **Ghadr-1,** began flight tests in 2004. It theoretically extends Iran's reach to about 1,600 km or 1,000 miles, which qualifies as a medium-range missile. But it carries a smaller, 750-kg warhead.

Although the Ghadr-1 was built with key North Korean components, Defense Minister Ali Shamkhani boasted at the time, "Today, by relying on our defense industry capabilities, we have been able to increase our deterrent capacity against the military expansion of our enemies."

Sajjil missiles: Sajjil means "baked clay" in Persian. These are a class of medium-range missiles that use solid fuel, which offer many strategic advantages. They are less vulnerable to preemption because the launch requires shorter preparation—minutes rather than hours. Iran is the only country to have developed missiles of this range without first having developed nuclear weapons.

This family of missiles centers on the **Sajjil-2,** a domestically produced surface-to-surface missile. It has a medium-range of about 2,200 km or 1,375 miles when carrying a 750-kg warhead. It was test fired in 2008 under the name, Sajjil. The Sajjil-2, which is probably a slightly modified version, began test flights in 2009. This missile would allow Iran to "target any place that threatens Iran," according to Brig. Gen. Abdollah Araghi, a Revolutionary Guard commander.

The Sajjil-2, which is unlikely to become operational before 2012, is the most likely nuclear delivery vehicle—if Iran decides to develop an atomic bomb. But it would need to build a bomb small enough to fit on the top of this missile, which would be a major challenge.

The Sajjil program's success indicates that Iran's long-term missile acquisition plans are likely to focus on solid-fuel systems. They are more compact and easier to deploy on mobile launchers. They require less time to prepare for launch, making them less vulnerable to preemption by aircraft or other missile defense systems.

Iran could attempt to use Sajjil technologies to produce a three-stage missile capable of flying 3,700 km or 2,200 miles. But it is unlikely to be developed and actually fielded before 2015.

Space program: Iran's ambitious space program provides engineers with critical experience developing powerful booster rockets and other skills that could be used in developing longer-range missiles, including ICBMs.

The Safir, which means "messenger" or "ambassador" in Persian, is the name of the carrier rocket that launched Iran's first satellite into space in 2009. It demonstrated a new sophistication in multistage separation and propulsion systems.

The Simorgh, which is the Persian name of a benevolent, mythical flying creature, is another carrier rocket to launch satellites. A mock-up was unveiled in 2010. It has a cluster of four engines and indicates that Iran's space program is making progress in its long-term goals.

Development of larger, more powerful launchers could also provide Iran with an ability to place communication and reconnaissance satellites into orbit, independent of foreign powers.

Factoids

- Iran has invested at least $1 billion in its missile programs since 2000, according to "Iran's Ballistic Missile Capabilities: A Net Assessment."

- Iran's space program aspires to place an astronaut into earth's orbit. Development of the Simorgh launcher is a key step towards this objective.

- Iran's universities and other technical centers are conducting basic and applied research in support of the missile and space launcher development programs.

Limitations

Iran's ballistic missiles have poor accuracy. The successful destruction of a single fixed military target, for example, would probably require Iran to use a significant percentage of its missile inventory. Against large military targets, such as an airfield or seaport, Iran could conduct harassment attacks aimed at disrupting operations or damaging fuel-storage depots. But the missiles would probably be unable to shut down critical military activities. The number of transporter-erector-launchers (TELs) available and the delays to reload them would also limit the impact of even a massive attack.

Without a nuclear warhead, Iran's ballistic missiles are likely to be more effective as a political tool to intimidate or terrorize an adversary's urban areas, increasing pressure for resolution or concessions. Such attacks might trigger fear, but the casualties would probably be low—probably less than a few hundred, even if Iran unleashed its entire ballistic missile arsenal and a majority succeeded in penetrating missile defenses.

Iran is also likely to face difficulties if it decides to develop a "second-generation" intermediate-range missile of 4,000 km to 5,000 km, or 2,500 miles to 3,100 miles, using solid-fuel technology. Its engineers would have to design, develop and test a much larger rocket motor. There is little reason to believe that the Islamic Republic could field such a missile before 2016. Moreover, Iran would still have to rely on imported technologies, components and technical assistance, and carry out a lengthy flight-test program.

Finally, Iran's past missile and space-launcher efforts suggest that Tehran would probably develop and field an intermediate-range missile before trying to develop an intercontinental ballistic missile capable of reaching the United States more than 9,000 km or 5,600 miles away. So an Iranian ICBM seems unlikely before 2020.

The future

- Although Iran's ballistic missiles are too inaccurate to be militarily effective when armed with conventional warheads, the regime likely believes that the missiles can deter and possibly intimidate its regional adversaries, regardless of warhead type.

- Iran's advanced engineering capabilities and commitment to missile and space launcher programs are likely, over time, to lead to development of additional missile systems. Export controls will slow, but not stop progress.

- There is no strong evidence that Iran is actively developing an intermediate-range or intercontinental ballistic missile. And a new system can't be deployed out of the blue. If Iran decides to pursue an intermediate-range capability, the necessary flight testing will provide a three- to five-year window for developing countermeasures.

Michael Elleman, senior fellow for missile defense at the International Institute for Stratgic Studies and a former U.N. weapons inspector, is co-author of "Iran's Ballistic Missile Capabilities: A Net Assessment."

20

Iran and the IAEA

Michael Adler

- Iran is a charter member of the Nuclear Non-Proliferation Treaty (NPT), the guide for the global fight against the spread of atomic weapons. Iran insists its nuclear program is for energy, not a bomb.

- Iran cites the NPT to justify its nuclear work, including uranium enrichment, which can be used to generate electricity or to make a bomb. Article IV guarantees "the inalienable right of all the Parties to the Treaty to develop research, production and use of nuclear energy for peaceful purposes without discrimination."

- Iran claims to honor the NPT obligations for monitoring its atomic program. It has been careful not to break the safeguards agreement that allows U.N. inspectors from the International Atomic Energy Agency to verify compliance with the NPT.

- But Iran has cut back on voluntary measures—such as inspecting its manufacture of centrifuges, the machines used for enriching uranium—that gave the IAEA more access to Tehran's nuclear work.

- The IAEA cited Iran for breach of safeguards, saying the Islamic Republic hid parts of its nuclear program and failed to answer questions on possible military work. This led the U.N. Security Council to impose sanctions to get Iran to provide data and to suspend enrichment to allay fears it seeks nuclear weapons.

Overview

Iran has been the subject of one of the most intensive investigations in the history of the International Atomic Energy Agency (IAEA). It was not always this way. Iran was an original signatory of the Nuclear Non-Proliferation (NPT) Treaty in 1968. The shah concluded an IAEA safeguards agreement in 1974.

After the 1979 revolution, revolutionary leader Ayatollah Ruhollah Khomeini initially opposed a nuclear program as a Western-oriented relic of the monarchy. But Iran and Iraq both did secret nuclear work during their 1980 to 1988 war. In August 2002, an Iranian resistance group revealed that Tehran was hiding two key nuclear plants—one in Natanz to enrich uranium, the other in Arak to produce plutonium. These fissile materials can be fuel for civilian power reactors, but also the raw material for atom bombs. The disclosure set off the current Iranian nuclear crisis.

Iran has since become a special focus for the IAEA. The U.N. agency, which is based in Vienna, issued 30 reports between June 2003 and September 2010 on Iran's nuclear program and its covert activities dating back to the 1980s. Tehran initially provided cooperation over and above regular safeguards, allowing inspections of non-nuclear sites, for instance. But on September 24, 2005, the IAEA's executive board found Iran in non-compliance with the NPT due to "failures and breaches of its obligations to comply with its NPT Safeguards Agreement," namely for hiding a wide range of strategic nuclear work. The board gave Iran time to answer crucial IAEA questions and to make key scientists available for interviews. It also called on the Islamic Republic to suspend uranium enrichment.

But with Iran moving to enrich, the board decided on February 4, 2006, to take the matter to the U.N. Security Council for possible punitive action. The Security Council has since imposed four rounds of sanctions to pressure Iran to suspend uranium enrichment, allow tougher inspections and cooperate fully with the IAEA. But as of September 2010, Iran continued to enrich uranium and defy the Security Council on grounds that it has the right to the full range of civilian nuclear work under the NPT.

The IAEA role

The IAEA was founded in 1957 as the U.N. branch of the "Atoms for Peace" program proposed by President Dwight Eisenhower. The idea was to make civilian atomic power accessible, in return for nations forswearing the pursuit of nuclear weapons. When the NPT went into effect in 1970, the IAEA became its verification arm. Headquartered in Vienna, Austria, the U.N. watchdog agency investigates national nuclear programs world-wide in order to guarantee that nuclear material is not being diverted for military use.

The IAEA is an essential player in the Iranian nuclear crisis, as it is the international community's eyes and ears monitoring the machines and scientists of the Iranian program. Its role has increased with the growing concern about Iran's atomic ambitions. Treating Iran as a special case, the IAEA has upped its inspections in the country, carrying out frequent visits to dozens of sites. It has an almost constant presence at key sites, such as the enrichment plant at Natanz. It uses remote cameras, as well as regular and unannounced inspections to verify that nuclear material being used and produced is not diverted for military purposes. Despite this, key questions about Iran's program remain, namely whether there was weapons work.

The IAEA has several tasks—and issues—with Iran:

- The IAEA is empowered to monitor all sites where there is nuclear material. But it is clashing with Iran over access to sites where nuclear material has not yet been introduced, such as at a reactor being built in Arak that could eventually make plutonium.

- The IAEA is particularly frustrated about Iran blocking access to key Iranian scientists, including Mohsen Fakhrizadeh, who has allegedly led Iran's atomic weapons work.

- The IAEA monitors Tehran's compliance with U.N. Security Council resolutions.

- It is also overseeing attempts to supply fuel to a research reactor in Tehran.

- In an attempt to better carry out an increasingly demanding verification agenda, the IAEA may seek to have its mandate expanded from its traditional focus on nuclear material to have the explicit authority to look into weaponization activities.

The IAEA investigation

In response to revelations about Iran's secret sites, IAEA chief Mohamed ElBaradei led an inspection of the Natanz enrichment site in February 2003. He issued his first special report on Iran in June 2003. The report gave a glimpse into 18 years of covert Iranian nuclear work. It found that Iran had "failed to meet its obligations under its [NPT] Safeguards Agreement with respect to the reporting of nuclear material, the subsequent processing and use of that material and the declaration of facilities where the material was stored and processed." These included "failure to declare the import of natural uranium in 1991."

More followed. The next report in August 2003 revealed that IAEA inspectors had found traces of enriched uranium on centrifuge machines in Natanz. Iran had told the agency, however, that it had not yet introduced nuclear material at this site, which was still under construction. The finding of the uranium particles raised suspicion that Iran was hiding yet more nuclear work. The IAEA called on Iran to make a complete disclosure of its nuclear activities by the end of October 2003.

As the IAEA investigation geared up and the revelations came out, the United States lobbied in Vienna to get the IAEA to declare the Islamic Republic in non-compliance with its safeguards obligations, thus clearing the way to U.N. sanctions. But leading western European states, as well as Russia, feared this could lead to an escalation of moves against Iran, and even war, as had happened in Iraq. The so-called EU-3—Britain, France and Germany—set out to parry U.S. pressure. They maneuvered for talks with Iran, and for keeping the Iran case away from the Security Council in New York.

In a diplomatic coup de theatre, the foreign ministers of Britain, France and Germany made a dramatic, surprise visit to Tehran on October 21, 2003, to strike a deal on resolving the nuclear crisis. Iran agreed to suspend enrichment and to make the requested full declaration to the IAEA about its activities. This kept talks alive and avoided sanctions.

The deal also kept an IAEA report the following November from having the impact the United States had been seeking, namely to be the catalyst for moving towards sanctions. The process begun by the EU-3 meant that Iran would be given more time to answer the IAEA's questions rather than be referred to New York for punitive measures. In addition, ElBaradei said in his report, in a conclusion the United States blasted as exonerating Iran, that there was no "evidence" Iran was seeking nuclear weapons. Yet, the report was strong.

It said, "Iran has failed in a number of instances over an extended period of time to meet its obligations under its Safeguards Agreement with respect to the reporting of nuclear material and its processing and use, as well as the declaration of facilities where such material has been processed and stored."

IAEA chronology

The evolution of the Iran nuclear crisis can be traced in the actions and reporting of the IAEA. Here is a brief chronology of events leading to Iran being taken to the U.N. Security Council:

- February 24, 2004: The IAEA reports that Iran is working to develop a more powerful centrifuge and on separating Polonium-210, which can be used in weapons.

- March 13, 2004: The IAEA board reprimands Iran for hiding possible weapons-related activities.

- March 17, 2004: Testifying before the U.S. Congress, IAEA chief Mohamed ElBaradei says the "jury is still out" on Iran's nuclear program.

- November 2004: In the Paris Agreement, European negotiators, the IAEA and Iran agree on the terms to suspend uranium enrichment.

- August 8, 2005: The IAEA reports that Iran had ended suspension and begun work to convert uranium into fuel for enrichment.

- September 2, 2005: The IAEA reports that there are still unresolved issues regarding Iran's nuclear program and says that full Iranian cooperation is "overdue."

- September 24, 2005: The IAEA board votes 22-1, with 12 abstentions, to find Iran in "non-compliance" with the NPT's Safeguards Agreement. This clears the way to report Iran to the Security Council for action.

- February 4, 2006: After failing to win Iran's cooperation, the IAEA board votes 27-3, with five abstentions, to refer Iran to the Security Council, pending one more report from ElBaradei.

- February 27, 2006: ElBaradei reports that the IAEA is still uncertain about both the scope and nature of Iran's nuclear program. The report is sent to the Security Council.

Case to the U.N.

After Iran was taken to the Security Council, and especially after the first sanctions were imposed in December 2006, the Iran dossier was divided between New York and Vienna. The IAEA continued monitoring Iran's activities, but the Security Council decided whether and how to punish the Islamic Republic. Iran reacted by reducing its cooperation with the IAEA. It followed strict safeguards measures, which verify the use of nuclear material. But it no longer allowed inspections at sites that may not have had nuclear material but that were crucial to the atomic program.

Iran and the IAEA were increasingly engaged in a cat-and-mouse game: Iran would build up credibility with concessions and cooperation, only to lose it after revelations of secret activities or failure to provide information about its activities. This pattern continued through September 2009, when the United States and its allies reported that Tehran had been hiding work on a second enrichment site, buried in a mountain near the holy city of Qom.

Iran consistently countered that it cooperated fully with the IAEA. Tehran said it resumed enrichment because the international community backtracked on its promises to help Tehran develop a civilian nuclear energy program and to remove Iran as a "special case" at the IAEA.

Four rounds of punitive U.N. sanctions did little to change Iran's position or its cooperation with the IAEA. In its September 2010 report, the IAEA said Iran had actively hampered its work by barring two inspectors from the country and even breaking seals on atomic material at Natanz. "Iran has not provided the necessary cooperation to permit the Agency to confirm that all nuclear material in Iran is in peaceful activities," the report said, in unusually blunt language. Tehran insisted that it had the right to vet inspectors and turn them away.

Factoids

- The IAEA was founded in 1957 as a direct result of the U.S. "Atoms for Peace" initiative to spread peaceful nuclear technology and stop the proliferation of atomic weapons. It has 151 member states.

- Iran had no centrifuges turning in 2003, when the IAEA investigation began. As of August 2010, it had 3,772 centrifuges enriching uranium and 5,084 more installed but not yet enriching, according to an IAEA report.

- Iran has cut down on cooperation with the IAEA. Since March 2007, Tehran has not implemented a Safeguards Subsidiary Agreement to give the IAEA notice as soon as it starts building a new nuclear facility.

- Since August 2008, Iran has "declined to discuss outstanding issues related to possible military dimensions of its nuclear program," according to an IAEA Safeguards Review.

The future

- Iran is likely to continue expanding its enrichment capabilities, even as it seeks diplomatic initiatives on its own terms, such as the Turkey and Brazil proposal on a fuel exchange deal.

- Tehran wants to maintain at least minimal cooperation with the International Atomic Energy Agency, since kicking out all inspectors could lead to a harsher international response, including more severe sanctions and even military strikes.

- But the Islamic Republic is also likely to continue to insist its nuclear program is strictly for peaceful nuclear energy, even if other secret sites or work are uncovered.

Michael Adler, a public policy scholar at the Woodrow Wilson International Center for Scholars, formerly covered the International Atomic Energy Agency for Agence France-Presse.

Iran's Economy

21

The Revolutionary Economy

Suzanne Maloney

- Iran has a strong foundation for rapid growth and development, with the world's second largest petroleum reserves, a young, well-educated population and a well-developed industrial and commercial infrastructure.
- But revolution, war, mismanagement and factional feuds over economic policy have undercut potential since the Islamic Republic's birth in 1979.
- The economy has been a central factor in shaping Iran's political evolution. Since the revolution, it has also been the primary target of U.S. sanctions and other international measures trying to influence Iranian policy.

Overview

Iran's revolutionaries inherited an economy in the throes of massive change and epic growth. In less than one century, Iran had been transformed from a small, predominantly agricultural economy run by a fading tribal dynasty into a modern centralized state with a booming manufacturing sector and a central role in international oil markets. Much of this transformation occurred during the reign of the Pahlavi monarchy, which sought state-led modernization modeled after the policies of Turkey's Kemal Ataturk.

Since the 1979 revolution, the Iranian economy has been beset by a costly eight-year war, unremitting international pressure and isolation, and ideological conflict. The revolutionaries clashed over what constituted an Islamic economy—and whether growth or social justice should be the top priority. Iran's reliance on oil revenues put the state at the mercy of energy market fluctuations, with prices below $10 per barrel in 1999 and above $145 per barrel in 2008. The Islamic Republic's approach to the economy is illustrated by the policies adopted during four distinct periods.

Revolution and economics

In the 1960s, Mohammad Reza Shah Pahlavi launched a far-reaching program that included sweeping land reforms, infrastructure development and huge investments in the country's industrial base. Iran's fortunes surged even more dramatically after the explosive rise in oil prices in the 1970s, helping fuel the shah's grandiose ambitions to overtake the French and German economies.

The Pahlavi economic program generated rapid growth, but the reforms also alienated influential constituencies, including the clergy, landlords and merchants or bazaaris. In addition, inflation and other problems spawned by the scope and pace of development created hardships for many Iranians. Economic grievances helped galvanize opposition to the monarchy, and revolutionary leaders such as Ayatollah Ruhollah Khomeini appealed to Iran's poor and its increasingly squeezed middle class.

Still, the economy was not the primary factor that mobilized opposition to the shah. After the monarchy's collapse, Khomeini dismissed its importance in the new order, remarking that, "Iran's Islamic Revolution was not about the price of melons." Consistent with Shiite tradition, Khomeini was a staunch defender of property rights and the role of the private sector, a view shared widely among clerics and reinforced by their alliance with the bazaar.

The clergy's economic conservatism unraveled during the chaos and competition that emerged as the Pahlavi regime imploded. Labor strikes and elite emigration paralyzed the industrial sector, and informal expropriations proliferated. Squatters were provoked by radicals hoping to accelerate the transfer of power and undercut the moderate provisional government. Iran's constraints intensified after the November 1979 seizure of the U.S. Embassy in Tehran, when Washington froze approximately $11 billion in Iranian assets and imposed other sanctions. After two years of disruptions to the economy, the post-revolutionary turmoil put the country on the brink of economic collapse.

Internal debate

The second factor that shaped the Islamic Republic's early approach to the economy was the fierce philosophical dispute within the revolutionary coalition itself. The powerful leftist component of the anti-shah movement, and even some clerics, had adopted 1960s-era Marxist dogma that sought an economy centered on "social justice."

Differences between Islamic leftists and traditional clerics roiled the policy debate throughout the 1980s, but the leftist influence won at the outset. Most major sectors of the economy were nationalized. The assets of the Pahlavis and other elite families were absorbed by newly-created semi-governmental organizations, broadly known as bonyads or foundations. They evolved into important and often unaccountable economic actors over the next 30 years.

The theocracy's enlargement of the state's economic role was to some extent an improvised response to circumstances. Yet the shift proved as consequential as any of its political, social and cultural changes. The state's economic takeover could not blunt the impact of the revolutionary unrest and uncertainty in the short term. All sectors of the Iranian economy experienced a marked decline during the first several years of the revolution.

The war years

Economic policies established during the revolution were strengthened after Iraq's 1980 invasion. The eight-year conflict provided a convenient excuse for expansion of the state sector and the precipitous decline in general living standards. Meeting the demands of major combat initially boosted Iran's manufacturing output. But the oil sector never fully recovered from the revolutionary turmoil. The 1985 collapse in oil prices severely constrained Iran's capacity to import goods required to maintain industrial production.

Throughout the war, sharp divisions persisted between the "Islamic socialists" and traditional conservatives. Proposals to nationalize foreign trade, expand land reform and establish new labor protections sparked fierce conflicts between the parliament and the oversight body empowered to vet all legislation. Iran's Guardian Council consistently favored a more conservative interpretation of Islamic law and rejected radically statist measures advanced by the Islamic leftists who dominated parliament.

Khomeini initially tried to balance the two camps. He eventually took steps that appeared to help the radicals but yet ultimately paved the way for greater pragmatism. In a decision with sweeping long-term political implications, he mandated that the interests of the state take precedence over either the constitution or Islamic law. This principle was institutionalized in 1988, with the establishment of the Expediency Council, which was empowered to mediate between parliament and the Guardian Council. Khomeini also sanctioned a wholesale reversal of his early pro-natalist policies that had boosted Iran's birth rate to the highest world.

The 1988 decision to accept a cease-fire with Iraq also reflected recognition that the country could not afford the war's toll on the economy or society. The costs were enormous: Productivity plummeted. Urban poverty doubled. Real per capita income dropped by 45 percent since the revolution. And price controls and strict rationing of basic consumer goods failed to prevent rampant inflation. Meanwhile, the factional battles over the economy polarized the political environment and eroded what was left of the private sector.

Rafsanjani and reconstruction

The cease-fire and Khomeini's 1989 death facilitated a major shift in the Islamic Republic's economic approach. Newly elected President Akbar Hashemi Rafsanjani sought to rebuild a country battered by a decade of revolution and a war with approximately $1 trillion in direct and indirect costs. Rafsanjani advocated a fundamental reorientation and liberalization of Iran's economy, along with efforts to reverse Iran's international isolation.

Rafsanjani's agenda included:

- Infrastructure development
- Privatization of state enterprises
- Foreign exchange liberalization
- Establishment of free-trade zones
- And elimination of subsidies and price controls.

To accomplish this ambitious program, he sought to utilize foreign lending as well as efforts to attract private domestic and foreign investment.

Reconstruction was initially strong. Post-war investment and relaxation of government restrictions helped generate robust growth in gross domestic product, government revenues and employment. The progress ran aground, however, as a result of policy miscalculations and political tensions. Massive increases in government spending and private consumption fanned inflation, prompting riots in a number of Iranian cities throughout this period. Iran's private sector proved hesitant to invest.

Foreign partners also remained deterred by political uncertainty and, after 1995, intensified U.S. sanctions. Meanwhile, soft oil prices from 1992 onward prompted a debilitating debt and currency crisis. Rafsanjani responded by rescheduling some external debt, reinstituting foreign exchange restrictions and shelving · infrastructure plans, as well as any move to rationalize subsidies.

Rafsanjani also had to deal with opposition at home, first from Islamic leftists who remained wedded to the state-centric economic model. They viewed any embrace of the free market as a betrayal of the revolution's ideals. After three years of tensions, Rafsanjani engineered their ouster from the parliament. But then his second term was stymied by traditional conservatives opposed to his relaxation of Islamic social and cultural restrictions. Reconstruction redressed some after-effects of the Islamic Republic's first decade. Yet the leadership's ambivalence toward market-based reforms hampered Iran's competitiveness.

The reform era

Leftists sidelined by Rafsanjani regrouped and reassessed the state they had helped create. Their efforts eventually helped produce the 1997 election of President Mohammad Khatami, and an ultimately ineffectual effort to reform the power structure. From the outset, this movement focused on social, cultural and political issues. It argued that strengthening the rule of law and regional détente represented necessary preconditions for growth and development. This strategy reflected the reformists' discomfort with the free market, a legacy of their leftist origins, as well as their frustration with the failings and repression of the Rafsanjani era. They also feared that the destabilizing impact of real economic liberalization might cost public support, which was their most powerful asset.

Once in office, however, Khatami found himself confronted with the onset of a global recession and a deep slump in oil prices. He also faced persistent inflation, unemployment, and mismanagement. His response was a typically cautious array of small-scale economic initiatives that bore modest fruit.

During his two terms, Khatami achieved a solid beginning to serious economic restructuring. Among his accomplishments:

- Unifying the exchange rate
- Establishing an Oil Stabilization Fund as a cushion against market volatility
- Authorizing the first post-revolutionary private banks
- Pushing through some improvements to the framework for foreign investment
- Stewarding the economy through a tumultuous period of unprecedented low oil revenues
- And luring new interest and investment from the West.

More ambitious plans, including efforts to reduce the costly energy subsidies, met opposition from conservative parliamentarians. They adopted an obstructionist approach to Khatami's economic agenda, as a means of subverting his political and cultural reforms.

Khatami and the reform movement can be credited with some stepping-stone economic reforms, but they failed to build and maintain public support for their agenda. Their political tribulations persuaded much of the Iranian public that press freedom ranked higher than job creation on their priority list. This strategic blunder left them vulnerable to a populist challenge, as the surprise 2005 election of Tehran mayor Mahmoud Ahmadinejad demonstrated.

Ahmadinejad's economy

Ahmadinejad's 2005 presidential campaign emphasized economic themes with populist appeal. He pledged to distribute oil revenues to the entire population and pointed to his modest lifestyle compared with his rivals. He assumed office at the height of a substantial increase in oil prices, which sustained illusory growth rates and brought an epic influx of revenues and foreign exchange. The other factor working in Ahmadine-jad's favor was the rise of Asia as a commercial counterweight to Iran's historic trade partners in Europe, which enabled Tehran to blunt the impact of U.S. and U.N. sanctions. After the United Arab Emirates, China became the largest source of Iran's imports. And Asia purchased more Iranian oil than any other region.

Ahmadinejad took an assertive and problematic role on policy by:

- Expanding credit and spending in a freewheeling fashion
- Feuding openly with a series of cabinet ministers and Central Bank chiefs
- Dismantling the planning bureaucracy
- Disempowering government technocrats
- And reveling in the reverberations of the global economic meltdown.

His provocative rhetoric on Israel and the regime's continuing defiance of U.N. Security Council resolutions on its nuclear program heightened the sense of political risk and persuaded some foreign investors to leave voluntarily.

Ahmadinejad did move boldly, however, to address longstanding distortions plaguing Iran's economy, such as subsidies and state dominance, but in a counterproductive way. Privatization benefited mainly state-affiliated companies, particularly those associated with the Revolutionary Guards, whose retirement funds took a majority stake in the state telecommunications firm in 2009.

Ahmadinejad's assiduous use of economic issues made him especially vulnerable. The mood inside Iran soured as the global economic slowdown began to impact Iran and the price of oil crashed to less than one-third of its 2008 high. Senior political figures and renowned economists were sharply critical of Ahmadinejad's spending and interventionist approach, while strikes by bazaaris in 2008 and 2010 forced the government to delay or abandon planned tax hikes.

The economy featured prominently in the 2009 presidential campaign. Ahmadinejad countered withering attacks on his record with misleading statistics and corruption allegations against his rivals. The post-election unrest aggravated Iran's economic dilemmas, intensifying the brain drain and capital flight. It also fueled European support for vigorous economic pressure. New U.N. sanctions in mid-2010 boosted the U.S. effort to cut off Iran's access to the international financial system. They also provided a platform for surprisingly robust measures by the European Union.

Paradoxically, the 2010 sanctions also provided a modest, temporary boost. The departure of foreign inves-tors opened opportunities for domestic firms, particularly those with Revolutionary Guard connections, and boosted the Tehran Stock Exchange. Sanctions also generated new pragmatism on economic liberalization. They galvanized support for previously unattainable reforms to the subsidies and even the investment framework. Yet early evidence suggests the 2010 sanctions may have hurt the regime, forcing costly and time-consuming shifts in banking and trade relations.

Factoids: IMF projections for 2010–2011

Gross Domestic Product (GDP)	$353.7 billion
Real GDP growth	3%
Unemployment	9.8%
Inflation (average CPI)	10.3%
Current account balance	$8.6 billion
Exports	$92.9 billion
Imports	$85.2 billion
Current account balance	$8.6 billion
External debt	$14.2 billion
Oil revenues	$64.4 billion
Oil production	3.7 million barrels per day (bpd)

The future

- The key uncertainty affecting Iran's economic future is the leadership's capacity to circumvent and mitigate sanctions, particularly restricting its banking relationships with Europe.

- Declining production from aging oil fields, together with political and logistical constraints on Iran's ability to monetize its gas resources, will begin to take a steeper toll on Iran's revenues and hard currency reserves.

- The government might be able to lure back some foreign investors by offering more attractive contracts. But changing the current "buy-back" system would likely entail a bruising internal battle.

Suzanne Maloney is a senior fellow at the Saban Center for Middle East Policy at the Brookings Institution. She is the author of Iran's Long Reach *(2008) and a forthcoming book on Iran's political economy since the revolution.*

22

The Oil and Gas Industry

Fareed Mohamedi

- The Iranian economy is heavily dependent on the lucrative oil and gas sector. But the vagueries of the oil markets and Iran's reliance on a single resource for most of its income has created disincentives to develop a more diversified and globally integrated economy. Consequently, the sector has been a source of periodic but persistent economic instablity.

- Iran's oil and gas sectors have critical structural problems. Subsidized prices and a population that has doubled since the 1979 revolution have created excessive demand. Supply has been stymied by underinvestment caused by financial constraints, technical shortages and sanctions. Iran is a net importer of gas and is under pressure to avoid becoming a net importer of oil.

- The government of President Mahmoud Ahmadinejad has asserted its control over the oil and gas sector. It has reduced the power of the "oil mafia," dominated by allies of former President Akbar Hashemi Rafsanjani, and replaced it with companies associated with the Revolutionary Guards.

Overview

In 1908, Iran was the first country in the Persian Gulf to discover oil. Petroleum has been the primary industry in Iran since the 1920s. Despite Tehran's attempts to diversify the economy, the oil and gas industry is still the critical engine of economic growth. Oil revenues accounted for 65 percent of government revenues in fiscal year 2008-2009, although it comprised only around 10 percent of the gross domestic product. This trend has remained fairly steady over the last few decades.

The Iranian government's dependence on oil revenues has resulted in prolonged patterns of rentierism—or dependence on a single natural resource—in its political economy. Some analysts suggest that Iran's "revenue autonomy" and access to large amounts of foreign exchange have helped fund an eight-year war with Iraq and extremist groups.

But Iran's oil sector has also suffered setbacks. Production was acutely affected during the revolution, especially by workers' strikes. During the Iran-Iraq War, the invasion of oil-rich Khuzestan and the port of Abadan severely impacted revenues. And Iran's support for militant movements led to sanctions that crippled its ability to buy badly needed equipment and new refineries from the West.

Vulnerabilities

The revolutionary government has struggled since the 1979 revolution to maintain oil production above 3.5 million barrels per day—just over one-half of production under the last shah. Iran produced 6 million barrels per day in the monarchy's final years. Production fell to a low of 1.5 million barrels per day in 1980. The long period of low oil prices between 1986 and 2000 also crippled Iranian revenues.

Iran's revenues have fluctuated due to the vagaries of the world's oil markets, periodically depressing government revenues. The government has often not been able to cut spending for political reasons and funded its deficits by borrowing from the Central Bank. Periodic bouts of lower oil prices have also led to foreign exchange shortfalls and a fall in imports, especially industrial inputs. Excessive domestic demand and disrupted industrial production has led to periods of high inflation.

Misuse of oil revenues has also caused long term-economic problems. After he was first elected in 2005, Ahmadinejad embarked on a populist spending program encouraged by higher oil prices. However, his plan has overcommitted the government to support social welfare, which Tehran will not be able to afford if oil prices remain low long-term. Iran has built up its foreign exchange because of higher oil prices over the past decade. But should oil prices fall, its reserves could be depleted rapidly. Ahmadinejad has already subverted the Oil Stabilization Fund, which was originally designed to save excess oil revenues in a rainy day fund. He tapped the fund to support higher spending levels.

Iran's longstanding subsidies—to support consumption of refined oil products and natural gas—have also become a huge burden on the Iranian budget and its balance of payments. Iranians pay as little as 38 cents for a gallon of subsidized gasoline. This has resulted in runaway consumption and rising imports of gasoline. Iran currently imports up to 40 percent of its refined oil needs, because its own refineries cannot handle the volume needed for domestic consumption. Gasoline imports, which have to be paid for in hard currency at world market prices, account for around 3 percent of gross domestic product (GDP). This, however, does not measure the true cost of subsidies. Total petroleum subsidies, including for consumption of those domestically produced, accounted for 20 percent of GDP.

Oil

Iran is the second largest OPEC producer and the fifth largest globally (after Russia, Saudi Arabia, the United States and China). In 2010, it produced some 3.7 million barrels per day. Its oil sector is one of the oldest in the world. Production started in 1908 at the Masjid-i-Suleiman oil field. As a result, Iran has one of the world's most mature oil sectors. About 80 percent of its reserves were discovered before 1965. Iran has already produced 75 percent of its reserves, so the likelihood of other major discoveries is low. Iran has made some important new discoveries in the past decade, such as the Yadavaran and Azadegan fields, but they have not been sufficient to alter the trend in oil reserves depletion.

The National Iranian Oil Company (NIOC) has held crude production within the 3.8 million to 4.0 million barrels per day range for the last several years. This has been a major achievement since most oil sectors with depletion rates of 75 percent usually witness steep declines in production. Indeed, Iran's base production is declining around 4 percent per year. The recently discovered new sources have allowed Iran to hold oil production relatively steady, and they may even help production levels to grow somewhat in the immediate future. But new sources will not be able to offset natural declines beyond the short-term. As a result, Iran will have to rely heavily on proven but undeveloped reserves, which will require major new investments. Production capacity is likely to fall because of geological constraints, the lack of domestic technical capacity, financial constraints and international sanctions.

In the 1990s, Iran attempted to attract foreign companies to develop its crude oil reserves, partly because it lacked the technical and financial resources to develop them. The contract terms were called buy-back arrangements, whereby foreign oil companies developed the field and were paid back in crude oil produced. The field under development was returned to NIOC's control after repayment was completed. These arrangements were unpopular with foreign companies, even though several large oil and gas fields were developed. The threat of renewed sanctions and Iranian refusal to provide better terms has led most private Western companies to leave.

In the last few years, Tehran has increasingly looked East to attract national oil companies into the Iranian upstream industry. The greatest activity has been with China, which has held talks on major projects since Sinopec signed the contract for the Yadavaran field in 2007. But proceeding to actual development has been slow, even for Yadavaran. It remains to be seen whether these other projects will move forward in the near term.

Refining capacity

Iran's refineries are operated by the National Iranian Oil Refining and Distribution Company (NIORDC). It operates nine refineries with a combined refining capacity of 1.775 million barrels per day. Capacity has almost doubled since the early 1990s and considerable work has been done on upgrading the refineries.

But a significant portion of what Iran's refines is low-value fuel oil. It still relies on imports of higher value-added refined products, such as gasoline, jet fuel and diesel, to accommodate the growing public appetite for subsidized fuels, especially gasoline and gas oil. In early 2006, NIORDC announced plans for a $16 billion program to expand and upgrade its refineries, with a goal of doubling its capacity to around 3.3 million barrels per day. As of mid-2010, several projects were underway, but the bulk of the program will not be completed in the next several years because of Iran's financial constraints and international sanctions.

Natural gas

Iran has the second largest gas reserves in the world after the Russian Federation. For two decades, its production growth has increased by an average of 10 percent, yet Iran has only depleted 5 percent of its gas reserves. Iran's problem is that its ability to produce has lagged behind its domestic needs. Demand has surged because of economic and population growth. Natural gas has also been liquified and used as a substitute for gasoline and other transport fuels. As its oil sector has become more mature, the government has had to use more gas for reinjection into maturing oil fields in order to maintain oil production.

Iran must continue to develop its reserves at a rapid rate to meet this demand. Iran's main asset is the giant off-shore South Pars field in the Persian Gulf, which it shares with Qatar. It is the world's largest gas field. Qatar has sped ahead with development of its field, but Iran has lagged way behind. Tehran has made some progress in developing several phases of the South Pars gas field in recent years. But achieving full potential of this giant field plus other fields will be a challenge over the near term because of technical and financial constraints.

Developing its natural gas sector also requires a heavy commitment to building the necessary infrastructure. Iran's gas production is in the south of the country, but the bulk of its demand is in the north. It has built an impressive pipeline network to transport this gas, but again growing demand has increased the need to expand domestic pipelines.

Since it can barely meet domestic demand, Iran will not be able to deliver on its ambitious gas export program beyond the current pipeline exports to Turkey. By 2010, none of the plans to export to Oman, the United Arab Emirates, India, Pakistan, Europe (all by pipeline) and China (by liquified natural gas) had even started. For its own needs, Iran will continue to rely on gas imports, mainly from Turkmenistan. These are getting more expensive, however, because of competition for this gas from China.

Industry structure and control

The Ministry of Petroleum, which has control over the National Iranian Oil Company, reports to the president with oversight from the parliament. But the dividing line between the ministry and Iran's oil company is often indistinct. The position of NIOC managing director was only established in 2000 as a separate post. But in reality, as a vestige of the past, the two institutions still share personnel and offices.

The Ministry also controls the National Iranian Gas Company, the National Iranian Petrochemical Company, and the National Iranian Oil Refining and Distribution Company. In 2006, the ministry submitted a bill to parliament proposing that NIOC manage all four companies. But the bill did not pass because Ahmadinejad's supporters did not want the ministry to create more autonomous companies.

For most of the revolution's first three decades, an "oil mafia" under the influence of former President Akbar Hashemi Rafsanjani controlled both the ministry of petroleum and the National Iranian Oil Company. Ahmadinejad initially failed to assume control over the sector after his election in 2005. Parliament rejected his first few choices for oil minister. In his second term, he has become more successful in prying control away from the oil mafia, especially after parliament approved Massoud Mir-Kazemi. In a reflection of the power shift, Mir-Kazemi has a strong background in the Revolutionary Guards and the defense ministry. He was former head of the IRGC think tank, the Center for Fundamental Studies.

Under Ahmadinejad, the Revolutionary Guards' influence has grown within NIOC, as well as in the service sector. Khatam ul-Anbia, the IRGC construction arm, has strengthened its role throughout the Iranian economy, including the oil and gas sector. In 2006, it won a contract to develop South Pars Phases 15-16. In 2009, it took over the Sadra Yard, a firm that has built many platforms in the Persian Gulf and the recently completed Alborz semi-submersible rig which will drill in the Caspian Sea. While the Revolutionary Guards' profile is growing, it also faces financing difficulties. International sanctions have deterred banks from funding Phases 15-16 due to its link with Khatam ul-Anbia.

The future

- International sanctions will slow investment in the oil and gas sector in the next few years, which could lead to a decline in output.

- A sharply lower oil price would destabilize the Iranian economy, since Iran balances its external accounts at around $75 per barrel.

• Falling oil and gas output and lower oil prices will weaken the government's ability to stimulate the economy, which could result in slower economic growth and higher unemployment.

Fareed Mohamedi is partner and head of oil markets and country strategies at PFC Energy, a Washington, D.C., based oil and gas consultancy.

23

The Subsidies Conundrum

Semira N. Nikou

- Iran has subsidized petroleum products, basic foodstuffs, medical goods and utilities since 1980, first to manage hardships during the eight-year war with Iraq, and then to prevent political and economic challenges after the war.

- Since the 1990s, three presidents have tried to cut back subsidies that are now estimated to cost Iran between $70 billion and $100 billion annually. President Mahmoud Ahmadinejad won parliamentary approval for a controversial plan to phase out subsides by 2015.

- Under the plan, universal price controls are to be replaced with small cash payments to families and direct support of industries. Some economists are concerned that lifting price controls will trigger dramatic rises in inflation and unemployment.

- The cutbacks come at a time the government already faces serious economic troubles and tougher international sanctions. For the public, the change is likely to produce the most economic disruption since the revolution. Economic reforms have triggered unrest in the past.

- If reform succeeds, however, the program could help reduce waste, shrink state outlays and enhance efficiency and productivity.

Overview

The 1979 revolution was carried out in the name of "the oppressed," and the Islamic Republic has been a welfare state committed to "social justice" ever since. The government introduced rationing soon after Iraq's 1980 invasion generated new economic hardships. To appease a war-weary society after the conflict, the theocracy kept consumer prices for energy, basic foods, medicines and utilities (water, power and sewage) well below market prices. But the economic burden soared as the new theocracy initially encouraged population growth, which almost doubled the population from 34 million to 62 million in a mere decade. The cost of subsidies, in turn, also soared.

The Islamic Republic has long been vulnerable economically. Politicians in both the executive and legislative branches have been reluctant to make badly-needed reforms for fear of political backlash. President Akbar Hashemi Rafsanjani's austerity plan in the early 1990s sparked riots across the country, forcing him to shelve free market reforms and subsidy cutbacks. President Mohammad Khatami was unable to mobilize support from conservatives in parliament for either subsidy reforms or a plan to gradually increase gasoline prices. Under Ahmadinejad, the announcement of gasoline rationing triggered unrest and attacks on gas stations in 2007.

Ahmadinejad proposed new subsidy reforms in 2008, but the plan was deferred until after the 2009 presidential election. He had to wage a heated political battle, and a compromise was eventually reached with the intervention of the supreme leader, in 2010. Yet for the first time, Iran's major political factions agreed that the burden of subsidies was unsustainable, despite fears of severe economic and political consequences.

The case for reform

Subsidies have been costly. They were estimated to eat up around 25 percent of Iran's gross domestic product (GDP) of $335 billion in 2009. Subsidies for energy products alone accounted for 10 percent of Iran's

GDP in 2010, according to the World Bank. Iranians pay as little as 38 cents for a gallon of rationed gasoline, cheaper than bottled water. Gas costs 10 center per liter, while a liter of bottled water costs around 25 cents.

Without reforms, costs would only continue to grow as Iran's population increases—even though innovative programs by previous presidents brought the population growth rate down, from a height of 3.9 percent in 1986 to 1.3 percent in 2008. In 2010, as he was simultaneously pushing subsidy reforms, Ahmadinejad also called for new population growth, including a $950 incentive for each new baby and a $95 annual stipend until the child turns 18. But a higher birth rate would be a further drain on the economy, and even conservatives moved to block institutionalizing his initiative.

The subsidies program has been plagued by two fundamental flaws. First, cheap prices have fostered wasteful behavior. Iran's energy consumption has increased five-fold in the past 30 years, while the population has only doubled, according to former International Monetary Fund economist Jahangir Amuzegar. Official Iranian figures claim energy consumption has actually increased nine-fold since 1976. Cheap gas has, in turn, contributed to chronic pollution, environmental decay and massive traffic overload in urban areas.

Second, subsidies have helped everyone, not just the poor. Those benefitting the most from subsidies are middle and upper income Iranians. Iran's richest 30 percent have reaped the benefits of 70 percent of government subsidies, according to Iran's ministry of economics and finance.

The plan

Subsidies will be phased out over five years, ending in 2015.

The government can cut back up to $20 billion of subsidies within the first year. In subsequent years, parliament will have to approve additional amounts through the annual budget process.

Immediate cutbacks affect the price of petroleum products, wheat, rice, cooking oil, milk, sugar, postal services, as well as airline and railway services. The government has discretion on which subsidies to cut first.

Medical services and products are not affected by the plan.

In lieu of subsidies, the government will distribute small sums of cash to individuals.

A new government body—a subsidy reform organization—will hold most of the funds that were once allocated for subsidies. It will plan and supervise the distribution of cash payments as a substitute for subsidies. Parliament insisted on making the organization subject to audit.

The funds accrued from subsidy cuts will be divided:

- 50 percent for direct cash payments to people who qualify for aid;
- 30 percent to industries that rely heavily on subsidies, and to improve the energy sector and public transportation;
- 20 percent directly to the Treasury to cover government costs of implementation and reduce dependence on oil revenues.

The politics

Ahmadinejad's reform plan is widely interpreted as a policy reversal. He won the presidency in 2005 on a platform of increased social services and aid to the poor—and putting Iran's oil wealth on the dinner table. But his cash handouts did little to improve living standards or reduce growing income gaps. The purchasing power of Iranians, particularly the poor and middle class, weakened as inflation spiked, hitting nearly 30 percent in 2008, according to the Central Bank of Iran. Critics argued that Ahmadinejad's profligate spending also drained the Treasury of billions from oil revenues, while contributing little to improve Iran's aged and ailing infrastructure.

Unlike his two predecessors, Ahmadinejad initially rebuffed proposals for reform by the World Bank and International Monetary Fund. But tough economic realities apparently changed his mind. His original proposal called for an even more drastic plan to eliminate subsidies within three years.

Many economists and members of parliament argued that Ahmadinejad's original shock-therapy strategy would have dire consequences. They urged a more gradual transition to avoid a dramatic spike in inflation for families and industries that relied on highly subsidized energy supplies and already faced a competitive disadvantage due to sanctions. Parliament also wanted supervisory power over distribution of funds, which Ahmadinejad rejected. After a year of intense debates, a compromise bill—lengthening the transition and creating the subsidy reform organization (SRO), which will be subject to parliamentary oversight through its audit authority—was passed in 2010.

Potential problems

The new scheme faces many dangers, especially in a fragile political climate following the disputed 2009 presidential election. First, the biggest danger is soaring inflation that could deepen poverty. Parliament's Research Center warned that Ahmadinejad's original plan could have produced inflation exceeding 60 percent, while the International Monetary Fund projected an increase of over 30 percent—figures the government rejects. Ahmadinejad's administration contends that the negative side effects will be transient and that the projections are based on out-of-date models.

Poverty is already a key political issue, and one reason Ahmadinejad first won the presidency in 2005 on a populist political platform. Figures vary widely, but both Iranian and U.S. sources say at least 9 million Iranians live in absolute poverty, with millions more living at the poverty line. Some economists say the plan's success will depend on gradual implementation to avoid too much economic disruption.

Second, Iran's industries could also suffer. Many have been able to compete with cheap imports—despite outdated equipment, inefficient practices and international sanctions—courtesy of low energy costs. Economists contend that the 30 percent in new aid for domestic industries is not sufficient to compensate for higher production costs. Industries are already at a competitive disadvantage because of the high cost of labor and overvalued exchange rate. Further danger is a ripple effect that impacts workers in an already restive labor climate.

A 2010 report by parliament noted that Iran already has the world's 17th worst unemployment rate, out of 208 countries and territories surveyed, despite a change in the definition of a worker. In his first year, Ahmadinejad altered the legal definition of employment to include anyone who works two hours a week. Previously, employment meant a minimum of two days of work each week.

Third, the new system for providing individual aid is wracked with flaws.

The government originally decided to divide the population into three income brackets and distribute financial assistance to the bottom two. But Iran does not have an effective data-collection system on family income. Most data were gathered by self-reporting to Iran's Statistical Center, and many families do not want to disclose their assets for tax and other reasons. The government then revised its plan and indicated it would distribute cash payments to a wider segment of society. It also encouraged people with financial means to forgo cash subsidies, but over 90 percent of the population signed up for aid. Trying to remove them from the list—now or later—risks a backlash.

Sanctions impact

The United Nations, the United States and the European Union all imposed tough new sanctions on Iran in 2010. One big unknown is how they may intersect with or impact the new subsidies cutbacks.

The regime is calculating that reducing subsidies and increasing petroleum prices will force consumers to change excessive consumption habits, thereby mitigating the effects of sanctions. Iran could also try to blame new hardships on international sanctions to divert public attention from its own controversial cutbacks. But if sanctions begin to bite, either the president or parliament could also try to delay or reschedule the phased cutbacks.

The future

- Iran is cutting back subsidies at one of the most precarious moments, politically and economically, since the 1979 revolution. To avoid a backlash, Tehran must avoid a further drop in unemployment, a slowdown in the economic growth rate and a significant increase in inflation. The growth rate of Iran's gross domestic product is already at its lowest point since 1989, after the war with Iraq ended.
- Ahmadinejad's poor economic track record has spawned concern about his administration's ability to implement such extensive reform in ways that are not politically disruptive and economically harsh, particularly on urban middle and working classes.

- The controversy over Iran's nuclear program could produce future setbacks. The Islamic Republic faces the danger of additional sanctions if there is no agreement with the international community to resolve growing tensions.

- Subsidy reform alone may not solve Iran's chronic economic problems. To improve Iran's overall fiscal health, the government also needs to pursue structural changes and other free market reforms to reduce inefficiencies plaguing state-owned or state-affiliated industries. The government otherwise may still be forced to support key sectors that depend on the state's protection or business.

Semira N. Nikou works for the Center for Conflict Analysis and Prevention at the U.S. Institute of Peace.

24

The Bazaar

Kevan Harris

- Iranian bazaars, especially Tehran's Grand Bazaar, have played central roles in the economic and political history of the country. "Bazaari" is a term applied to Iran's heterogeneous commercial class located in historical urban centers.

- Bazaaris have often allied with other social groups, including the clergy, in anti-government protests when their grievances have overlapped.

- Under the monarchy, the bazaar prospered as an institution because of state neglect. But under the Islamic Republic, individual bazaaris were given key positions of power.

- Bazaaris have adapted to the new constraints that a state-dominated economy have created and the opportunities that a global economy has provided.

- There is no such thing as a single "bazaari mentality," since bazaars reflect and respond to the political and economic developments of contemporary Iran.

Overview

Bazaars in Iran are more than local markets for the truck and barter of traditional goods and handicrafts. They are urban marketplaces where national and international trade is conducted, political news and gossip is shared, religious and national symbols are on display and various social classes mingle. Iran's largest bazaar, located in central Tehran, has been central to the country's economic and political history since the late 19th century, most notably as a major force in the 1979 revolution.

The bazaar has long occupied the imagination of intellectuals, politicians, and travelers inside and outside Iran. For many, its customs and attitudes represent the traditional qualities of the nation's culture. One frequently hears the need to understand "the bazaar mentality" in analyses of Iranian statecraft and foreign policy. In reality, however, bazaars in Iran have continually changed with the times.

Under the reign of Mohammad Reza Shah Pahlavi, bazaars benefited from a long period of economic growth, but they were also alienated by the monarchy's rapid modernization agenda. After the 1979 revolution, some supporters of the Khomeini regime from the bazaar were given more control over commerce and trade, but increased state management of the economy and an unpredictable environment did not benefit the bazaar as a whole. The links between Iranian bazaars and the international economy are densely connected, as smuggling through the United Arab Emirates and other Middle East entrepôts (trading posts) created major routes to supply domestic consumers with cheap East Asian goods. As urban areas have grown, commercial shopping areas well beyond the downtown bazaar have emerged to meet the desires of Iran's new middle classes. Instead of being a bastion of tradition that represents an ancient way of life, the bazaar in contemporary times is remarkably different than in previous periods of Iranian history.

Bazaar history

Like the Athenian agora, the Arabic souk, or European fairs of trade, the Persian bazaar is central in understanding the development of political dynasties and economic enterprise in the areas where they are embedded in daily life. Notable pre-Islamic bazaars appeared in Bukhara and Khuzestan, and bazaar layouts adapted urban innovations from Roman and Byzantine cities.

After the advent of Islam, bazaars from Samarkand and Kabul, to Isfahan and Baghdad, bordered the main thoroughfares of trade-linked Central Asian cities, usually located near ruling palaces or citadels and the largest Friday mosques. In fact, Friday became the day of congregational prayer in Islam because it was the day when merchants and townspeople would assemble in a weekly bazaar in the Arabian Peninsula.

As sites where merchant families accumulated wealth, prestige and power, by being situated at the major nodes of regional and global trade routes, bazaars also became central locales of political organization in supporting or opposing the many rulers of Iran. The concentration of merchants, middlemen and wholesalers in densely packed alleys under covered roofs created a social space where common grievances could quickly coalesce, even between rich merchants, poor workers and diverse ethnicities.

The bazaaris of Tabriz and Isfahan who took part in the 1905-1911 Constitutional Revolution became local legends, and many Tehran bazaaris supported Prime Minister Mohammad Mossadegh in his attempt from 1951 to 1953 to nationalize the production of Iranian oil and take it away from foreign control.

The revolution

The Pahlavi monarchy cared little for bazaars, preferring modern shopping centers and channeling financial support to heavy industry. But the oil-fueled economic growth of the 1960s and 1970s still benefited the bazaar. The shah mostly neglected the 100,000 merchants and workers and 20,000 shops in the Tehran bazaar until 1975, when the state initiated an anti-profiteering campaign and price controls against bazaar stores.

Disparate political tendencies of various bazaar merchants soon united against the shah's government. Bazaaris participated in and supported protests and demonstrations in the spring of 1977, well before most social groups—including the clergy—had joined the revolutionary surge.

Bazaaris and clerics

Although Bazaaris eventually mobilized through local mosques during the revolution, this temporary partnership did not lead to a permanent bazaar-mosque alliance as the political backbone of the Islamic Republic. During the 1980s war years, the state nationalized major industries, restricted trade and controlled credit. Key bazaari supporters of the Khomeini regime were given high positions in government and rewarded with coveted import licenses.

Yet the prolonged turmoil and uncertainty severely hindered the ability to export Iranian goods to lucrative Western markets, or privately engage in long-term planning for the domestic market. As a result, many bazaaris felt detached from their supposed representation—the conservative Motalefeh faction—in government.

Today, there are indications that many bazaaris, most likely a majority, have been disenchanted with the Islamic Republic's policies for quite some time. Anecdotal evidence shows that many voted for Mohammad Khatami in 1997 and 2001, and also Mir Hossein Mousavi in 2009. However, compared to students, workers and women, bazaaris have rarely protested in public against the regime, even when other groups took to the streets.

This seemingly changed in October 2008 and again in July 2010, when bazaars in major Iranian cities closed down in protest over the Ahmadinejad government's attempts to raise and collect more taxes from bazaar shops. Both protests resulted in the government backing down to the demands of the bazaaris.

Yet the absence of bazaari activity during the Green Movement demonstrations of June and July 2009 indicates that broader links between the bazaar as a social entity and democratic social movements in Iran have not developed. This is perhaps because bazaars today seldom exhibit the collective identity and public solidarity that occurred in past moments of Iranian political history. This stems partially from the new cleavages in bazaar networks that resulted from the Islamic Republic's management of the economy and the picking of politically subservient economic winners. However, it also derives from significant changes in relations between the bazaar and the global economy.

The bazaar and globalization

Many bazaar merchants are still wealthy, but networks of Iranian commerce and trade have shifted in the past 30 years, reducing the bazaar's central importance to economic life. Both legal and smuggled imports entered the country through major ports such as Bandar-e Abbas or free trade zones such as the islands of Kish and Qeshm. As East Asian merchandise rose in quality and lowered in price, it easily outsold Iranian-manufactured products inside the country. An expanded and educated Iranian middle class preferred international goods that reflected Western prestige and status, even in knockoff form. A small but growing number of superstores and shopping malls exist in Iran. And increasing urbanization and congestion have meant that fewer wealthy Iranians living far from downtown are willing to travel to the bazaar to make major purchases.

Bazaaris have accustomed themselves to these new challenges. Many work with fellow Iranians in Dubai, for example, to ship a wide variety of fashionable products to their stores. They maintain necessary contacts with important individuals in government ministries and agencies, in order to acquire goods in a timely manner. The extent of smuggling in Iran is not entirely known. But almost every large government bureaucracy allegedly either looks the other way or has members who are actively engaged in smuggling, including the armed forces and Revolutionary Guards, the religious foundations and supervisory trading bodies.

Commercial profits in the bazaar are mostly short-term and precarious. And there is a high incentive to transfer wealth out of the bazaar and into speculation on land and real estate, which many bazaaris have done since the 1980s. While Iran's urban bazaars may have more employees, stores and goods now, compared to before the revolution, their social role and centrality to the country have diminished.

Romanticizing the bazaar

European visitors to Iran since the 16th century have identified the bazaar with the traditional culture of the country, conjuring up notions of piety, honesty and community on the one hand, shiftiness, gluttony and irrationality on the other. Many commentators on Iran today still lamentably employ timeless and hackneyed descriptions of a "bazaar mentality" to explain everything from Iranian statecraft to Persian literature and films. These clichés are not only insulting but also empirically inaccurate, given the adaptation and diversity within bazaar networks over the arc of modern Iranian history.

Factoids

- The director of the National Union of Clothing estimated in 2009 that over 70 percent of the foreign clothing for sale in Iran was illegally smuggled into the country, mostly to avoid a 100 percent tariff by the state.

- Tensions between the bazaar-founded Motalafeh coalition and the Ahmadinejad government are strong. In 2005, one member described Ahmadinejad as a "political midget," which he said did not refer to the president's height.

- *Resalaat* is a conservative newspaper associated with the Motalefeh faction. It frequently features opinion pieces on the Iranian economy arguing for more laissez-faire policies that would remove state tariffs and regulations on trade and benefit the bazaar.

- Bazaari merchants and their employees are now eligible to enroll in the Social Security Organization's self-employed pension program, one of the most generous pensions in the world for retirees.

Individuals and organizations

Islamic Coalition Association (Jamiyat-e Motalefeh-e Islami or ICA) is a pro-Khomeini opposition group that originated in the bazaar in the early 1960s. It had to compete with other more popular political elements in the bazaar, including the Liberation Movement of Iran associated with Mehdi Bazargan. After 1979, ICA members were placed in high government posts and took staunchly conservative positions in factional battles.

Habibollah Asgarowladi is from a bazaar merchant family. He was a founding member of the ICA, served as minister of commerce (1981 to 1983) and was the supreme leader's representative in the Imam Khomeini Relief Committee. He helped other ICA members get top positions in state-created Centers for Procurement and Distribution of Goods during the Iran-Iraq War. He was removed from his ministerial post after allegations of nepotism. Still an important voice in conservative politics today, his brother Asadollah is director of the Iran-China Joint Chamber of Commerce.

Mohsen Rafiqdoust joined the ICA as a teenager while working in the vegetable bazaar. He was nicknamed the "Imam's driver" because he picked up Khomeini from the airport in Tehran upon his arrival from exile in February 1979. He later became the Revolutionary Guards minister and then the head of the Foundation for the Oppressed and Disabled, a large state-funded charity, in the early 1990s. He faced widespread charges of embezzlement and mismanagement. Reportedly one of the richest men in Iran, he is now active in the private sector.

Society of the Islamic Associations of Tehran's Guilds and Bazaar was established by Mohammad Beheshti in late 1980s to serve as a vehicle for uniting the Islamic Associations, which helped distribute goods during 1979's revolutionary turmoil. It later acted as a monitoring organization for anti-regime bazaari activity and profiteering. Its head until 2001, Sa'id Amani, was a founder of the ICA. Amani's nephew, Asadollah Badamchian, was also a founder of the ICA and today is a conservative member of parliament.

The future

- Deeper government encroachment or further economic deterioration could lead the bazaaris to protest again.

- Yet the bazaar is unlikely to be a potent force in undermining the regime, due to multiple cleavages in bazaar networks and dependence on the state for livelihoods.

- Privatization of state-owned companies in Iran has been transferred mostly to state-linked organizations, pension funds, and notable elites in an opaque manner. Bazaaris with clout will likely take part in this transfer of state assets.

- The bazaar as an institution will depend less on territorial location and more on connections to other centers of economic and political power.

Kevan Harris is a Ph.D. candidate in the Department of Sociology at Johns Hopkins University who recently spent a year doing economic research in Iran.

Sanctions

25

U.S. Sanctions

Patrick Clawson

- The United States has had sanctions on Iran for most of the period since the 1979 Islamic revolution, with sanctions becoming broader since 1995 and expanded further since 2005.
- U.S. sanctions have been controversial on many scores, with vigorous debates about their impact and their negative side effects.
- U.S. sanctions have been maintained largely because the alternatives were less attractive.

Overview

Sanctions have been a regular feature of U.S. policy toward Iran for more than three decades. Washington first imposed sanctions on Iran over the 1979 U.S. Embassy seizure and then lifted them after the 1981 hostage release. Embargos were gradually re-imposed after 1984, at first because of Iranian sponsorship of terrorism and then because of concern about Iran's ambitions to acquire weapons of mass destruction.

In the 1990s, the Clinton administration imposed much broader sanctions, which became a high-profile issue in U.S. relations with Europe and Russia. Since 2005, sanctions and related restrictions—such as on the sale of militarily-useful items—have been more vigorously enforced. The Bush administration launched complementary banking sanctions.

In the vigorous U.S. debates about sanctions, all parties agree in principle to target the regime rather than the Iranian people, to encourage Iran to engage and compromise, and to urge other governments to join a coordinated approach towards Iran. But analysts and policymakers do not agree about how to use unilateral U.S. sanctions to help achieve these goals.

In the 1990s, U.S. sanctions created deep friction with Europe. But Washington and its allies have moved closer on policy since 2007, when Tehran failed to cooperate with the international community. A broad international consensus in favor of sanctions developed largely because other approaches accomplished even less. At the same time, few analysts or policymakers are enthusiastic about sanctions in general or those on Iran in particular.

Five major rounds

Five administrations have imposed sanctions on Iran, all in response to Iranian actions.

The Carter administration: Washington had no sanctions against Iran after the 1979 Islamic revolution until the takeover of the U.S. Embassy in Tehran nine months later. President Carter imposed an escalating series of sanctions, beginning with a ban on Iranian oil imports, followed by blocking all $12 billion in Iranian government assets in the United States. In April 1980, the administration imposed an embargo on U.S. trade with Iran and on travel to Iran.

One provision of the January 20, 1981, Algiers Declaration under which Iran released the U.S. hostages was, "the United States will revoke all trade sanctions which were directed against Iran in the period November 4, 1979, to date." The asset freeze was more complicated: Some $5 billion was released to repay debts Iran owed to U.S. banks. Another $1.1 billion went into an escrow account held by the Algerian central bank to settle claims by Americans against the Iranian government. The assets of the royal family remained frozen until Iran's claim to them could be heard. And the rest of the frozen assets were returned to Iran. The agreement also set up the Iran-U.S. Claim Tribunal, based in The Hague, to hear claims by Americans against Iran and by Iran against Americans and the shah. The tribunal still exists, even though it has issued no judgments since 2003.

The Reagan administration: After the 1983 bombing of U.S. Marine peacekeepers in Lebanon, which produced the largest loss of U.S. military life in a single incident since World War II, the Reagan administration declared Iran a sponsor of international terrorism. In 1984, Washington imposed various restrictions, such as U.S. opposition to World Bank loans to Iran.

During the Iran-Iraq War, the administration also imposed increasing restrictions on exports to Iran of dual-use items that could be adapted for military use. The embargo was extensive, including even scuba equipment. In 1987, Congressional criticism of U.S. purchases of Iranian oil for the U.S. Strategic Petroleum Reserve was a factor in President Reagan's order banning all U.S. imports from Iran.

The Clinton administration: U.S. sanctions on Iran expanded considerably during the Clinton administration. In March 1995, after Iran announced a $1 billion contract with Conoco, a U.S. oil company, to develop selected oil and gas fields, Clinton banned all U.S. participation in Iranian petroleum development. Two months later, he broadened the sanctions to encompass a total trade and investment embargo on Iran.

In 1996, Congress overwhelmingly passed the Iran and Libya Sanctions Act, (ILSA) to press foreign companies not to invest in Iran's oil and gas industry, the main source of the regime's income.

The Bush administration: Since 2005, the United States has issued a series of orders to freeze the assets of firms and individuals said to be involved in Iran's support for terrorism, in Iran's role in threatening stability in Iraq, and in Iran's nuclear and missile programs. The president's authority in this last area was significantly expanded in 2006 by the Iran, North Korea and Syria Nonproliferation Act.

The United States has frozen the assets of numerous Iranian officials and Iranian firms, especially those affiliated with the Revolutionary Guards. Washington has also imposed sanctions on dozens of foreign entities, particularly Chinese and Russian companies, for helping Iran's nuclear and missile programs. The U.S. government formed a unit in the Justice Department to more vigorously prosecute individuals or companies charged with selling arms and weapons parts to Iran. More than 30 arrests were made between 2008 and 2010.

The Obama administration: In June 2010, Congress overwhelmingly passed and President Obama signed the Comprehensive Iran Sanctions, Accountability, and Divestment Act (CISADA). It tightened U.S. sanctions in several areas and enacted numerous legal restrictions previously made under presidential executive orders. But CISADA significantly expanded sanctions by targeting the supply of refined petroleum products sent to Iran by non-U.S. firms. Iran imports about 30 percent of its refined gasoline because of the poor state of its own refineries.

The president has the power to waive nearly all CISADA provisions. But several major international oil firms announced a cutoff of refined products to Iran because of CISADA's provisions, combined with growing approval among European governments and some Gulf Arab governments to increase pressure on Iran. For example, BP refused to sell Iran Air fuel at European airports.

At congressional urging, the Securities and Exchange Commission also requires firms to provide information about their activities in Iran. It ruled that such activities constitute a risk, about which investors should be aware.

State sanctions

In addition to sanctions imposed by the federal government, many states—by some counts, more than half—now restrict their pension funds from investing in firms active in the Iranian market or firms with ties to Iran's weapons programs, or human rights abuses. After the brutal suppression of protests following the contested 2009 presidential election, some states and cities debated whether to purchase goods from Western firms allegedly involved in assisting Iranian repression, such as Internet censorship.

Sanctions impact

There has been strong disagreement about whether Iranians blame their government for causing economic problems, or whether they blame the West. Evaluating the impact of sanctions is complicated by disagreement over what sanctions are meant to achieve. Different policymakers and analysts stress different objectives. The many objectives they cite include:

• Taking a moral stance against human rights abuses in Iran

- Deterring other countries from taking the same nuclear route as Tehran
- Signaling international disapproval
- Delaying and disrupting Tehran's nuclear and missile programs
- Helping the democratic opposition
- Crippling the country, or at least the government
- Using sanctions as leverage to open fruitful negotiations on the nuclear issue or perhaps on a broader set of issues
- Persuading Iran to halt its uranium enrichment efforts

Evaluating what sanctions accomplish depends on whether the benchmark is progress on the more modest objectives, or full achievement of the more far-reaching goals.

Imposing sanctions has also carried costs. In the 1990s, U.S. sanctions created serious friction with Europe, which objected to both the policy on Iran and U.S. punitive measures on European companies. A crisis over ILSA was averted only when Washington agreed to waive ILSA on European investments in Iran; in return, Europe restrained export of dual-use items to Iran.

A new consensus

After years of failed diplomatic efforts to negotiate with Iran, European officials concluded that sanctions were necessary to get Iran to comply with its international obligations, including the Nuclear Non-Proliferation Treaty. Since 2007, Europe has been as involved as the United States in diplomatic efforts to secure U.N. sanctions on dual-use items useful for Iran's nuclear and missile programs.

By late 2010, U.S. sanctions on Iran were no longer an outlier; other major Western industrial countries imposed similar sanctions. As countries acted, major multinational firms decided that Iran's market was not worth the trouble. U.S. firms such as Caterpillar and GE decided that their foreign affiliates—which were not covered by U.S. sanctions—would pull out of Iran. So did foreign firms such as Siemens and Toyota.

Few policymakers in either the United States or Europe are actually enthusiastic about sanctions, especially after the experience with the crippling sanctions on Iraq between 1990 and 2003. Sanctions have gained momentum largely because the tougher alternative of using force is so unpalatable. Yet sanctions have had some successes. One factor in the 1981 release of 52 U.S. Embassy hostages was Iran's desire to end the assets freeze and trade embargo so it could prosecute the war with Iraq. More recently, the International Atomic Energy Agency reported that Iran's nuclear program has been held back by lack of access to foreign inputs and technology.

Factoids

- Sanctions on Iran allow much more people-to-people exchange than embargos on Cuba. U.S. restrictions on exports and imports do not cover travel (or travel-related payments), donations of articles intended to relieve human suffering (such as food, clothing and medicine), gifts valued at $100 or less, or "informational materials" defined broadly to include films, posters, photographs, CDs and artwork.
- Some U.S.-Iran trade continues, especially in food. Iran is a large wheat importer; some years, it buys as much as $200 million in U.S. wheat. From 1998 to 2010, Americans could legally buy Iranian handicrafts and foods. U.S. purchases never reached $50 million in a year; the main item was rugs. Some Iranian products faced other restrictions: Caviar was limited by the international agreement for conserving the endangered Caspian sturgeon, and pistachios faced a stiff countervailing duty imposed after California pistachio growers complained about dumping.
- Some trade is surprising. U.S. airlines pay several million dollars a year in fees to the Iranian government for air traffic control services while overflying Iran. Taking advantage of the peculiar U.S. classification of tobacco as a food for trade purposes, Iran bought large amounts of American cigarettes one year.
- While Iran has often complained that the United States does not allow Iran Air to buy spare parts for its aging Boeings, in fact, the Bush administration issued a license for such exports but Boeing has been unable to make a sale.
- In 1992, before the Clinton administration toughened sanctions, the United States was Iran's sixth largest source of imports; U.S. exports were $748 million.

Useful resources

The Treasury Department's Office of Foreign Assets Control (OFAC) website provides much information about the rules it administers.

Periodic reports from the Congressional Research Service explore the history of U.S. sanctions and proposals for additional actions.

The future

- U.S. sanctions on Iran have drawn harsh criticism over the years, but sanctions have intensified under five presidents, indicating a broad bipartisan consensus that, for all their faults, sanctions are an important part of the U.S. policy mix towards Iran.

- U.S. sanctions were widely criticized in the 1990s for being unilateral, yet U.S. action was eventually a spur to a broad international consensus, including a series of U.N. sanctions since 2007. By 2010, European governments that had long criticized U.S. sanctions policy had adopted much the same approach, imposing restrictions on wide swatches of the Iranian economy.

- There is no agreement among U.S. officials on the specific objectives of sanctions on Iran, which makes it hard to judge how successful they have been. Sanctions have facilitated some goals. But they have not had any success in persuading Iran to fully cooperate with the International Atomic Energy Agency on its controversial nuclear program.

Patrick Clawson is deputy director of research at the Washington Institute of Near Easy Policy, where he directs the Iran Security Initiative. He is the co-author of Eternal Iran: Continuity and Chaos.

26

The U.N. Resolutions

Jason Starr

- Since 2006, the U.N. Security Council has passed six resolutions critical of Iran for its controversial nuclear program. Each resolution was designed to increase pressure on Tehran to suspend its uranium enrichment and ballistic missiles development programs, two of three critical steps in obtaining a nuclear weapons capability.

- U.N. sanctions have progressively targeted officials, government branches and businesses linked to Iran's nuclear program and military. The resolutions have included travel bans and asset freezes on individuals, front companies, and banks.

- U.N. resolutions have also increasingly targeted the Islamic Revolutionary Guard Corps (IRGC), an elite branch of Iran's military and an alleged driver of the country's nuclear program.

- With each resolution, U.S. and European powers faced mounting difficulty winning international consensus to expand sanctions against Iran, particularly from Russia and China.

Overview

International concern over Iran's nuclear intentions escalated in August 2002, after an Iranian dissident group revealed a secret uranium enrichment facility at Natanz and a heavy-water facility at Arak. The International Atomic Energy Agency (IAEA) launched an investigation into Iran's nuclear program. In November 2003, the U.N. nuclear watchdog agency determined that for the previous 18 years, Iran had secretly developed technologies to produce highly enriched uranium. The IAEA reported that Iran had failed to declare several of its nuclear-related activities as required by the 1970 Nuclear Non-Proliferation Treaty.

In October 2003, during the IAEA investigation, Britain, France and Germany negotiated an agreement with Iran known as the Tehran Declaration. The Islamic Republic agreed to voluntarily suspend uranium enrichment during negotiations over its nuclear program, fully cooperate with the IAEA, and implement additional protocols to build confidence in its peaceful nuclear intentions. A key part of the deal was Iran's agreement to provide details on its secret program over the previous 18 years. But negotiations stalled in February 2005 over Iran's right to uranium enrichment. The United States and the European powers wanted Iran to permanently relinquish uranium enrichment; Iran said it would not stop a process granted to all signatories to the Nuclear Non-Proliferation Treaty (NPT). Tehran claimed the demand challenged its sovereign rights.

Tensions that ultimately led to U.N. sanctions began in 2005. After negotiations with Britain, France and Germany broke down, Iran resumed its uranium enrichment program in mid-2005 under newly-elected President Mahmoud Ahmadinejad. The IAEA Board of Governors voted in February 2006 to report Iran to the U.N. Security Council for non-compliance with the NPT, which Iran had signed in 1968. On July 31, 2006, the Security Council adopted Resolution 1696, the first of what grew into six resolutions demanding that Iran cooperate with the IAEA and stop enriching uranium. Iran indicated a willingness to negotiate but refused to suspend enrichment.

U.N.S.C. Resolution 1696

The Security Council passed Resolution 1696 by a 14 to 1 vote on July 31, 2006. The resolution demanded that Iran suspend its uranium enrichment and reprocessing activities within one month. It did not impose sanctions but vowed that the Security Council would adopt "appropriate measures" if Iran failed to comply. Russia expressed concern that the resolution could be interpreted as authorization for the eventual use of military force against Iran. The final resolution addressed this issue by specifying that the council was acting under Article 41 of the U.N. Charter, which empowers it to use measures not involving the use of armed force to enact its decisions. Qatar voted against the resolution after voicing concern about its potential effects on Middle East stability in the middle of the 2006 Israel-Hezbollah war in Lebanon.

Iran called the resolution unlawful, destructive and unwarranted. Its U.N. envoy noted that Iran's supreme leader had issued a religious decree in August 2005 against the development, production, stockpiling or use of nuclear weapons. He said nuclear weapons had no place in Iran's military doctrine. Tehran did not comply with the resolution's deadline.

U.N.S.C. Resolution 1737

Resolution 1737 was unanimously passed on December 23, 2006. It imposed the first U.N. sanctions on Iran for failing to comply with the international community. It directed all U.N. member states to adopt measures to prevent the supply, sale or transfer of materials to Iran that could be used for nuclear or ballistic missile programs. The resolution called on member states to freeze the financial assets of 22 corporations and individuals involved in these programs. Among the individuals designated was General Yahya Rahim Safavi, then the Revolutionary Guards commander, for his alleged involvement in both Iran's nuclear and ballistic missile programs. Resolution 1737 also called on members to "exercise vigilance" to prevent individuals involved in Iran's proliferation or missile programs from entering or transiting their territories. Russia was initially reluctant to adopt sanctions, in part because of its estimated $1 billion contract to complete Iran's first light-water reactor for peaceful nuclear energy at Bushehr. In order to win Russian support, the final resolution exempted light-water reactor items from its list of "proliferation sensitive" materials.

In response, the Iranian foreign ministry spokesman warned that cooperation with the IAEA would worsen. And Iran's U.N. ambassador accused the Security Council of attempting to force Iran to abandon its rights under the Nuclear Non-Proliferation Treaty. He said the council should instead focus its attention on Israel, which had not rejected the use of nuclear weapons or declared its secret program.

U.N.S.C. Resolution 1747

The Security Council unanimously adopted Resolution 1747 on March 24, 2007. It prohibited member states from procuring combat equipment or weapons systems from Iran and called on states to "exercise vigilance and restraint" in supplying such items to Iran. It also called on member states and global financial institutions not to enter new financial commitments with Iran's government—including grants or concessional loans—except for humanitarian and developmental purposes. Resolution 1747 added the names of 18 individuals, companies and banks associated with Iran's nuclear and ballistic missile programs. It also added seven individuals linked to the Revolutionary Guards, including Mohammad Reza Zahedi, the commander of IRGC ground forces; Morteza Safari, the commander of the IRGC navy; and Qasem Soleimani, the commander of the elite IRGC Qods force. Finally, it strengthened the previous resolution's travel ban provision by requiring any member state to notify the Security Council whenever an Iranian official designated for ties to Iran's nuclear or missile program entered or transited its territory.

Russia agreed to support Resolution 1747 after accusing Iran of delinquency in payments for Bushehr. Iranian Foreign Minister Manouchehr Mottaki charged that in passing the resolution, the Security Council had taken "unnecessary and unjustifiable action" against a peaceful nuclear program that "presents no threat to international peace and security and falls, therefore, outside the council's charter-based mandate."

U.N.S.C. Resolution 1803

The Security Council passed Resolution 1803 on March 3, 2008, by a vote of 14-0-1 after intense debate. A U.S. National Intelligence Estimate issued in December 2007 concluded "with high confidence" that Iran's nuclear program had been suspended in the fall of 2003. As a result, several council members initially questioned the need for further sanctions against Iran. Libya, South Africa, Indonesia and Vietnam were especially hesitant to pursue new punitive measures, arguing that Iran had begun to cooperate with IAEA inspections. However, U.S. and European officials wanted to tighten existing measures because of Iran's failure to comply with earlier resolutions.

Resolution 1803 contained several suggested measures for member states but few mandatory actions. It called on states to "exercise vigilance" when providing export credits, guarantees and insurance to Iranian entities. It also called on states to voluntarily limit their interaction with Iranian banks operating in their territories. The resolution specifically urged states to cut ties with Bank Melli and Bank Saderat, which the United States accused of providing financial services for Iran's nuclear and ballistic missile programs, in addition to facilitating money transfers to terrorist organizations. Resolution 1803 subjected 13 individuals and 12 companies to travel restrictions and asset freezes. Finally, it authorized inspections of air and sea cargo traveling to or from Iran if "reasonable grounds" suggested the vessel was transporting illicit materials.

Indonesia, the world's largest Muslim country, abstained from the vote on Resolution 1803. Iran's ambassador to the IAEA called the resolution "irresponsible" and described the agency's information on its nuclear program as "forged and fabricated."

U.N.S.C. Resolution 1835

The Security Council unanimously adopted Resolution 1835 on September 27, 2008. It imposed no new sanctions and merely reaffirmed the four earlier resolutions. Resolution 1835 was issued in response to a September 2008 IAEA report that Iran was resisting the agency's investigation into its nuclear program. The report also said that Tehran was making progress in developing and operating centrifuges for uranium enrichment. In response to these charges, Resolution 1835 called on Iran to comply "fully and without delay with its obligations" under previous resolutions.

Resolution 1835 was the weakest of the Security Council's six resolutions on Iran. In its final U.N. measure on Iran before leaving office, the Bush Administration was forced to accept a compromise resolution after Russia balked at more sanctions. Washington claimed Resolution 1835 showed the council's mutual resolve in confronting Iran, while Moscow argued it would encourage a political solution to the nuclear impasse. Iran's chief nuclear negotiator described the resolution as "not constructive" and said it would only cause further mistrust.

U.N.S.C. Resolution 1929

Resolution 1929 passed on June 9, 2010, by a 12-2-1vote, after months of intense and sometimes bitter diplomacy. Negotiations over the resolution followed two key events: First, revelations in September 2009 that Iran had built a secret uranium enrichment facility at Qom. And second, Tehran's rejection in October 2009 of a deal designed both to meet Iran's pressing medical needs and serve as a confidence-building measure to allow time for negotiations over the long-term nuclear controversy. The plan called for Iran to send uranium enriched at a low level to Russia for further enrichment and then to France to be turned into nuclear fuel rods. Iran would receive the finished rods, which would be extremely difficult to use in a nuclear weapon, but would fulfill its energy and research needs. After Iran rejected the offer, U.S. and European officials pushed for new sanctions. Russia and China initially balked but ultimately agreed to support a new resolution—the first under President Barack Obama. In last-ditch diplomacy, Turkey and Brazil won Iran's approval for a modified "fuel swap" arrangement, but key nations said the deal fell short because it did not account for the near doubling of Iran's enriched uranium since October 2009. Turkey and Brazil opposed the resolution, and Lebanon abstained.

Resolution 1929 required U.N. member states to prevent the transfer of missile-related technology to Iran. It prohibited Iran from acquiring commercial interest in uranium mining or producing nuclear materials in other countries. It enhanced previous travel sanctions by requiring states to prevent designated individuals from entering their territories and calls on states to inspect ships bound to or from Iran if they suspect banned cargo is aboard. The resolution especially targeted the Revolutionary Guards and the Islamic Republic of Iran Shipping Lines (IRISL), a state-owned shipping conglomerate that was allegedly involved in transporting items related to Iran's nuclear and ballistic missile development. It called on the international community to refuse financial and insurance services to both the IRGC and IRISL. Finally, it urged member states to ban new branches of all Iranian banks in their countries and prevent financial institutions operating in their territories from doing business in Iran.

In addition to imposing new sanctions, the Security Council listed several proposed areas of cooperation with which it would be willing to engage Iran to end the nuclear impasse. The proposal, which was initially presented to Tehran by the permanent five Security Council members plus Germany in mid-2008, offered several energy, economic, agricultural, civil aviation, political and humanitarian incentives, if Tehran agreed to verifiably suspend uranium enrichment. Iran's U.N. ambassador responded that no amount of pressure would break his nation's determination to pursue its legal and inalienable right to enrichment.

The future

• The six U.N. resolutions designated a total of 75 organizations and 41 individuals for their involvement in Iran's nuclear or ballistic missile programs or for their affiliation with the IRGC. The list includes seven individuals and 18 organizations linked to the IRGC. But Iran has been clever in creating new front companies to replace those subject to sanctions.

• If Iran continues to defy earlier resolutions, the United States and its European allies may feel compelled to push for additional international sanctions—one of the few remaining options short of military force.

• Tehran has leverage as one of the world's primary petroleum exporters, which will influence international interest in sanctioning Iran for years to come.

• China's expanding role in the global economy and its status as one of the world's foremost consumers of petroleum will render it an increasingly important player—or spoiler—in the course of future negotiations over Iran sanctions resolutions.

Jason Starr, a former research assistant at USIP, is currently a presidential management fellow at the U.S. Department of State. Any views expressed herein are the author's own and not necessarily those of the Department of State or the U.S. government.

27

Financial Sanctions

Matthew Levitt

- Since 2005, the United States has incrementally imposed financial sanctions on Iranian banks for helping finance Iran's nuclear and ballistic missile programs and terrorist groups. Sanctions are also a response to Iran's deceptive financial practices, which threaten to undermine the stability of the international banking system.

- U.S. measures also include informal actions to leverage market forces by highlighting the reputational risk of doing business with a bank engaged in illicit financial conduct.

- Banking sanctions alone will not solve the problem of Iran's nuclear program. But, coupled with diplomatic and military tools, they can disrupt Iran's illicit activities, deter third parties from facilitating those activities and induce Iran to reconsider its pursuit of illicit activities.

- In today's globalized economy, even unilateral U.S. financial measures against Iran complicate Tehran's ability to engage in international business, commerce and finance. But multilateral efforts are still preferable for the international legitimacy they confer and their constricting effects.

Overview

Punitive financial measures represent the strongest non-military tactic available to disrupt Iran's nuclear program in the short term. They are also the most viable tactic to convince the regime that it cannot afford to carry out destabilizing proliferation activities in the long term. Financial sanctions have proven an effective tool in disrupting the illicit activities of other rogue regimes, like North Korea. But Tehran is even more susceptible to punitive financial measures than Pyongyang because the Islamic Republic is fully integrated in the global financial system. Thus, denying Iran access to it is a powerful tool.

Iran sanctions extend as far back as 1979. But the United States launched more extensive efforts after the 2005 election of President Mahmoud Ahmadinejad. Shortly after he took office, the regime resumed uranium enrichment efforts, abruptly ending an agreement Tehran made with Britain, France and Germany to suspend its controversial program.

In response, Congress passed a bill in April 2006 extending and strengthening the August 1996 Iran Sanctions Act (ISA). (The Clinton administration had weakened ISA in 1999 and 2000 in an attempt to engage the previous reformist government.) A modified version of this bill was signed into law on September 30, 2006, three weeks after the U.S. Treasury Department cut off Iran's Bank Saderat from the U.S. financial system for transferring funds to terrorist organizations. A round of United Nation sanctions followed on December 23, 2006.

"Targeted" sanctions

The financial measures levied against Iran have focused on specific illicit conduct and specific illicit actors—what are known as "targeted sanctions"—not the entire regime. The sanctions started small. They gradually became more severe as Iran continued to engage in three types of activities:

- Refused international inspections of its nuclear facilities

- Engaged in deceptive financial conduct harmful to the international financial system

- Rejected diplomatic overtures and negotiations.

Sanctions imposed since 2006 represent a marked improvement over the broad-based, country-wide sanctions levied against Iraq that President Saddam Hussein easily evaded and abused. Targeted sanctions against

Iran have been enacted with three goals in mind: First, they aim to disrupt Iran's illicit activities. Second, they seek to deter third parties from acting as enablers for Iran's illicit activities. Third, they aim to force Iran to recalculate the cost-benefit ratio of—and reconsider continuing—its illicit activities. Targeted measures have been directed at specific Iranian companies, sectors and individuals engaged in illicit conduct.

Targeted sanctions against Iran are graduated—they have been implemented in stages, each round building on the previous ones in order to gradually constrict the regime's air supply, leaving it gasping for breath and desperate to acquiesce. The graduated approach, which includes both multilateral and unilateral efforts, is intended not simply to punish, but to encourage the Iranian regime to alter its behavior.

U-turns

Targeted financial restrictions include blocking "U-turn" transactions. Iranian banks are prohibited from engaging in financial transactions with American banks under sanctions passed after the 1979 seizure of the U.S. Embassy in Tehran. But U.S. banks had been allowed to process certain dollar transactions for Iranian entities simply for the purpose of clearing those transactions. This authorization was referred to as a U-turn exception. It applied as long as no U.S. bank directly debited or credited an account of an Iranian party. In 2006, however, the U.S. Treasury Department denied Bank Saderat access to this U-turn, effectively cutting off its ability to do business in dollars, the international currency for oil markets.

The Treasury Department cited the bank's ties to terrorism, specifically evidence that Bank Saderat had facilitated Iran's transfer of millions of dollars to Hezbollah and other extremist groups for several years. The so-called "U-turn license" remained available to all other Iranian banks for the next two years. But in late 2008, after Iran's illicit activities continued, the Treasury Department ended the U-turn license. This new restriction effectively denied all Iranian banks the ability to use dollars for any transactions related to the international oil economy.

Targets

As of September 2010, the Treasury Department had targeted 16 Iranian banks. They include:

Bank Mellat: A state-owned commercial bank meaning "bank of the nation," Mellat was formed in 1980. It was designated in October 2007 for moving funds for Iran's nuclear program and providing financial services for the Atomic Energy Organization of Iran and Novin Energy Company. Treasury targeted Mellat's Malaysian subsidiary, First East Export Bank, in November 2009, as well as the Mellat-linked Mellat Bank SB CJSC (Armenia) and Persian International Bank PLC (United Kingdom) in October 2007.

Bank Melli: Iran's first national bank, formed in 1927, Melli is now the country's largest commercial retail bank. Melli provides a wide range of financial services for entities involved in Iran's nuclear and ballistic missile programs, among its other illicit activities. It was designated in December 2008. Arian Bank (Afghanistan), Bank Kargoshee (Iran), Bank Melli Iran ZAO (Russia), Future Bank (Bahrain) and Melli Bank PLC (United Kingdom) have also been designated for being controlled or owned by Melli.

Bank Sepah: First opened in 1925, the Iranian Army pension fund provided its original capital. The bank was designated in January 2007 for servicing designated Iranian firms involved in proliferation activities. Sepah is Iran's fifth largest state-owned bank. Treasury targeted its wholly-owned subsidiary, Bank Sepah International PLC (United Kingdom), the same day it targeted Sepah.

Bank Saderat: One of Iran's largest banks, it was the first to be cut off entirely from the U.S. financial system in September 2006. Treasury targeted the state-owned Saderat for transferring funds to Hezbollah and other terrorist organizations. Saderat was founded in 1952.

Further, Treasury designated **Banco Internacional de Desarollo**, C.A. (Venezeula) and the **Export Development Bank of Iran** in October 2008, as well as **Post Bank** in June 2010.

Islamic Revolutionary Guard Corps (IRGC): The IRGC has also been a major focus of both U.S. and U.N. sanctions. The Revolutionary Guards are deeply involved in the country's ballistic missile and nuclear and weapons proliferation activities. They also maintain a special branch, called the Qods Force, which provides funds, weapons and training to terrorist groups.

In recent years, the Revolutionary Guards have become one of the largest economic actors in Iran, controlling vast financial assets and resources. Most of the IRGC's actual funds and assets lie beyond seizure in Iran, but its business and industrial activities—particularly those connected to the oil and gas industries—are heavily dependent on the international financial system. Targeted financial measures against the IRGC represent the kind of regime-hostile, people-friendly initiative that punishes those engaged in offensive behavior, without harming the average Iranian citizen.

Multilateral sanctions

Multilateral sanctions against Iran's financial institutions are an extremely effective tool in the fight against Iran's illicit activities. For instance, U.N. resolution 1929, passed on June 9, 2010, designated 40 Iranian entities linked to Tehran's nuclear and ballistic missile programs, including Bank Mellat's Malaysian subsidiary, First East Export Bank.

Multilateral bodies such as the Financial Action Task Force (FATF) have also been used to target Iran. Based in Paris, FATF is an international organization created in 1989 to establish standards to combat money launder-ing and terrorism financing. Its membership includes 34 countries and regional groupings. In a series of warn-ings between 2007 and 2009, FATF instructed its members to urge their financial institutions to use "enhanced due diligence" when dealing with Iran. In 2009, it went further and urged countries to begin developing "countermeasures" to deal with Iran's illicit financial activities. FATF also dismissed Iran's purportedly updated financial legislation, calling the changes "skimpy" and noting their "big deficiencies."

The risk factor

Sanctions are most effective when they are multilateral. But achieving consensus is difficult, and the resulting action often represents the lowest common denominator. As such, complementary measures—including regional efforts by bodies such as the European Union and individual actions such as U.S. designations—are critical in raising the risks of doing business with Iran. Unilateral sanctions are felt internationally because of integrated and globalized market forces.

The reputations of international banks, multinational corporations and insurance companies depend on their due diligence. The risks of engaging with an entity that has been publicly exposed for illicit activity often outweigh the potential profit margins. Executives of foreign corporations have opted to stop dealing with unilaterally sanctioned entities, even if they have no explicit legal obligation to do so.

After President Barack Obama signed a unilateral sanctions bill in mid-2010, Lloyd's of London denied insur-ance or re-insurance to petroleum shipments destined for Iran. Lloyd's' general counsel acknowledged, "The U.S. is an important market for Lloyd's.... Lloyd's will always comply with applicable sanctions." Iran's ability to develop its vast—and extremely lucrative—energy reserves has also been hard hit by investment cutbacks following unilateral U.S. and European actions.

U.S. measures have also led to several high-profile cases against major international financial institutions. In early 2009, Lloyds Banking Group was fined $350 million for processing payments that originated in Iran. In December 2009, Credit Suisse Group paid a $536 million settlement over similar charges. In August 2010, Barclays agreed to pay $298 million to settle charges that it altered financial records to hide payments from sanctioned countries, including Iran.

The actual cost of U.S. fines may not hurt large financial institutions, but firms are wary of the costs to their reputations for being associated with rogue regimes. Foreign financial institutions and private industries increasingly incorporate the Treasury Department's designation lists into their databases, not because they are required to do so, but out of their own fiduciary interests. Tehran's ability to do business as usual has taken a severe hit as banks, multinational corporations and insurers end their business relationships with Iran.

Informal sanctions

The Treasury Department has also embarked on an ambitious information campaign. Senior Treasury officials have met with private sector leaders around the world to outline Iran's deceptive financial conduct and the risks they pose for banks and businesses. Treasury provided evidence, for example, that Bank Sepah asked other financial institutions to remove its name from transactions when processing them through the interna-tional financial system. Informed of the risks, market forces have led many banks and corporations to forgo business with Iranian institutions.

In light of growing evidence, the Paris-based Organization for Economic Cooperation and Development, comprising the world's 32 strongest economies, raised Iran's risk rating in early 2006. In addition, a growing number of banks and corporations wanting to conduct business in the United States have concluded that putting their U.S. business at risk is not worth the investment in Iran.

Offense and defense

Financial sanctions targeting Iran have also included offensive and defensive measures. Offensive tactics such as designations target actors engaged in illicit activity, from terrorism to weapons proliferation. The U.S. Treasury Department or its counterparts abroad proactively deny these companies or individuals access to the international financial system.

Defensive tools, on the other hand, protect markets by denying entry to banks, companies or individuals who continue to engage in business with risky entities such as Iran, despite knowing the risks. Section 311 of the U.S.A. Patriot Act, for example, gives the Treasury Department the authority to deny risk-prone entities—defined as entities either exposed or involved in money laundering or terror financing—access to the U.S. financial system. Defensive tools do not aggressively target offending companies or individuals but, rather, serve as stop-gap measures to protect the U.S. financial system from abuse. The consequences of being denied access to one of the most important world markets can be severe.

The future

- To succeed, targeted financial measures must be credible. This may require follow-up efforts—ranging from additional sanctions to the possibility of military action—in the event that Iran fails to comply with its international obligations on its controversial nuclear program.

- Finding the right combination of financial sanctions is critical. The tool kit includes unilateral, multi-lateral and regional sanctions; formal and informal sanctions; offensive and defensive measures; and targeted and country-wide sanctions.

- Due to insufficient refining capacity, Iran still imports 30 percent of its oil from foreign refineries for domestic consumption. Limiting Iran's ability to import refined petroleum could be a powerful tool in exploiting one of the regime's primary vulnerabilities.

Matthew Levitt is director of The Washington Institute for Near East Policy's Stein Program on Counterterrorism and Intelligence and a lecturer in international relations and strategic studies at Johns Hopkins University's Paul H. Nitze School of Advanced International Studies.

U.S.–Iran

28

The Carter Administration

Gary Sick

- When President Jimmy Carter took office in January 1977, he inherited a unique relationship with the shah of Iran, who had been returned to his throne by a U.S.-British covert action and who had accepted the role of protecting U.S. interests in the Persian Gulf. The shah had some of the most sophisticated arms in the U.S. inventory.

- When the monarchy was overthrown, the United States and other countries in the world got their first real introduction to radical political Islam, not only during the revolution against the shah but also in the 444-day captivity of American diplomats in Tehran. That experience shaped the U.S. relationship with Iran for decades thereafter.

- The Algiers Accords ending the hostage crisis returned only a fraction of Iran's frozen assets. It created a claims tribunal that settled hundreds of U.S. claims against Tehran. Those costs, plus Iran's alienation from much of the world, suggests the hostage model is not likely to be repeated.

- The Carter administration's effort to build an independent military capability in the Gulf established the initial framework that was completed by its successors.

Overview

When President Jimmy Carter took office in January 1977, he inherited a unique relationship with Iran and its imperious and ambitious ruler Mohammed Reza Shah Pahlavi. That relationship was the product of interaction dating back to World War II and included a U.S.-British covert operation in 1953 to remove Prime Minister Mohammad Mosaddegh and return the shah to the throne.

Most importantly, during the eight years before Carter's election, President Richard Nixon and his foreign policy adviser, Henry Kissinger, had created a unique and unprecedented relationship with the Iranian ruler. As part of what was dubbed the Twin Pillar policy, the shah was identified as the primary guardian of U.S. interests in the Persian Gulf. (Saudi Arabia was the other pillar.) In return, the shah was permitted to purchase whatever non-nuclear U.S. military technology he wished.

The explosion of oil prices in the preceding four years had given the shah a windfall of revenues, and he used this money to fund a massive economic and military buildup. Tens of thousands of U.S. technicians were provided to install and maintain an enormous arsenal and to train Iranians to use it. But when oil prices declined, Iran was hugely over-extended. Disaffection with the shah's rule, which had been simmering for years, burst into the open.

The revolution

During the first two years of the Carter administration, Iran went through a wrenching societal transformation that steadily gathered momentum. Both Washington and the shah's own forces were constantly surprised at the speed of events, and the shah could not maintain control. Opposition forces, led from abroad by Ayatollah Ruhollah Khomeini, took over the streets of Tehran in December 1978, and the shah left the country the following month.

Khomeini returned to Tehran on February 1, 1979, and 10 days later the monarchy fell and was replaced by an Islamic revolutionary government. This was the first contact between the United States and radical, political Islam. It set the tone for future dealings with Iran and other radical Islamic states.

The United States attempted to develop a working relationship with the new government. Some modest progress was made in the summer of 1979 with the relatively secular, technocratic provisional government of Prime Minister Mehdi Bazargan and Foreign Minister Ibrahim Yazdi.

U.S. Embassy seizure

But in October 1979, President Carter reluctantly permitted the shah, who was desperately ill with lymphoma, to enter the United States for medical treatment. This triggered a violent reaction in Tehran. Mobs of students invaded the U.S. Embassy on November 4, taking its occupants prisoner and demanding the return of the shah and his financial assets to Iran. Khomeini threw his support behind the students, and the Bazargan government was dismissed, thus beginning a 444-day siege usually referred to as the hostage crisis.

When the students attacked the U.S. Embassy, Khomeini and his clerical circle were facing an internal problem of their own. They were pressing for adoption of a new constitution that would permanently enshrine the concept of an Islamic Republic, with direct clerical oversight of the government. Many, if not most, Iranians who had joined forces against the shah had not anticipated that the monarchy would be replaced by a theocracy, and opposition was growing.

The conflict with America—the hated Great Satan—rallied the public behind Khomeini. The referendum on Islamic rule was passed by a nearly unanimous vote one month after the hostages were taken. Khomeini subsequently referred to the taking of the U.S. Embassy as a second Iranian revolution.

The fallout

Iran publicly considered withdrawing all its deposits from Western banks, but the United States responded by freezing all Iranian assets on deposit in the West—some $12 billion. The massive arms purchasing program started by the shah was also frozen. Many of the weapons systems—including major warships—that were under construction were cancelled or sold to other parties. The proceeds were used to pay termination costs of the many contracts. Other materiel was placed in storage. The magnitude and disposition of this account (managed entirely by the United States) would later become a point of bitter legal contention between Iran and the United States.

President Carter was primarily motivated in his decision-making by concern for the welfare of the hostages. When Iran threatened to put them on trial, he sent a private note to Iran's leaders warning that if any of the hostages were harmed, the United States would interrupt Iran's commerce. Iran never acknowledged the message, but talk of trials ceased. When one hostage, Richard Queen, was diagnosed with multiple sclerosis, Iran quickly returned him to U.S. custody.

But it was also an election season in the United States. The hostage issue initially became a rallying point for Americans in support of their government. But as popular frustration mounted with both with the hostage impasse and a stagnant economy, the continued imprisonment of U.S. diplomats became emblematic of a loss of confidence in Carter's leadership.

The squeeze

One of the most extensive diplomatic campaigns in American history was mounted to pressure Iran's revolutionary government to release the hostages. Nations around the world and key Islamic statesmen were persuaded to intervene with Iran's leadership on the grounds that the taking and holding of diplomatic prisoners were clear violations not only of international law but also of Islamic law and practice.

The Palestine Liberation Organization interceded in the early days of the conflict and succeeded in securing the release of 13 blacks and women held at the embassy. Tehran apparently believed that this gesture would convince Americans about the justice of their cause. When it did not, they were never willing to repeat the process. Iranian relations with the PLO progressively soured, taking them out of the picture.

The United Nations repeatedly condemned the Iranian action, although the Soviet Union vetoed Security Council resolutions that would have penalized Iran. The Carter administration brought a case against Iran in the World Court. Washington established secret negotiating channels to the Iranian government leadership, leading to a tentative agreement in which Iran would be given an international forum to express its grievances against the shah in return for transfer of the prisoners from the students to government control as the first step toward release. To that end, both the U.N. Secretary General and a formal U.N. fact-finding commission traveled to Tehran to meet with victims of the shah's regime.

Despite many efforts, however, Washington never succeeded in developing contacts with Ayatollah Khomeini or the clerical circle. In the end, Khomeini vetoed all diplomatic initiatives.

Failed rescue

The administration contemplated a rescue mission from the earliest days of the crisis but rejected it as unworkable. The 52 hostages were being held inside a fortified complex in the heart of a hostile city far from any U.S. military facilities. But in early 1980, several developments made a rescue more feasible. U.S. intelligence had developed a network of agents in Iran. Reconnaissance had also identified a number of Iranian facilities that could be used to support such a mission. Special Forces had trained for months for the actual breaching of the embassy walls, and new information was available about the specific location of each hostage within the embassy compound.

In late March 1980, Khomeini rejected a negotiated settlement of the crisis, after a comprehensive plan had been accepted by Iran's provisional president and foreign minister. Negotiations seemed at a dead end, and U.S. political pressure was mounting to do something about the hostages after five months of futile efforts. So Carter broke diplomatic relations with Iran and secretly approved a complex rescue plan. Secretary of State Cyrus Vance vehemently opposed any use of force. When his objections were overridden, he told Carter that he would resign after the mission, regardless of the outcome, and he did.

The mission took place on the night of April 24-25. It involved eight large military transport helicopters launched from a U.S. carrier in the Gulf of Oman. Six were required to complete the mission. Other fixed wing aircraft, bringing a Delta Force team and supplies, were to rendezvous with the helicopters at a site dubbed Desert One, a small abandoned airstrip some 200 miles from Tehran.

The mission ran into early trouble. The helicopters encountered a massive dust cloud (invisible to the satellites that were the only available source of weather information) almost as soon as they crossed the coastline into Iran. One helicopter developed mechanical problems and had to stop. Another helicopter's warning light indicated a possible cracked rotor, and it decided to turn back just short of the landing site. A third was found to have an irreparable hydraulic problem upon arrival at Desert One, thus bringing the number below the necessary six.

The commander at Desert One made the agonizing decision to abort the mission, and the president accepted his judgment. As the helicopters maneuvered in the dark and dust to refuel for the return trip, one of them clipped the wing of a transport aircraft and both aircraft burst into flames, killing eight U.S. servicemen. Carter went on radio early in the morning to announce the mission's failure and to clarify that this was a limited rescue mission, not a military invasion. Until his announcement, Iran was unaware of the operation.

The endgame

On September 12, 1980, after the establishment of an Iranian cabinet and parliament, Iran sent an emissary to Germany to propose negotiating an end to the crisis. Initial talks, under German auspices, were held in mid-September. But the process was interrupted by Iraq's invasion of Iran on September 22. Although some expected Iran to be forced to come to the United States for arms and spare parts, the Iran-Iraq War was more of a distraction than a boon to the hostage negotiations. In the end, Iran solved its military problems without U.S. government assistance.

After the Reagan landslide over Carter in November, Iran nominated Algeria to act as the intermediary for talks to end the hostage impasse. Washington accepted. The talks were tortuous and continued to the very last second of the Carter administration. Unraveling the various strands of the problem, and particularly the frozen assets, was immensely complicated.

In the end, Iran paid off its various loans at incredible financial cost and agreed to establish a claims tribunal in The Hague to adjudicate commercial claims against Iran. In the Algiers Accords of January 1981, the United States promised not to interfere in Iran's internal politics and not to bring claims against Iran on behalf of the hostages.

The agreement was criticized for being negotiated under duress, but it has been validated by every succeeding U.S. administration. The claims tribunal has resulted in payment by Iran of hundreds of millions of dollars to dozens of companies that had contracts under the shah's regime. The shah died in Egypt in July 1980, and his assets were not returned to Iran.

After paying off the loans and setting up an escrow account at The Hague, Iran received only $4 billion or roughly one-third of its original assets. The cash loss to the Iranian treasury amounted to about $150 million per hostage, or roughly $300,000 per day for each hostage. The financial cost, and the incalculable loss of international legitimacy that has dogged Iran ever since, suggest that the hostage episode is not a model that is likely to be attractive to other countries and is unlikely to be repeated.

The aftermath

- The Iranian revolution and the hostage crisis dramatized to U.S. policymakers the gap between U.S. regional interests and its ability to project force.

- The shah had been anointed as the substitute for a robust U.S. military presence at a time when U.S. forces were tied down in Southeast Asia and the American public was opposed to any new overseas commitments. When the shah fell, the United States was left strategically naked, without a safety net.

- The Carter administration began to rebuild a regional capability in the form of the Rapid Deployment Joint Task Force and to undertake urgent negotiations with regional states for operating facilities.

- At the end of Carter's four-year term, however, those plans were more intention than reality. They would be completed by his successors.

Gary Sick, principal White House aide for Iran and the Persian Gulf on the Carter administration's National Security Council, is now executive director of Gulf/2000, an international online research project on the Persian Gulf at Columbia University.

29

The Reagan Administration

Geoffrey Kemp

- U.S. relations with Iran during the Reagan administration went through four stages—indifference, hostility, cooperation and finally confrontation that even included some limited combat.
- U.S. policy was shaped largely by three events: The 1980-1988 Iran-Iraq War, the 1982 Israeli invasion of Lebanon, and the abduction of American hostages in Beirut.
- A scandal in the mid-1980s—involving secret arms sales to Iran in exchange for release of American hostages held by Iran's allies in Lebanon—nearly destroyed the Reagan presidency.
- By 1988, U.S. support for Iraq and its military operations against Iran contributed to the end of the Iran-Iraq War and a de facto defeat for the Islamic Republic.

Overview

Ronald Reagan was sworn into office on January 20, 1981, just as Iran released 52 Americans held hostage at the U.S. Embassy in Tehran for 444 days. The timing was deliberate. The young revolutionary regime did not want the hostages freed until after Jimmy Carter, who had supported the shah and allowed him into the United States, left office. At the same time, Tehran wanted to clear the slate in the face of a new Republican administration that had vowed to take a tougher stand on terrorism and hostage-taking. But Iran also had bigger problems. Four months earlier, on September 20, 1980, Iraq had invaded, and Iran was embroiled in a life-or-death struggle. For the first 18 months of the war, virtually all the fighting took place on Iranian territory.

As one of the last Cold War presidents, President Reagan was also preoccupied with the Soviet Union, especially its military threats and its ties to radical states like Libya and Syria. In the Middle East, the White House focus was on advancing the 1978 peace pact between Israel and Egypt. Before the 1979 revolution, Iran had been pivotal to U.S. interests. It was a frontline state sharing a 1,200-mile border with the Soviet Union; it served as a listening post for the CIA. And it was one of the few Muslim countries to recognize Israel—and sell it oil. After the revolution, however, Iran became peripheral to these U.S. priorities.

Over the next eight years, U.S. and Iranian interests would both intersect and conflict violently. The Reagan administration produced unorthodox diplomatic contacts between Washington and Tehran. But it also witnessed the first military confrontation. The 1980s generally marked the most volatile period in relations between the United States and Iran during the revolution's first three decades. The White House faced four major challenges.

Israel's 1982 invasion of Lebanon

The first turning point was Israel's 1982 invasion of Lebanon, which triggered a series of events that played out over the rest of the Reagan presidency. Israel invaded to push Palestine Liberation Organization (PLO) guerillas away from its borders. The Israelis were initially embraced as liberators by the predominately Shiite population in southern Lebanon, where the Palestinians had alienated the local population. But the welcome was short-lived. The heavy-handed Israelis were soon regarded as occupiers.

The summer-long war, symbolized by the siege of Beirut, was complicated by the intervention of foreign forces. Shortly after the invasion, Iran dispatched more than 1,000 Revolutionary Guards to Lebanon in a sign of support. The Iranians never directly engaged the Israelis, but they fostered the birth of Hezbollah, a Shiite resistance movement, and armed its new members. Over time, Hezbollah became a far more potent enemy than the Palestinians.

To help end hostilities, U.S. mediation produced a deal for the withdrawal of Palestinian guerrillas in exchange for an end to the Israeli siege of Beirut. A multinational force of U.S., French and Italian troops was dispatched to oversee the PLO pullout. The Western coalition was forced to deploy in Beirut a second time for an open-ended stint due to violence among the Lebanese. For the next 18 months, Iran and the United States both had troops in tiny Lebanon.

Armed and aided by Iran, Hezbollah was responsible for the first suicide bombings against American targets in 1983 and 1984 on two U.S. Embassies in Beirut and the U.S. Marine peacekeepers barracks. The Marines suffered 241 dead, the highest loss of U.S. military personnel in a single incident since Iwo Jima during World War II. In 1984, the Marines first redeployed to ships offshore and a few months later sailed home. Lebanon's civil war raged on for 11 years. Israeli troops remained in Lebanon for another 16 years. Iran's Revolutionary Guards were the last to close down their base in the Bekaa Valley.

In 1982, Hezbollah also began abducting Americans and other Westerners, in another attempt to force the United States to end its political and military involvement in Lebanon. Among the hostages was CIA station chief William Buckley, who was picked up in 1984, and eventually tortured and killed. Between 1982 and 1991, at least 96 hostages from 21 nations were kidnapped.

The Iran-Iraq War, 1980-1988

The second challenge was the Gulf War. Iran liberated its territory and repelled Iraqi forces in 1982. But Tehran was loath to let Saddam Hussein remain in power in Baghdad. So the theocrats pushed the war across the Shatt-al-Arab waterway into Iraq. The war's shifting tide led the United States to rethink its neutrality, for fear Iran might threaten the weak oil-producing Gulf sheikhdoms, Jordan and even Israel. Reagan opted to tilt in favor of Iraq. Washington provided critical tactical intelligence to Iraq to hold off Iran's offensive.

In early 1983, the United States also orchestrated Operation Staunch, a worldwide effort to block arms supplies to Iran, including U.S. spare military parts for a military that had been trained and armed by the United States during the monarchy. Iran was running out of spare parts and missiles in the midst of an offensive that required a significant amount of new weaponry.

The Iran-Contra scandal

During its second term, the Reagan administration made secret contacts with Iran. The outreach was based on the erroneous belief that Iran's regime included some "moderate" politicians who were prepared to do a deal with the United States—at a time when other Iranians were pushing for an alliance with the Soviet Union.

In 1985, Reagan signed a secret finding authorizing a covert program to provide weapons, funneled initially through Israel, to Iranian forces squeezed by Operation Staunch. Washington hoped the Iranians would in turn help free American hostages held in Lebanon by Hezbollah. (In a twist, unbeknownst to Reagan, money generated by the arms sales to Iran was secretly deposited in Swiss banks to fund the Contras, an anti-communist group fighting the Nicaraguan government). Details of the covert Iran-Contra affair were revealed in 1986 and nearly brought down the Reagan presidency. And in the end, the effort failed. Three American hostages were released in exchange for several shipments of TOW and HAWK missiles. But then Hezbollah simply abducted three more Americans in Beirut.

U.S. forces in the Gulf

The final challenge was ensuring free passage for oil from the Gulf. The Iran-Iraq War spawned deepening instability that spilled over into Gulf shipping lanes. At the end of Reagan's first term, the so-called Tanker War erupted when Iraq attacked Iranian oil tankers and its oil terminal at Kharg Island. Iran retaliated against tankers carrying Iraqi oil.

In mid-1987, the Reagan administration launched Operation Earnest Will to protect Kuwaiti ships carrying oil from Iranian attack. Since American law prevented the U.S. Navy from escorting foreign ships, the Kuwaiti ships were re-registered under the American flag. On October 16, 1987, the re-flagged tanker *Sea Isle City* was struck at anchor in Kuwaiti waters by an Iranian silkworm missile, wounding 18 people.

In 1988, in retaliation for a minor attack against the *USS Samuel B. Roberts* in April 1988, the United States launched Operation Praying Mantis. U.S. warships sunk an Iranian frigate and shelled two Iranian oil platforms near the Strait of Hormuz. The military encounters climaxed on July 3, 1988, when the *USS Vincennes* accidentally shot down Iran Air flight 655, a commercial jet carrying 290 passengers and crew. All perished. The warship mistook the plane for a fighter. Operation Praying Mantis, combined with the Iran Air tragedy, pressured the regime to reluctantly agree to the terms of a U.N. cease-fire with Iraq on August 20, 1988. Ayatollah Khomeini said accepting the cease-fire was comparable to drinking poison.

The aftermath

- U.S. aid to Iraq in the name of defeating Iran backfired somewhat. Tehran was weakened, but Iraq emerged stronger and more belligerent than anticipated. Two years after its war with Iran ended, Saddam Hussein invaded Kuwait—precipitating a major war with a U.S.-led coalition.

- Reagan left office with several Americans still in captivity in Beirut. Iran still had hundreds of Revolutionary Guards deployed in Lebanon. And Israeli forces in Lebanon were under growing pressure from Hezbollah.

- Reagan's legacy was shaped most by the dramatic change in relations with the Soviet Union, including a friendship between Reagan and Mikhail Gorbachev. This rapprochement led to the break-up of the Warsaw Pact in 1989, and the collapse of the Soviet Union in 1991. But the Cold War's end also had some benefits for Iran. It removed one longstanding threat, dating back to Soviet occupation of Iran during and after World War II. And it opened up diplomatic and economic access to a new bloc of Muslim countries that had been Soviet republics.

Geoffrey Kemp, the director of Nixon Center's regional strategic programs, served on the National Security Council during the first Reagan administration. His latest book is The East Moves West: India, China, and Asia's Growing Presence in the Middle East.

30

The George H.W. Bush Administration

Richard N. Haass

- The Bush administration's policy on Iran was shaped largely by three factors: Iraq's 1990 invasion of Kuwait, American hostages held by Iranian allies in Lebanon and a new round of Arab-Israeli peace talks.

- The U.S. strategic priority after Iraq's invasion was liberating Kuwait and making sure that Saddam Hussein could not dominate the oil-rich region. Iran was an indirect beneficiary of the war, which was a by-product of U.S. policy, but not an objective. The administration was mindful of the threat posed by Iran and worked to ensure any gains from Iraq's defeat would be distinctly limited.

- The 1991 Madrid Peace Conference—the first face-to-face meeting between Israeli and Arab authorities—was a signal accomplishment for U.S. foreign policy. But Iran viewed it as a major threat to its regional standing and interests.

- Iran's failure or inability to bring about the release of the American hostages held in Lebanon until mid-1991 (and its continuing support for acts of terrorism) squandered much of the "good will" offered in President Bush's inaugural address.

Overview

George H.W. Bush entered the White House during a period of rapid and historic global change. The main development was the end of the Cold War, which for four decades had been the defining feature of the international environment. This shift opened up possibilities for U.S.-Soviet—and, subsequently, U.S.-Russian—cooperation. It also muted competition even when cooperation proved elusive.

The Cold War's end loosened up the international system and increased the room for maneuver—in ways that at times were anything but benign—by other states and non-state entities. The Soviet Union's demise helped create a moment in which U.S. primacy in the world was stark, a reality that led the 41st president to speak openly about a "new world order" based on stronger international institutions and a considerable degree of cooperation among states.

But the emergence of the United States as the world's dominant power did not alter the decade-old tensions between Washington and Tehran. Hezbollah, the Lebanese militia sired and armed by Iran, had held several American and other Western hostages dating back to the mid-1980s. Since the late 1980s, Tehran had also aided the Palestinian Islamic Jihad and Hamas, who were challenging both Israel and the Palestine Liberation Organization—and adding a new dimension to the conflict.

Early expectations

Ironically, the Middle East region was not expected to play a major role in the Bush 41 presidency. The one possible exception was trying to broker peace between Israel and the Palestinians and/or Syria. Iran and Iraq, the region's principal contenders for power, had just ended eight years of brutal warfare. Sifting through the ashes of devastated cities, recovering from the hundreds of thousands of dead and wounded, and beginning the slow process of social and economic rebuilding would, it was presumed, preoccupy leaders in both countries.

The Bush administration, for its part, was at once distrustful of the Islamic Republic of Iran, yet open to improving relations. (One sign of this openness was President Bush's telephone conversation in February 1990 with someone he believed to be Iranian President Akbar Rafsanjani, but who proved to be an imposter.) The continued holding of American hostages in Lebanon by Iranian-backed Hezbollah, however, cast a long shadow over U.S. relations with Tehran. Nevertheless, President Bush referred to the hostage situation in his 1989 inaugural address in a positive way. If Iranian assistance were to be shown, he said, it would not go unnoticed. "Good will begets good will. Good faith can be a spiral that endlessly moves on."

Hostages released

The Bush administration worked quietly with and through the United Nations to gain the hostages' release. There was some progress, but in the end, the hostage issue became another in the long line of missed opportunities between Washington and Tehran. Hezbollah had begun seizing Americans in 1982, and many had already languished in captivity for years. Lt. Col. William Higgins, who had been taken years earlier while serving in Lebanon with the United Nations, was killed in 1989.

Making matters worse from the American perspective was the 1989 *fatwa* issued by Ayatollah Ruhollah Khomeini against Salman Rushdie, author of *The Satanic Verses.* His edict further limited potential for political progress, as did the assassination in August 1991, in Paris, of former Iranian Prime Minister Shapour Bakhtiar by Iranian agents.

The last American hostage was released in 1991, but by then the opportunity to improve U.S.-Iranian ties had largely disappeared. Iran's leaders were reportedly angry and frustrated that their efforts to end hostage-taking did not meet with American goodwill, namely in a relaxation of sanctions or blaming Iraq for initiating the Iran-Iraq War.

From the American perspective, though, it was a case of too little, too late. Splits within Iran's leadership, which had become more pronounced after the June 1989 death of Ayatollah Khomeini, may have made it impossible for Iran to release the hostages and end acts of terrorism. But what was behind the policy mattered less than the policy itself to officials in the Bush administration.

The Gulf War

Tehran's commitment to exporting its revolution throughout the region, via its terrorist clients if necessary, remained an ongoing and serious threat to regional stability. A formal review of U.S. Persian Gulf policy, finalized in National Security Directive 26 and signed by the president in October 1989, reaffirmed the existing view that Iran, and not Iraq, posed the greater threat to U.S. interests in the region. As a result, President Bush supported a policy, which was consistent with what he inherited from President Reagan, of trying to build a political and commercial relationship with Iraq, in the hopes of moderating its behavior and offsetting Iranian power.

By the spring of 1990, the U.S. effort to work with Iraq was increasingly running up against the reality of Saddam's bad behavior. What little was left of the policy of constructive engagement came to an end with Iraq's August 1990 invasion and occupation of Kuwait. The strategic implications of Iraq's actions were grave. If Saddam's aggression was allowed to stand, an American diplomat noted at the time, "he would control the second- and third-largest proven oil reserves with the fourth-largest army in the world." Saddam's influence in OPEC's decision-making on production levels and prices would be markedly greater, which would allow him to increase oil prices—and provide even larger revenues to spend on his military. Other states in the region would think twice before standing up to Iraq. Allowing Iraq to control Kuwait would also set a terrible precedent for international relations, setting back hopes that something better would emerge after the Cold War's end.

For six months, from August 1990 through mid-January 1991, the United States and much of the world tried diplomacy and sanctions to persuade and pressure Saddam to withdraw Iraqi forces from Kuwait and accept its independence. All this made for an interesting moment for the U.S.-Iran relationship. The two countries had stumbled on a rare moment of seeming agreement.

The widespread international opprobrium, crippling economic sanctions and, eventually, military action against Iraq were weakening Iraq far more than Iran could ever hope to do alone. Moreover, Iran had to do little to help. It made some small contributions, such as grounding a significant number of Iraqi fighter jets that landed on its territory and largely respecting the embargo. But by and large, Iran's leaders simply waited for the coalition to weaken its primary rival for regional power.

The degree of overlap between American and Iranian policy should not be exaggerated. The United States defeated Iraq but deliberately chose not to decimate it or march on to Baghdad. The administration calculated that an Iraq strong enough to balance Iran—but hopefully not strong enough to intimidate or conquer its

Arab neighbors—was strategically preferable. U.S.-Iranian interests began to diverge even more clearly after the war. One reason the Bush administration mistrusted and opted not to aid the Shiite uprising in southern Iraq was because of Iranian involvement. Iran encouraged the uprising and sent Iranian-trained militias to join the rebels. Washington was concerned about long-term Iranian influence in Iraq.

Madrid Peace Conference

One of the Bush administration's original goals in the Middle East was establishing formal peace talks among the Israelis, the Palestinians and their Arab neighbors. The timing was arguably even better after the Gulf War, given soaring U.S. prestige, the absence of a rival superpower, improved ties with many of the Arab states, and the weakening of the Palestine Liberation Organization after its decision to side with Iraq. It was a moment of unique American leverage.

The conference itself was unprecedented. President Bush and Soviet President Mikhail Gorbachev co-hosted the first face-to-face meetings between Israel and its Arab neighbors, including Syria, Egypt, Jordan, Lebanon and the Palestinians. It began a years-long series of talks designed to secure a lasting and stable peace between old and wary enemies. To Iran, however, the Madrid summit also represented an unprecedented challenge.

The new peace process not only legitimized the existence of Israel—a state Iran viewed as an illegal and hostile imposition on the region—in the Arab world. It also threatened Iran's ties with its most important allies. Syria, a participant in the Madrid Conference, was Iran's principal ally in the region. A separate peace between Syria and Israel would remove a shared strategic goal and undermine the entire relationship. Hezbollah's refuge in Lebanon could be similarly threatened by a deal between Lebanon with Israel. Disarming and potentially even disbanding Hezbollah would almost certainly have been among the terms of any agreement, an outcome that would remove much of Iran's influence in the area.

The peace process spurred Iran's support of a number of Palestinian terrorist groups, not least Hamas. It also encouraged cooperation among the groups, particularly Hamas, Palestinian Islamic Jihad and Hezbollah. Tehran's investments paid off, as a spate of fresh terror attacks in the Middle East and beyond shook efforts at peace. It also built relationships with Islamist movements across the Middle East, from Egypt and Algeria to the Gulf states and Lebanon, and invited these hostile forces to work against the peace process in general, and the United States and Israel, in particular.

The aftermath

- The U. S.–Iran relationship was largely stagnant during the Bush administration, with little contact and less progress.

- Iran and its support for terrorist groups posed a significant threat to efforts designed to promote peace and secure Israel's place in the region.

- U.S. opposition to Iraq after Operation Desert Storm—a hostility that lingered for more than a decade until the 2003 war and Saddam Hussein's removal—did not translate into better U.S. ties with Iran. In the Middle East, the enemy of your enemy can still be your enemy.

- Many of the same issues that had dogged U.S.-Iranian relations before President Bush took office in 1989—including differences about Israel, the use of terrorism as a tool of policy, and Iraq—were still problems when President Bush was succeeded by President Clinton.

Richard N. Haass, president of the Council on Foreign Relations, was the National Security Council staff director in charge of the Middle East during the George H. W. Bush presidency.

31

The Clinton Administration

Bruce O. Riedel

- In 1993, William Jefferson Clinton inherited almost 15 years of troubled relations with Iran, impeded by no diplomatic ties, deep animosity on both sides and layers of sanctions. He left office in 2001 with no breakthrough in relations but an improved atmosphere that offered an opening for further progress.

- This shift happened despite Iran's suspected involvement in the 1996 attack on the U.S. barracks in Khobar, Saudi Arabia. But the terror attack heavily influenced U.S. policy toward Iran in the Clinton years. The White House refrained from military retaliation but signaled that additional terrorism could lead to conflict.

- Clinton sought to build a relationship with President Khatami after his surprise 1997 election but was thwarted by the Khobar legacy and internal Iranian politics. Clinton and Khatami encouraged reciprocal people-to-people exchanges to reduce animosity and prepare the groundwork for improved relations.

- The Clinton administration hoped for a breakthrough in government-to-government dialogue and eventual diplomatic relations. It offered on several occasions, via different interlocutors, to set up a direct dialogue without conditions, but Iran refused.

Overview

When President Clinton took office in 1993, the United States had no direct diplomatic relations with Iran. Any prospect of improvement was complicated by sanctions dating back to the 1979 U.S. Embassy takeover and an American public intensely distrustful of the Islamic Republic's policies. Iran was also the major patron of Lebanon's Hezbollah, which actively opposed the Middle East peace process and engaged in regular clashes with Israeli forces in Lebanon. It no longer held American hostages, however, and it suspended direct anti-American terrorist attacks.

Shortly after the inauguration, the administration announced that its policy toward Tehran would be part of a larger "dual containment" in the Gulf, to limit the threats posed by both Iraq and Iran to U.S. interests and allies. Containment was based on the premise that both Iraq and Iran were hostile powers and that the balance of power in the Gulf was inherently unstable. In the 1980s, the United States had tried to play the two countries off against each other. But Iraq emerged from the 1980-1988 war with Iran as the more powerful country, unchecked by any of its neighbors. The imbalance allowed Baghdad to invade Kuwait in 1990 and claim the oil-rich city-state as its 19th province.

The new containment strategy acknowledged the many substantive differences between the threats from Iran and Iraq; it recommended diverse tactics to deal with each. Iran would be contained by a military deterrent based in the Gulf states, targeted economic sanctions to discourage foreign investment in Iran, and diplomacy to discourage Iranian support for terrorism and pursuit of a nuclear capability. But Clinton left on the table the Bush administration's offer to engage in direct government-to-government talks without preconditions.

The Lebanon problem

Throughout both terms, the Clinton administration faced several crises in Lebanon between Israel and the Iranian-backed Hezbollah. Hezbollah seemed determined to undermine Israel's separate negotiations with the Palestinians and Syria, one of Clinton's highest foreign policy priorities. Tensions repeatedly heated up in Lebanon at critical junctures.

Washington suspected the Iranian Revolutionary Guards, who had been deployed in Lebanon since 1982, of fomenting trouble, although Israeli actions occasionally played into Hezbollah's hands. The White House often had to rely on Syria, Iran's ally, to defuse crises in Lebanon. This specter of Iranian-backed terror grew worse at the end of Clinton's first term.

Khobar Towers attack

On June 25, 1996, a truck bomb exploded at the U.S. Air Force facility in Khobar, Saudi Arabia, killing 19 Americans and wounding over 350 Americans, Saudis and other nationals. Intelligence indicated the bombing was the work of Hezbollah al Hijaz, a Saudi Shiite group with close links to Iran's Revolutionary Guards and Lebanon's Hezbollah. But the intelligence was uncertain about the Iranian senior leadership's involvement. The Clinton administration prepared to conduct military retaliation against Iran but quickly recognized any operations could escalate and even trigger full-scale war.

The White House instead sought additional intelligence on Iran's role, while warning Iran to desist from further attacks, hardening American installations in the Gulf, and deploying U.S. warplanes to a remote air base in the Saudi desert. The administration also took targeted actions against the Revolutionary Guards and Iranian intelligence personnel around the world. In early 1997, the CIA's Operation Sapphire identified Iranian intelligence officers in numerous countries and disrupted their activities. Iran never acknowledged its role in Khobar, but the Hezbollah al Hijaz organization was dismantled in the late 1990s. In 2001, the Justice Department charged that several members of the group were involved. The indictment noted the support of Iran's Revolutionary Guards and Lebanon's Hezbollah in the attack.

Dialogue of civilizations

The surprise victory of Mohammad Khatami in the 1997 presidential elections offered the second Clinton administration an opportunity to restore U.S.-Iran relations. In a widely publicized CNN interview, Khatami signaled early in his term that he was open to a new relationship and wanted to bring down the "wall of mistrust" with the American people. President Clinton and his national security team were eager to take advantage of this possible opening.

Over the next three years, Clinton sent a series of public messages affirming his interest in improving people-to-people relations. His messages at Nowruz (the Iranian new year) and Eid al Fitr (end of Ramadan feast) expressed appreciation for Iranian culture. On the Eid, in January 1998, Clinton said in a videotaped message that the United States "regrets the estrangement of our two nations ... and I hope that the day will soon come when we can enjoy once again good relations with Iran." U.S.-Iran sports exchanges received high-level attention at the White House; an American wrestling team that traveled to Iran was photographed with the president in the Oval Office. Sanctions on imports of various Iranian goods, including carpets and pistachio nuts, were also gradually eased.

Clinton wanted to go further and open direct diplomatic relations with Tehran. Several efforts were made during his second term. The administration sent one message through the Swiss Embassy in Tehran, which hosted the U.S. Interest Section, in October 1997. It invited Iran to meet with three U.S. officials—Undersecretary Thomas Pickering, Special Assistant to the President Bruce Riedel, and Deputy Assistant Secretary of State David Welch—without pre-conditions at a venue chosen by Iran. The message was leaked to the press in the United States; Iran did not respond with a positive answer.

Another attempt was made via Saudi Arabia. During a May 1998 visit to the kingdom, Vice President Al Gore asked Saudi Crown Prince Abdullah to broker direct dialogue between Washington and Tehran. Again the Iranians deferred and stressed that people-to-people dialogue needed to precede official talks.

The United States and Iran did talk directly in multilateral forums. The most active discussions centered on Afghanistan at the United Nations. The so-called 6-plus-2 dialogue brought together Afghanistan's six regional neighbors with the United States and Russia. Secretary of State Madeleine Albright attended one meeting after the United Nations pledged to persuade her Iranian counterpart to attend, thus encouraging a high-level dialogue. But he did not show up for the meeting.

The Clinton administration was frustrated by Khatami's preference for people-to-people rapprochement, a limitation produced by an internal power struggle with Iranian hardliners who opposed an official dialogue. When further evidence developed of Iranian involvement in the Khobar bombing, Clinton faced mounting pressure to get Iran to take action against the Revolutionary Guard elements involved in the attack.

The Omani gambit

In June 1999 Clinton sent Bruce Riedel and Martin Indyk to Fontaine-le-Port, France, to carry written and oral messages to Khatami to be delivered by Oman. They met with Sultan Qaboos at his chateau and asked him to send his Foreign Minister Yusuf bin Alawi to Tehran to deliver the messages. The written message—which has been declassified—said the United States had evidence Revolutionary Guard members were "directly involved in the planning and execution" of the Khobar bombing, activity unacceptable to the United States. The Guards' involvement in ongoing terrorist activity was a "cause of deep concern." While Washington sought better relations with Iran, it could not allow the murder of American citizens to pass unaddressed. Clinton asked for assurances that Iran would cease involvement in terrorist attacks and that those responsible for Khobar would be brought to justice. Alawi delivered the message to Khatami in July 1999.

Khatami told Alawi he appreciated Clinton's efforts to improve relations; he promised to look at the Khobar issue. The Islamic Republic did not formally respond for six weeks. In September 1999, Iran told the Omanis that it had conducted a "reliable investigation and serious scrutiny" of the Khobar attack and concluded that U.S. allegations about the Revolutionary Guards were "inaccurate" and "fabricated." Iran also accused the United States of failing to take action against the crew of the *USS Vincennes* for its 1988 attack on an Iran Air passenger plane. Tehran charged the American warship had deliberately shot down the airbus, killing all 290 passengers and crew on board.

Yet the Iranian message also said Iran "bears no hostile intentions" toward America and posed "no threat" to U.S. interests. Once again, a U.S. initiative to set up a direct dialogue with Khatami failed. Nonetheless, the Khobar attack was not repeated, and the Saudi Hezbollah al Hijaz group was eventually dismantled.

Albright's speech

In a major speech on March 17, 2000, Albright formally apologized for the CIA's role in the 1953 coup that overthrew Prime Minister Mohammad Mossadegh's government and restored the monarchy, a major Iranian demand for years. She also announced the lifting of sanctions on imports of Iranian food and carpets and approval for export of spare parts for Iran's aging Boeing aircraft. She also offered to settle outstanding legal claims on Iranian assets frozen in U.S. bank accounts since the 1979 U.S. Embassy seizure. A few days later, Iranian Supreme Leader Ayatollah Ali Khamenei dismissed Albright's remarks as worthless. He also accused the United States of backing Iraq in the Iran-Iraq War and refused any official dialogue with America.

Despite the rebuffs, Khatami and Clinton continued to make public statements about the need to reconcile Iran and the United States. Clinton took the unusual step of staying in the U.N. General Assembly after his own speech in September 2000 to listen to Khatami speak, a gesture to signal a continued interest in direct dialogue. But Khatami's domestic political problems ultimately prevented any tangible progress.

The aftermath

- By the end of the second Clinton term, the United States and Iran had moved from the precipice of armed conflict in 1996, after the Khobar attack, to an indirect dialogue. The climate had improved, but policy differences remained wide.

- Tensions over Iran's role in terrorism, its ties to Hezbollah and its pursuit of nuclear technology were the most serious differences. But a new effort to defuse tensions between Washington and Tehran had begun.

Bruce Riedel, a senior fellow at the Brookings Institution's Saban Center, was special assistant to the president and senior director for Near East and South Asian Affairs at the National Security Council during the Clinton administration.

32

The George W. Bush Administration

Stephen J. Hadley

- The Bush administration's engagement with Iran began positively. The two nations worked together to form a new Afghan government after the 2001 ouster of the Taliban.

- But efforts to cooperate on Iraq after Saddam Hussein's overthrow foundered. Iran increasingly provided training, weapons and support to terrorists and insurgents, first in Iraq and later in Afghanistan.

- U.S. and international concern about Tehran's nuclear activity increased dramatically in 2002, when an exile group revealed that Iran had secretly built a facility in Natanz capable of enriching uranium for use in nuclear weapons as well as civilian nuclear power reactors.

- After Iran reneged on an agreement to suspend uranium enrichment in 2005, the White House backed an international campaign offering Iran a choice: aid and engagement or economic pressure. Tehran balked.

- As part of its "freedom agenda," the administration supported greater political opening in Iran through presidential speeches, Persian language broadcasts and aid to civil society groups.

Overview

The Bush administration had perhaps the most significant public engagement with Iran since the 1979 revolution, mainly on Afghanistan and Iraq. But it was short-lived. Iran's growing support for extremist groups and new revelations about its secret nuclear facilities soon produced some of the deepest tensions between Washington and Tehran since relations originally ruptured.

On Iran's nuclear program, Bush administration strategy was to rally the international community to confront the Iranian regime with a strategic choice. Tehran could transparently and verifiably give up its pursuit of a nuclear weapons capability, especially its enrichment facility at Natanz. If it did, the international community would respond with substantial diplomatic, economic and security benefits. These would include the relaxation of existing economic sanctions and active international support for a truly peaceful civilian nuclear program, including the supply of nuclear fuel so Iran would not need an enrichment facility. If it rejected this choice, the regime would only be further isolated diplomatically, incur increased economic sanctions, and run the risk of military action.

The Bush approach can be summarized as the "two clocks" strategy: First, try to push back the time when the Iranian regime would have a clear path to a nuclear weapon. And second, try to bring forward the time when public pressure would either cause the regime to change its nuclear policy (and suspend enrichment) or transform it into a government more likely to make the strategic choice to deal with the international community.

Engaging Iran

The Bush administration was aware of Clinton administration efforts to engage the Iranian regime and improve relations. But the lack of a sustained positive response from President Mohammad Khatami was taken by the Bush administration as evidence that he was either unable or unwilling to deliver. Despite skepticism engendered by this history, the Bush administration engaged the Iranian regime after the 9/11 attacks. Tehran had long backed the Northern Alliance, the main Afghan opposition force, which Washington also supported to help oust the Taliban. U.S. and Iranian envoys then worked together at the Bonn conference in December

2002 to establish the first post-Taliban government in Afghanistan. The Iranian team was pivotal in convincing the Afghan opposition to support the U.S.-backed candidate for president, Hamid Karzai.

After the 2003 ouster of Saddam Hussein in Iraq, Tehran and Washington again sought to cooperate to stabilize Iraq internally in the face of increasing terrorist and insurgent violence. In 2004, U.S. and Iranian envoys held three meetings in Baghdad, two at ambassadorial level. But little was accomplished. In the years that followed, diplomatic engagement on Iraq and Afghanistan went downhill. Iran increasingly trained, armed, and aided Shiite extremists in Iraq and later Taliban militants in Afghanistan. Other engagement efforts had little merit or success. In 2003, a fax purportedly from Iranian sources offering a diplomatic breakthrough arrived on a State Department fax machine. It was later determined to be the result of freelancing by a Swiss diplomat hoping to be the one to make peace between Iran and the United States.

Terrorism

Iran continued throughout this period to support other terrorist groups such as Hezbollah, Palestinian Islamic Jihad and Hamas. Tehran provided them with increasingly advanced weaponry, all for use against Israel. Iran's support contributed to both the 2006 war between Israel and Hezbollah in Lebanon (sparked by the kidnapping of Israeli soldiers) and the 2008 Israeli incursion into Gaza (in response to rocket attacks launched from Gaza into Israel). The Bush administration staunchly defended Israel's right to defend itself against these terrorist threats, while at the same time using its diplomacy to extricate Israel from each of these conflicts.

The Bush administration considered Hezbollah the "A-team" of terrorist groups. It had killed and kidnapped Americans during two previous administrations. The White House took steps to enhance U.S. capability to deal with this threat. But Hezbollah did not undertake terrorist activity directed against Americans or provoke a confrontation with the United States during President Bush's tenure.

"Axis of evil"

The Bush administration placed a high priority on fighting terrorism and countering nuclear proliferation. The scope and sophistication of the al Qaeda attack on September 11, 2001, increased concern that these two dangers would merge, and nuclear terrorism would pose an even more ominous threat. Iran was one of three countries—with Iraq and North Korea—that sponsored terrorist groups and were widely believed to be pursuing nuclear weapons.

President Bush sought to dramatize this risk in his State of the Union speech on January 29, 2002. He called these three states "an axis of evil," because each represented a potential link between terrorists and weapons of mass destruction. The administration was criticized for using the word "axis," suggesting a World War II-style alliance among these three states and sounding as if Washington was threatening them with war. The criticism colored how the speech was received, particularly abroad, and gave it a war-mongering cast. Yet the speech did not prevent the subsequent constructive cooperation between the United States and Iran on Afghanistan.

Nuclear deal

After revelations about Iran's secret nuclear sites, the International Atomic Energy Agency (IAEA) pressed Tehran in 2002 and 2003 for greater access, particularly to the Natanz uranium enrichment facility. It sought answers to outstanding questions about the regime's nuclear program and called on the regime to suspend all further enrichment activity. About the same time, Britain, France and Germany—the EU-3—sought to engage Iran in a political dialogue.

In October 2003, the EU-3 foreign ministers and Iranian officials in Tehran issued a statement in which Iran agreed to cooperate fully with the IAEA and voluntarily suspend all uranium enrichment activities. It separately agreed to provisional implementation of the IAEA Additional Protocol, which gave the IAEA enhanced access to Iran's nuclear-related facilities. The statement was codified in the Paris Agreement signed on November 14, 2004, after a year of attempted Iranian backpedaling. In support of EU-3 diplomacy, the United States announced in March 2005 that it would drop its objection to Iranian membership in the World Trade Organization and consider licensing spare parts for aging Iranian civilian aircraft.

Nuclear setback

After he took office in 2005, President Mahmoud Ahmadinejad promptly accused Iranian diplomats who had negotiated the Paris Agreement of treason and began to restart Iran's nuclear activities. In April 2006, Tehran announced that uranium enrichment had resumed at Natanz.

The administration did not give up on efforts to engage the regime. It backed international overtures, including an EU offer in August 2005 to provide extensive, long-term political, economic and civilian nuclear cooperation, if Tehran suspended enrichment. It supported Moscow's plan to enrich fuel in Russia for Iran's new nuclear power reactor at Bushehr and then take back the spent fuel rods to ease international concern about the reactor.

The White House also extended its own offer. In May 2006, Secretary of State Condoleezza Rice announced that the United States would join the EU-3's talks with Iran once Tehran suspended all enrichment-related activities. The next month, the so-called P5+1 offered additional incentives. (The P5+1 included the five permanent U.N. Security Council members—Britain, China, France, Russia and the United States—plus Germany.) EU foreign policy chief Javier Solana launched a series of meetings with Iranian nuclear negotiator Ali Larijani. But whenever they seemed to be making progress, Ahmadinejad publicly attacked the process. In 2007, Larijani resigned in frustration. A final P5+1 diplomatic effort offered a "refreshed" incentives package in Geneva in 2008, with U.S. Under Secretary of State William Burns in attendance. It went nowhere. The Iranian regime gradually expanded its nuclear activities.

Sanctions

As Iran balked, the administration and its European allies won international support for a sequence of four separate U.N. Security Council resolutions: 1737, 1747, 1803 and 1835. They sanctioned Iranian missile and nuclear-related entities and persons, imposed asset freezes and travel bans, and required international vigilance regarding arms sales to Iran. Separately, the United States unilaterally sanctioned the Islamic Revolutionary Guard Corps (IRGC) and Iranian state-owned banks. Sanctioning official Iranian government entities sent a signal of increased seriousness, and including the IRGC meant attacking a principal security pillar of the regime—and the one it relied upon to keep the Iranian people in line.

The administration also launched a unique global campaign to get major foreign banks to stop doing business with Iran because it violated international banking practices. The Treasury Department convinced banks and later multinational businesses that dealing with Iranian banks or supplying goods and services to the government carried reputational risks, due to the potential that these entities engaged in any of three practices: Facilitating nuclear proliferation, supporting terrorism, or money laundering needed to finance these activities. More than 90 major international banks in dozens of countries signed on. The combination of economic sanctions and banking restrictions led major multinational companies to pull out of contracts with the Iranian government. The international Financial Action Task Force and the Organization for Economic Co-operation and Development later issued their own warnings about dealing with Iranian financial institutions.

National Intelligence Estimate

In 2007, the director of national intelligence released the unclassified judgments of a National Intelligence Estimate confirming that Iran had had a covert program to develop nuclear weapons. The program included covert nuclear weapon design, weaponization (including marrying a nuclear warhead with a ballistic missile delivery system) and uranium enrichment-related work. The NIE judged this covert work to have been suspended in the fall of 2003 at roughly the same time that Iran agreed to suspend its overt enrichment activity at Natanz. The release of the NIE judgments seriously set back Bush administration efforts during 2008 to convince the international community to impose further sanctions on Iran.

The NIE concluded that the covert program "probably was halted in response to international pressure." Other events in 2003—the U.S. invasion of Iraq over its suspected nuclear weapon activities and the interception of the German cargo ship *BBC China* carrying uranium enrichment centrifuge components to Libya—may have helped convince the Iranian regime that its covert program was too risky. (Libya ended up handing over all elements of its nuclear weapon and other weapons of mass destruction programs to the United States.) When the Bush administration left office, there were questions about whether Iran's covert nuclear weapons activities remain suspended.

U.S. support for Iranian freedom

Over this period the Iranian regime increasingly pursued a more repressive policy at home, sidelining reformers and pragmatists and cracking down on regime opponents. The Bush administration wanted to show that it stood with the Iranian people, but without discrediting Iranian political activists or subjecting them to the charge of being American agents. Washington had to deal with the Iranian regime diplomatically but without enhancing its legitimacy.

The administration sought to strike the right balance in several ways. In presidential speeches and other statements, it made a distinction between the Iranian people (which it supported) and the regime (which it challenged to give its people more political freedom). Senior officials blamed regime policies for the isolation and hardships suffered by the Iranian people. President Bush spoke directly to the Iranian people on the Iranian new year, expressing respect for Iranian history, culture and traditions and explicitly expressing American support for their struggles.

In 2002, the United States began to increase the flow of news and information into Iran. The Voice of America (VOA) established what later became its Persian News Network (PNN). Radio Free Europe/Radio Liberty and VOA jointly established Radio Farda. For the 2003 Afghan election and the 2005 Iraqi vote, provisions were made so that refugees of both countries living in Iran would be able to vote in their nation's respective elections. It was hoped that their example would encourage Iranians to demand more free and fair elections from the Iranian regime. In 2008, Congress appropriated $60 million for programs to promote democracy, the rule of law and governance in Iran.

The aftermath

- The Bush administration added to the long history of attempted engagement with Iran, having some initial success, but growing disillusioned over time as Iran failed to respond positively.

- The administration left behind a robust international framework for coordinating incentives to encourage positive behavior from the Iranian regime, as well as diplomatic and economic pressure if it failed to comply with U.N. resolutions.

- The administration developed a new set of tools to exert economic pressure by cutting off Iran from the international financial system and persuading multinational businesses to sever ties with the regime.

- The administration enhanced the U.S. military presence in the Middle East, encouraged and facilitated increased defense cooperation among Arab allies—on air defense, missile defense and in other areas— and worked to enhance the defense capabilities of individual friends and allies.

- As the Bush administration left office, there was increasing debate within Iran about the wisdom of the regime's foreign policy, its economic performance and the lack of political freedom.

Stephen J. Hadley was national security adviser for President George W. Bush during his second term and assistant secretary of defense under President George H.W. Bush. He is currently senior adviser for international affairs at USIP.

33

The Obama Administration

John Limbert

- During his campaign and after taking office, President Obama repeatedly declared his determination to break the 30-year downward spiral in U.S.-Iranian relations.

- During his first two years in office, Obama twice wrote Iranian Supreme Leader Ali Khamenei but did not receive a response to his second letter. Iranian President Mahmoud Ahmadinejad twice wrote Obama but did not receive a reply.

- Iran, beset by internal political battles, has had trouble changing the patterns of the past. At the same time, the Obama administration faced congressional pressure to take tougher action against Tehran.

- Both sides claim the other is not responsive to its messages, and both risk falling into the familiar, dysfunctional ways of the past when confronted with perceived intransigence by the other.

Overview

President Obama inherited 30 years of hostility in U.S.-Iran relations. During the previous decade, the two longstanding rivals had engaged in unofficial outreach. Track II diplomacy had included exchanges of scholars, athletes, filmmakers, scientists and artists. But the unofficial meetings could not diminish the underlying tensions, and, in some cases, even increased suspicion.

One of Obama's first foreign policy initiatives was outreach to the Islamic world, including Iran. But reconnecting with Tehran proved difficult and frustrating. Diplomacy was complicated by political turmoil in Iran. As in the past, new diplomatic efforts between Washington and Tehran foundered on mutual suspicion, political ineptitude, misreading signals, bad timing and the power of inertia. Officials on both sides seemed unable to get beyond their classic responses, including:

- Never say yes to anything. You will look weak. Insist the other side must change first.

- Anything the other side proposes must contain some subtle trick. Its only goal is to cheat us.

- The other side is infinitely hostile, devious, and irrational. Its actions prove its implacable hostility.

- Whenever the smallest progress is made, someone or some diabolical coincidence will derail it.

A new message

Six days after his inauguration in January 2009, Obama said in an interview with Al-Arabiyya that "negative preconceptions" lay at the heart of Middle East disputes. He did not mention Iran specifically, but his meaning was clear: As long as Americans and Iranians assumed the worst of each other, there would be little chance of ending their 30-year estrangement. He made that point explicitly to Iran in his March 2009 message marking the Iranian new year (*Nowruz*). For the first time, an American president spoke directly to the government of "the Islamic Republic of Iran" as well as to its people. He called for "engagement that is honest and grounded in mutual respect" and quoted from 13th century Persian poet Sa'adi,

> The children of Adam are limbs of one body,
> Which God created from one essence.

In his June 4, 2009, Cairo speech to the broader Muslim world, Obama spoke of a "new beginning" between the United States and Muslims, "based upon mutual interest and mutual respect." Referring to Iran, he acknowledged the difficulties in overcoming "decades of mistrust," but he pledged to proceed with "courage, rectitude and resolve." He said Washington was willing to move forward "without preconditions on the basis of mutual respect."

Iran's disputed presidential election took place just one week later, followed by six months of sporadic protests and a brutal crackdown. The turmoil complicated diplomacy. Iranian opposition voices that had advocated engagement were now changing their position and urging Obama to take a tougher line. The administration was judicious in its public statements, balancing outreach to the Islamic Republic with defense of human rights. The statements emphasized universal rights, insisting that the Iranian people have the right to choose their leadership freely and the right to express themselves without fear of intimidation.

Obama persevered, despite Iran's unfolding political drama. He referred to Iran in his Oslo speech accepting the Nobel Peace Prize in December 2009. He said relations with repressive regimes were important even when engagement "lacks the satisfying purity of indignation." In other words, the United States was giving priority to the larger interest of changing an unproductive relationship.

The White House sent another Nowruz message to Iran in March 2010. Obama's tone was positive, although not as warm as the previous year. He again called for better relations, but he also issued a challenge to evoke something more positive or concrete from Tehran. "We know what you're against," he said. "Now tell us what you're for."

A nuclear proposal

Obama backed his words with action designed to jumpstart diplomacy on the most serious issue dividing the two countries—Iran's controversial nuclear program. In mid-2009, Iran contacted the International Atomic Energy Agency to ask for help finding fuel for the small U.S.-built Tehran Research Reactor. The facility produces radioisotopes for medical procedures that treat about 10,000 patients a week. Supplies of the medical isotopes were scheduled to run out by the end of 2010. In a deal brokered largely by the United States, the International Atomic Energy Agency proposed a formula to provide fuel to Tehran while offering safeguards. Iran would ship 1,200 kg of low-enriched uranium to Russia, where it would be enriched, then sent on to France for conversion into fuel rods for Tehran's reactor.

The proposal was appealing to Washington because it would transfer about 80 percent of Iran's known stock of low-enriched uranium outside the country. It would take about a year for Iran to replace that amount in its own enrichment facilities. The proposal initially appealed to Tehran because it would also provide at least tacit acknowledgment of its right to enrich uranium—a long disputed issue.

But more importantly, the deal was also designed to build confidence among all parties and pave the way for comprehensive talks on all aspects of Iran's nuclear program during that intervening year. Talks also carried the prospect of a broader dialogue on a wide range of issues of mutual concern. To prove good intentions, Obama allowed a senior State Department official to hold a rare meeting with Iran's chief nuclear negotiator on the sidelines of talks about the deal in Geneva in October 2009. Tehran initially accepted the deal, but within weeks it collapsed.

The deal appears to have fallen through for a variety of reasons, both domestic and foreign. The biggest problem may have been Iran's internal political fighting. President Ahmadinejad initially embraced the deal. "We welcome fuel exchange, nuclear co-operation, building of power plants and reactors, and we are ready to co-operate," he said live on state television. But the reactor deal was soon criticized by Iran's new Green Movement opposition as well as conservatives in the regime, both largely for political reasons. Ahmadinejad's opponents did not want the president to get credit for any agreement favorable to Iran. Some leaders also may have feared that any change in the Islamic Republic's underlying anti-Americanism would threaten the existence of their system.

Turkey–Brazil diplomacy

After Iran reneged on the Tehran Research Reactor deal, the Obama administration began what it called a dual-track policy: Keeping engagement as a possibility, while pushing for new sanctions. Turkey and Brazil, two rising middle powers with seats on the U.N. Security Council, made one last attempt to revive the diplomatic initiative. As the United Nations moved toward a vote on sanctions, the prime minister of Turkey and the president of Brazil negotiated with Ahmadinejad in Tehran. The three signed a tripartite deal on May 17, 2010. The package included many features from the original Geneva deal. But Tehran found it more attractive because its low-enriched uranium would go to Turkey, a Muslim country with which it had better relations, instead of Russia. Iran also felt it could enlist Turkey and Brazil's support in opposing the new sanctions resolution at the Security Council.

But the last-ditch diplomacy ended up a classic case of bad timing. Terms acceptable in October 2009 were not acceptable in May 2010. In the intervening seven months, Iran had enriched more uranium. The original deal called for Iran to transfer 1,200 kilograms, which then represented an estimated 80 percent of its stock. By May, the same amount was only about one-half of its stock. Nor did the new agreement deal with the 20 percent enriched uranium Iran had produced in the interim. The Obama administration—along with Russia and France, the original parties to the Geneva deal—viewed the revised package primarily as an Iranian attempt to avoid U.N. sanctions. By then the sanctions process had acquired too much momentum for the Turkey-Brazil deal to reverse.

New U.N. sanctions

The administration continued to work with Britain, France and Germany—the three countries that had led international diplomatic efforts with Iran—on measures in a new sanctions package. Unlike previous resolutions, however, the Obama administration wanted the resolution to include the long-promised incentives that Iran would receive if it cooperated with the international community and suspended its uranium enrichment altogether. After six months of complex negotiations, the Security Council passed Resolution 1929 on June 9, 2010. The final vote was 12 in favor, two opposed (Turkey and Brazil), and one abstention (Lebanon).

Resolution 1929 requires U.N. members to block the transfer of technology related to either missiles or nuclear weapons and to cut off commercial access to uranium mining or nuclear materials production in their territories. It also imposes new restrictions on travel by Iranian officials associated with proliferation. It targets Iranian shipping lines affiliated with Iran's Revolutionary Guards and calls on member starts to refuse them financial and insurance services. Resolution 1929 also calls on member states to block new branches of certain Iranian banks in their territories.

The aftermath

- Obama was willing to go further than any previous administration in normalizing relations with Iran. Despite repeated setbacks, Washington continued to look for opportunities to crack the diplomatic door open.

- But the road ahead is likely to be frustrated by Iran's fears, internal political friction and mutual hostility built up over 30 years without communication.

John Limbert is the distinguished professor of international affairs at the U.S. Naval Academy. He previously served as deputy assistant secretary for Iran in the State Department's Bureau of Near Eastern Affairs.

Iran and the Region

34

Iran and Iraq

Michael Eisenstadt

- The overthrow of the Saddam Hussein regime provided Iran with a historic opportunity to transform its traditional Iraqi enemy into a partner or ally.

- A long, porous border and extensive political, economic, religious and cultural ties provide Iran the potential for significant influence in Iraq.

- Iranian attempts to wield this influence, however, have often backfired, leading to a nationalist backlash by Iraqis and tensions with the Iraqi government.

- As the United States withdraws its forces from Iraq, the uncertain security situation will present both risks and opportunities for Iran.

Overview

Since ancient times, Iraq and Iran have been the seats of rival states and empires. Mesopotamia, today's Iraq, was home to the Assyrian, Babylonian and medieval Abbasid empires. The Achaemenid, medieval Safavid and early-modern Qajar dynasties ruled in Persia.

Iraq has also held special significance for Iran ever since the Safavid dynasty made Shiism the state religion in the 16th century. Shiite Islam was born in Iraq. The holy Shiite cities of Najaf and Karbala are traditional Shiite centers of learning and destinations for religious pilgrims. For centuries, the holy cities have had a strong Persian presence. As a result, Iran views southern Iraq as part of its historic sphere of influence.

This ancient rivalry has continued into modern times. The newly established Islamic Republic tried to export its Islamic ideology to Iraq, providing Saddam Hussein a pretext for his 1980 invasion. The Iraqi leader in turn tried to strike a fatal blow against his foremost regional rival and to seize its oil wealth. Instead, the invasion produced a long, bloody and inconclusive eight-year war that killed and wounded well over 1 million people. The toppling of Saddam Hussein in 2003 by U.S. and coalition forces thus constituted a historic opportunity for Iran to expand its influence in Iraq and to transform it from an enemy into a partner or ally.

Political strategy

Since the fall of Saddam Hussein in 2003, Iran has tried to influence Iraqi politics by working with Shiite and Kurdish parties to create a weak federal state dominated by Shiites and amenable to Iranian influence. Tehran has also supported Shiite insurgent groups and militias and enhanced its soft power in the economic, religious and informational domains.

Iran's goal is to unite Iraq's Shiite parties so that they can translate their demographic weight into political influence, thereby consolidating Shiite primacy for the first time. Tehran has encouraged its closest allies—the Islamic Supreme Council of Iraq (ISCI), Dawa and the Sadrists to participate in politics and help shape Iraq's nascent institutions. It has backed a range of disparate parties and movements to maximize its options and ensure its interests are advanced, no matter which Iraqi party came out on top.

Local allies

The Islamic Supreme Council of Iraq (ISCI) was established in Tehran in 1982 by expatriate Iraqis and was based there until returning to Iraq in 2003. Its militia, the Badr Corps, was trained and controlled by the Islamic Revolutionary Guard Corps and fought alongside Iranian forces during the Iran-Iraq War. After 2003, thousands of Badr militiamen entered southern Iraq from Iran to help secure that part of the country. Many were subsequently integrated into the Iraqi security forces, particularly the army and the national police.

Dawa, founded in the late 1950s, enjoyed the Islamic Republic's support during the latter phase of its underground existence in Iraq. After 2003, Dawa joined the political process, but its potential was limited due to its lack of an armed militia. Its leader, Nuri al-Maliki, was selected by the more powerful ISCI and Sadrists as a compromise choice for prime minister in 2005, but he has since used this position to build a power base in the government and the army—parts of which now function as a personal and party militia.

Maliki shares a general affinity with Tehran's Shiite Islamist worldview, but not its doctrine of clerical rule. Mindful of his dependence on Washington for survival, he has tried to tread a middle path between Tehran and Washington and has avoided a full-fledged embrace of Tehran.

The Sadrists have emerged as a major force in politics and the Iraqi street since 2003. Their leader, Muqtada al-Sadr, has played on his family name as the sole surviving son of the revered Ayatollah Muhammad Sadiq al-Sadr, who was murdered by regime agents in 1999. His populist, anti-American rhetoric, and the muscle and patronage offered by his Jaysh al Mahdi (Mahdi Army) militia, have gained him support among the Shiite urban poor.

Though politically aligned with ISCI and Dawa, the Sadrists have also had a contentious and violent relationship with both parties. Sadr fled to Iran in 2007 to avoid being targeted by U.S. and Iraqi forces and to pursue his religious studies. He reportedly hopes to become an ayatollah to acquire the key religious leadership credential he currently lacks.

Kurdish parties—the Kurdish Democratic Party (KDP) and the Patriotic Union of Kurdistan (PUK)—have long-standing ties with Iran. Kurdish guerillas (Peshmerga) fought alongside Iran during the Iran-Iraq War. And Tehran armed the PUK during its fighting with the KDP from 1994 to 1998. Iran continues to enjoy close ties with the PUK and KDP, as well as Iraq's northern Kurdistan Regional Government (KRG). But Tehran has conducted occasional cross-border artillery strikes against Iranian Kurdish guerillas based in northern Iraq.

Modes of influence

Iran exercises its influence through its embassy in Baghdad and consulates in Basra, Karbala, Irbil and Suleimaniyah. Both of its post-2003 ambassadors—Hassan Kazemi-Qomi and Hassan Danaifar, who was born in Iraq but whose family was expelled by Saddam Hussein—served in the Islamic Revolutionary Guard Corps' (IRGC) elite Qods Force. Their appointments reflect the role Iran's security services play in formulating and executing policy in Iraq. The Qods Force is the IRGC unit in charge of Iran's most sensitive covert foreign operations.

Iran reportedly tried to influence the outcome of the 2005 and 2010 parliamentary elections and 2009 provincial elections by funding and advising its preferred candidates. Qods Force commander Qasem Soleimani reportedly played a key role in negotiations to form an Iraqi government in 2005. He also reportedly brokered cease-fires between the Supreme Council and the Mahdi Army in 2007, and between the Iraqi government and the Mahdi Army in 2008. Iran unsuccessfully encouraged ISCI, Dawa and the Sadrists to run for the 2010 elections in a unified bloc. Following the 2010 election, Iranian Majles Speaker Ali Larijani reportedly played a key role in prodding these parties to form a coalition government.

Iran has also been vying for Iraqi "hearts and minds" through Arabic language news and entertainment broadcasts into Iraq (and the Arab world) over the al-Alam television network. The programs reflect Tehran's propaganda line on news relating to the region. Al-Alam was launched on the eve of the U.S. invasion of Iraq in 2003.

Militias and insurgents

Iran has encouraged its Iraqi political allies to work with the United States. But its Qods Force has armed, trained and funded militias associated with these parties, as well as radical insurgent groups that attack U.S. forces. These groups could provide Tehran the means to retaliate against U.S. forces in Iraq, should the United States or Israel attack Iran's nuclear facilities.

After 2003, Iran initially focused resources on its traditional allies in ISCI's Badr Corps. But it soon expanded its aid to include the Sadrists' Mahdi Army, associated special groups and even some Sunni insurgent groups. It sometimes used Arabic-speaking Lebanese Hezbollah operatives to facilitate these efforts.

Iran's support for the Mahdi Army has proven particularly problematic. The Sadrist militia underwent a dramatic expansion after 2003, which led it to incorporate many criminal elements. The militia's radical agenda and its competition for power within the Shiite community soon brought it into conflict with both the Supreme Council and the Iraqi government, thereby undermining Iranian efforts to unify the Shiite community.

Iran has also reportedly facilitated the activities of the Ansar al-Islam, a Salafi jihadist group in northern Iraq, which provided leverage over the Kurdish regional government and an entrée into Sunni jihadist circles.

By 2010, Iran had narrowed its support to three armed Shiite groups: Sadr's Promised Day Brigade—the successor to the Mahdi Army—and two special groups: Asa'ib Ahl al-Haqq (League of the Righteous) and Kata'ib Hezbollah (Battalions of Hezbollah). Iranian advisers reportedly returned to Iraq in mid-2010 with Kata'ib Hezbollah operatives trained in Iran to conduct attacks on U.S. forces as they drew down. Their goal was to create the impression that the United States was forced out of Iraq.

Trade

Iran has strengthened trade and economic ties with Iraq for financial gain and to obtain leverage over its neighbor. Iran is Iraq's largest trade partner. Trade between the two countries reportedly reached $7 billion in 2009. Iranian exports to Iraq—the lion's share of the total—is mainly fresh produce and processed foodstuffs, cheap consumer goods and cars. Iraqi exports to Iran include crude and refined oil products, sulfur and iron. Iranian investors and construction firms are also active in Baghdad, predominantly Shiite southern Iraq and Kurdistan.

Iranian dumping of cheap, subsidized food products and consumer goods into Iraq, however, has undercut Iraq's agricultural and light industrial sectors, and generated resentment among Iraqis. Iran's damming and diversion of rivers feeding the Shatt al-Arab waterway has also undermined Iraqi agriculture in the south and hindered efforts to revive Iraq's marshlands. And while Iran has made up for Iraq's electricity shortages by supplying about 5 percent of its needs (the proportion is actually much higher for several provinces that border Iran), many Iraqis believe that Iran manipulates these supplies for political ends.

Religious influence

Iran has been working to ensure the primacy of clerics trained in Qom, steeped in the Islamic Republic's official ideology, over clerics trained in the relatively non-political "quietist" tradition of Najaf's academies. Its goal is to ensure that its version of Islam is the dominant ideology among Shiites worldwide.

Iran may now be poised to achieve this goal, due to:

- Its lavish use of state funds for the activities of its politicized clerics.

- The 2010 death of Grand Ayatollah Hussein Fadlallah, an influential Lebanese cleric trained in Najaf.

- And the advanced age of Grand Ayatollah Ali Sistani—the foremost member of the Najaf school and *marja*, or source of emulation, for perhaps 80 percent of all Shiites. He was born in 1930 and is reportedly ailing.

Iraq has also become a major destination for Iranian religious tourists. Some 40,000 Iranians visit holy sites in Najaf, Karbala, Kadhimiya and Samarra each month. Iran reportedly invests tens of millions of dollars annually for construction and improvement of tourist facilities for its pilgrims.

Limits of influence

Despite significant investments to expand its influence in Iraq, Iran's efforts have yielded only mixed results. The goal of Shiite unity in Iraq has proven elusive. Relations among its Iraqi clients have frequently been fraught with tensions and violence, and it has spent much time and effort mediating among them. Tehran's meddling in Iraqi politics has also been a liability for its local allies, contributing to the Supreme Council's extremely poor showing in 2009 provincial elections and 2010 parliamentary elections.

Tehran also failed to block two key pacts—the Security Agreement and the Strategic Framework Agreement—between Iraq and the United States. It did succeed in obtaining a provision in the Security Agreement ensuring that Iraq would not be used as springboard for an attack on Iran. But these agreements mean that Iran faces the possibility of Iraq having a long-term strategic partnership with the United States.

Finally, various Iranian policies have stoked anti-Iranian sentiment in Iraq. They include the dumping of subsidized products on the Iraqi market; the diversion of rivers feeding the Shatt al-Arab; occasional artillery strikes on northern Kurdish villages; and provocations, such as the temporary occupation of an oil well in the Fakka oil field in Maysan province in December 2009.

Outstanding issues

Iraq and Iran have made some progress in recent years in resolving sources of tension and conflict dating to the Iran-Iraq War. Both now accept the terms of the 1975 Algiers Accord for demarcating land and water boundaries. Since the 1990s, they have been exchanging the bodies of war dead, although 75,000 remain unaccounted for. In 2005, Baghdad accepted responsibility for starting the Iran-Iraq War. But Iran is seeking reparations for war damages, and Iraq is still seeking the return of 153 civilian and military aircraft flown to Iran at the start of the 1991 Gulf War.

The fate of the 3,400 Iranian members of the oppositionist Mujahedin-e Khalq Organization (MEK) located in Camp Ashraf, in Iraq, remains unresolved. The MEK is the largest Iranian opposition group in exile. Iran would like Iraq to close the camp down and turn over members of the group for trial. Many Iraqis would also like them to be deported, as they are accused of helping the former regime put down popular uprisings in the Kurdish north and the Shiite south in 1991.

The future

- Iran-Iraq relations will continue to be bedeviled by a variety of unresolved issues dating to the Iran-Iraq War and by an Iranian tendency to pursue policies viewed as harmful to Iraqi interests.

- Geography, politics, economics and religion ensure that Iran will retain a modicum of influence in Iraq. And there will always be some Iraqis willing to work on behalf of Iran, for ideological and mercenary reasons.

- The most powerful constraints on Iranian influence in Iraq are Iran's own policies and high-handed behavior, Iraqi nationalism and U.S. information activities that highlight Iranian meddling in Iraq.

- Over the long-term, Iraq's relations with Iran will depend largely on its security situation, the political complexion of its government, and the type of long-term relationship it forges with the United States and its Arab neighbors.

Michael Eisenstadt is senior fellow and director of the Military and Security Studies Program at The Washington Institute for Near East Policy.

35

Iran and Afghanistan

Mohsen Milani

- Like the United States, Iran seeks a stable Afghanistan free of the Taliban and al Qaeda, which it considers a strategic menace. It also supports the government of President Hamid Karzai, contributes to Afghanistan's reconstruction and fights against its narcotics trafficking.
- Yet Iran's policies toward Afghanistan are linked to its fierce strategic competition with the United States for a dominant role in the Islamic world.
- Having gained strategic depth in Afghanistan, Iran has developed asymmetrical capability to disrupt U.S. operations or retaliate against American troops, should Iran's nuclear facilities be attacked.
- Iran has called on foreign forces to leave Afghanistan and has reportedly provided limited military support to anti-American forces as the Taliban.
- Iran has created a sphere of influence and a security buffer zone in the Herat region, the industrial heart of Afghanistan and its most secure region. Most of Iran's pledged reconstruction assistance, estimated at $660 million, is in Herat.
- Iran is now among the top five exporters and importers of goods to and from Afghanistan.

Overview

Iran has been an influential force in Afghanistan. Dari, the Afghan dialect of Persian, is one of Afghanistan's two official languages and is used by intellectuals and the elite. Until 1857, Herat was part of Iran, and only after Iran and Britain signed the Paris Treaty of 1857 did Iran abandon its claim—although it reserved the right to send forces to Afghanistan "if its frontier is violated."

From Afghan independence in 1919 until 1979, Iran's relations with Afghanistan were friendly. After the 1979 revolution, Iranian policy on Afghanistan went through four phases. In the first phase, which coincided with the 1979-1989 Soviet occupation, Iran called for a Soviet withdrawal and aided Afghan Shiites. In the second phase, after the Soviet Army withdrew, Iran helped the non-Pushtun ethnic groups form a united front. During the Afghan civil war, Iran, Pakistan and Saudi Arabia supported different warlords. In the third phase, when the Taliban seized power in 1996, Iran refused to recognize the government and instead provided military support to the Northern Alliance opposition.

In the fourth and current phase, since the U.S.-backed Northern Alliance ended Taliban rule, Iran has developed friendly relations with the Karzai government. It has engaged in reconstruction of Afghanistan, continued supporting its traditional allies and pressed for the withdrawal of all foreign troops from the country.

Historic ties

In 1979, the destinies of Iran and Afghanistan were irrevocably altered. A revolution overthrew the monarchy in Iran, and the Soviet Union invaded Afghanistan. Iran condemned the Soviet occupation of Afghanistan and demanded its withdrawal, but Tehran was cautious not to antagonize Moscow. Iran refused to become a frontline state against the Soviet occupation and refused to participate in the "Washington-Islamabad-Riyadh" axis that financed and managed the Afghan resistance. Iran saw the Soviet Union as a counterweight to U.S. influence in the region.

Iran was also concerned about the spread of Saudi "Wahhabism," which Ayatollah Khomeini called "America's Islam." In the beginning, Iran's Afghan policy was Shiite-centric. Tehran generously supported the oppressed Hazara Shiites, who constituted about 20 percent of the population, and more than 1.5 million Afghan refugees who fled to Iran—many of them Hazaras.

After the 1989 Soviet pullout, Washington and Moscow pledged not to interfere in Afghanistan. That decision turned the war-ravaged country into a battleground for a proxy war among Iran, Saudi Arabia and Pakistan. The Saudis wanted to use Afghanistan as a springboard to spread their version of Islam throughout Central Asia and to neutralize Iran's revolutionary message. Pakistan sought to install a Pushtun-dominated government and gain "strategic depth" against India, its nemesis. Iran, having ended its eight-year war with Iraq, sought to establish a friendly government in Kabul that reflected Afghanistan's rich ethnic diversity. Tehran encouraged all Dari-speakers and non-Pushtuns to form a united front.

In 1992, an alliance that included the Tajiks, Uzbeks and Shiites, under the leadership of legendary Tajik commander Ahmad Shah Massoud, overthrew the caretaker government left behind by the Soviets. This was the first time non-Pushtuns had dominated the government—a victory for Iran. Iran's role in the putsch is unclear, but Massoud's victory without Iran's support would have been difficult.

Afghan civil war

The victory was short-lived, as Afghanistan descended into a devastating civil war. The Pushtuns, Pakistan and Saudi Arabia all rejected the new realignment of power and undermined the government which they believed was close to Tehran. The government itself was paralyzed by lingering in-fighting among its supporters, and its stubborn refusal to share power with the Pushtuns and Shiites. In addition, the Afghan warlords, who rose to prominence as they fought against the Soviets, fueled the civil war. Having created their own fiefdoms, they formed fleeting alliances of convenience with the highest bidder, including regional powers.

Independently, and through work with the United Nations, Iran called for peaceful resolution of the conflict. It appealed to the government to share power with Pushtuns and Shiites. But Tehran had neither the diplomatic skills nor the resources to bring peace to Afghanistan. Kabul also had serious tensions with Tehran, as it tried to appease Pakistan and Saudi Arabia.

During the civil war, Iran pursued inconsistent policies. It supported the Kabul government but also covered its bets by supporting Shiites who worked both for and against the regime. It also backed rival warlords, including Ismail Khan from Herat, a Tajik; General Abdul Rashid Dostom, an Uzbek; and Gulbuddin Hekmatyar, a Pushtun.

Iran and the Taliban

Amid the chaos, the Taliban, an obscure group of young Pushtun religious students, rose to power. Their ideology was a strange combination of Wahhabism and Deobandism. Iran was astonishingly slow to recognize the Taliban's dazzling rise and the pivotal support provided by Pakistan and Saudi Arabia. In 1995, Herat fell to the Taliban, and a year later, they overthrew President Rabbani—a major defeat for Iran and a clear victory for Saudi Arabia and Pakistan.

Iran, unlike Pakistan and Saudi Arabia, refused to recognize the Taliban and sought to return Rabbani to power. It participated in the U.N. "Six Plus Two" talks on Afghanistan's future, but Iran's strategic investment was to generously support the Northern Alliance made up of Tajiks, Uzbeks and Shiite fighters. India and Russia supported the alliance, but Iran was its principal source of military assistance.

Broken relations

Iranian support for the Northern Alliance, the Taliban's most formidable rival, created serious animosity between Tehran and Kabul. They severed diplomatic relations in 1997. Iran accused the Taliban of being "narco-terrorists," whose antediluvian ideology and draconian laws made Afghanistan a huge prison. Iran's relations with Pakistan and Saudi Arabia also deteriorated.

Iran provided key support for the Northern Alliance when the Taliban tried to capture its interim capital at Mazar-e Sharif. The Taliban initially was pushed back. But with Pakistani support, the Taliban ultimately prevailed, killing more than 2,000 people. They also kidnapped and killed eight Iranian diplomats and one journalist, which led Iran and Afghanistan dangerously close to war. Tehran massed some 200,000 troops on its eastern border, but the threat only made the Taliban more belligerent. They raided Iran's cultural center in

Mazar-e Sharif and set its library ablaze. Thereafter, Tehran increased support for the Northern Alliance while the Taliban ruled most of Afghanistan.

Washington's gift

After al Qaeda's 9/11 attacks, Iran was the recipient of an unintended strategic gift from Washington. The Taliban, who had developed a symbiotic relationship with al Qaeda, were forcefully removed from power after the United States provided air power and intelligence for the Northern Alliance, Iran's ally. Iranian military advisers rubbed shoulders with U.S. military personnel in the Northern Alliance areas. Tehran even said it would give sanctuary for distressed U.S. military personnel inside its territory. It also allowed the United States to transport humanitarian goods to Afghanistan through Iranian land. Iran reportedly suggested the best targets for U.S. bombers.

Iran also participated in the U.S.-sponsored Bonn Conference in December 2001. U.S. and Iranian envoys worked together at the conference—the most fruitful encounter between the two since the 1979 revolution. Both wanted Afghanistan free of the Taliban and al Qaeda. Iran favored the return of President Rabbani, but it agreed to support U.S.-backed Hamid Karzai. The tactical cooperation between the United States and Iran continued, even as they were competing for greater influence in a new Afghanistan. Iranian cooperation with the United States ended in 2002, after President George Bush cited Iran as a member of the "axis of evil."

Iran and the new Afghanistan

Iran has four major goals in Afghanistan:

- To collaborate with Karzai without abandoning supports for other Afghan allies
- To invest in Afghan reconstruction to create a "sphere of influence" and a security zone in the Herat region
- To avoid direct confrontation with the United States, while pressuring Kabul to distance itself from the United States and ensure that Afghanistan is not used to attack Iran
- To reduce and, if possible, control the flow of narcotics to Iran.

Karzai has been in a precarious position, as an ally of the United States also seeking friendly relations with Iran. On many occasions, he has paid tribute to Iran's "unforgettable support" and for behaving "like the brother of the Afghan people." He has visited Tehran many times and has signed economic, cultural and security agreements with Iran. He was one of the first leaders to congratulate Ahmadinejad after the disputed 2009 presidential election.

There are a few sources of tension between the two countries:

- Iran has called for the withdrawal of foreign troops, who back Karzai.
- The issue of an Iranian pipeline going through Afghanistan is not settled.
- Iran has expressed concern about Karzai's policy of Pushtun-ization, which has somewhat marginalized the Tajiks, Uzbeks and Hazaras.
- Iran is home to 1.5 million Afghan refugees, whose treatment is disputed.
- Narcotics trafficking from Afghanistan has created a chronic drug problem in Iran.

On drug trafficking, Iran blames the Karzai government and the United States for failing to curb opium production. Iran is one of the major consumers of Afghan opium, and a favorite corridor for shipping narcotics to Europe and the Persian Gulf. While addiction to opium has increased alarmingly in Iran, revenues from narcotics have financed much of the anti-American insurgency in Afghanistan. Hundreds of Iranian security agents have been killed in clashes with traffickers. Iran claims that Jundallah, a terrorist group responsible for killing scores of Iran's Revolutionary Guards, is closely tied to trafficking.

Sphere of influence

One of Iran's main objectives is to create an economic sphere of influence in Herat and turn it into a security buffer zone. Iran ultimately wants to become the hub for transit of goods and service between the Persian Gulf, Afghanistan, Central Asia, China and India. At the International Pledging Conference in Tokyo in 2002, Iran committed $560 million to Afghan reconstruction, making Iran one of the leading contributors. At the London Conference on the reconstruction of Afghanistan in 2006, Iran pledged an additional $100 million.

The bulk of Iran's reconstruction investments lie in the Herat region and involve infrastructure projects, road and bridge construction, education, agriculture, power generation and telecommunication projects. Iran has been working on building a 176-kilometer railroad from Iran to the city of Herat. It has upgraded a tax-free trade route linking the Iranian port of Chabahar, located at the southern end of the Sistan va Balochstan province, near the Oman Sea, to the southwestern border post of Malik in Afghanistan, and to Kandahar and Kabul. The road would shorten the distance from the Persian Gulf to Afghanistan by 700 kilometers and would significantly diminish the importance of the Karachi-Kandahar road, which is Afghanistan's traditional roadway to international waters.

Iran and the Taliban—again

Iran and the Taliban are ideological enemies, and restoring power to the Taliban in Afghanistan would pose a grave national security threat to Iran. Yet in 2007, NATO claimed that it had intercepted a shipment of explosively formed projectiles from Iran, destined for Afghan insurgents. (It is possible that rogue elements were responsible for the flow of the arms, as there is a huge black market in arms dealing. For example, Gulbuddin Hekmatyar, the Afghan warlord, claims that an antimissile can be bought for $100.) If the Taliban is getting support from Iran, both parties know that is not because Iran likes the Taliban or vice versa. It is because, as the saying goes, the enemy of my enemy is sometimes my friend.

Iran is clearly concerned about reports that the United States and NATO have reached out to some Taliban. Many in Tehran believe Washington would have established ties with the Taliban had it not been for the Taliban providing sanctuary for al Qaeda. Iran is also concerned that successful negotiations between the Taliban and the United States would involve Pakistan and Saudi Arabia—and once again empower them in Afghanistan. Iran wants America to bleed, but its reported support for the Taliban appears to be tactical and limited, as Iran is determined to avoid any direct military confrontation with the United States.

The future

- Iran will continue to be an influential player in Afghanistan. As Iran's role in reconstruction of Afghanistan is likely to increase, and as more Iranian-educated Afghan refugees return to Afghanistan, Iran's influence is likely to increase in the coming years.

- Peace in Afghanistan is more likely to be realized through a regional approach, in which the strategic and economic interests of Iran, as well as Pakistan, are not ignored.

- Compared with other aspects of its foreign policy, Iran's policy toward Afghanistan has been relatively moderate. That policy is likely to change, however, if there is a discernable increase in the level of animosity between Iran and the United States.

Mohsen Milani is chairman of the department of government and international affairs at the University of South Florida.

36

Iran and the Gulf States

Afshin Molavi

- The Persian Gulf states hold some two-thirds of the world's proven oil reserves. Saudi Arabia is the largest Gulf oil producer, Iran a distant second.

- Iran's population of 74.5 million is roughly equal to the seven other Gulf states combined.

- A large population of Iranian nationals lives in the emirate of Dubai, Iran's most important regional trade partner. Smaller populations live and work in Kuwait, Qatar and Bahrain.

- In the post World War II era, Gulf geopolitics have been dominated by a triangular balance of power among Iran, Saudi Arabia and Iraq.

- The region has experienced three "Gulf wars": the Iran-Iraq War of 1980-1988 fought to a brutal stalemate, the successful 1991 U.S.-led coalition to roll back Iraq's invasion of Kuwait, and the 2003 U.S.-led war to remove Saddam Hussein from power.

- Persian Iran is the only non-Arab country in the Gulf region. Its predominant religion, Shiite Islam, is shared by a majority of Iraqis and Bahrainis and significant minorities in other Gulf states.

Overview

Modern Iranian leaders—from shahs to ayatollahs—have sought a dominant role in the Gulf region because of Iran's economic and demographic weight, as well as the value of Persian Gulf oil shipping lanes. In the 1960s and 1970s, Iran was the pre-eminent Gulf power and guarantor of U.S. national interests in the region.

Iran's 1979 revolution dramatically altered Tehran's regional stance. Revolutionary leader Ayatollah Ruhollah Khomeini called for the overthrow of existing pro-American monarchs in the Gulf. Iraq's 1980 invasion of Iran pulled the Gulf Arabs and the United States into the brutal eight-year conflict, mostly on Baghdad's side.

The end of the Iran-Iraq War in 1988, the death of Ayatollah Khomeini in 1989, and the rise of more pragmatic leadership in Tehran led to an easing of tensions between Iran and the Gulf Arab states. The two subsequent "Gulf wars" in 1991 and 2003 weakened Iraq, thereby strengthening Iran's relative regional power. Iran's relationship with the smaller states of the lower Persian Gulf has historically been centered on trade. The emirate of Dubai has emerged as Iran's most vital Gulf trade partner and an occasional outlet to skirt sanctions.

The monarchy, 1941–1979

In 1968, Britain declared its intention to abandon all military outposts in the Persian Gulf. Mohammed Reza Shah Pahlavi sought to fill the British vacuum and become the "policeman of the Gulf." Washington encouraged Tehran by adopting a "twin pillar" policy, anointing both Saudi Arabia and Iran as guarantors of U.S. national security interests in the region. The Nixon administration opened the floodgates to U.S. arms purchases to Iran.

Although they were all pro-Western regimes, the Persian monarchy had tense exchanges with the Arab sheikhs across the Gulf. In 1968, the shah declared Bahrain a historic Iranian territory, only to pull back after a U.N. mission found that Bahrainis preferred independence. In 1971, Iran seized three strategic Persian Gulf islands—Abu Musa and the Greater and Lesser Tunbs—claimed by the newly formed union of seven emirates, known as the United Arab Emirates. The shah also refused to participate in the Arab oil embargoes of 1967 and 1973. He continued to sell oil to the West and Israel, a source of contention between Riyadh and Tehran.

The shah also had serious ideological differences with socialist and Soviet-allied Iraq. The two countries had a serious dispute over the Shatt al-Arab waterway that required international mediation to resolve in 1975. Yet the shah's Iran—with its large conventional army, high-tech weapons, large population and strong ties to Washington—seemed like the biggest power on the bloc in the 1970s.

Decade of conflict, 1979–1988

Iran's 1979 revolution dramatically altered the regional geopolitical balance in the Persian Gulf. Ayatollah Khomeini declared his intent to overthrow Gulf monarchs. Iran was implicated in a coup plot in Bahrain, unrest in Kuwait, and attacks on U.S. facilities in the Gulf states. In 1980, Iraqi President Saddam Hussein, sensing weakness from revolutionary chaos, attacked Iran to prevent the newly formed Islamic Republic from inspiring Iraq's own Shiite majority and to gain strategic depth on its border.

The Iran-Iraq War turned out to be a defining feature of Iran-Gulf Arab relations throughout the 1980s. In 1981, the five smaller states of the Gulf—Bahrain, Kuwait, Oman, Qatar, and the United Arab Emirates (UAE)—joined with Saudi Arabia in what was billed a security and political alliance, known as the Gulf Cooperation Council (GCC). The Gulf states sided largely with Iraq, although each state—and even emirates within states—charted their own path regarding Iran.

Saudi Arabia and Kuwait underwrote Saddam's war efforts to the tune of an estimated $40 billion. The new UAE federation was split. The emirates of Dubai, Sharjah and Umm Al-Quwain remained neutral, fearful of jeopardizing trade and commercial links with Iran. Indeed, Dubai flourished as a re-supply entrepot (trading post) for the Iranian military. But the UAE capital, Abu Dhabi, supported the Saudi-Kuwaiti position.

After 1984, Saudi Arabia and Kuwait were pulled into the war after Iraq struck Iran's main oil export terminal and Iran retaliated by striking at tankers of Gulf nations allied to Iraq. The United States intervened by re-flagging Kuwait and Saudi tankers, which in turn raised tensions between Tehran and Washington. After a U.S.-flagged ship was hit, the U.S. Navy bombarded an Iranian oil platform in October 1987. U.S.-Iran tensions ultimately led to the accidental shooting down of an Iranian civilian passenger plane by the *USS Vincennes,* killing 290 passengers and crew, in July 1988.

The war finally ended when Iran accepted U.N. Resolution 598 in August 1988. Ayatollah Khomeini said accepting the terms was akin to drinking "a poisoned chalice." There was no clear victor, but the triangular balance of power between the Gulf big trio—Iraq, Iran and Saudi Arabia—largely remained intact.

Rafsanjani's bridge-building, 1989–1997

Shortly after he assumed the presidency in 1989, Akbar Hashemi Rafsanjani proclaimed, "Iran needs to stop making enemies." He signaled a substantive shift in foreign policy from an aggressive revolutionary state to a new pragmatic coexistence. Rafsanjani saw the GCC states not as ripe pawns to be toppled, but as cash-rich investors to entice. Prince Saud al-Faisal, the Saudi foreign minister, suggested shortly thereafter that the two countries could see "a future of positive relations."

But the third piece of the triangular balance of power, Saddam Hussein's Iraq, seethed at the sight of his fellow Arab states making conciliatory gestures to Iran. He also seethed at the war debt that he accrued, which he expected Kuwait to forgive since he had fought the dreaded "Persian menace" and "the scourge of Khomeini" on behalf of all Arabs. Unable to come to terms with Kuwait, Saddam Hussein invaded in August 1990.

President George H. W. Bush organized an international coalition to liberate Kuwait and protect its Saudi ally. Iran treaded a fine line during the 1991 Gulf War, neither siding with Washington nor hindering its war effort, despite U.S.-Iran tensions. Tehran's neutrality in the Gulf War did not sway Washington. In 1993, the Clinton administration announced its policy of "dual containment," targeting both Iraq and Iran. But Rafsanjani's position did alter GCC perceptions of Iran. Trade increased. Direct flight links were restored. And money began flowing more freely across borders. The Rafsanjani era offered Iran and the region a soft landing from the war's ravages and the revolution's zealotry.

Khatami's rapprochement, 1997–2005

The 1997 election of Mohammad Khatami introduced a period of outreach in his attempt to launch a "dialogue of civilizations." In December 1997, Tehran hosted the Organization of Islamic Conference (OIC) summit. Among the delegates was Crown Prince Abdullah, the de-facto Saudi head of state, and the most senior Saudi visitor to Iran since the 1979 revolution. The Saudi-Iran détente was accelerating. When President Clinton also initiated an outreach to Iran, several GCC states lined up to play intermediary between Washington and Tehran, although a breakthrough never occurred.

The September 11, 2001, terrorist attack on New York City and Washington, D.C., altered the dynamics of U.S.-Iran relations. Within the next two years, President George W. Bush launched two wars on Iran's borders—in Afghanistan in 2001 and in Iraq in 2003. The U.S. ouster of Saddam Hussein particularly rocked the region—and ended up dramatically changing the balance of power in Iran's favor.

For Iran, the U.S.-led war knocked out a primary rival. Tehran also sensed an opportunity to shape and influence post-Saddam Iraq. Over the next two years, Iran's Islamic Revolutionary Guard Corps (IRGC) and ministry of intelligence began a sophisticated campaign using both hard and soft power. Tehran's growing role distressed the GCC states. In 2005, Saudi Foreign Minister Prince Saud Al-Faisal expressed some of the frustration, "We fought a war together to keep Iran from occupying Iraq after Iraq was driven out of Kuwait. Now we are handing the whole country over to Iran without reason."

Rising oil prices also gave Tehran new economic leverage. Flush with new cash, Iranians looked for regional investment opportunities and increasingly turned to Dubai, which emerged as Iran's offshore business center—its Hong Kong.

By the end of Khatami's term in 2005, most of the GCC states were again wary of Iran. Iraq was being shaped more by Iran than any other regional state. Sunni Arab states from as far as Egypt and Jordan began to whisper about fears of a Shiite crescent taking hold of the region. The Gulf was in deep flux.

Ahmadinejad's brinkmanship, 2005-

The surprise election of the populist Mahmoud Ahmadinejad in 2005 again changed the dynamics of Iranian foreign policy—this time back to the hardline positions of the early revolution. The regime immediately announced a resumption of uranium enrichment. And Iran's controversial nuclear program immediately became the focal point of its foreign policy and world diplomacy. Iran's Gulf neighbors were at least as alarmed as Israel and the United States.

Saudi Arabia and Iran increasingly found themselves vying for regional influence in proxy battles in Lebanon, the Palestinian territories, Iraq and even Afghanistan. The days of détente seemed a distant memory. In Iraq, Saudi Arabia's Sunni monarchy tried to protect the Sunni minority while Iran worked with an array of Shiite groups and the two major Kurdish parties to influence the budding Iraqi state. Iraq's March 2010 elections seemed to indicate that Iran's efforts had paid off. Immediately after the disputed elections, three of the top four candidates turned up in Tehran for "consultations" with Iranian officials.

A microcosm of the rivalry played out in the United Arab Emirates. For years, Iran's one GCC ally was oil-less Dubai in the UAE, the Gulf's rising commercial center, which was home to as many Iranians as Emiratis. Tehran's rival was oil-rich Abu Dhabi, the politically powerful UAE capital allied with the United States. Dubai's 2008 financial crisis and Abu Dhabi's subsequent bail-out of its over-leveraged brother tipped the balance in Abu Dhabi's favor.

Factoids

- In 2009, Dubai-Iran trade was estimated at $10 billion, a fall from the estimated $12 billion figure in 2008, due to the global financial crisis and tighter controls by UAE authorities on Iran trade. New rounds of sanctions and more stringent oversight by Abu Dhabi are expected to lower the trade numbers further in 2010, but Iran remains the UAE's fourth largest trade partner after China, the United States and India. Most trade represented goods from around the world that land in Dubai ports and are re-exported to Iran.

- Iran and Oman serve as joint "policemen of the Strait of Hormuz," the world's most important oil choke-point. Some two-fifths of the world's globally traded oil passes through the Strait, which at its narrowest point is only 21 miles wide.

- Iran's threats to "close down the Strait" in the event of U.S. or Israeli strikes ring hollow, as a closure would damage Iran's own oil industry, the most vital source of state revenues.

- Qatar has increasingly reached out to Iran, even discussing ways to bring Tehran into regional security discussions.

- The name of the body of water linking these eight states has occasionally sparked diplomatic spats. For Iranians, it is indisputably the Persian Gulf. For many Arab states, it is either "the Gulf" or, more provocatively, "the Arabian Gulf." Most official atlases refer to the body of water as the Persian Gulf.

The future

- An Israeli attack on Iran's nuclear facilities could spark a wider regional war with dramatic repercussions for the Persian Gulf region, leading to a skyrocketing oil prices and potential conflict between Iran and America's key Gulf Arab allies, Saudi Arabia and the United Arab Emirates.

- The world's major oil players have largely abandoned Iran but are active in Iraq. If Iraq achieves its ambitious oil targets, it could surpass Iran as the Gulf's second largest producer within a decade. This would have repercussions for the regional balance of power.

- The Iran-Dubai trade relationship will be tested by sanctions and U.S. pressure. But historic links are too deep to imagine a drastic reduction in trade, even though Iranian merchants may not feel as welcome as in the past.

Afshin Molavi is a senior fellow at the New America Foundation.

37

Iran and Turkey

Henri J. Barkey

- Relations between Iran and Turkey have long been defined by mutual suspicion and competition, despite a 312-mile border that has remained unchanged since 1639.
- Close allies during the monarchy, relations soured after the 1979 revolution. Ankara felt threatened by Tehran's ambitions to change the regional order. Iran in turn perceived Turkey as a close ally of the West and therefore potentially hostile.
- Adding to tensions, Tehran and Ankara have diametrically opposed worldviews: Turkey is a constitutionally secular state where the military is the self-appointed guardian of secularism. Iran is a theocracy in which Islamic law rules and clerics play decisive roles, including control over the military.
- Yet the two governments have cooperated when necessary, especially on energy and Kurdish issues. Relations improved after the 2002 election of Turkey's Justice and Development Party, which has Islamist roots.

Overview

In many ways, Turkey and Iran are mirror images. They share geography, culture, religion and a long history of conflict and cooperation. They both straddle multiple geopolitical regions. Between the two, they span two continents and border five of the world's most volatile regions—the Middle East, the Caucasus, the Balkans, Central Asia and the South Asian subcontinent. They are both descendants of empires with hegemonic histories that occasionally pitted them against each other. In the 16th century, Persia converted to Shiite Islam in part to distinguish itself from the Sunni caliphate of the Ottoman Empire. Both countries today are also profoundly insecure about real and imaginary enemies at home and abroad. As inheritors of great civilizations, they both feel their importance has been largely unappreciated.

Yet the two countries also symbolize two opposite poles in the Islamic world. For the first two decades after Iran's 1979 revolution, Turkey behaved as a status quo power. Its enduring secular Kemalist ideology was named for the founder of modern Turkey, Mustafa Kemal Ataturk, who turned Turkey toward the West. Ankara changed little in its alliance commitments or political structures dating back to the Cold War. In contrast, Iran became a leading agitator for change. It persistently pushed its ambitious Islamic ideology directly and through a new network of surrogates. Tehran also wanted Muslim countries to form their own bloc independent of either East or West. So each viewed the other as a menace.

The 2002 victory of Turkey's Justice and Development Party (AKP) changed Turkey dramatically—and led to role reversal between Ankara and Tehran. As it shed its inward economic and political policies, Turkey emerged as a local superpower ruled by a party willing to muscle its way into the Middle East and beyond. Turkey is also fully integrated into the global economic system, while Iran finds itself increasingly isolated politically and economically.

Three phases

Relations between Ankara and Tehran have gone through three broad phases:

Phase 1: Post-revolution

The Iranian Revolution shocked the international system and, along with the 1979 Soviet invasion of Afghanistan, increased Turkey's importance to the West. Turkey's strategic value was especially enhanced because the

United States lost its early warning stations in Iran to monitor Soviet missile tests.

Turkey quickly recognized Tehran's new regime and did not participate in U.S. sanctions imposed after the hostage crisis. A Turkish junta assumed power in a September 12, 1980, military coup and had no time to formulate a new policy on Iran when Iraq invaded Iran 10 days later. Turkey, which bordered both countries, remained neutral during the eight-year conflict. But the war provided an important boost to the Turkish economy, which had undergone one of its worst crises to date. Both countries relied on Turkey for basic goods. By 1983, Turkish exports to Iran constituted 19 percent of all Turkey's exports, surpassing Germany, which was then Turkey's leading trading partner. As the war petered out, so did Turkish exports, although they remained higher than in the late 1970s.

Phase 2: The 1990s

Iranian-Turkish relations became more confrontational after the Iran-Iraq War ended, in part because of ideological differences. Each viewed the other through the narrow prism of their secular-religious divide. The Turks were particularly suspicious of Iranian support for fundamentalist movements in Turkey. The Iranian ambassador to Ankara was declared persona non grata after he criticized Ankara's ban on Muslim women wearing headscarves in universities and government offices, and even participated in demonstrations against the ban. Ankara was also bitter about Iranian aid to insurgents in the Kurdistan Workers' Party (PKK), which operated bases deep in Iranian territory. In 1991, Turkey detained an Iranian-flagged vessel on suspicion of carrying weapons destined for the PKK.

Iran harbored parallel suspicions of the Turks. Ayatollah Ruhollah Khomeini once quipped that secular Kemalism was worse than communism. The Turkish regime, he charged, held on to power largely through the power of bayonets. Echoing Turkey's concerns, Tehran specifically complained that Ankara was not doing enough to control Iranian dissidents operating on Turkish soil. Iran was also suspicious of Turkish interference in its own province of Azerbaijan, as well as in the post-Soviet republic of Azerbaijan. The Azeri populations in both have close linguistic ties to Turkey.

But Iran focused more on Turkey as an external threat. As a member of NATO, Turkey brought the world's mightiest military alliance to their common border. After the Soviet Union's collapse, the West also turned to Turkey to counter Iranian influence in the newly independent Central Asian states that had been part of Moscow's empire. They also differed seriously on Iraq, despite agreement about containing Kurdish ambitions in Iraq. Turkey wanted Saddam Hussein to cooperate with the international community to end economic sanctions. Ankara also wanted Baghdad to reestablish control over all Iraqi territory. But after its eight-year war with Iraq, Iran wanted the Baghdad regime weakened and hamstrung by stringent U.N. sanctions.

Phase 3: Erdogan and the AKP

The AKP, which had Islamist roots, took a different approach to the Middle East. Anxious to develop new trade opportunities and become the leading actor in regional politics, Ankara developed a policy based on "zero problems" with its neighbors, including Iran. Even deep sectarian differences—Turkey is overwhelmingly Sunni, Iran is largely Shiite—were not obstacles to improving relations. Ankara's new vision of the Middle East seemed less antagonistic to Iran and Iranian allies, demonstrated by frequent visits by both Turkish and Iranian heads of state.

The Turks provided Iran with important support at its most vulnerable time. Ankara was one of the first governments, along with Russia and Venezuela, to offer unqualified support for President Mahmoud Ahmadinejad after the disputed June 2009 elections. The Turkish government was also silent when the Iranian regime violently suppressed Green Movement protesters to regain political control.

Iran also slowly shifted its stance, particularly on the sensitive Kurdish question. After years of tolerating PKK activities in Iran, Tehran gradually began to prevent the movement's access to its territory. Tehran's policy shift emerged after a PKK affiliate, the Free Life Party of Kurdistan (PJAK), successfully attacked Iranian security forces. In response, Iran launched artillery strikes against both the PKK and PJAK in their hideouts in northern Iraq's remote Qandil mountains. Iran's new policy was a way to begin intelligence cooperation and ingratiate itself with Turkey; it was also a way to embarrass the United States, which occupied Iraq at the time but had been reluctant to militarily act against the PKK.

Nuclear diplomacy

Turkey's changed approach has been most apparent on Iran's nuclear controversy. The Turks have historically been ambivalent about Tehran's program. In 2010 President Abdullah Gül expressed misgivings about the Islamic Republic's ultimate objectives. At the same time, Prime Minister Recep Tayyip Erdogan publicly vouched for Tehran's peaceful intentions on nuclear energy at a time the international community and Turkey's allies expressed growing alarm about the dangers of Iran developing a nuclear weapon. Erdogan repeatedly argued that Iran's program was not the real problem and instead tried to make Israel the issue, to the annoyance of the United States. This would prove to be an important psychological boost to Tehran since the central issue was its lack of compliance with international safeguards and rules.

In May 2010, Turkey and Brazil negotiated an agreement with Iran to ship 1,200 kg of low enriched uranium to Turkey for safekeeping. In exchange, the Iranians would receive fuel rods for the Tehran Research Reactor, which produces isotopes for medical use. This was part of Ankara's strategy to burnish its diplomatic credentials internationally and establish itself as a major actor capable of resolving some of the world's most difficult problems. The deal was heralded in Turkey. But it was rejected by the United States and Europeans because it represented a watered down version of their own proposal, which Iran had walked away from eight months earlier. In the first deal, 1,200 kg represented some 80 percent of Iranian stocks. But Tehran had produced so much more low enriched uranium in the intervening months that 1,200 kg was closer to 50 percent when Iran accepted the Turkey-Brazil package.

The new diplomacy played out just as the U.N. Security Council was about to vote to impose new sanctions on Iran. The deal was widely interpreted as an attempt to derail sanctions and give Tehran more breathing room. Turkey argued that sanctions were counterproductive; it said persuasion was more effective than punitive measures in getting Tehran to change its behavior. (Turkey also believed it they would suffer disproportionately from sanctions on Iran.) The United Nations went ahead with the vote on new sanctions. Turkey, which had one of the 15 Security Council seats, voted against the resolution. Turkey's decision to side with Iran at the expense of its traditional Western allies caused a major crisis of confidence with the United States.

Factoids

- Iran accounts for 20 percent to 30 percent of Turkey's gas imports. But the Iranians have not been reliable partners. Twice in 2010, for example, cold weather forced Iran to indefinitely suspend deliveries, which led the Turks to look for alternative supplies.

- Trade between Turkey and Iran totaled $10 billion in 2008. Iran exported $8.2 billion in goods, mostly hydrocarbons. Turkey exported $2 billion. In 2009, Iranian exports to Turkey declined precipitously to $3.4 billion, although Turkish exports remained stable. Turkey's exports to Iran represent no more than 2 percent of its total exports.

- Turkey has the largest Kurdish population, estimated to be up to 20 percent of the population or 14 million. Iran has the third largest population, estimated at almost 5 million. The two Kurdish communities have little contact.

- Turkey is one of the few countries Iranians can travel to without a visa.

- Iran and Turkey are members of the Economic Cooperation Organization, a 10-nation alliance created in1985, with members stretching from Turkey through Central and South Asia. Tehran and Ankara are also members of the Developing-8, an association of mid-income Muslim nations created by the Turks in the 1990s.

Balance of power

Turkey and Iran have emerged as the two rival models for much of the Islamic world. They represent disparate ways of blending Islam and democracy. Turkey has engaged in gradual evolutionary change. Its ruling party has Islamist roots but governs a strictly secular system. Its foreign policy has become increasingly multifaceted. It is already a member of the world's most powerful military alliance, NATO, and is a candidate to join the European Union. It is a rising mid-level power. And its economic reforms have made it the 16th largest economy in the world.

In contrast, Iran's political transformation was fraught with turmoil throughout its first three decades. Its foreign policy long defied both East and West. Its closest allies were often militias rather than governments. Vast oil resources produced wealth, but international sanctions made it increasingly difficult to develop. By

2010, its failure to compromise with the international community led to growing isolation.

Relations between the two are also uneven. Turkey's AKP government, with its boundless self-confidence, has been an enigma to Iran. The Turks stood up to their own allies to extend Iran an economic lifeline and support Tehran's nuclear program. Yet Turkey's growing regional ambitions challenge Tehran's alliances. The Iranians have the upper hand in Iraq, Lebanon and Syria, for example, but the Turks are challenging them in all three countries. In the Arab world, public opinion polls now indicate that Turkish Prime Minister Erdogan is the single most admired leader.

The future

- Turkey's principal concern is the stability of the Iranian regime. President Ahmadinejad's erratic behavior has irritated Ankara, but the AKP government is unlikely to be sufficiently offended to disrupt its bourgeoning ties with Tehran.

- Yet the current Turkish government—despite its sympathies and expectations of greater trade opportunities—is not an ally of Iran. It sees itself in a long-run competition with Iran for influence.

- In the region, Turkey can use its assets, its improved diplomatic position, a robust economy and a willingness to engage with all parties to eclipse Iran. Turkish inroads into Syria have the long-term ability to influence Syrian society. Ankara has opened its borders to Syrians, and Turkish border towns are doing brisk business with Syrians.

- Iran rhetorically welcomes Turkey's attempts to mediate, especially when they weaken international consensus. In reality, however, Tehran also perceives itself as a rising power of great significance that ought not need a mediator, especially by a mid-level power or neighbor.

Henri J. Barkey is the Cohen Professor of International Relations at Lehigh University and is nonresident senior associate at the Carnegie Endowment for International Peace.

38

Iran and Israel

Steven Simon

- Israel and Iran have interacted since Israel's birth in 1948. Although ideology has played a role, their respective regional strategic interests have largely shaped their relationship.

- Relations between the two countries were relatively close until the 1979 revolution. Arms transfers from Israel to Iran continued for a short time, but there have been no publicly acknowledged deals since 1982.

- The 1982 Israeli invasion of Lebanon mobilized the Shiites. Iranian troops deployed in Lebanon and sired Hezbollah to fight Israel. Through a proxy, Iran now faces Israel across a common border.

- Iran also armed and funded Islamic Jihad, which carried out terrorist attacks within Israel in the 1990s and from Gaza since the 1980s.

- Iran's controversial nuclear program has raised the stakes for both sides in their regional rivalry. Some Israelis believe that their security justifies military action to ensure Iran does not acquire a bomb.

Overview

Iran was a focal point of Israeli foreign policy almost as soon as the new state was established in 1948. After initial stumbles, the two countries developed a close relationship based on shared interests in keeping the Soviets out and pan-Arabism down. Various types of diplomatic, military and trade ties endured for some three decades; Iran was an important source of oil for Israel. But the mutual interests that sustained relations withered after the 1979 Iranian revolution and the Soviet Union's collapse in 1989. The theocracy began seeking regional influence by doing more than the Arabs to aid Israel's enemies, while the Americans replaced the Soviets as the mullahs' bête noir.

Despite its enmity toward the Jewish state, Iran secretly bought weapons from Israel after Iraq's 1980 invasion. The sales ended in the mid-1980s without producing the rapprochement that some Israelis had hoped for. Relations deteriorated further as Iran took a front line position against Israel by training and equipping Lebanon's Hezbollah and encouraging Palestinian attacks on Israel from Gaza and the West Bank. In 2006, Israel and Hezbollah fought Israel's longest war. Due partly to Iran's rearming of Hezbollah, Israel's northern border remains a serious flashpoint.

By 2010, tensions had reached unparalleled heights due to the combination of Iran's suspected pursuit of a nuclear weapons capability and its virulent rhetoric, which stressed Israel's illegitimacy and even its disappearance. Israel has considered unilateral military action to impede Iran's nuclear efforts, although its leaders would prefer the United States and the international community persuade or compel Iran to abandon any program that could be used to develop a nuclear weapon.

Origins

After the Israeli War of Independence, Iraq cracked down on its Jewish population. As the prospect of pogroms grew, Israel sought ways to smuggle Jews out of Iraq, which had forbidden emigration. Iran provided an exit route for Jews, at a price. Israeli agents were deployed to Iran to facilitate the rescue of Iraqi Jews, but also to cajole Iranian officials to establish diplomatic relations with new state, mainly through bribery. These initial efforts failed, owing largely to domestic opposition orchestrated by Ayatollah Ruhollah Khomeini. But Israel maintained a permanent delegation in Tehran that served as a de facto diplomatic mission. Ambassadors were ultimately exchanged in the 1970s.

Israeli outreach to the Pahlavi regime was defined by the "periphery doctrine," devised by Israeli Prime Minister David Ben Gurion, diplomatic adviser Reuven Shiloah and Mossad chief Isser Harel. They were motivated by the Eisenhower administration's spurning of Israel after the 1956 Suez War and the need to replace the lost backing of a great power with some other source of support. The underlying concept was that Israel could leapfrog hostile Arab regimes on its borders by cultivating de facto alliances with non-Arab states at the edge of the Arab world and vulnerable non-Muslim ethnic groups within it: Turkey to the north, Iran to the east and predominantly Christian Ethiopia to the south were the key regimes. Lebanese Maronites and Iraqi Kurds were the essential ethnic groups.

Israel's strategy hinged on a common interest in resisting the spread of pan-Arabism, unleashed by popular Egyptian President Gamal Abdel Nasser, and in winning Washington's favor by aligning with the United States against Soviet encroachment. Young Reza Shah Pahlavi appreciated these advantages, but he also believed that friendship with Israel would foster U.S. support. Jews, he thought, were a powerful influence on American policy.

Deepening ties

As relations matured, thousands of Israelis went to Iran to work in the defense industry as military advisers—with the SAVAK intelligence as mentors—and in the agricultural and health sectors as technical consultants. The expatriate community became large enough to warrant the creation of an Israeli school in Tehran. Israelis helped the shah pursue his highest priorities, including:

- Creating a powerful military to deter Soviet aggression

- Exerting Iran's influence in the Persian Gulf, where Tehran was to occupy islands—claimed by the UAE—astride large oil deposits

- And advancing the goals of his White Revolution.

For Israel, the burgeoning relationship was a clear success story for Ben Gurion's strategy of the periphery. It:

- Reduced its diplomatic isolation

- Aligned it with the United States

- Strengthened Iraq's main adversary

- Facilitated the rescue of Iraqi Jews

- Ensured the security of Iran's large Jewish population

- And yielded a cash bonanza.

In the late 1970s, Mossad concluded Iranians were angered by the shah's domestic policies but believed he could suppress opposition. Jerusalem, therefore, was as surprised as Washington by the monarch's collapse. The revolutionary regime immediately severed diplomatic ties with Israel, turning over the Israeli Embassy to the Palestine Liberation Organization. But Israel hoped that the status quo ante would be restored once revolutionary fervor faded and the new regime recalculated its strategic interests.

Iraq's 1980 invasion of Iran fulfilled this hope, for a time. Iran's desperate military, decimated by purges and the loss of Western military assistance, forced the regime to turn to Israel for crucial supplies. Weapons, munitions, aircraft spare parts and combat engineering equipment were transferred to Iran in an extensive covert operation that later meshed with the Iran-Contra conspiracy launched by the Reagan administration. By 1982, it became clear that weapons sales were not going to renew Iranian friendship, but the profits retained Israel's interest. Transfers continued until the mid-1980s, when they petered out, in part because Iran's failure to pay on time undermined the incentives of middlemen.

Allies to enemies

Israel adjusted to the loss of Iran as a partner. The Camp David peace agreement ended the threat of renewed Arab-Israeli war, which diminished the need for a periphery strategy and close relations with Iran. The Iran-Iraq War weakened both countries, in turn improving Israel's strategic environment. And Tehran's efforts to incite revolution and undermine secular Arab governments, except for Syria, distracted Israel's adversaries.

The 1988 cease-fire between Iran and Iraq removed any basis for secret engagement with Israel. The Soviet Union's demise in 1991 also ended Tehran's fear of a "smash and grab" attack aimed at the Khuzestan oilfields and a warm water port. The Islamic Republic's interests shifted to seducing Arab and Muslim public opinion, which meant an even harder line toward the Jewish state. Iran's realpolitik hostility toward Israel was reinforced by ideological and obsessive enmity. President Mahmoud Ahmadinejad is the most visible purveyor of anti-Semitic notions, but such beliefs have circulated among Iran's leadership since the revolution. Israel's support for the *ancien regime* inflamed these views. A confluence of strategic interest and religious rivalry has shaped Iran's severely negative attitude toward Israel.

Hezbollah

In 1982, Israel invaded Lebanon to destroy the PLO, sideline Syrian influence, and install a friendly Christian government in Beirut. Within days, Tehran deployed Revolutionary Guard Corps (IRGC) in eastern Lebanon to show support for their Shiite brethren. The IRGC never directly confronted Israeli troops. But Israel's prolonged occupation alienated the southern Shiites and opened the door for greater Iranian intervention.

Iran trained and equipped a small Shiite splinter group that evolved into a highly capable Hezbollah militia with a network of social services for Lebanon's largest sect. Hezbollah soon became Israel's deadliest threat, responsible for dozens of attacks against Israeli troops in Lebanon. By 2000, Israel decided its interests would be better served by withdrawing from Lebanon—marking the first voluntary Israeli withdrawal from occupied Arab territory without a peace treaty.

Proxy war

Tehran's role in Hezbollah's emergence as a serious regional foe put Iran on Israel's borders by proxy. In the decade following its 2000 withdrawal, Israel concluded that Iran was, in effect, at war. In 2002, the Israeli Navy seized the Karine A, a ship owned by the Palestinian Authority which had been loaded with a vast array of weapons, explosives and ammunition at Iran's Kish Island. Since the mid-1990s, Iran had been funding Palestinian Islamic Jihad and training Palestinians at the Dara Kazwin barracks outside Tehran. But a large arms shipment to the Palestinian Authority was a quantum leap.

During this period, Israel and the United States also tracked large Iranian arms shipments to Lebanon's Hezbollah via Syria. Hezbollah acknowledged these shipments as part of "resistance" against Israel. In 2006, Hezbollah guerrillas attacked an Israeli patrol along the border and seized two soldiers. A new Israeli government, eager to demonstrate resolve and convinced Hezbollah was acting as a tool of Iran, responded harshly. In the 34-day war, Israel's longest conflict, an Israeli ship was nearly sunk by an Iranian cruise missile and northern Israel was inundated by rockets supplied by Iran to Hezbollah. The war reinforced Israeli views that Lebanon had become Iran's frontline against it.

Nuclear threat

Iran's nuclear program intensified Israeli anxieties. In 2005, President Mahmoud Ahmadinejad's denial of the Holocaust and statements about Israel's disappearance added an apocalyptic dimension. The prospect of a nuclear-armed Iran was widely seen as an existential threat. Israeli Prime Minister Benjamin Netanyahu reportedly compared Iran to the Amalekites, whom the Bible says tried to exterminate the Israelites. Most Israelis do not believe that Iran would attack using nuclear weapons. Rather, they fear that a nuclear-armed Iran would be emboldened to take risky actions that could lead to war. Israelis also fear their best and brightest will emigrate, rather than live under an Iranian nuclear shadow.

In 2009, Israel appealed publicly—somewhat quixotically—to the Arab world to cooperate against Iran. Limited cooperation had already started, with the transit of Israeli submarines through the Suez Canal allegedly en route to the Persian Gulf. Reports of discussions between Israelis and Saudis in third countries also surfaced. Israel even staged a large-scale exercise over the Mediterranean Sea. The force deployments and flight profiles in this exercise closely resembled what would be required for a raid on Iranian nuclear facilities. In addition, the 2007 Israeli air raid that destroyed Syria's unfinished nuclear reactor was widely seen as a statement of Israel's intention to prevent the rise of a hostile nuclear power in the Middle East.

Prospects for conflict

Israel's position as of September 2010 was that Iran's nuclear program is a problem for the international community. Netanyahu has told numerous audiences that he expected the United States to block Iranian progress toward a threshold or weapons capability. Israelis have little confidence, however, that sanctions will suffice. Nevertheless, Israel's incentives to strike will vary with several factors:

- The effectiveness of sanctions and covert operations to hobble Iranian efforts
- A consensus that diplomatic efforts have been conclusively and irrecoverably exhausted
- Confidence that a strike would set back Iran's program by three to five years
- Assessment of the effect of a strike on U.S.-Israel relations
- Availability of an uncontested flight path to the target
- The quality of targeting data.

In the fall of 2010, there was no agreement on some of these factors, especially on the feasibility of an attack. The IDF Chief of Staff, Gen. Gabi Ashkenazi, openly shared his skepticism about Israel's ability to carry out a successful strike. Military action is not likely in the near term, given the pace of diplomacy, the lead time for sanctions to bite and ongoing talks between the United States and Israel on the way forward. The wild card is an outbreak of fighting with Hezbollah that leads to an Israeli attack against Iran. This scenario might happen, for example, if rockets supplied by Iran to Hezbollah killed a large number of Israeli civilians.

Factoids

In the heyday of Israel-Iran relations during the 1970s, Israel sold Iran about $500 million per year in weapons and planned to launch a $1 billion joint program to develop a surface-to-surface missile.

After the revolution, between 1980 and 1983, Israeli sales totaled an additional $500 million, including TOW anti-tank missiles, spare parts for armor and aircraft and large amounts of ammunition.

Hezbollah has approximately 45,000 rockets and anti-ship cruise missiles for use against Israel.

Iran provides significant financial aid to Hezbollah for military and non-military purposes. Estimates range from $25 million to more than $100 million per year. In 2010, the Pentagon speculated that Iran provided as much as $200 million annually to Hezbollah.

Israel is thought to have 200 nuclear warheads and an accurate intermediate range ballistic missile capability in the Jericho 2.

If Israel were to attack Iran, it could deploy over 100 long-range fighters and ground attack aircraft as well as the necessary refueling, reconnaissance, and combat search and rescue assets. Israel also has large stocks of JDAMS, the precision-guided bomb that was developed by the United States to attack the kind of facilities that Israel would target.

Iran has 45 SA-2 and 10 SA-5 high altitude surface-to-air missiles it could use to defend against an Israeli attack. Simulations suggest that these would be insufficient to foil an Israeli attack.

The future

- Iran and Israel will remain at odds for the foreseeable future, assuming that the current regime remains in power. As long as Iranian rhetoric stresses the disappearance of Israel while the regime pursues a nuclear capability, Israel will seek ways to reduce the implied threat to its existence or, less dramatically, its viability.

- Israel is capable of launching an attack against Iran's nuclear-related infrastructure but could not sustain an offensive or have high confidence in a successful outcome.

- In the past, Israel acted when its leaders believed they were isolated and the country's back was against the wall. Although these fears are again in the air, they have not yet gained sufficient traction to impel action. Concerted international pressure on Iran would probably stave off such concerns.

- Lebanon is a flashpoint for Israeli-Iranian conflict. A confrontation between Hezbollah and Israeli forces could escalate. As of September 2010, the parties seemed well aware of the danger and were careful to avoid provocative actions—or reactions.

Steven Simon is adjunct senior fellow for Middle Eastern Studies at the Council on Foreign Relations, adjunct professor of security studies at Georgetown University, and senior adviser at Good Harbor Consulting, LLC. He is coauthor of The Sixth Crisis: America, Israel, Iran and the Rumors of War *(2010).*

39

Iran and the Palestinians

Rachel Brandenburg

- After the 1979 revolution, Iran ended its alliance with Israel and started supporting the Palestinians, symbolized by turning over the Israeli embassy in Tehran to the Palestine Liberation Organization.

- As part of its campaign to export the revolution, the theocracy also aided emerging Palestinian Islamic groups, notably Islamic Jihad and Hamas. Both sent representatives to Tehran.

- Iran generally opposed the U.S.-backed Middle East peace process. During the 1997-2005 reform era, however, President Mohammad Khatami indicated that Tehran might accept any decision embraced by the Palestinian majority. But that sentiment was short-lived.

- Tehran has trained many Palestinian militants and provided a significant proportion of the weaponry used against Israel. For Shiite Iran, the Palestinian groups are among its most important Sunni allies.

Overview

Between Israel's birth in 1948 and Iran's revolution in 1979, the two countries had close relations based on common strategic interests, particularly as the two non-Arab countries in the Middle East. Iran became an important source of oil for Israel, and Israel became an important source of weapons for Iran. Thousands of Israeli businessmen and technical experts aided Iranian development projects. But after the shah's ouster, relations deteriorated and envoys went home. Israel remained a source of Western arms during the early years of Iran's 1980-1988 war with Iraq. But by the mid-1980s, even commercial ties had ended.

Tehran's new theocrats refused to recognize Israel as a state or even use its name, instead calling it the "Zionist entity" or the "Little Satan." Leftists opposed Israel because of anti-imperialist sentiment and its relationship with the United States. The religious right viewed Israel as an illegitimate occupier of Muslim land and a threat to Islam and Islamic justice. Shortly after the revolution, Ayatollah Ruhollah Khomeini designated the last Friday of Ramadan as a new national holiday—Qods Day, or Jerusalem Day—to "proclaim the international solidarity of Muslims in support of the legitimate rights of the Muslim people of Palestine." Qods Day is honored across the Muslim world.

During the revolution's first decade, Iran's primary focus in the Arab-Israeli conflict was aiding and arming its Shiite brethren in Lebanon's new Hezbollah. But Tehran's involvement with the Sunni Palestinians deepened progressively with three major turning points: The Palestinian Liberation Organization's call for peace talks with Israel in 1988, the second *intifada*—or uprising—in 2000, and the election of Hamas in 2006.

The PLO

During the monarchy, the Palestinian Liberation Organization (PLO) had close ties with the Iranian opposition. Many Iranian dissidents trained at PLO camps in Lebanon in the 1970s. The PLO also backed the 1979 revolution. Days after the revolution, PLO chief Yasser Arafat led a 58-member delegation to Tehran. Prime Minister Mehdi Bazargan hosted the official welcome ceremony, where the keys to the former Israeli embassy were handed over to the PLO. The road in front of the mission was renamed Palestine Street. Arafat traveled throughout Iran to set up PLO offices, which members of his delegation stayed to manage for more than one year.

Khomeini did not welcome Arafat with open arms, however. During their two-hour meeting on Feb. 18, 1979, the ayatollah criticized the PLO for its nationalist and pan-Arab agenda. He appealed to Arafat to model the

PLO on the principles of the Islamic revolution. Arafat was an observant Muslim, but he rebuffed Khomeini. Arafat and Khomeini never met again.

Relations between Iran and the PLO eroded further when Arafat joined the Arab world in supporting Iraq during its 1980-1988 war with Iran. In 1988, Tehran also condemned Arafat after he recognized Israel's right to exist, renounced terrorism, called for peace talks with Israel and began a dialogue with the United States. Iran's new Supreme Leader Ayatollah Ali Khamenei denounced the PLO chief as a "traitor and an idiot" in 1989. Arafat did not visit Iran again until 1997, when Tehran hosted the Organization of the Islamic Conference. The PLO maintained a diplomatic presence in Tehran, but Iran did not actively aid the PLO again until 2000.

Intifada and Karine A

The second Palestinian intifada, or uprising, erupted in September 2000 after the collapse of Middle East peace talks at Camp David and Ariel Sharon's visit to Jerusalem's Temple Mount, or Haram al Sharif in Arabic, home of the Al Aqsa Mosque, the third holiest site in Islam. To support the uprising and heighten pressure on Israel, Arafat released Hamas and Islamic Jihad militants held by the Palestinian Authority. Iran lauded Arafat and his Fatah party for their resistance. In 2001, Iran hosted a second "Support for the Palestinian intifada" conference, attended by Palestinian parliamentarians and representatives from Hezbollah, Hamas and Islamic Jihad. Ayatollah Khamenei praised the intifada for restoring Palestinian unity.

Iran's renewed support for Arafat's Palestinian Authority was evident when Israel captured the Karine A, a ship reportedly destined for Gaza, in 2002. The ship carried 50 tons of advanced weaponry—including Katyusha rockets, rifles, mortar shells, mines, and anti-tank missiles—that had been loaded in Iranian waters. It was interdicted by an Israeli commando raid in the Red Sea. Arafat denied any involvement; the arms were a clear violation of Palestinian-Israeli agreements. But Israel interpreted the shipment as a sign of Iran's renewed support for the PLO resistance.

Islamic Jihad

Islamic Jihad (PIJ) is the smallest but most violent Palestinian group—and long the closest to Iran. The underground movement was founded by Fathi Shikaki, a young physician and Gaza refugee, in the late 1970s as an offshoot of Egypt's Muslim Brotherhood. PIJ endorsed the Iranian revolution. Shikaki shared Khomeini's belief that "Islam was the solution and Jihad was the proper means." The Sunni Muslim group also adopted the suicide tactics used mainly by Shiite militants, justified as martyrdom for the greater cause. Since 1989, it has carried out more than a dozen major suicide attacks against Israeli targets. Unlike other Arab and Sunni groups, Islamic Jihad supported Shiite Iran during its long war with Iraq.

The group's leadership was forced out of Gaza in 1988, first to Lebanon, then to Syria, where it is now based. Ramadan Abdallah Shallah became secretary general after Shikaki's assassination in 1995. He has met frequently with Iranian officials both in Tehran and Damascus, often in meetings with other major Palestinian militant groups. Shallah reportedly attended a meeting in Tehran in 1996, when he coordinated with the Qods Force, an elite wing of the Revolutionary Guards that handles Iran's foreign operations. PIJ maintains a representative in Iran. Iran has armed, trained and funded PIJ, although its aid is reportedly modest compared with support for Hamas or Lebanon's Hezbollah.

Hamas

Hamas, an acronym in Arabic for "Islamic resistance movement," emerged out of the first Palestinian intifada, or uprising, in 1987. It was co-founded by Sheikh Ahmed Yassin and six others, originally as a local offshoot of Egypt's Muslim Brotherhood. Hamas and Iran both wanted to see Israel replaced by the Islamic state of Palestine. Yet Hamas initially had little connection to Iran due to sectarian differences, Tehran's ties to Islamic Jihad, and the Hamas desire to be an independent resistance movement.

Relations between Iran and Hamas developed after the PLO called for making peace with Israel. In 1990, Tehran hosted a conference on support for Palestine, which Hamas attended but Arafat did not. In the early 1990s, a Hamas delegation led by Mousa Abu Marzouk held talks Tehran with key officials, including Ayatollah Khamenei. Iran pledged military and financial support—reportedly $30 million annually—as well as advanced military training for thousands of Hamas activists at Revolutionary Guard bases in Iran and Lebanon. Hamas also opened an office in Tehran and declared that Iran and Hamas shared an "identical view in the strategic outlook toward the Palestinian cause in its Islamic dimension."

Tehran continued support for Hamas throughout the intifada. Aid steadily increased after Arafat's death in 2004 and Israel's withdrawal from Gaza in 2005. But Hamas's surprise victory in the 2006 Palestinian elections dramatically transformed its relations with Iran. Tehran stepped in to rescue the nearly bankrupt Palestinian Authority in Gaza, now under Hamas control, after foreign aid dried up. When Hamas Prime Minister Ismail Haniyeh visited Tehran in December 2006, Iran reportedly pledged $250 million in aid.

Iran reportedly provided military aid and training for dozens of men in Hamas's military wing, the Izz ad-Din al Qassam Brigades. Iran also allegedly supplied much of the military equipment that Hamas used against Israel in the December 2008 Gaza war. Hamas leader Khaled Mashaal visited Tehran in February 2009, after the war ended, to thank Iran for its help during the conflict, citing Iran as a "partner in victory."

Palestinian Authority

The ebb and flow of relations between Iran and the many Palestinian factions often correlated with the status of peace efforts. After the U.S.-orchestrated peace process resumed in Washington in 2010, President Mahmoud Ahmadinejad told a rally in Tehran that talks were doomed to fail. He also lambasted Palestinian President Mahmoud Abbas, calling him a hostage of Israel. Abbas, who was Arafat's successor, shot back.

In a pointed reference to Ahmadinejad's disputed win in 2009 elections, Abbas spokesman Nabil Abu Rudeineh said, "He who does not represent the Iranian people, who forged elections and who suppresses the Iranian people and stole the authority is not entitled to talk about Palestine, or the president of Palestine. We have fought for Palestine and Jerusalem. And the Palestinian leadership has provided thousands of martyrs and tens of thousands wounded and prisoners [and] did not repress their people, as did the system of Iran led by Ahmadinejad."

Middle East peace process

Iranian politicians all condemn Israel, and the regime has opposed the peace process since the 1993 Oslo Accords launched sporadic diplomacy. But the language of the leaders has varied, albeit slightly.

Ayatollah Khomeini: In 1981, he said, "To liberate Qods [Jerusalem], Muslims should use faith-dependent machine guns and the power of Islam and keep away from political games which reek of compromise. . . . Muslim nations, especially the Palestinian and Lebanese nations, should punish those who waste time indulging in political maneuvers."

Former **President Akbar Hashemi Rafsanjani:** In 2005, he said, "We want all the Palestinians back in their homeland, and then there can be a fair referendum for people to choose the form of state they want. Whoever gets the majority can rule."

Former **President Khatami:** In 1998, he said, "The root of tension in the region is the Zionist regime." He also said, Iran "morally and logically" does not recognize Israel but would not interfere in the Israeli-Palestinian peace process.

President Mahmoud Ahmadinejad: In September 2010, he told a Qods Day rally in Tehran, "Who gave them [Mahmoud Abbas's negotiating team] the right to sell a piece of Palestinian land? The people of Palestine and the people of the region will not allow them to sell even an inch of Palestinian soil to the enemy. The negotiations are stillborn and doomed."

Supreme Leader Ayatollah Ali Khamenei called Israel a "cancerous tumor" and urged Palestinians to unite and model their resistance against Israel on Hezbollah. In 2005, he said, "Palestine belongs to the Palestinians, and the fate of Palestine should be determined by the Palestinian people."

Iran's Palestinian allies

Ramadan Abdallah Shallah: Islamic Jihad secretary general and British-educated economist who briefly taught at the University of South Florida and took over after Shikaki was assassinated in 1995. "Our ties with Iran date back to the first days of our movement, just after the Islamic revolution took over in Iran," he once said. Shallah is also on the FBI's most wanted terrorist list.

Khalid Mashaal: Hamas leader based in Damascus. After the 2006 Hamas victory, Mashaal visited Tehran and said, "Just as Islamic Iran defends the rights of the Palestinians, we defend the rights of Islamic Iran. We are part of a united front against the enemies of Islam."

Ismail Haniyeh: Hamas leader who became prime minister of the Gaza half of the Palestinian Authority after Hamas's 2006 election victory. Later that year he visited Tehran, where he told a Friday prayer service, "The world arrogance (US) and Zionists ... want us to recognize the usurpation of the Palestinian lands and stop jihad and resistance and accept the agreements reached with the Zionist enemies in the past. . . .We will never recognize the usurper Zionist government and will continue our jihad-like movement until the liberation of Jerusalem."

Sheikh Ahmed Yassin: Hamas co-founder and spiritual guide. The quadriplegic cleric was hosted by Supreme Leader Ayatollah Ali Khamenei and President Mohammad Khatami during a 1998 visit to Tehran. After meeting the sheikh, Ayatollah Khamenei said, "The Palestinian nation's jihad is a source of honor for Islam and Muslims. . . .God's promises will undoubtedly come true, and the Islamic land of Palestine will someday witness the annihilation of the usurper Zionist rule." He died in an Israeli helicopter gunship attack in 2004.

The future

- For the foreseeable future, Iran will have the means to play primary spoiler in the Middle East peace process through its proxies in Hamas, Islamic Jihad and Hezbollah.

- As long as it has substantial financial and military support from Iran, Hamas can in turn refuse to work with Fatah and other parties to form a single Palestinian government in the West Bank and Gaza. The split between the two halves of the Palestinian Authority seriously complicates peace efforts since only two of the three parties to the conflict have been negotiating.

Rachel Brandenburg was a Middle East program specialist at USIP.

40

Iran and Syria

Jubin Goodarzi

- Since 1979, the alliance between Syria and Iran has had significant impact in both shaping Middle East politics and thwarting the regional goals of the United States, Israel and Iraq.

- Syria and Iran are the two parties most responsible for spoiling U.S.-backed peace efforts between the Arabs and Israel in order to promote their own Arab and Islamic interests. For the United States, they were also the most troublesome countries during the U.S. intervention in Iraq because they aided, abetted or armed insurgents.

- The two regimes share common traits. They are both authoritarian and defiantly independent, even at a political or economic cost. Iran is predominantly Shiite. Although Syria is predominantly Sunni Muslim, its ruling family is Alawite, a Shiite sect.

- At the same time, they are odd political bedfellows. Syria's Baathist ideology is strictly secular and socialist. Iran's ideology is rigidly religious and, in principle, opposed to atheist communism and its offshoots. Yet their common strategic goals have held the alliance together for three decades, despite repeated attempts to rend them apart.

Overview

The Iran-Syria alliance grew out of common cause—and common enemies. Since Iran's 1979 revolution, the two regional powerhouses have pooled political leverage and military resources to enhance their position, build a network of surrogate militias and frustrate the plans of opponents. Together they ensured Saddam Hussein's Iraq, which bordered both countries, would not become the predominant regional power. They forced U.S. peacekeepers out of Lebanon in 1984 and thwarted Israel's effort to bring Lebanon into its orbit during an 18-year occupation that finally ended in Israel's unilateral withdrawal in 2000. The odd bedfellows together sired or supported Hezbollah, Hamas, Palestinian Islamic Jihad and an array of radical Palestinian groups. All reject peace. And together they have inflicted repeated setbacks on six American presidents.

The alliance also reflects a common need. Together the regimes stand a better chance at survival—without having to accommodate either domestic or foreign demands for change—than they would without each other. Together they also stand a better chance of achieving their long-term goals. Syria wants to regain the strategic Golan Heights, lost to Israel in the 1967 War, and keep its veto power over Lebanese politics. Iran wants to be the preeminent regional player in the Persian Gulf and ensure its allies rule in Iraq. Both also want to protect Arab interests (in the case of Damascus) and Islamic interests (in the case of Iran) throughout the region.

The six phases

Relations between Iran and Syria have gone through six distinct phases.

Phase 1: The new alliance, 1979-82

Syria was the first Arab country to recognize the provisional government of Prime Minister Mehdi Bazargan after the shah's ouster, and third overall, after the Soviet Union and Pakistan. Damascus provided invaluable diplomatic and military support to Tehran after Iraq's 1980 invasion of Iran. The alliance was formalized in March 1982 when a high-level Syrian delegation, headed by then Foreign Minister Abd al-Halim Khaddam visited Tehran and concluded a series of bilateral agreements on oil and trade, and a secret pact on military matters.

Phase 2: The zenith of Syrian-Iranian power, 1982-85

The high point of bilateral cooperation was in the Levant. After Israel's 1982 invasion of Lebanon and rout of Syrian forces there, Syrian President Hafez Assad enlisted Iran's influence among the Lebanese Shiites to wage a campaign of subversion, terror and guerrilla warfare against their mutual opponents in Lebanon—the Christian-dominated government, Israeli occupation forces and the U.S. and French peacekeeping forces. Together they orchestrated a series of devastating blows: President Bashir Gemayel was assassinated in September 1982. Israeli military headquarters in Tyre were bombed in November 1982. The first modern Muslim suicide bombers hit the U.S. Embassy in west Beirut in April 1983. The barracks of U.S. Marine and French contingents of the Multinational Force were bombed within minutes of each other in October 1983. Israeli headquarters in south Lebanon were again bombed in November 1983. And a second U.S. Embassy was bombed in east Beirut in September 1984. Unable to fulfill its mission, U.S. forces withdrew in early 1984. The 1983 Israeli-Lebanese peace treaty was scrapped. And Israel began a partial withdrawal of its troops from most of the territory it initially seized in 1985.

Phase 3: Alliance tensions and consolidation of the axis, 1985-88

The late 1980s marked the most problematic phase of the Syria-Iran partnership. The Lebanese civil war and the Iran-Iraq War drained their resources and undermined the clout of the Damascus-Tehran nexus. Iran and Syria also developed conflicting agendas in Lebanon, particularly in picking their Shiite allies. Syria backed Amal, the political party and militia that was the longstanding representative of Lebanon's Shiites. Damascus backed a secular and multi-confessional state that fell within its sphere of influence. Iran backed Hezbollah, the underground extremist movement. Iran favored greater power for Lebanon's Muslim majority, particularly Shiites, the largest of the country's 17 recognized sects.

Their rival visions played out on the ground. The Syrians backed the Amal-led siege of Palestinian refugee camps between 1985 and 1987, much to Iran's dismay. Iran tried to mediate a peaceful end to the confrontation. Tehran and Damascus eventually reached an understanding on key issues: Syrian interests took precedence in the Levant, while Damascus would defer to Tehran in the Gulf.

Phase 4: Containment of Saddam Hussein's Iraq, 1988-1991

Cooperation focused on checking Iraqi power and crushing President Michel Aoun's anti-Syrian revolt in Lebanon in 1988-1989. During the 1990-1991 Gulf War against Iraq, Syria contributed troops to the U.S.-led coalition, and Iran remained neutral. Damascus hoped to reap the benefits of having its agenda included in subsequent Middle East peace efforts, while Iran did not try to check the growing U.S. military presence, in hopes it would ultimately weaken Baghdad's power in the region.

Phase 5: Alliance cooperation in the post-Cold War period, 1991-2003

As the Cold War ended and the United States became the world's dominant power, Tehran and Damascus grew increasingly important to each other. They cooperated in development of ballistic missiles. They collaborated in arming and abetting Hezbollah and Hamas to pressure Israel, as well as to influence events in Lebanon and the Palestinian Authority. Their aid was instrumental in enabling Hezbollah to wage a guerrilla campaign throughout the 1990s against Israel, which opted to withdraw in 2000.

Both Syria and Iran flirted with the United States during this phase. Damascus participated in sporadic U.S. peace efforts. And under reformist President Mohammed Khatami in the late 1990s, Tehran proposed bringing down the "wall of mistrust." But neither effort produced any progress.

Phase 6: Reinvigoration of the alliance after the 2003 Iraq war

Cooperation between Iran and Syria increased markedly after the U.S.-led invasion of Iraq in 2003. Both countries welcomed the ouster of Saddam Hussein, their mutual foe. But the speed of the U.S. military victory also initially raised fears that either Iran or Syria might be the next target in the Bush administration's "War on Terror." Both provided significant aid to an array of domestic and foreign forces in Iraq, challenging the U.S. military and the new government in Baghdad.

Their roles in Iraq evolved, especially after the Obama administration announced plans to withdraw. Tehran cultivated ties with major Iraqi political parties and militias, particularly the Shiites, to ensure Baghdad would not again become hostile. And Damascus sporadically limited the flow of insurgents across its border. Neither country wanted Iraq to plunge into anarchy or civil war. But nor did either want U.S. allies in political control of Baghdad.

The balance of power

The balance of power in the Syrian-Iranian alliance has shifted since 1979. Syria was the dominant partner in the 1980s. Iran is the stronger partner today.

From 1976 to 2005, Syria was the more dominant player in Lebanon due to its military presence. But its leverage weakened after Damascus was forced to pull out troops in 2005. Hezbollah, the pro-Iranian party and militia, has since become the most influential ally in Lebanese politics. During the 1980s, Syria's regional role was also magnified when Egypt was banished from the Arab fold after the 1979 Camp David Accords. And both Iraq and Iran were weakened by their costly eight-year conflict. Syria enjoyed the political, military and economic patronage of the Soviet Union until its dissolution in 1991.

The balance of power between the two shifted in part because of arms. Syria was a conduit for arms shipments to Iran during the Iran-Iraq conflict. This was particularly important after Iran's relations with Moscow deteriorated in 1982 and Washington orchestrated a widespread arms embargo in 1983. Iran responded by developing its own arms industry in the 1980s, and in the 1990s it had the lead role in joint efforts with Syria to develop ballistic missile capabilities. Iran now exports arms to Syria and helps finance Syrian arms purchases from Russia, Belarus, North Korea and elsewhere.

Iran needed the alliance with Syria during the 1980s to prevent becoming isolated in the Middle East. But after Iraq's invasion of Kuwait, Iran mended fences with many Arab countries. Despite its uneasy relations with key Arab governments, Iran is more popular on the Arab street. Its position has been enhanced by its posturing on the nuclear issue, relatively high oil prices, and the backlash against U.S. forces in Iraq and Afghanistan.

An enduring marriage

The Syria-Iran alliance has survived in part because it has been primarily defensive in nature. For three decades, it has been aimed largely at neutralizing Iraqi and Israeli capabilities and preventing American encroachment in the Middle East. Defensive alliances which have fixed and limited objectives are often more durable.

Their distinctive ideological differences, ironically, have also helped the relationship endure. Syria and Iraq were intense political rivals, and often came close to military blows, because they shared the same Ba'athist ideology. The political elites in Tehran and Damascus were never competing.

Their respective agendas also have jived: Iran has vied for leadership of the Islamist bloc in the Middle East and beyond, a role in which secular Syria has no interest. Syria has long sought to be "the beating heart of Arabism," a role in which Iran, a non-Arab country, has no interest. Except for a brief period of rival ambitions in Lebanon, the two countries have never been in competition—ideologically, economically or militarily. Neither has tried to upstage the other.

The future

- Despite multiple attempts to wean Syria from Iran, the alliance between Tehran and Damascus remains strong. It would take a major catalyst—such as progress in the Arab-Israeli peace process that addresses Syria's demands—to seriously undermine their cooperation.

- In part by default, Iran and Syria still have strong influence in the region for several reasons: Their militia allies have become major political players, particularly in Lebanon and the Palestinian Authority. Mideast peace efforts have not produced major new pacts since the mid-1990s. And U.S. attention has been focused elsewhere.

Jubin Goodarzi, a professor of international relations at Webster University, Geneva, Switzerland, is author of Syria and Iran: Diplomatic Alliance and Power Politics in the Middle East.

41

Iran and Lebanon

Emile Hokayem

- Iran's 1979 revolution transformed relations with Lebanon and politics within Lebanon, especially after Tehran sired Hezbollah in 1982.

- Iran now considers Hezbollah its primary Lebanese interlocutor, followed by the Shiite community, and only then the state.

- Iran has poured billions of dollars and tons of increasingly sophisticated weaponry into Hezbollah, the most successful example of the theocracy's campaign to export its revolutionary ideals.

- Hezbollah, the Party of God, is an extension of Iran's foreign policy and an instrument of its security policy, especially against the United States and Israel. Yet it also has its own Lebanese and regional agenda and is no longer just an obedient proxy of Iran.

- Iran's use of Lebanon and Hezbollah to challenge Israel, often at great cost, has spawned widespread anger and suspicion among many other Lebanese parties and religious sects. Lebanese views of Iran reflect the country's political and sectarian fault-lines.

Overview

Iran has long had ties to Lebanon through its Shiite community, the largest of Lebanon's 18 recognized sects. Many Lebanese clerics came from Iran, trained under Iranians, or had strong Iranian connections. The first leader to mobilize Lebanon's Shiite community was Musa al-Sadr, an Iranian-born cleric from a prominent family of Lebanese theologians. He trained in Iran's holy city of Qom. In 1974, he founded the Movement of the Disinherited to aid Lebanon's Shiites. It formed an armed wing called Amal during Lebanon's civil war. Sadr disappeared on a trip to Libya in 1978, but Amal remains one of Lebanon's two major Shiite parties.

Iranian-Lebanese relations were transformed after Tehran fostered the birth of Hezbollah in 1982. Iran's operational and financial support shaped Hezbollah into a powerful militia and an important deterrent against Israel. The Lebanese Shiite militia's symbolic and strategic successes against Israel have in turn made Iran a pivotal player in Levantine politics and broadened Iran's appeal generally in the Arab world. Over the years, Hezbollah has also provided support for Iran's external operations. Hezbollah is now a full-fledged partner in a rejectionist front including Iran, Syria and militant Palestinian factions opposed to peace with Israel.

Hezbollah's political ascendance as the second major Shiite party is due to its advocacy of Shiite rights, its social services and political patronage and its resistance against Israel. Its activism over time translated into cross-confessional appeal and even an alliance with a Christian party. Yet Hezbollah's ties to Iran have upset Lebanon's fragile political balance and heightened sectarian tensions.

Early connections

Iranian-Lebanese relations predate the establishment of modern Lebanon. In the 16th century, the Safavid dynasty recruited Shiite clerics from Jabal Amel, a region of south Lebanon, to help spread Shiism as a state religion. Clerical and family exchanges flourished as a consequence. Later, the growth of Beirut as a major Middle East commercial and cultural center attracted Iranian elites. Two of the last shah's prime ministers were schooled there.

In the second half of the 20th century, Iranian opponents of the monarchy also found refuge in Lebanon. Some were active in Lebanese politics and even trained in Palestinian camps before and during the Lebanese civil war.

Hezbollah's birth

The 1982 Israeli invasion of Lebanon provided Iran with an opportunity to deepen its engagement among Lebanon's Shiites and export the ideology of revolutionary leader Ayatollah Ruhollah Khomeini. At war with Iraq and isolated by many Arab governments, Iran was looking for a way to open a new front.

Iran's intervention was spearheaded by some 1,500 Revolutionary Guards deployed in Lebanon's eastern Bekaa Valley. They helped create, arm and fund a shadowy organization that initially went under disparate names and later became Hezbollah, or the Party of God. In 1983 and 1984, its militants bombed two American embassies as well as U.S. and French peacekeeping troops for meddling in Lebanon and siding with Lebanon's Christian-dominated government. In 1982, following the disappearance of four Iranian diplomats in Lebanon, the precursor to Hezbollah also launched a campaign of kidnappings. Among the nearly 90 Western hostages was American University of Beirut President David Dodge, who was abducted in Beirut and held for one year in Iran.

Hezbollah also inflicted severe blows on Israeli occupation forces in Lebanon. Suicide bombers regularly attacked Israeli headquarters and military posts. In 1985, Israel withdrew from most of Lebanese territory it occupied except for a "security zone" in the south. Hezbollah is now unquestionably the foremost Shiite party.

Iran's influence

It is tempting to infer from arms and financial flows that Iran determines Hezbollah's behavior. By arming Hezbollah with sophisticated weaponry, Iran has built a powerful force to deter Israel and to hit Israeli targets in the event of another regional conflict. Hezbollah's arsenal reportedly includes some 40,000 rockets and missiles, including the mid-range Zelzal 1 and Zelzal 2 with a range of 95 miles to 130 miles, and a variant of the Fateh 110 with a range of 155 miles.

In return, the Party of God movement has supplied operatives and logistics when requested, providing Tehran with deniability. Argentine prosecutors have charged Hezbollah and Iran in the 1994 bombing of a Jewish community center in Buenos Aires. The Party of God has allegedly helped Iraqi Shiite militias allied with Iran as well. At least one Hezbollah operative was picked up by U.S. forces in Iraq.

Yet support for Hezbollah does not necessarily translate into allegiance to or unequivocal support for Iran. Lebanese Shiites appreciate Iran's support in forcing Israel's withdrawal. But they hold widely diverse views about Iran as a political model; many have concerns about its long-term intentions. Hezbollah's power also relies on its standing at home and regional image, both of which have suffered from appearing to be a mere proxy of Iran.

As a conventional political party, Hezbollah has to work with dozens of other political parties and organizations. As a welfare agency with tens of thousands of clients, it has to deal with other Lebanese sects. And as a militia, it has to consider the regional balance of power when engaging in resistance. So its relationship with Iran is dynamic rather than unidirectional, with Hezbollah also informing and influencing Iranian policy.

The Lebanese state

Iran is obligated under U.N. resolutions to end arms transfers to Hezbollah and to respect Lebanese sovereignty. But given Hezbollah's political and military power, the weak state of Lebanon has ambiguous relations with Tehran. When the Beirut government is antagonistic toward Hezbollah, as happened between 2005 and 2009, Iran adopts a distance. When the government accommodates Hezbollah, as in 2009 and 2010, Iran warms up.

In mid-2010, Hezbollah's leader suggested that Iran could arm the Lebanese military. Iran's defense minister responded that "Lebanon is a friend, and its army is our friend […] We are prepared to help them should there be a request."

The Syrian factor

Iran-Hezbollah relations have always had to factor in Syria. As the geographic link to Lebanon, Damascus leveraged Iran's quest for influence in Lebanon to enhance its own power and position. But Syria also often limited Iran's role for two reasons: First, in order to maintain paramount Syrian control over Lebanon. And second, to preserve its relations with Western and Arab countries.

During its early years, Hezbollah had testy interactions with Damascus, which disliked its revolutionary and fundamentalist agenda. Syria also favored other, more pliable Shiite groups such as Amal. Yet Hezbollah operated in areas under Syrian control. And for isolated Iran, the alliance with Syria remained a priority. So the military and political balance of power tilted in Damascus's favor. The one target all three could agree on was targeting Israeli forces in Lebanon.

In the early 1990s, Syria began a rapprochement with the United States and participated in international peace talks with Israel. But to preserve leverage over Israel, Syria imposed a Lebanese consensus to allow Hezbollah to remain armed. In exchange, Hezbollah downgraded the Islamist facets of its political program, abandoned revolutionary rhetoric, entered Lebanese political life and abided by Syrian edicts. An inward-looking Iran seeking regional détente facilitated this evolution.

Throughout the 1990s, with Iranian weaponry and Syrian guidance, Hezbollah grew into an increasingly competent guerilla force. Twice, in 1993 and 1996, it resisted Israeli onslaughts, gradually changing the balance of power by elevating the human cost for Israel. Israel finally withdrew from southern Lebanon in 2000, the first time it pulled out of Arab territory unilaterally and without a peace treaty. As Hezbollah's power reached new heights, however, it also faced growing questions at home and in the region about its weapons and the value of continued resistance. Iran officially remained committed to aiding and abetting the Party of God, but public enthusiasm appeared to wane.

Hezbollah challenges

In 2005, Lebanon's political landscape underwent rapid and profound changes. Hezbollah was both an instigator and a casualty. The assassination of former Lebanese Prime Minister Rafik Hariri triggered mass protests demanding that Syria end its 29-year military occupation of Lebanon. The Syrian withdrawal in turn allowed for massive public debate over Hezbollah's armed status. The Party of God also faced new pressure from other Lebanese sects for its ties to Iran. Hezbollah responded by raising its profile as a political champion of the Shiite community. Although it had been in parliament since 1992, it joined the government and took cabinet positions for the first time.

Hezbollah faced a second challenge in July 2006, when again it was both instigator and casualty. It launched a daring raid into Israel to capture Israeli soldiers to exchange for long-held Lebanese prisoners. The gambit backfired, instead igniting a massive Israeli retaliation. Hezbollah demonstrated considerable military prowess, checking Israeli ground forces while showering rockets onto northern Israel without interruption. But the 34-day war also produced billions in damages, mainly in Lebanese civilian areas, and serious loss of Hezbollah military forces.

Despite its losses, the 2006 summer war provided a political boost for Hezbollah at home and in the region. The militia's self-declared "divine victory" restored some of its image by fighting Israel for over one a month. Iran benefited by association and as Hezbollah's political patron and arms supplier. Hezbollah illustrated the viability of the strategy of confrontation preached by the hardline government of President Mahmoud Ahmadinejad. Iran supplied vast sums of money to help Hezbollah allay Shiite suffering after the war. Iranian engineers worked with the Jihad al-Binaa, Hezbollah's construction arm, to rebuild homes and infrastructure. Iran reportedly also helped rebuild Hezbollah's military infrastructure.

Notables in Lebanon-Iran relations

Hassan Nasrallah is Hezbollah's secretary general. A charismatic leader who took over the movement in 1992, he is widely admired in the Arab world and more popular than any Iranian leader.

Musa al-Sadr was the Qom-trained scion of a prominent Lebanese clerical family that moved to Tehran. Al-Sadr, the architect of the awakening of Lebanon's then-disenfranchised Shiite community, disappeared before the Iranian revolution. His mobilization of the Shiite sect paved the way for greater Iranian political, social and military presence in Lebanon.

Imad Mughniyah was the former Hezbollah security chief who collaborated with Iranian security. The closeness of Iranian-Hezbollah ties was evident by the large presence of Iranian security personnel at his funeral after he was killed in a car bombing in Damascus in 2008.

Grand Ayatollah Mohammad Hussein Fadlallah captured the complex nature of Lebanese Shiite-Iranian relations. Fadlallah, long the senior Lebanese Shiite cleric with a following worldwide, was once a spiritual reference for Hezbollah militants. Yet he openly contested the Iranian concept of *velayet-e faqih,* the basis of rule by a supreme religious leader. He often clashed theologically and politically with Iran and Hezbollah. He also ran a social services network that catered to the same Shiite constituency. His passing in 2010 left the field open for greater Iranian clerical influence.

The future

- Hezbollah is valuable to Iran, but Iranians have also begun to grumble about the financial and political costs of supporting the Lebanese militia. Hezbollah's fate now depends more on Lebanese politics and tensions with Israel than on Iran.

- Hezbollah will be a major component in any conflict involving Iran. Yet its participation may not be automatic. Hezbollah will weigh domestic considerations, including a war's impact on the Shiite community.

- Peace between Israel, Lebanon and Syria will require Hezbollah's transformation into a peaceful political party. Yet this will require Iranian acquiescence, which seems unlikely outside some form of U.S.-Iranian rapprochement.

Emile Hokayem is the senior fellow for regional security at the International Institute for Strategic Studies.

42

Iran and China

John S. Park

- Iran is a linchpin in China's regional energy security strategy. Iran has a strategic commodity essential to China's primary goal—sustainable economic development. The more China grows, the less it acts like a responsible stakeholder due to its energy needs.

- Iran has focused on rebuilding its refinery capabilities, hedging against U.S.-led sanctions and advancing its nuclear energy capabilities. China plays an important role as a major commercial and political partner.

- An unintended consequence of U.S.-led sanctions is more opportunity for Iran and China to cooperate. For China, fewer European and Asian investors means less competition for its companies in Iran and more access to Iranian energy. For Iran, China provides a coping mechanism amid international efforts to squeeze Tehran.

- Deepening symbiotic relations raise the prospect of a nuclear Iran and a less responsible Chinese stakeholder. Beijing's economic priorities will make it less able to substantively support global attempts to halt Iran's nuclear program.

Overview

Iran and China established diplomatic relations in 1971, but trade started in 1950. Since 1982, Sino-Iranian economic and technological cooperation has progressed significantly. In 1985, they set up the Joint Committee on Cooperation of Economy, Trade, Science and Technology to collaborate on energy, machinery, transportation, building material, mining, chemicals and nonferrous metal.

The symbiotic Iran-China relationship dates to the early 1990s, when Beijing became a major oil importer. As Chinese economic growth accelerated, Beijing's energy needs increasingly defined its political ties with Tehran. By 2009, Iran provided 11 percent of China's oil imports, ranking third after Saudi Arabia and Angola, according to Chinese customs data.

Trade between Iran and China soared from $4 billion in 2003 to over $20 billion in 2009, according to the International Monetary Fund. China's major exports to Iran have been machinery and equipment, textiles, chemical products and consumer goods. A significant portion of Chinese shipments has reportedly been funneled to Iran through China's trade with the United Arab Emirates. China has also been selling refined gasoline to Iran, which lacks the refineries to meet its domestic needs.

Strategic implications

Growing commercial ties have significant strategic implications, with Beijing reaping the larger immediate benefits. China's engine of economic growth is relatively well developed and maintained by a leadership group dominated by able technocrats. China, with a population of 1.3 billion, is increasing the living standards of more of its citizens each year. Iranian oil helps keep this engine running. In contrast, Iran's economy has contracted as a result of ineffective government policies. Sanctions have compounded—but not caused—this economic decline.

Iran's economic difficulties—including an acute shortage of refined gasoline capabilities—have created unique opportunities for China. Beijing's noninterventionist foreign policy principle enables it to pursue a commercial policy that has no linkage to human rights or nuclear proliferation. So the Iranian nuclear issue has not affected commercial Sino-Iranian relations, despite Tehran's widely suspected weapons development activities. China's support of the fourth round of U.N. sanctions on Iran in June 2010 has not halted Chinese firms' commercial activities with Tehran. Beijing says these commercial interactions are not related to Iran's nuclear program. This trend is unlikely to change, despite new unilateral U.S.-led sanctions announced in August 2010 to penalize some foreign firms doing business with Iran.

Chinese investment in Iran will alleviate some of Iran's economic difficulties, but it will not reverse years of Tehran's economic mismanagement. The longer Iran's own engine of economic growth remains dysfunctional, the greater the likelihood of internal political instability in an Islamic Republic of approximately 74 million. For China, that would constitute a direct threat to its energy security.

Turning points

Sino-Iranian relations have been defined by three issues:

First: China's political shift

Premier Deng Xiaoping's introduction of economic reforms in 1979 set the stage for a major transformation of China. Deng's changes in the legal and political foundation of China's economy gradually unleashed the Chinese people's march toward a xiaokang ("well-being") society, where the majority of the population has joined the ranks of the middle class through economic development. Deng promoted slogans like "To be rich is glorious" and "It doesn't matter if a cat is black or white, so long as it catches mice" to motivate his compatriots to use capitalist means to achieve socialist goals.

After major setbacks following Tiananmen Square in 1989, Chinese economic development began to gain momentum again in the early 1990s. In 1992, delegates to the 14th Communist Party Congress officially endorsed Deng's renewed push for a market-oriented economy. China began to import oil after the influx of foreign investment, the growth of its export sector, and the expansion of the middle class. During this period, Beijing intensified efforts to secure energy resources from the Middle East. Commercial ties with Iran became a top priority. Beijing fed its increasing need for Iranian oil, while Tehran imported more Chinese manufactured goods.

Second: China's Muslims

Despite shared economic and geopolitical interests, Beijing and Tehran have clashed over China's treatment of Uighur Muslims in Xinjiang province. Tensions have risen between the wealthy Han majority and the Uighur minority as a result of Beijing's efforts to promote Han migration to Xinjiang. In July 2009, ethnic riots erupted in the provincial capital of Urumqi after the killing of two Uighur workers in Guangdong province. More than 150 people were killed, 800 injured, and over 1,000 arrested. Most of those involved were Uighurs. Tehran sided with its Muslim brethren. Ayatollah Jafar Sobhani said, "In that part of the world, the unprotected Muslims are being mercilessly suppressed by yesterday's communist China and today's capitalist China." And Iran's Foreign Ministry expressed support for "the rights of Chinese Muslims." A Chinese diplomat in Tehran countered that the Xinjiang riots were encouraged by foreign separatist groups and were not connected to religious or ethnic issues.

Both Iran and China sought to defuse tensions. Within days, an Iranian Foreign Ministry spokesman said that Tehran balanced concerns for Muslims with bilateral relations with China. But Iranian concerns about China's Muslim population continued to fester, despite a meeting between foreign ministry officials to discuss the ethnic unrest. Beijing's approach to dealing with the Uighurs is likely to remain unchanged, engendering future ethnic unrest—and tensions with Tehran over a sensitive Chinese core interest.

Third: U.N. sanctions on Iran

After a year of negotiations amid growing Iranian defiance, the Obama administration secured Chinese and Russian support for the fourth round of U.N. sanctions on Iran in June 2010. U.N. Resolution 1929 restated the Council's longstanding demand that Iran suspend its uranium enrichment activities and peacefully resolve outstanding concerns over the nature of its nuclear program. The additional sanctions primarily targeted Iran's military and financial sectors.

In early August, Chinese Vice Premier Li Keqiang reassured Iranian Oil Minister Massoud Mirkazemi that China would maintain cooperation with Tehran on existing large-scale projects in the energy sector, even after the United States directly called on Beijing to observe sanctions. With more than 100 Chinese state-owned enterprises operating in Iran, Beijing continues to expand its presence in the Iranian market and invest heavily in Iran's energy sector. Gaps left by Western and other Asian firms forced out by sanctions present Chinese companies with strategic opportunities to enlarge their share of key sectors amid reduced competition.

Common regional interests

Two major trends in the growing Sino-Iranian relationship could help bolster regime stability in Iran.

Caspian Sea: The first trend is China's intensifying efforts to gain access the energy resources of the Caspian Sea region. China's major energy security initiative is to reduce its heavy reliance on maritime oil imports from Persian Gulf states. Iran is a linchpin in this Chinese regional strategy. Beijing's plan to build pipeline access to the Caspian Sea region via Iran reinforces the symbiotic relationship between Tehran and Beijing. In this respect, China has a strong interest in seeing a secure Iranian regime.

Shanghai Cooperation Organization: The second trend is Iran's increasing participation in the Shanghai Cooperation Organization (SCO). It was originally formed in 1996 to demilitarize the border between China and the former Soviet Union. It evolved into a wider regional organization after the Soviet Union's break-up and the independence of Central Asian countries. Since 2005, Iran has had observer status in the SCO. In 2008, Tehran announced it would seek full SCO membership. Despite its limited activities, the SCO could provide Iran an organizational context to forge closer relations with states vital to its interests in Central Asia. Iran reportedly views the SCO as a potential guarantor of its future security.

Greater involvement in the SCO might also further President Mahmoud Ahmadinejad's "Look East" policy, which seeks to build stronger economic, political, and cultural cooperation with non-Western countries. In support of Iranian efforts, President Hu Jintao said in 2009, "Tehran and Beijing should help each other to manage global developments in favor of their nations; otherwise the same people who are the factors of current international problems will again rule the world."

Diplomacy

The regular exchange visits of senior Iranian and Chinese leaders highlight the mutual importance of bilateral relations. Iranian leaders who visited China include:

- Speaker of the Iranian Islamic parliament Akbar Hashemi Rafsanjani (June 1985)

- President Ali Khamenei (May 1989)

- Speaker Mehdi Karroubi (December 1991)

- President Akbar Hashemi Rafsanjani (September 1992)

- First Vice President Hassan Habibi (August 1994)

- President Mohammad Khatami (June 2000)

- President Mahmoud Ahmadinejad (June 2006)

- First Vice President Parviz Davoodi (October 2008)

- First Vice President Mohammed Reza Rahimi (October 2009)

Chinese leaders who visited Iran include:

- Chairman of the National People's Congress Wan Li (May 1990)

- Premier Li Peng (July 1991)

- President Yang Shangkun (October 1991)

- Chairman of the National People's Congress Qiao Shi (November 1996)

- State Councilor Wu Yi (March 2002)

- President Jiang Zemin (April 2002)

- Foreign Minister Li Zhaoxing (November 2004)

- Foreign Minister Yang Jiechi (November 2007)

The future

- Beijing's growing energy needs are likely to only deepen Iran-China relations for the foreseeable future. China will be relying on the Middle East for 70 percent of its oil imports by 2015—up from 44 percent in 2006, according to the International Energy Agency.

- As Beijing's energy dependence on Tehran grows deeper, its ability to substantively support the international community's efforts to halt Iran's suspected nuclear weapons development activities will be further constrained.

- Without some compromise between Tehran and the international community on its controversial nuclear program, the Iranian leadership is likely to turn increasingly to China to help it cope economically and politically.

- Iran's chronic domestic economic and political challenges pose the greatest threat to regime stability in Tehran and energy security for Beijing.

John S. Park is a USIP senior research associate focusing on Northeast Asian security, economic and energy issues, and U.S. foreign policy toward the region.

43

Iran and Russia

Mark N. Katz

- Despite their shared suspicions of the United States, Russia and Iran have long had a contentious relationship and do not cooperate well with each other.

- Moscow is worried about Iran's nuclear program, but it is more concerned about maintaining and building lucrative economic ties with Tehran. Trade between the two countries has increased steadily since the Soviet Union's collapse.

- Moscow's willingness to cooperate with Washington in imposing sanctions on Iran over the nuclear controversy is limited.

Overview

Relations between Russia and Iran have long been difficult—and appear likely to remain so. Tensions date back to the early 19th century, when Iran lost territory to the Russian Empire. Tsarist Russia intervened militarily against Iran's 1905-1911 Constitutional Revolution. The Soviet Union supported the secession of the "Gilan Soviet" in northwestern Iran at the end of World War I, and of Iranian Azerbaijan and Kurdistan at the end of World War II. The Soviet Union (and Britain) occupied Iran during World War II. And Joseph Stalin's subsequent refusal to withdraw Soviet troops led to one of the first crises of the Cold War. Soviet support for the Tudeh, Iran's Communist Party, angered both the monarchy and theocracy. And the Soviet Union armed and aided Iraq during its 1980-1988 war with Iran. Even now, the Iranian press routinely refers to these events as reasons why Tehran should not trust Moscow.

Since 1989, however, cooperation has increased between Moscow and Tehran. Russia agreed to complete the nuclear reactor at Bushehr, which was started by the German firm Siemens during the monarchy, but stopped after the 1979 revolution. Russia also began selling weapons, including missiles, to Iran. Both countries supported the opposition Northern Alliance against the Taliban in the 1990s. And along with China, Russia tried to weaken and delay U.S. and European efforts to impose U.N. sanctions on Iran over its nuclear program.

Yet several issues continue to trouble relations. Russia's completion of the Bushehr reactor lagged years behind schedule. Moscow delayed delivering weapons, notably the S-300 air defense system. The two countries differ on rights to the Caspian Sea, which affects dividing up everything from its petroleum resources to its caviar. Iran has been angered by Moscow's improved ties with both Israel and the United States. And while it has acted to weaken them, Russia has ultimately gone along with the West in imposing some U.N. sanctions on Iran.

Three phases of relations

Moscow's relations with the Islamic Republic can be divided into three distinct periods:

Phase one: 1979 and 1989

The first phase, which coincided with the rule of revolutionary leader Ayatollah Ruhollah Khomeini, was especially hostile. Tehran viewed Moscow as hostile for reasons both past and present. The ayatollah, who called the United States "the Great Satan," dubbed the Soviet Union "the Lesser Satan." As an atheist ideology, communism was also anathema to the Islamic revolutionaries. Khomeini often said Iran should be aligned with "neither East nor West."

The fragile new regime was also angered by Soviet support for its opponents both at home and in the region. During the power struggle that erupted after the revolution, the Soviets backed Iran's Tudeh Communist Party and other leftists against the radical Islamists. Iran also paid a heavy price during the decade-long Soviet occupation of Afghanistan, when it absorbed some 2 million refugees who fled the conflict. And Soviet weaponry was pivotal to Iraqi President Saddam Hussein's eight-year military campaign against Iran. Moscow, in turn, feared Tehran's Islamic ideology might spread to its own Muslim republics, including some that bordered Iran. The Soviet Union had one of the world's largest Muslim populations.

Phase two: 1989 and 1999

The second phase was a relatively friendly period as Presidents Mikhail Gorbachev and Boris Yeltsin pursued rapprochement with Tehran. Tensions eased after four turning points in the late 1980s:

- The Iran-Iraq War ended in 1988.

- Khomeini died in mid-1989.

- The Soviet Union withdrew from Afghanistan in early 1989.

- And communism collapsed in Eastern Europe later that year.

The shifts ushered in the friendliest decade ever in Russian-Iranian relations. Moscow began selling weapons to Tehran and promised to complete the unfinished Bushehr nuclear reactor. After years of trying to export its Islamic ideology, Tehran opted not to side with fellow Muslims during Moscow's first war with Chechen rebels between 1994 and 1996. Iran pointedly expressed support for Russia's territorial integrity in the face of secessionist movements—a problem the theocracy also faced.

In the mid-1990s, Russia and Iran also worked together to end the 1992-1997 civil war in Tajikistan between Moscow's former communist allies and a democratic-Islamist alliance. Iran supported a truce that favored Moscow's allies. Moscow and Tehran also both supported Afghan forces opposing the Taliban.

Differences still remained. Tehran was not pleased with the 1995 Gore-Chernomyrdin agreement—named for the U.S. vice president and Russian prime minister—in which Russia agreed to limit the amount of weaponry and nuclear know-how it provided Iran. The agreement did not seriously impinge on Russian-Iranian relations, as it reportedly did not cover agreements "in progress"—even though Washington and Moscow disagreed about what was "in progress." With the Soviet Union's demise, the Caspian acquired three new littoral states: Kazakhstan, Turkmenistan and Azerbaijan. The five countries bordering the resource-rich sea were (and remain) unable to agree on how to divide its petroleum riches.

Phase three: 1999–

The third phase has fluctuated between antagonism and friendship. It began shortly after Vladimir Putin assumed office in 1999 and initially looked like it might lead to a formal or informal Russian-Iranian alliance. Putin publicly repudiated the Gore-Chernomyrdin agreement in October 2000. Moscow then announced new arms sales to Tehran, as well as a renewed Russian commitment to completing the Bushehr reactor. And in March 2001, Mohammad Khatami became the first Iranian president to visit Russia since the 1979 Islamic Revolution.

In July 2001, however, Iranian gunboat diplomacy halted an effort by British Petroleum (BP) to explore for oil off Azerbaijan's Caspian coast, in an area that Tehran also claimed. The incident did not directly threaten Russia, but it undermined Russian interests by leading Azerbaijan to turn to the United States and Turkey for support. Moscow also feared that Khatami's call for a "dialogue of civilizations" might lead to rapprochement with the United States—and limit Russian influence in Tehran.

In 2005, Moscow welcomed the election of Mahmoud Ahmadinejad as Iran's new president, expecting that his hardline anti-American views would prevent rapprochement with Washington. But the new president's views did not translate into greater cooperation with Moscow. Putin apparently believed his various offers to have Russia enrich uranium to commercial grade for Tehran would resolve the nuclear crisis: Iran could acquire uranium for its nuclear reactor. Western concerns about Iran subverting enriched uranium for a weapons program would be assuaged. And both sides would value Russia for brokering a resolution. But Tehran insisted on enriching its own uranium, instead heightening international tensions over Iran's program.

Since 2006, Russia has repeatedly pushed to dilute or defer a series of U.N. sanctions resolutions against Iran. Its diplomacy appears designed to convey to Tehran that Moscow can protect Iran from the West if Tehran cooperates with Russia—but also that Russia can side with the West against Iran, if Tehran does not cooperate with it.

Factoids

- Russian exports to Iran have grown steadily, according to the Russian Federal State Statistics Service:

  $249 million in 1995

  $633 million in 2000

  $1.9 billion in 2005

  $3.3 billion in 2008

- Iran's exports to Russian also grew steadily, the Russian Federal State Statistics Service reported:

  $27 million in 1995

  $57.6 million in 2000

  $125 million in 2005

  $401 million in 2008

- In November 2009, the Russian news service RIA Novosti published the results of a poll showing that 93.5 percent of Iranians have a negative opinion of Russia.

- Russia was the first country to formally recognize Ahmadinejad's re-election as president in the disputed 2009 vote.

- In December 2009, Ahmadinejad began calling on Moscow to pay compensation for the Soviet occupation of northern Iran during World War II, which produced a backlash from the Russian press.

- In early March 2010, Tehran ordered all Russian commercial pilots working in Iran to leave within 60 days. Iranian sources blamed Russian pilots for Iran's numerous plane crashes.

Interested parties

The two most important players in Russian foreign policy on Iran are President Dmitry Medvedev and Prime Minister Putin. Medvedev appears inclined to seek good relations with America and the West, and to see Iran as a problem. Prime Minister Putin, in contrast, appears to see America as an adversary and Iran as a highly lucrative potential partner for Russia. The two men, however, work closely together. Some differences may be more reflective of a policy debate than a power struggle.

Important organizations that seek to shape Russian policy on Iran include:

Rosoboronexport, the Russian arms export agency, which sells weapons to Iran and wants to keep doing business. It is an influential organization committed to good Russian-Iranian relations.

Atomstroyexport, the Russian atomic energy power equipment exporter that is working on the Bushehr nuclear reactor, also has a vested interest in Russian-Iranian relations. Atomstroyexport wants to obtain other contracts to build additional nuclear reactors in Iran. Tehran periodically dangles the prospect of contracts for five or even ten more reactors.

Gazprom, and the Russian petroleum industry in general, wants to invest in Iranian oil and gas projects. Gazprom in particular has strong political influence in Moscow.

Flashpoints

But Moscow also wants to improve diplomatic and military ties with some of Iran's rivals. The Russian Ministry of Defense is interested in purchasing sophisticated weapons from abroad that its arms industry either does not produce or produces poorly. It has already begun buying unmanned aerial vehicles from Israel and has signed a contract to buy two Mistral class warships from France.

Defense officials do not want Moscow to get too friendly with Tehran, as this could damage relations with Israel and France, which have both led the international campaign to prevent Iran from acquiring a nuclear capability. The Ministry of Defense also wants Moscow to exercise restraint in selling arms to Tehran so that Israel will not sell arms to Georgia, which it had begun doing but then stopped at Moscow's request after the outbreak of the 2008 Russia-Georgia conflict.

The future

- Moscow does not want Tehran to acquire nuclear weapons, but it is not as concerned as is Washington. Moscow is far more concerned about maintaining and building Russia's economic relationship with Tehran, especially in the area of petroleum, atomic energy and weaponry.

- Russia has cooperated with the United States on the Iranian nuclear issue for two reasons: First, to placate Washington, with which it wants good relations, and second, to create enough incentive for Washington to continue pursuing a multilateral diplomatic approach.

- Moscow understands that it cannot prevent the United States or Israel from taking military action against Iran. Moscow wants to position itself so that Tehran won't blame Russia or harm Russian interests if either the United States or Israel strikes Iran.

Mark N. Katz, professor of government and politics at George Mason University, is a visiting scholar at the Middle East Policy Council in Washington, D.C., in 2010.

44

Iran and the European Union

Walter Posch

- Since the early 1990s, relations between the European Union and Iran have correlated with Iran's domestic situation. Relations have grown closer during times of political openings in Tehran and tenser when the regime becomes more repressive.

- To address political, economic and human rights issues, the European Union has preferred to conduct relations with Iran in a dialogue format, instead of through the usual Trade and Cooperation and Political Dialogue Agreements.

- Britain, France and Germany have taken the diplomatic lead on nuclear negotiations with Iran. They established a framework that kept the door open for indirect and direct negotiations between the United States and Iran.

- Since 2005, the nuclear controversy has surpassed all strategic issues—energy, Middle East security, trade and even human rights—in EU-Iran relations. As a result, the EU policy has increasingly resembled U.S. policy on Iran. A decade of independent and imaginative EU policy ended with the passage of U.N. Resolution 1929 in June 2010.

Overview

For decades, the European Union's policy of engaging Tehran differed markedly from the U.S. policy of containing or isolating Iran. At the height of European engagement, EU foreign policy chief Javier Solana often acted as negotiator with Iran on behalf of the entire international community. The EU's main function in the nuclear crisis was accomplished when the United States expressed willingness to talk directly to Iran. But the more the Iranians stalled, the more the EU followed the U.S. lead and intensified sanctions against the Islamic Republic—even when it ran counter to Europe's own economic and strategic interests in the region.

The Rafsanjani era, 1989-1997

After a decade of war and revolutionary turmoil, President Akbar Hashemi Rafsanjani began pushing Iran toward normalcy in both domestic and foreign policy when he was elected in 1989. Iran's new tone, combined with its geopolitical and economic importance, convinced the European Union—as distinguished from individual member states—to consider intensifying relations. In 1992, the European Council made the formal decision to reach out to Iran. A host of issues still caused serious tensions, including Ayatollah Ruhollah Khomeini's 1989 fatwa calling for the death of Salman Rushdie, author of *The Satanic Verses*. So the EU initiated a "critical dialogue," rather than try to establish formal ties through a Trade and Cooperation Agreement or a Political Dialogue Agreement—as the EU would with other countries.

The "critical dialogue" reflected both components of the new EU policy: It was critical because the Europeans brought up the most worrisome issues with Iran—its abysmal human rights record, support for terrorism, opposition to the Middle East peace process and proliferation issues. But it was still a dialogue in which Europeans and Iranians talked and listened to each other.

The "critical dialogue" came under fire from many in Europe, the United States and Israel. The main complaint was that the diplomatic dialogue was cheap cover for booming European business relations with the oil-rich Islamic Republic. Yet the "critical dialogue" did force the Iranians to look at human rights issues—and admit that there was an issue at all. But over the next five years, EU-Iran relations deteriorated again. A 1997 German court's verdict against Iranian officials for involvement in terrorist activities was the turning point. Iran's unacceptable reaction to the verdict led to the pull-out of all European ambassadors from Tehran. Relations seemed beyond repair, at least from the EU vantage point.

The reformist era, 1997–2002

The surprise election of President Mohammad Khatami in 1997 changed the Iranian political climate at home and with the outside world. His new reform agenda made reengagement possible. The EU decided to revamp the "critical dialogue" and launch a new "comprehensive dialogue." Within this format, EU and Iranian officials met twice a year at the level of under-secretary of state. The range of issues was enhanced; human rights and non-proliferation issues were put higher on the agenda.

After Khatami's 2001 re-election, the EU moved to further intensify the relationship. It pressed for significant positive steps on the thorniest issues between Iran and the outside world. During this period, EU-Iran relations flourished at all levels—economic, social, academic and cultural. Impressed by the serious debate inside Iran on democracy and human rights, many Europeans hoped that further engagement—including Trade Cooperation and Political Dialogue Agreements—would facilitate even more democratic openings in Iran.

But this second diplomatic effort also suffered a serious setback after revelations in 2002 that Iran had undeclared nuclear sites at Natanz and Arak. From then on, Iran's controversial nuclear program took priority over all other policy issues.

Nuclear issues, 2002–

Iran became a critical diplomatic test case for the young EU after the 2003 U.S. invasion of Iraq. Given the disclosure of a secret Iranian nuclear program, European decision makers could not rule out another unilateral U.S. military attack, this time on Iran. But many Europeans were concerned that American unilateralism might also weaken the system of controls and verification conducted by the Vienna-based International Atomic Energy Agency (IAEA). The EU felt pressure to use its contacts with both Iran and the United States to prevent another Middle East war and also prove that it could act as a united, important and independent actor on the international stage. Combining these partially conflicting agendas was not easy in light of the often cumbersome and consensual EU decision-making processes.

In the autumn of 2003, the EU's "Big Three"—Britain, France and Germany—launched an initiative to defuse the crisis created by Iran's secret nuclear program. The three foreign ministers travelled to Tehran to convince the regime to take three pivotal steps: suspend uranium enrichment, detail the full scope of its nuclear program and facilities and sign the Nuclear Non-Proliferation Treaty's Additional Protocol, which provided for more intrusive IAEA inspections. The European Council's secretary general and foreign policy chief, Javier Solana, joined the negotiating team. The EU-3 finalized the Paris Agreement with Iran on Nov. 15, 2004. The Paris Agreement was a major turning point, proving the effectiveness of joint EU diplomacy. The EU-3 initiative became the EU's main modus operandi for transatlantic diplomacy with the United States, as well as nuclear diplomacy with Iran.

For the Europeans, the Khatami presidency was a mixed blessing. He appeared to be willing to deal with the international community, but he also faced a growing backlash with each compromise. After Iran signed the Paris Agreement, the nuclear issue became the most divisive foreign policy issue among Tehran's many factions. Hardliners argued that the nuclear program was the key to Iran's technological progress as well as the symbol of its sovereignty and international standing. They accused the reformists of selling out Iranian national interests.

The diplomatic tide turned after Mahmoud Ahmadinejad won Iran's 2005 presidential election. Tehran effectively renounced the Paris Agreement. The new government instead announced plans to again enrich uranium, the most controversial step in its nuclear program. The rejection was not simply due to a new president. The regime also had a basic disagreement with the outside world on its rights under the Nuclear Non-Proliferation Treaty.

Diplomatic escalation

Ahmadinejad had an impact on relations with Europe in other ways. His inflammatory remarks on Israel and denial of the Holocaust, which are particularly sensitive issues in Europe, poisoned the diplomatic climate. They also destroyed the inroads achieved during the Khatami presidency. Iran's supreme leader ultimately makes key decisions. Yet there was a striking difference in tactics once Ahmadinejad was elected. During Khatami's presidency, Iran meticulously avoided actions on its nuclear program that would lead Iran to be referred to the U.N. Security Council. But Ahmadinejad proved a bold risk-taker.

In early 2006, Iran was referred to the U.N. Security Council because of its failure to provide information on its past covert nuclear program. The EU continued to take the lead in trying to convince Tehran to cooperate with the international community. Solana, the EU foreign policy chief, became the sole negotiator with the Iranians. In 2006 and in 2008, Solana presented offers for a negotiated solution that included several economic and diplomatic incentives, in both cases backed by the United States and the U.N. Security Council. Tehran rejected both packages, even though the price was a new round of sanctions.

In 2009, the EU and the United States jointly made a third offer to help Iran at talks in Geneva, the first time an American envoy was present. This time the deal introduced a two-step plan. The first phase would provide badly needed fuel for Iran's research reactor, which it used to produce isotopes for medical purposes, in exchange for Iran transferring some 80 percent of its enriched uranium abroad for reprocessing into fuel rods. The process would allow time for step two, which centered on talks about Iran's entire nuclear program. Tehran initially embraced the offer, but soon backed down under pressure from both conservatives and reformers at home.

Trade relations and sanctions

The post-war normalization under Rafsanjani created a relatively friendly business environment. European enterprises were ready to engage in what has been a promising market. The Europeans imported mainly oil from Iran and hoped to be able to invest in Iran's vast gas supplies. Iran, in turn, bought mostly machinery. Yet business relations with Iran faced many practical obstacles, including an overbearing bureaucracy, a weak legal system and the absence of a European Trade and Cooperation Agreement. Business relations became more complicated under the Ahmadinejad government; international sanctions also had an impact. Between 2008 and 2009, EU exports to Iran declined by some 45 percent. In 2010, sanctions were expected to produce further declines.

EU exports to Iran in 2009:

• 18.4 billion Euros, down 45 percent compared to 2008

• Machinery and transport equipment–4 percent

• Manufactured goods–16.9 percent

• Chemicals–12.1 percent

EU imports from Iran in 2009:

• 10.3 billion Euros, fairly constant

• Energy and energy related products–90 percent

Since 2006, Europe's Iran policy has increasingly been reduced to nuclear issues. Actions have in turn been increasingly focused on sanctions. Since the United States has long had a wide array of sanctions on Iran, the new U.N. resolutions have impacted Europe far more. But the one-issue focus has had two other negative effects: First, it prevents the EU from formulating a cohesive Iran strategy that would also factor in human rights, regional issues and energy. Second, sanctions ceased to be a tool because they became both the EU's strategy and policy on Iran. The array of sanctions imposed under four U.N. resolutions since 2006 have progressively moved toward a containment policy. For Europe, they are also effectively irreversible without U.S. consent. From that perspective, the EU has out-sanctioned itself from having any influence with Iran.

The future

• The EU is committed to getting Iran to negotiate in good faith, despite repeated setbacks and deteriorating bilateral relations.

• Iran's performance on human rights will be a key to EU actions. Further deterioration on rights issues could lead to additional EU travel bans against officials tied to abuses. The human rights issue could also increase the European parliament's role in shaping the European debate on Iran policy.

• EU actions on Turkey will be influenced by what Ankara does with Iran. Turkish-Iranian relations will be closely watched. And the question of whether Turkey acts European or drives "eastward" will become an increasingly crucial question for European decision makers and academia.

Walter Posch is a senior research fellow working on Iranian domestic, foreign and security policy at the German International and Foreign Policy Institute in Berlin.

45

Iran's Alternative Allies

Steven Heydemann

- Iran has aggressively pursued diplomatic, economic and strategic relations with an eclectic array of non-Western states. It also expanded activity within regional and international organizations for developing countries.
- Iran's alliance strategy is intended to undermine international sanctions, sustain its nuclear program and thwart Western efforts to isolate Tehran.
- Iran's cultivation of "alternative allies" reflects deep pragmatism. It has cultivated ties with regimes that share an anti-Western or non-aligned perspective, without regard for their political or ideological orientation.
- But Iran's alliance strategy is anchored in a distinct vision of global governance, in which a coalition of non-Western states is needed as a counterweight to Western power.

Overview

Iran has developed close ties with a wide range of alternative allies in Latin America and Africa. These relationships serve several purposes. They impede U.S. and European efforts to maintain effective sanctions. They provide Iran with material to sustain its nuclear enrichment program. They bolster markets for Iranian oil. They also weaken U.S. efforts to isolate Iran in international institutions.

Non-Western powers such as Russia and China figure prominently in Iran's alliance strategy. Yet Iran has also increasingly sought close ties with regional powers such as Brazil and Nigeria and non-democratic governments, including the regimes of Hugo Chavez in Venezuela and Robert Mugabe in Zimbabwe. Tehran has become increasingly active in regional and international organizations that represent the economic and political interests of non-Western states, including the Non-Aligned Movement, which will hold its 2012 Annual Summit in Tehran, as well as organizations of oil and gas producers, Central Asian and Asian countries and the Muslim world.

Alliance strategy

Iran's alliance strategy reflects a deep pragmatism. Its leadership has sought closer ties with governments without regard for their political or ideological orientation. Iran's Islamic regime has little in common with the populist authoritarianism of Hugo Chavez. Nonetheless, Venezuela is among Iran's closest partners in its new network of alternative allies.

Iran's alliance strategy also expresses a clear and distinctively anti-Western vision of global governance. It is rooted in the views of revolutionary leader Ayatollah Ruhollah Khomeini, who defined Tehran's foreign policy as "neither East nor West."

Yet the new alliance strategy today goes well beyond Khomeini's go-it-alone version of non-alignment. It is anchored in the conviction that non-Western states share an interest in balancing U.S. and Western power in the international system. Only by coordinating policies and acting collectively can non-Western states defend their sovereignty, security and international interests. President Mahmoud Ahmadinejad said, "We [non-Western nations] have to develop a proper coordination…to wriggle ourselves from the domination of Western powers."

Global goals

Iran's leaders have adroitly exploited concerns among developing nations about U.S. dominance. They have tried to enhance Iran's influence by advocating a more just distribution of power and resources in the international system. They accuse the United States and its allies of using globalization as an instrument of Western power and to impose their will on non-Western states. Ahmedinejad calls it "forced globalization."

Ahmadinejad defends Iran's alliance strategy as a means to reclaim globalization from the West. In August 2010, Ahmedinejad told students that the "real battlefield in the world is over global supremacy and globalization. Today, Iran supports globalization more strongly than Westerners." This view has been echoed by many of Iran's alternative allies, including Chavez, Mugabe and also Brazil's President Luiz Inacio Lula da Silva.

Iran's alliance strategy includes economic, strategic and diplomatic elements. In each, Iran has tried to establish organizations, bilateral agreements, and formal economic arrangements as a way to institutionalize alternative networks of power in the international system.

Short-term, the Iranian regime has effectively utilized a global network of alternative allies to expand its diplomatic room for maneuver, impede U.S. and European efforts to tighten international sanctions, and sustain its enrichment program. Longer term, its aim is to establish alternative frameworks of global governance that will permit non-Western nations to trade, invest, borrow, and provide for their sovereignty and national security without recourse to the West.

Iran–Venezuela alliance

The massive expansion of Iranian-Venezuelan ties since 2000 is an extreme but representative case of how Iran's alliance strategy has unfolded. Before 2000, bilateral exchanges were sporadic. President Khatami's visit to Caracas in 2000 was the first by an Iranian head of state in 23 years. Over the next seven years Iranian and Venezuelan heads of state visited one another no less than 14 times.

In 2002, Iranian-Venezuelan trade was trivial, only $1.5 million annually. Between 2001 and 2007, Venezuela and Iran signed more than 181 trade agreements worth at least $20 billion. The agreements covered cooperation in steel and oil production, automobile production, manufacturing ammunition and oil exploration. The two countries have jointly lobbied OPEC members to price oil in Euros instead of U.S. dollars. A few weeks after the United Nations approved sanctions on Iran, Tehran and Caracas called for a cut in oil production by OPEC members.

In 2007, Iran and Venezuela announced they would establish a $2 billion fund aimed at financing projects in the developing world "to help thwart U.S. domination." Chavez described the fund as "a mechanism for liberation." Ahmadinejad said the fund would promote cooperation in Third World countries, especially in Latin America and Africa. In 2009, they agreed to establish an Iranian-Venezuelan Development Bank funded at $200 million.

The theme of building international support against American power recurs frequently in official Iranian-Venezuelan exchanges. During a 2007 visit, Chavez held up Ahmadinejad's hand and said that the two nations would "unite and create a multipolar world. …united, we are going to help defeat U.S. imperialism, and that's why…they get worried in Washington when they see the two of us shaking hands."

Chavez is an ardent supporter of Iran's nuclear enrichment program. Venezuela was one of only three countries at the International Atomic Energy Agency (IAEA) to vote against referring the Iranian nuclear file to the U.N. Security Council. Chavez has threatened to suspend crude oil exports to the United States if it attacks Iran and has offered to supply Iran with F-16 fighter jets. Security cooperation extends well beyond the nuclear issue. Venezuela has reportedly entered into military projects with Iran, and they are seeking to jointly produce an unmanned aircraft similar to the U.S. Predator. Reports indicate Iran's Revolutionary Guards are training Venezuelan police and secret services.

Latin American allies

Iran has used its alliance strategy across Latin America over the past decade. After the Security Council approved sanctions against Iran in 2006, Ahmadinejad embarked on a tour of Latin American countries critical of U.S. policies, including Bolivia, Nicaragua and Ecuador. He attended the swearing-in of President Rafael Correa, who had pledged during his campaign not to renew a lease for a U.S. air base in Ecuador. In 2006, Bolivian President Evo Morales announced plans to establish diplomatic ties and forge energy cooperation with Iran—on Chavez's advice. A high-level Bolivian official told the press, "Iran is seeking to gain geopolitical control in the Western Hemisphere with the aid of Venezuela. They will eventually be able to place and replace governments."

The deepening of Iranian-Brazilian ties followed a similar pattern, absent vitriolic anti-Americanism. Bilateral relations date to the early days of the Islamic Republic but have expanded significantly since 2000. In 2010, Brazil was Iran's largest trade partner in Latin America, hitting $1.3 billion in 2008—an increase of over 80 percent in one year. In 2010, Lula da Silva took more than 300 political and business leaders to Tehran. He and Ahmadinejad agreed to expand bilateral trade to $10 billion and signed 11 economic cooperation agreements.

In 2010, Brazil had a central role in international efforts to ensure that Iran does not acquire a nuclear weapons capability. With Turkey, Brazil won Iranian support for a deal to swap low enriched uranium for more highly enriched uranium intended for use in a nuclear medical facility. The deal complicated but did not derail U.S. efforts to secure new U.N. sanctions against Iran. Brazil voted against the sanctions but agreed to abide by them, reflecting the limits of Iran's strategy with governments that are nonaligned, rather than anti-American.

African connections

Iran has worked assiduously to expand its influence in Africa. Sudan and Zimbabwe share Iran's anti-Western orientation and its critique of the international system. Iran was among the few states to oppose sending U.N. peacekeepers to Darfur. It has supported Mugabe's regime in Zimbabwe with technical and humanitarian aid following the collapse of its economy in 2008 and the 2009 imposition of economic sanctions. Heads of government have visited one another's capitals. They have also signed several economic agreements since 2005.

During a visit to Tehran in November 2006, Mugabe echoed Ahmadinejad and Chavez in calling for radical change in an "evil" international system. "Countries who think alike must come together and work out mechanisms to defend ourselves," he told a press conference. In 2007, Iran and Zimbabwe created an international "coalition for peace in response to the aggression of global bullies" after President George W. Bush criticized both governments.

In the absence of political and ideological compatibility, Iran has strengthened economic ties, increasing investments and facilitating trade, aid and humanitarian support. South Africa is among Iran's largest trading partners, to the tune of $20 billion annually in recent years. Iran supplied some 40 percent of South Africa's oil. In the late 1990s, South Africa offered to sell Iran nuclear technology for the purpose of developing a nuclear energy capacity. It strongly supports Iran's right to enrichment, even while opposing nuclear proliferation.

Economic ties with West African states have expanded enormously in recent years, although they remain far lower than Iran-South African trade. A 2010 study from the American Enterprise Institute noted that 2009 exports to Côte d'Ivoire, Niger and Senegal was roughly 2,700, 2,800 and 3,600 percent higher (respectively) than 2000 exports.

Limits of alliances

Tehran has also faced setbacks reflecting the limits of its policy. In 2010, Russia and China agreed to support a fourth round of U.N. sanctions after trying to water them down. Nigeria voted for sanctions. Brazil voted against but said it would comply with the new restrictions.

In Latin America, some governments allied with the United States have expressed suspicion, if not alarm, about Iran's intentions in the region. In North Africa, Morocco broke off diplomatic relations with Iran in 2009 over charges of Iranian interference in its religious affairs. In West Africa, a number of states that have benefited from increasing trade with the United States continue to participate in American counterterrorism programs.

Iran has played a weak hand effectively to strengthen its international influence. Yet its track record reflects only partial success. Its vision of a radical restructuring of the international system has limited appeal. And its economic influence is constrained by the growing reach of U.N., U.S., and EU sanctions.

The future

- Iran's alliance strategy will remain a tool in its diplomatic and economic arsenal to gain leverage internationally.

- Iran's leaders articulate a vision of the international system that will continue to resonate with many non-Western nations. These relationships help insulate Tehran from the full impact of harsh economic sanctions.

- Iran's ambitious diplomacy will continue to pose a major challenge to the United States and its Western allies in their efforts to prevent Iran from acquiring a nuclear weapons capability.

- But Iran's efforts to cultivate alternative allies are not always successful. And economic aid or ties are not always sufficient to generate political support from developing nations.

Steven Heydemann is vice president of USIP's Grant and Fellowship Program and a specialist on the comparative politics and political economy of the Middle East.

Policy Considerations

46

Reading Iran

Ellen Laipson

- The United States has had trouble reading Iran since the break in diplomatic relations in 1980. A basic lack of understanding, compounded by missed signals at critical junctures, deepened estrangement and set back efforts to rebuild relations.

- Two problems deepened the divide: For decades, the United States has had no diplomatic presence in Tehran, while Iran has had an Interests Section in Washington. And visa policies are not reciprocal: Many more Iranians are able to visit the United States than the reverse. Iran's secretive political system is not accessible, especially to Westerners. The absence of communication—at any level—often fostered worst-case assumptions.

- More than three decades later, Washington still has trouble discerning Iran's strategic intentions. Is Iran driven more by religious ideology or the practical interests of the state? Is it committed to becoming a hegemonic regional power at U.S. expense? Or can its leaders, under the right conditions, seek accommodation with the United States?

Overview

Reading Iran is critical to U.S. policymaking to understand the threats and dangers as well as changing conditions that create opportunities for engaging Tehran. But U.S. government analysts, even those with strong academic credentials and language skills, have struggled to understand Iranian politics and the constantly shifting balance of power among its many factions. Limited access has impeded accurate assessments. From the start, the revolutionary regime condemned the West and limited contacts because of U.S. support for the monarchy. Iran's culture also values secrecy. And Shiite tradition honors *taqiya*, or deception, in the name of survival. All three factors have made it even harder to provide reliable answers on which to base government action.

U.S. intelligence has been more successful in tracking Iran's foreign relations, social and economic conditions and developments in the energy sector. Analysis is based on a synthesis of information from international institutions, allies with embassies in Tehran and independent academics and journalists who engage with a wide variety of Iranians during travel to Iran.

So the record of reading Iran's often volatile domestic scene and fickle foreign policy has been mixed—beginning with the revolution itself. The revolution's first decade from 1979 until the death of revolutionary leader Ayatollah Ruhollah Khomeini in 1989 was the toughest period. Key U.S. assessments proved partially wrong, contributing to policy missteps. In the 1990s, tentative Iranian attempts to reengage with the world after the Iran-Iraq War occurred alongside Iranian support for extremism. Determining Iran's real intent was tricky. The reform era from 1997 to 2005 pitted factions within the regime against each other, often making it hard to tell who had the upper hand. The rise of hardliners in 2005 and 2009 elections led to crackdowns on the opposition, academics and the media, in turn further restricting information about conditions inside Iran. Five major events illustrate the challenges of reading Iran—and the impact of getting it wrong.

Missing the revolution

In 1978, the critical year of political upheaval, few U.S. analysts believed that the shah was in trouble or that a revolution was brewing. Analysis was misguided by interests, ideology, and ignorance. Washington clung to three myths: The shah was pro-American. The shah was loved at home. And the opposition was small and easily controlled. Analysis was further hampered by two factors:

First, the shah had begun to have the upper hand in relations with Washington. In the early 1970s, he even persuaded the Nixon administration to scale back its intelligence collection inside Iran to ensure continued cooperation on regional problems. So by the late 1970s, U.S. Embassy reporting to Washington was less robust than the circumstances and stakes warranted.

Second, U.S. analysis looked at Iran primarily as a bastion against Soviet expansion, which colored its assessments. In the run-up to the revolution, Washington was more focused on leftist opposition to the shah, which it thought could be managed by Iranian security forces, rather than on the growing Islamic opposition.

After the shah's ouster, American diplomats in Iran tried to warn Washington about the challenges of dealing with the proud but insecure new regime. In August 1979, three months before the U.S. Embassy takeover, ranking American diplomat Bruce Laingen described Tehran's pervasive unease about the nature of the world and belief that hostile forces abound. The Carter administration, he wrote in a diplomatic cable, should not expect Iran's new leaders to see the advantages of a long-term relationship based on trust. "Good will for good will's sake is a waste of effort," he wrote.

Laingen also warned the White House that it had to choose between allowing the shah into the United States for medical treatment or strengthening relations with the new government. Carter opted to admit the shah, despite dangers to the U.S. Embassy. The shah entered the U.S. for medical treatment in October 1979. Less than three weeks later, students seized the sprawling American compound and held 52 hostages 444 days, an event that has framed tensions between Washington and Tehran ever since.

Iran-Contra affair

In the mid-1980s, the Reagan administration was drawn into complicated intrigue with Iran involving U.S. (and Israeli) arms transfers to Iran in exchange for the release of American hostages in Lebanon. The immediate U.S. goal was to convince Tehran to use its influence with a surrogate militia to end years of abductions of U.S. citizens in Beirut. The immediate Iranian goal was to acquire badly needed arms to hold off the Iraqi army during their eight-year war.

But the stakes were higher. The logic of the initiative was based in part on a U.S. intelligence assessment about Soviet designs on Iran. To counter the presumed Soviet push to build its influence in the Persian Gulf region, Washington wanted to use the arms-for-hostage swap to possibly improve its own relations with Iran through contact with reputed "moderates."

In the end, Washington again misread Iranian politics, underestimating the internal divisions. While some Iranian leaders appeared interested in exploring the possibilities, others sabotaged the effort—leaking news of a high-level U.S. visit and the arms swap. In the end, Iran's Lebanese allies only picked up more hostages. And the U.S. overture sparked a serious political crisis at home. The diplomatic drama also had lingering impact, making the United States and Iran suspicious of all back-channel initiatives and public outreach.

The Conoco deal

In 1995, the government of President Akbar Hashemi Rafsanjani offered a $1 billion contract to U.S. oil company Conoco to develop offshore Iranian oil and gas fields. The Conoco contract was the most lucrative petroleum deal ever offered by Iran, under the monarchy or the theocracy. It could provide significant economic benefit to the United States. Iran also had economic incentives: It was engrossed in reconstruction after the eight-year war with Iraq, the deadliest modern Middle East conflict. Its ravaged economy needed new revenue sources. Rafsanjani also appeared interested in thawing relations with the West, which had been troubled with the United States since the 1979 hostage crisis and with Europe since a 1989 *fatwa* imposing the death sentence on author Salman Rushdie for his book *The Satanic Verses*.

But Washington was surprised and had difficulty interpreting the sincerity of the overture. U.S. assessments suggested that Tehran had ulterior motives—and wanted to neutralize the damage from the Clinton administration's dual containment policy on both Iran and Iraq. Washington was pressuring European capitals and businesses to deny Iran any revenue that could fuel its support to extremists, so such a deal would make Washington look hypocritical and undermine its overall policy.

In the end, the White House issued two executive orders in spring 1995 banning U.S. investment in Iran's energy sector. The Conoco deal was dead. Rafsanjani later claimed the United States missed a major opportunity to improve relations. "This was a message to the United States which was not correctly understood," Rafsanjani said in an interview with ABC's Peter Jennings.

The reform era

After the 1997 election of President Mohammed Khatami, U.S. analysts struggled to understand whether reformers could liberalize Iran's labyrinthine institutions and political culture. The reform era initially witnessed a freer press, burgeoning civil society, vibrant women's movement and an overture to the outside world to bring down the "wall of mistrust." For Washington, the issue was whether it was sustainable enough to try to re-engage Iran. In unclassified threat assessments, U.S. intelligence over those eight years kept adjusting their assessments of the prospects for genuine reform in Iran:

1997: "Opposition to clerical rule lacks a charismatic leader or an institutional power base."

1998: "Genuine struggle is now underway between hardline conservatives and more moderate elements represented by Iran's new President Khatami."

2000: "Change in Iran is inevitable. …The path will be volatile at times as the factions struggle to control the pace and direction of political change."

2001: "Events of the past year have been discouraging for positive change in Iran. …They have begun to push back hard against the reformers."

2002: "Reform is not dead. …The people of Iran have demonstrated in four national elections since 1997 that they want change and have grown disillusioned with the promises of the revolution."

2003: "We are currently unable to identify a leader, organization or issue capable of uniting the widespread desire for change."

In 2000, the Clinton administration made a tentative gesture to Tehran in hopes of launching rapprochement. Secretary of State Madeleine Albright publicly apologized for the 1953 CIA operation that ousted a democratically elected prime minister and put the shah back on the throne. She also lifted sanctions on Iranian carpets and foodstuffs and offered to expedite resolution of Iranian and U.S. assets frozen since the 1979 U.S. Embassy takeover. But Iran's supreme leader dismissed the offer. After years of mistrust, any overture ran the risk of being seen as support for one faction over another, and Iran's political system was unable or unwilling to respond.

Nuclear intentions

The toughest challenge for U.S. intelligence agencies has been monitoring Iran's controversial nuclear program. Analysts have provided empirical evidence about Iran's current activities as well as strategic assessments about its long-term intentions, which are judgments rather than provable facts. This range of knowledge—some well documented, some speculative—has created uncertainty about what is actually known.

For more than one decade, U.S. intelligence officials have publicly discussed the prospects of Iran becoming a nuclear power. In 1996, for example, Director of Central Intelligence John Deutch said that Iran could produce a nuclear weapon by the end of the decade, with outside assistance. Six years later, DCI George Tenet focused on indigenous production and judged that by 2010, Iran could produce enough fissile material for a bomb.

More recently, U.S. assessments have occasionally conflicted with the estimates of allies and the International Atomic Energy Agency (IAEA), which has consistently resisted making a definitive judgment about whether Iran in fact has a weapons program.

In 2007, the U.S. government released unclassified judgments of a National Intelligence Estimate on Iran. Its key points included:

"We judge with high confidence that in fall 2003, Tehran halted its nuclear weapons program; we also assess with moderate to high confidence that Tehran at a minimum is keeping open the option to develop nuclear weapons."

"We continue to assess…that Iran does not currently have a nuclear weapon."

"The program was probably halted primarily in response to international pressure. …"

But in early 2010, the annual threat assessment to Congress had a different tone. Its key points included:

"Iran is keeping open the option to develop nuclear weapons in part by developing various nuclear capabilities. …"

"There is a real risk that its nuclear program will prompt other countries in the Middle East to pursue nuclear options. …"

"We judge Iran's nuclear decision-making is guided by a cost-benefit approach, which offers the international community opportunities to influence Tehran."

Analysis can provide important insight into the opportunities and the potential risks of engaging Iran. It can never provide absolute confidence that one American course of action will produce the desired results, but it is an essential input to diplomatic decisions.

The future

- Given the longstanding gap in access, policymakers trying to either address the threat from Iran or pursue diplomacy are unlikely to have all the knowledge they seek before making hard choices.

- But integration of information from more diverse sources, language skills, access to Iran and openness to multiple points of view would add greater value to the analysis needed by U.S. decision makers.

- Successful diplomacy with Iran will particularly require a deeper understanding of the stakes for Iran and the intentions of its leaders.

- In the end, however, even the best analysis does not ensure successful policies. There is no substitute for relationships to communicate and build trust in international relations. Contacts among diplomats, the military and civil society groups all contribute to the ability to read Iran.

Ellen Laipson, president and CEO of the Stimson Center, worked on Iran and other Middle East issues on the National Security Council, the National Intelligence Council and at the Congressional Research Service.

47

Engaging Iran

James Dobbins

- Under President George W. Bush, the United States and Iran twice engaged in extended and substantive diplomatic talks.

- In the immediate aftermath of 9/11, bilateral U.S.-Iranian contacts produced the most significant cooperation since the 1979 revolution, as Iranian officials helped the United States form a new Afghan government. Despite this, only weeks later, President Bush included Iran in the "axis of evil" and threatened to use force to halt its nuclear program.

- Iran persisted for more than a year to offer assistance to the United States, first in Afghanistan and then Iraq. But Washington failed to accept any of Tehran's offers.

- In 2007, talks were held between top U.S. and Iranian envoys in Iraq. These exchanges were highly confrontational, but Iranian behavior in Iraq did moderate somewhat thereafter.

- During his first year in office, President Barack Obama tried unsuccessfully to open a high-level dialogue with Iran, while at the same time seeking to bypass the populist and confrontational President Mahmoud Ahmadinejad in favor of the supreme leader, Ayatollah Ali Khamenei.

Overview

The 9/11 attacks opened a brief period of cooperation between the United States and Iran. Tehran had long opposed both the Taliban and al Qaeda. Iran publicly condemned these attacks on the United States and privately offered to assist American efforts to overthrow the Taliban regime. Iran had considerable influence with the Northern Alliance, the insurgency that had been battling the Taliban since the mid-1990s. Tehran used this influence to help the United States secure agreement among all elements of the Afghan opposition on a new government that took office in Kabul in December of 2001, only a few weeks after the Taliban's ouster.

A month later, President Bush called Iran, along with North Korea and Iraq, the new "axis of evil" and threatened to use military force to halt their nuclear programs. The Iranian government nevertheless continued to offer cooperation on Afghanistan, volunteering to help the United States raise and train a new Afghan army. The Bush administration ignored this offer, as it did an even more far-reaching proposal of cooperation a year later, after the U.S. invasion of Iraq.

In 2005, the hardline mayor of Tehran, Mahmoud Ahmadinejad, replaced reformist President Mohammad Khatami. Over the next five years, Tehran showed little interest in cooperating with the United States. Ahmadinejad wrote to both Bush and Obama, but neither responded. Bush authorized a series of talks in Baghdad in 2007 between the U.S. and Iranian ambassadors, which involved a well-publicized exchange of complaints. But Iranian behavior did moderate somewhat thereafter. Since his election, Obama has made several overtures to open a dialogue, particularly on Iran's nuclear program. In 2009, Ahmadinejad initially agreed to a U.S.-backed proposal for a compromise deal on Iran's controversial nuclear program but then backed off when criticized at home from opponents on both the right and left.

The Bonn talks

There is a popular perception in the United States that in the aftermath of 9/11, the United States formed a coalition and overthrew the Taliban. Actually, in the aftermath of 9/11, the United States joined an existing coalition that had been trying to overthrow the Taliban for almost a decade. The coalition consisted of India,

Russia, Iran and the Northern Alliance. With the addition of American airpower, that coalition succeeded in ousting the Taliban.

The quick success in forming a successor regime was also thanks to this coalition, which met with others in Bonn to help forge a future for Afghanistan. The 10-day conference had representatives from the major Afghan opposition factions and from all principal regional states—Russia, India, Pakistan, Iran and the United States—that had been playing the so-called Great Game in Afghanistan for 20 years.

On two pivotal issues, Iran played a highly constructive role. At the conference, the United Nations circulated the first draft of the Bonn Declaration, which became Afghanistan's interim constitution. It was the Iranian envoy who noted that the constitution had no mention of democracy. "Maybe a document like this ought to mention elections," he suggested. The Iranian delegation also proposed that the document should commit the Afghans to cooperate against international terrorism.

On the last night of the conference, all major elements had been decided—except who was going to govern Afghanistan. The Afghan factions had agreed on the interim constitution, but they were still arguing about the composition of a new coalition government. The Northern Alliance insisted on occupying 18 of the 26 ministries; the other Afghan factions insisted that this was too many.

Again, Iran made a major contribution to forge a solution. U.N. Negotiator Lakhdar Brahimi assembled representatives from Russia, India, Iran and the United States, the four countries that had supported the Northern Alliance. For two hours, the four envoys pressed Northern Alliance representative Younnis Qanooni to give up several ministries. Qanooni remained obdurate. Finally, the Iranian envoy took him aside and whispered to him for a few moments. The Northern Alliance envoy returned to the table and said, "Okay, I agree. The other factions can have two more ministries. And we can create three more, which they can also have." Four hours later, the Bonn Agreement was formally adopted. Ten days thereafter, Hamid Karzai was inaugurated in Kabul as the head of the new Afghan government.

Further cooperation

In early 2003, Japan held an international conference to raise money for Afghan reconstruction. Iran pledged $500 million in assistance. The American pledge, by comparison, was $290 million.

At the January conference, Iranian diplomats approached U.S. representatives bilaterally and through the Japanese government to express an interest in broadening their dialogue with the United States to include issues beyond Afghanistan. But in his first State of the Union address days later, President Bush characterized Iran, along with Iraq and North Korea, as an "axis of evil." He threatened all three states with preemptive military action intended to halt their acquisition of weapons of mass destruction.

The Iranian regime nevertheless persisted in its efforts to expand cooperation with the United States. In March 2002, Iranian and American representatives met bilaterally on the fringes of yet another multilateral meeting about Afghanistan in Geneva. The Iranian delegation included a uniformed general who had been the commander of security assistance to the Northern Alliance throughout its insurgency campaign against the Taliban. The general said that Tehran was prepared to participate in an American-led program to raise and train a new Afghan national army. As part of this effort, he explained, Iran was prepared to house, pay, clothe, arm and train up to 20,000 Afghan troops in a broader program under American leadership.

The offer was briefly considered by Secretary of State Colin Powell, Secretary of Defense Donald Rumsfeld and National Security Adviser Condoleezza Rice. But no positive decision was made, and the Iranians never received a response.

The Iraq invasion

In June 2003, three months after the American invasion of Iraq, Iran made an even more sweeping offer designed to address the full range of issues dividing the two countries. The proposal came from the Iranian foreign ministry; it was transmitted by the Swiss government, which represented American interests in Tehran in the absence of a U.S. Embassy.

The American invasions, first of Afghanistan and then of Iraq, had left the Tehran regime both grateful and fearful. They were grateful that the United States had removed their two principal regional opponents—the Taliban and President Saddam Hussein. But they were also nervous that Iran might be next. American troops were by then deployed to their north in Central Asia, to their east in Afghanistan, to their south in the Gulf and to their west in Iraq. Iran was virtually surrounded.

While these developments encouraged Tehran to improve relations with the United States, they had the opposite effect in Washington. Rapid victories, first in Afghanistan and then in Iraq, had made the U.S. government confident—and somewhat overconfident—about its successes and future influence in the region. The Bush administration therefore saw no rush to deal with Iran and failed to respond to the Iranian overture.

The Baghdad talks

For several years after the 2003 offer, Iran's position strengthened, while the U.S. military position weakened and its diplomatic leverage diminished. In 2001 and 2003, Tehran feared that the United States might invade Iran and overthrow its regime. By 2004, this fear had receded, as American troops became bogged down battling rising insurgencies in both Afghanistan and Iraq.

In August 2005, Mahmoud Ahmadinejad replaced Mohammad Khatami as president. Hard-liners replaced reformers in the foreign ministry and other key national security posts. Despite his tougher language on the United States, Ahmadinejad did not prove personally adverse to contacts with the American leadership. He wrote a letter to President Bush, full of tendentious religious references, and subsequently sent a congratulatory message to Barack Obama on his election as president. Neither of these missives received a response.

In 2007, the United States faced steadily mounting violence in Iraq, which Iran was partly responsible for feeding. The Bush administration authorized Ambassador Ryan Crocker in Baghdad to meet with his Iranian counterpart in trilateral talks hosted by the Iraqi government. Three sessions were held in May, June and August of 2007.

The meetings consisted largely of an exchange of complaints. No agreements resulted. But Iran's support for extremist Shiite militia groups—a major U.S. complaint—did begin to moderate somewhat. Aggressive steps by the U.S. military to limit Iranian activity may have been a more important factor. So was pressure from the Shiite-led Iraqi government on Tehran. Nevertheless, the Baghdad talks, while entirely unproductive on the surface, at least did no harm. They may even have contributed to more restrained Iranian behavior.

Obama and engagement

When he took office in 2009, President Obama made several attempts to follow through on a campaign promise to try and engage with Iran and other rogue regimes. But he also sought to bypass the provocatively outspoken Ahmadinejad, who had written to him after his election. Obama instead wrote to the supreme leader, who ultimately makes all major domestic and foreign policy decisions. (The Clinton administration had tried the same tactic in reverse more than a decade earlier. It addressed overtures to then President Khatami and took a more critical position toward the supreme leader. That effort yielded little.)

Obama made an initial overture to the Iranian people and government in a broadcast on the Iranian new year in March 2009. He also sent two private messages to Ayatollah Khamenei. The State Department also announced that it was inviting Iranian diplomats to various U.S. Embassy Fourth of July celebrations, only to revoke the invitation a few days later in reaction to rising controversy in Iran over the disputed reelection of Ahmadinejad.

In the fall of 2009, senior U.S. and Iranian officials met briefly in Europe for multilateral talks on Iran's controversial nuclear program. The American and Iranian envoys talked briefly on the sidelines of the meeting. Those larger talks produced a tentative interim agreement, which Ahmadinejad initially endorsed. Iran subsequently pulled back from the deal due to opposition from both conservative quarters and the reformist opposition.

The future

- In both Tehran and Washington, engagement comes at a heavy domestic political cost.

- A breakthrough on the nuclear front could expand the room for dialogue on other issues.

- Yet since Ahmadinjad's disputed reelection, Iran's leadership has become even more heavily factionalized, with hard-line elements associated with the Revolutionary Guard gaining greater influence, making any breakthrough more difficult.

James Dobbins, a former U.S. Ambassador and assistant secretary of state, directs the RAND Corporation's International Security and Defense Policy Center and was a senior official at the Bonn talks with Iran.

48

Track II Diplomacy

Suzanne DiMaggio

- In the absence of formal U.S.–Iran relations, which were severed in 1980 following the U.S. Embassy takeover, Americans and Iranians have held track II meetings to discuss contentious issues that divide their governments.

- "Track II" refers to unofficial interactions usually carried out by non-governmental actors with access to decision makers. In contrast, "track I" denotes diplomacy conducted by government officials.

- U.S.–Iran track II exchanges expanded under President Mohammad Khatami between 1997 and 2005, particularly during his second term. They provided the space to talk informally about issues that the two governments were not ready or able to address.

- But the impact on official policies was limited, largely due to the volatile environment between Tehran and Washington that impeded the transfer of track II results to track I.

- Since President Mahmoud Ahmadinejad's election in 2005, Tehran has stepped back from track II, and opportunities for Americans to engage Iranians in informal settings have been limited.

Overview

The term "track II diplomacy" refers to frank, off-the-record interactions, often between members of adversarial countries outside of official negotiations. An early example of track II was the Dartmouth Conference, which brought together Americans and Soviets in 1960 after the breakdown of the 1959 Eisenhower-Khrushchev summit. Track II diplomacy can also be multilateral, with the aim of addressing specific issue areas. Other examples include regional dialogues focused on the Asia-Pacific (North Korea), the Middle East (Arab-Israeli or Gulf security) and South Asia (the status of Kashmir and nuclear proliferation).

U.S.-Iran track II initiatives are unique because they occur in the absence of official relations, which ceased in 1980. Even during the height of the Cold War, when the United States and the Soviet Union had formal relations, track II efforts were able to complement track I diplomacy.

The U.S.-Iran case presents a distinct set of challenges, including the inability to coordinate activities with official negotiators to advance progress. At the same time, the lack of opportunities for Americans and Iranians to interact at the official level makes the socialization, learning and confidence-building aspects of track II particularly valuable. Several American participants in past track II initiatives hold key positions in the Obama administration, which has offered Iran an opening on engagement.

The Khatami years, 1997–2005

During his first term, President Khatami encouraged a "dialogue of civilizations," as a counterargument to Samuel Huntington's theory of a "clash of civilizations." The new mood in Tehran increased the opportunities for Americans to engage in unofficial exchanges with influential Iranians. Tehran's tolerance of track II was seen as an attempt to move Iran's foreign policy in a more conciliatory direction with the United States and the West generally.

On the Iranian side, the primary convener was often the Institute for Political and International Studies (IPIS), the foreign ministry's think tank. The Center for Strategic Research (CSR), a policy institute affiliated with the Expediency Council that advises the supreme leader's office, also played a convening role.

A core group of reform-minded diplomats, policy advisers and scholars participated in these discussions. The members of this group remained fairly consistent during the Khatami presidency. Most shared the experience of living in the United States as university students. They also shared the view that rapprochement in U.S.-Iran relations offered a way to advance Iranian interests over time.

By participating in track II, the Iranian reformists often risked their careers and reputations in the process. By early 2008, hard-line elements in the Iranian government began to charge members of this group with a pro-U.S. agenda. Most have since faced censure; some faced prosecution. Pressure on them increased after the disputed 2009 presidential election. Their ability to participate in international conferences and travel abroad has since been restricted. Some professors at Iranian universities have been subjected to downgrading of positions or altogether stripped of their teaching duties.

The Ahmadinejad years, 2005–

During the early part of Mahmoud Ahmadinejad's presidency, IPIS continued to convene track II events that included Americans and other Westerners. This began to change after IPIS hosted the International Conference to Review the Global Vision of the Holocaust in Tehran in December 2006, which included the participation of David Duke, former grand wizard of the Knights of the Ku Klux Klan, and other Holocaust deniers. After the conference, several dozen policy institutes and think tanks, mostly in Europe, Australia and the United States, severed relations with IPIS in protest.

In the fall 2007, Iranian Foreign Minister Manouchehr Mottaki met with a group of Americans in New York to inform them that Iran's participation in track II discussions would be put on hold while the Iranians reassessed their objectives. He also indicated that the composition of the Iranian group would be reconfigured to better reflect the changing power realities in Tehran.

Since then, U.S.-Iran track II diplomacy has been in transition, with significantly less activity and a change in Iranian participation. Instead of a core group organized by IPIS or another Iranian institute, the interactions have been more ad hoc. They usually involve officials connected to various Iranian power centers, such as the president's office, the foreign ministry or the Supreme National Security Council. Current participants are conservative policymakers and advisers who represent Iran's "new political order." Many served on the front lines during the Iran-Iraq War. Most lack exposure to the United States and have had limited contact with Americans.

The future of track II was further complicated in early 2010, when Iran's Ministry of Intelligence and Security (MOIS) identified a number of American and European organizations associated with track II as "subversive" and part of a "soft war" against the Islamic Republic.

American organizers

Over the past decade, most track II initiatives have been multilateral in scope and conducted as regional dialogues, where Iranians and Americans have had opportunities to meet on the sidelines. The University of California, Los Angeles (UCLA) along with the University of California's Institute on Global Conflict and Cooperation, has been organizing regional dialogue groups that meet three times each year in Europe. They include as many as 250 participants from a range of countries. They also organize smaller, specialized working groups.

The Pugwash Conferences on Science and World Affairs also has been bringing together Iranians and Americans in a multilateral context. In 2008, Pugwash convened four meetings in The Hague and Vienna that included the participation of currently serving Iranian officials and former American officials. Discussion topics included security in the broader Middle East and, specifically, Iran's nuclear program.

From 2006 to 2007, the Stanley Foundation organized "The Future of Gulf Security" project, which brought together representatives from Gulf Cooperation Council (GCC) states, Iran, Iraq, Yemen, the European Commission, Italy, the United Kingdom, Pakistan, Japan and the United States. The discussions centered on Iran's nuclear program, Iran-Arab-U.S. relations, Iraq and cooperative multilateral regional security frameworks.

Other track II efforts have been carried out by American organizations with European partners. The Nixon Center, together with the International Institute for Strategic Studies and the Geneva Center for Democratic Control of Armed Forces, have organized track II sessions with Iran in Geneva.

The United Nations Association of the USA in partnership with the Stockholm International Peace Research Institute convened one of the longest running track II efforts. From 2002 to 2008, they held 14 meetings, mostly in Stockholm. These discussions focused on U.S.-Iran bilateral relations, Iran's nuclear program and regional security issues, including Afghanistan, Pakistan, Iraq and Israel-Palestine. The core group of reform-minded Iranians participated in these meetings, as well as in the vast majority of track II initiatives held during this time frame. Over 20 influential Americans participated in one or more of these meetings; many were former senior government officials. In 2005, the Americans and Iranians jointly wrote a paper, "The U.S.-Iran Relationship: Breaking the Stalemate," which aimed to provide the foundation and agenda for beginning official discussions. The paper, which was written in English and translated into Farsi, was distributed to select senior officials in Washington and Tehran. It was not released publicly.

Another form of track II diplomacy is citizen-to-citizen exchanges that focus on non-political aspects of U.S.-Iran relations. Search for Common Ground has been organizing exchanges in the areas of sports, film, the environment and health. Third parties have also hosted track II exchanges. The University of Toronto's Munk Center for International Relations and more recently the University of Ottawa have played the "honest broker" role, convening Europeans, Americans and Iranians for discussions.

Measuring success

Measuring the success of past and current track II efforts is difficult because there is usually not an immediate breakthrough or impact on policy. Current and past track II exchanges generally have taken a long-term approach geared toward socializing elites with access to and influence on policymakers. The goal is to shape the policy debate by presenting a more nuanced picture of problems and possible options for cooperative solutions.

The key contributions of current and recent U.S.-Iran track II efforts fall into the following five areas:

- Serving as an informal forum to identify common interests, generate ideas, vet proposals and think though policy options.

- Providing reality checks that lead to the clarification of intentions and the correction of misperceptions.

- Communicating insights and analyses to key decision makers in Tehran and Washington.

- Forging important relationships over time, particularly between key Iranian advisers and officials and former U.S. officials/diplomats with access to American decision makers.

- Providing a reliable channel for unofficial communications on sensitive issues and during times of heightened tensions.

Discretion is vital to ensuring the continuation of U.S.-Iran track II dialogues. Participants usually agree in advance not to release any information to the public or the media. Individuals commonly prefer to maintain a low profile and even preserve anonymity. So success stories are not revealed or celebrated.

The future

- After years of steady interactions, the future of U.S.-Iran track II diplomacy is in a state of flux. Valuable efforts are still underway, but it is not yet clear whether they can be sustained over time. In light of Iran's power struggles, it is also unclear which individuals and organizations have the capacity or authority to carry out track II.

- But given tense relations between the governments of Iran and the United States, track II exchanges continue to be one of the few bridges that bring together Americans and Iranians for dialogue.

- If Tehran and Washington move toward formal talks, track II efforts are also likely to gain new traction. This is the optimal scenario, since track II diplomacy on its own is insufficient to address the decades of deep mistrust.

Suzanne DiMaggio is the director of policy studies at the Asia Society, where she leads the Society's Iran Initiative.

49

Containing Iran

Kenneth M. Pollack

- Since the 1979 revolution, containment has been the default policy of the United States toward Iran. It has never been a policy eagerly embraced by any U.S. administration.

- Containment has had some successes. It has been effective in partially isolating Iran. It has hamstrung Tehran's efforts to develop a capable military. It has limited Iran's ability to play an influential role in the geopolitics of southwest Asia. And it has constrained Iran's economic growth.

- But containment has also had limits. It has not prevented Iran from supporting a wide range of violent extremist groups. Tehran has continued to develop an arsenal of ballistic missiles and a nuclear enrichment program. And the Islamic Republic has stoked instability in several Middle East countries.

- Unless the Iranian regime collapses or evolves into something quite different—or the United States wages a third major war in the Middle East—containment is likely to remain the cornerstone of U.S. policy on Iran for some time.

Overview

The Carter administration attempted to develop normal diplomatic ties with the Islamic Republic after the revolution. But the White House reluctantly shifted to a policy of containment after the seizure of the U.S. Embassy in Tehran 10 months later. Containment has remained America's core strategy toward Iran because every administration since Carter has opted to pay as little attention to Iran as possible without jeopardizing U.S. interests in the Middle East. But several presidents deliberately avoided describing their policies as containment.

Containment endures because it is a minimalist strategy. It is a default position when engagement at any level is blocked and warfare is too costly or unattractive. Containment is predicated on two assumptions: First, the United States is not willing to expend the blood and treasure to remove the Tehran regime by force. Second, Iran is not interested in a peaceful relationship with Washington and, if left to its own devices, would try to overturn the current Middle East order to America's disadvantage. Containment's goal is to minimize Tehran's ability to cause mischief beyond its borders, destabilize the region, and hurt America's allies. Containment allows the United States to devote far fewer resources than would be needed to overthrow the regime.

Understanding containment

At the beginning of the Cold War, George Kennan introduced the idea of "containing" an unfriendly state in his work on U.S. policy toward the Soviet Union. It was based on two assumptions: For both ideological and geostrategic reasons, the United States and the Soviet Union would always be adversaries. And the United States would not try to eliminate the communist regime by force because of the unacceptable costs of war in the nuclear age. Containment was an alternative strategy to block political expansion, undermine the economy and prevent military aggression until the regime collapsed from its own defects in 1991.

Because of containment's success with the Soviet Union, the United States adapted it for a host of other challenges, including China, North Korea, Cuba, Libya, Iraq, Nicaragua, Angola, Ethiopia and Afghanistan. It has become the default policy whenever normal diplomatic relations are impossible. It is useful because it is highly flexible. Washington has pursued aggressive versions, as in Iraq between 1991 and 2003, and passive versions, as in Afghanistan between 1989 and 2001.

Containment options

With Iran, Washington's use of containment has been erratic, ranging from passive isolation to highly confrontational. The core elements of U.S. containment of Iran have remained largely unchanged, although the intensity has varied markedly. These include:

- Diplomatic efforts to isolate Tehran and enlist as many countries as possible to help the United States in containing Iran.

- Sanctions to prevent Iran from becoming economically or militarily powerful. These have especially focused on preventing or dissuading Iran from acquiring ballistic missiles or weapons of mass destruction, particularly nuclear weapons.

- Covert action to support various groups inside Iran that have opposed the regime politically and/or militarily.

- "Red lines," spelled out either explicitly or implicitly, that would trigger the use of U.S. force if Tehran crossed them.

- Military deployment, such as basing U.S. forces along the Persian Gulf to defend American allies, deter an Iranian attack, and enforce the red lines.

Five presidents: A brief history

The Carter administration tried to roll back the revolution by dispatching a senior U.S. general with close ties to Iranian military leaders to encourage them to seize power. When that gambit failed, Washington reversed gears, reached out to the new regime and offered to establish normal relations. That policy went up in smoke in November 1979, when Iranian students seized the U.S. Embassy in Tehran, kicking off the 444-day hostage crisis.

Carter considered a range of military options but eventually settled for a policy of pressuring Iran through economic sanctions and diplomatic isolation. Responding to fears of U.S. allies in the Persian Gulf, Washington also increased its military assets in the region to deter or defeat any Iranian attempt to spread its revolution by force. In effect, if not original intent, it was a policy of containing Iran—limiting its ability to cause harm beyond its borders and hindering its ability to generate greater power.

The Reagan administration was deeply critical of its predecessor, yet still adopted containment as its own policy. It showed a remarkable reluctance to confront Iran during both terms, despite its aggressive "cowboy" reputation and repeated Iranian provocations. Washington opted not to respond militarily even after Iranian Revolutionary Guards deployed to Lebanon, created Hezbollah, and facilitated the 1983 and 1984 suicide bombings of two American embassies and the U.S. Marine peacekeepers barracks in Beirut, the latter killing 241 Marines. Iran also had a role in the abduction of several American hostages in Beirut.

Reagan's containment tactics included building up U.S. military forces in the Gulf and increasing arms sales to Saudi Arabia and other Gulf Cooperation Council sheikhdoms. Washington also tilted toward Iraq in 1982, after Iran's battlefield victories in the war allowed it to push into Iraq. Tehran vowed to topple Saddam Hussein and march to Karbala and/or Jerusalem. The United States renewed diplomatic relations with Iraq, which Baghdad severed during the 1967 war. It also provided Iraq with trade credits and critical intelligence on Iran's military. And it encouraged European allies to supply Iraq with weapons paid for by U.S. Gulf allies.

The Reagan administration departed briefly from containment when it attempted a tactical rapprochement with Tehran in the mid-1980s to help free American hostages held by its allies in Lebanon. The subsequent arms-for-hostage swap ended in humiliation when Iranian hard-liners leaked news of the secret diplomacy. The United States then reverted to a restrained version of containment.

Washington was initially reluctant to defend Gulf Arab oil tankers that came under attack from Iranian forces in the Persian Gulf. When it finally agreed to deploy additional U.S. ships to defend the tankers in 1986-87, the administration issued tight rules of engagement. Washington intervened repeatedly to prevent conflict with Tehran. Iranian attacks on U.S. ships provoked limited U.S. counterstrikes, although the disparity in strength was so great that the U.S. Navy still sunk about one-half of Iran's major surface warships.

The administration of George H. W. Bush took office looking to improve relations with Iran. Bush suggested in his inaugural address that "good will begets good will." But when Iran helped win freedom for the last American hostages in Lebanon, Washington did not respond and his initiative came to naught. Other demands—the fall of communism, the crisis with China over Tiananmen Square and the 1990-1991 Persian Gulf War—led Bush to rely on passive containment of Iran. Washington ended up virtually ignoring Tehran.

The Clinton administration proclaimed a strategy of "dual containment" toward both Iran and Iraq. President Clinton believed a comprehensive Arab-Israeli peace was finally possible but feared Saddam Hussein's Iraq and revolutionary Iran would try to undermine the process. So Washington sought to limit the damage from either regime. Iran pushed back with an aggressive asymmetric campaign against U.S. interests and allies, which led Washington to get tougher. Goaded by Congress, the administration imposed comprehensive unilateral sanctions on Iran, threatened secondary sanctions on non-American companies doing significant business with Iran's oil industry, and rejuvenated the moribund covert action campaign against Iran. Clinton's first term witnessed the most aggressive containment pursued against the Islamic Republic.

But Clinton's second term overlapped with the 1997 election of reformist Mohammad Khatami as president and a slow shift in policy. Khatami reached out to the United States to try to bring down "the wall of mistrust." The Clinton administration hoped Khatami's opening offered the potential to end two decades of hostility and tried a string of unilateral gestures to try to help Khatami. But once again, Iran's hard-liners killed the budding reconciliation.

The administration of George W. Bush embraced containment after the rejected U.S. overture, although it demonstrated some flexibility after the 9/11 attacks. Washington and Tehran cooperated extensively, first in helping the Northern Alliance oust their mutual adversaries, the Taliban and al Qaeda, and then in forging an interim government in Afghanistan. Some in Tehran apparently hoped to turn tacit cooperation into a wider opening. But tentative diplomacy died after President Bush's 2002 State of the Union address lumped Iran with Iraq and North Korea in an "axis of evil." The United States again settled into a containment strategy, especially after the U.S. invasion of neighboring Iraq triggered new tensions between Washington and Tehran.

Nuclear complications

U.S. complacency was shattered in 2002, with revelations about secret facilities that indicated Iran was making greater progress in acquiring a nuclear capability than previously believed. Washington feared Iran's progress would seriously undermine containment, increase regional instability, and even endanger conflict. In response, the Bush administration and then the Obama administration tried a "carrot and stick" approach to convince Iran to halt its nuclear program. In both instances, Washington and its allies offered Tehran economic and diplomatic incentives to halt the program, while threatening more stringent sanctions if it refused.

The shift was intended to shore up containment and prevent Iran from increasing its military might with weapons of mass destruction. But both Bush and Obama also expected the strategy to deepen the policy debate in Tehran. They hoped that pragmatists willing to accept restrictions on Iran's nuclear program in return for concessions would prevail over hard-liners unwilling to give up the nuclear program at all. This gambit also calculated that a victory by pragmatists might lead to their ascendance—and in turn new openings for rapprochement.

The future

- Many fear that Iran's eventual acquisition of a nuclear capability could fatally compromise containment. It could eliminate the ultimate deterrent of an American conventional military attack as a restraint on aggressive Iranian efforts to destabilize the Middle East.

- Others believe that making containment work will be more important than ever once Iran achieves a nuclear capability because it will once and for all rule out an American invasion of Iran but could in turn make Tehran feel more secure in confronting the United States—and therefore less inclined to improve relations.

- A nuclear Iran would create additional challenges for containment by potentially convincing some of Iran's neighbors to acquire nuclear capabilities of their own.

- It would also create potentially worrisome interactions between Iran and Israel, which might engage in unconventional warfare against each other that would likely provoke dangerous nuclear stand-offs between Jerusalem and Tehran.

Kenneth M. Pollack, director of the Saban Center for Middle East Policy at the Brookings Institution, is the lead author of Which Path to Persia? Options for a New American Strategy toward Iran.

50

The Military Option

Dov S. Zakheim

- Iran's controversial nuclear program is nearing a crisis point. A combination of factors—progress in enriching uranium, years of defying U.N. resolutions and bellicose rhetoric—has led to growing talk about a military option.

- Israel is independently concerned about Iran's program, given statements by President Mahmoud Ahmadinejad denying the Holocaust and challenging Israel's existence.

- But any military operation against nuclear facilities in Iran, the world's 18th largest state, would be starkly more difficult and more dangerous than Israel's air strikes on Iraqi and Syrian nuclear reactors.

- A single bombing raid, even several raids, is not likely to terminate the Iranian program.

- The international community is also likely to be deeply divided over a military operation, with opposition from key allies and major powers such as Russia and China. It could even be unpopular in a war-weary American society.

Overview

Since the mid-1990s, the international community has claimed Iran was engaged in a clandestine uranium enrichment program that could be used to develop a nuclear weapons capability. Calls for more decisive international action increased after revelations in 2002 that Iran had built a secret enrichment facility in Natanz and a heavy-water facility at Arak. If sanctions fail to force Iran to abandon the program, Israel particularly has suggested the military option.

But a military strike would be more difficult than the 1981 Israeli attack on Iraq's Osirak reactor or the 2007 Israeli attack on a Syrian nuclear facility, which was alleged to be a weapons-grade reactor. Iraq and Syria had only one target, while Iran has several targets, some underground and all dispersed throughout its much larger territory. Iran could have other secret nuclear sites, although Tehran denies it. In mid-2010, Tehran announced plans to build 10 additional sites for enrichment, the first one to begin in March 2011. All were to be built inside mountains. Even Israel admits that a military strike would yield only limited, short-term results. And an American strike, even a series of strikes, might ultimately not be any more successful in putting a permanent halt to the Iranian program.

Targets

Iran's geographic area is one of the world's largest; it ranks 18th among all nations. Its known nuclear facilities are geographically dispersed:

- The Natanz facility is 130 miles southeast of Tehran.

- The Qom enrichment facility, identified in 2009, is southwest of the Iranian capital.

- The Arak heavy-water plant is about 150 miles south of Tehran.

- The Isfahan nuclear technology research center is in central Iran, 210 miles south of Tehran.

- The Karaj radioactive storage facility is 100 miles northwest of Tehran.

- The Bushehr reactor is on the Gulf, more than 500 miles from Tehran.

Any strike, or series of strikes, may also have to target many other Iranian military facilities to eliminate the danger of retaliatory attacks against U.S. forces in Afghanistan, Iraq, the Gulf or elsewhere in the Middle East. There are hundreds of potential targets, which could include:

- Medium range ballistic missile sites near Iraq
- Cruise missile sites
- 14 airfields with shelters
- Naval facilities and especially diesel submarines
- Two chemical plants
- The major petroleum refinery at Kharg Island could constitute another major target for American forces.

Forces and weapons

To conduct a massive aerial campaign against Iran, the United States could use B-2 bombers launched from Diego Garcia. It could also employ F-22s and F-16s from the territories of one or more of its Gulf allies, carrier-based F-18s and the support aircraft that would accompany them: AWACS, electronic warfare aircraft and tankers. The United States could also call on special operating forces to provide targeting and other support.

U.S. forces could employ a variety of weapons to ensure the destruction of underground as well as above-ground facilities. These include BLU 113 bunker buster penetrators and BLU-118 hyperbaric weapons for deep penetration attacks as well as more conventional munitions. In addition, aviation units could be supplemented by Tomahawk land attack missile strikes from Trident submarines based in the Indian Ocean.

Military challenges

One major operational decision confronting both policymakers and military planners will be the actual number and location of potential Iranian targets. If there are secret underground enrichment facilities—and the U.S. intelligence record on Iran has not been consistently stellar—local Iranian dissidents or minorities are unlikely to provide much targeting support. The majority of the population supports the broader nuclear energy program and could rally around the Ahmadinejad regime in the event of a foreign attack, as it did in support of Ayatollah Ruhollah Khomeini after Iraq's 1980 invasion.

Targeting would therefore have to rely primarily on two sources:

- Satellites, which may not have detected underground facilities
- Special forces, whose best-known operation in Iran, the April 1980 Desert One rescue attempt, was an unmitigated failure. How well and freely such forces might operate in Iran 30 years later is a major uncertainty.

Uncertainty about the location of all facilities would also influence the number of attacks to be launched against Iranian targets. While the United States could easily control the skies over Iran for a single massive attack, it is unclear whether and to what extent such an attack would succeed, given both uncertainty about the location of all potential targets, and difficulty achieving rapid and certain battle damage assessments. Multiple aerial attacks may therefore be necessary.

Depending on the number of targets and sorties involved, an aerial strike could require a very large number of attack aircraft, including several air force fighter/attack wings, three to four aircraft carrier wings, bombers and support aircraft. Aircraft, particularly carrier aviation, may have to be diverted from other missions, notably in East Asia. And if the United States undertakes an ongoing series of strikes, a longer operation would result in a significant redeployment of forces back to the Gulf region.

Neighboring states

Any U.S. operation against Iran involving land-based fighter aircraft would require the cooperation of Iran's neighbors. Such cooperation cannot be taken for granted, especially for forces deployed in Iraq. The Baghdad government, which is likely to be led by Shiite political parties for the foreseeable future, would almost certainly object to U.S. forces using its territory against its larger and more powerful Shiite neighbor. Article 27 of the 2009 U.S.-Iraq Status of Forces Agreement explicitly prohibits the use of "Iraqi land, water and airspace as a route or launching pad for attacks against other countries." The costs of violating that agreement—on many fronts—would be high.

The nervous Gulf sheikhdoms would be equally hesitant to do anything more than grant American forces overflight rights. To permit U.S. aircraft to operate from their soil would amount to an invitation to Iran to destabilize their own regimes. Each country has its own concerns:

Bahrain, which is headquarters for the U.S. Fifth Fleet, has a restive Shiite majority that is split between Arabs and Persians.

Saudi Arabia has a significant Shiite population in its eastern province, the country's oil-producing heartland, that would certainly not want to be seen as cooperating with the United States.

Qatar, host to the U.S. Combined Air Operations Center, maintains decent relations with Tehran.

Oman and Kuwait, which host prepositioned materiel for U.S. forces, also either have dealings with Iran or would want to avoid igniting new tensions in the Gulf.

The United Arab Emirates, which continues to contest the shah's seizure of Abu Musa and the Tunbs islands, might be willing to provide overflight rights. Even so, Dubai's tight trading relations with Iran would probably put a brake on just how far the UAE was prepared to go in support of an American strike.

It is even less likely that the United States could conduct aerial strikes from Incirlik or other bases in Turkey. The Turkish parliament denied Washington access to deploy its Fourth Infantry Division against Saddam Hussein in 2003. Nothing more could be expected from the parliament in the event of a proposed attack in Iran. The government of Prime Minister Recep Erdogan has been outspoken in opposing sanctions on Iran and would probably oppose any cooperation with U.S. forces on Iran even more vociferously than it did on Iraq in 2003.

The bottom line is that any aerial strike against Iran's nuclear facilities would have to be conducted primarily by long-range bombers and naval aviation. And it would be difficult, especially for the carrier forces, to sustain ongoing strikes over a period of time due to the strain on a declining carrier force.

Other options, other targets

The United States could employ Trident-based cruise missiles to attack Iranian nuclear facilities. Doing so would avoid some of the political complications in the region. But cruise missile strikes also tend to be one-off affairs. In addition, they would have uncertain results against underground targets. Finally, it would be difficult to obtain battle damage assessments, particularly about underground targets.

The United States could pressure Iran militarily without actually attacking its nuclear facilities. For example, it could strike the Kharg Island oil refineries, or some other major military or economic targets. These strikes could be carried out by a number of different forces, including carrier-based aircraft, bombers or cruise missiles.

Another option is for the U.S. Navy to impose a blockade on Iranian exports. A blockade or any other use of naval forces operating inside the Gulf would almost certainly provoke an Iranian naval response, possibly swarm attacks by coordinated Iranian Navy and Revolutionary Guard Naval forces. The U.S. Navy could ultimately repel such attacks, using both air and surface forces to destroy the attacking boats. But some Iranian forces may be able to break through the U.S. naval defense and inflict damage. Iran could also circumvent the blockade, at least to some extent, by trading or smuggling goods through Turkey, Central Asia and even Russia.

Finally, the United States could deploy Special Forces, as well as intelligence units, to conduct covert and clandestine operations against elements of the Iranian nuclear program. There have been repeated reports of Israeli attempts to sabotage the program, with some degree of success, which is how the Israelis sabotaged the Egyptian program in the 1960s. These types of operations may not be as dramatic or as immediate as military strikes, but they would lessen the likelihood of retaliation by Iran or its regional allies. At the same time, Special Forces operations also run the risk that Americans could be captured in Iran.

Political repercussions

The United Nations is unlikely to support a military attack. Even the British and the French are unlikely to support anything more than sanctions, while China and Russia have been reluctant even to support serious sanctions.

The biggest danger may be backlash in the Muslim world, especially after prolonged U.S.-led wars in Iraq and Afghanistan. A U.S. strike could certainly stir up sympathy for Iran in the Muslim world, especially among the Shiites in Iraq, Saudi Arabia and Bahrain, and on the Sunni street in the southern Gulf, the Arab Middle East and potentially South Asia. Even quiescent Muslim communities, notably India's Shiite community (who number in the tens of millions), might react strongly against the United States. India has staunchly resisted sanctions against Iran, for geopolitical reasons. Both countries are wary of Pakistan's anti-Shiite extremists. But

Pakistanis of many sects are anti-American and could react violently against U.S. targets in Pakistan. The U.S. Embassy in Islamabad was attacked and burned to the ground in 1979—tied in part to Iran.

Whether Israel or the United States attacked Iranian nuclear facilities, Tehran would see both as the same. Tehran could retaliate in a variety of ways. It could attack U.S. targets not only in Iraq and Afghanistan, but worldwide. The regime could urge Hezbollah and Hamas to launch rocket strikes against Israel, although whether either would do so is uncertain since Israel has indicated it would in turn retaliate against Lebanon and Gaza in unrestrained fashion. Syria, Iran's only real Arab ally, could even enter a war. The bottom line is that the possibility of a U.S. or Israeli attack prompting a wider Middle East war cannot be ruled out.

The future

- An Israeli attack on Iranian nuclear facilities is unlikely to stop the Iranian program for very long. An American aerial strike might be more successful, but it also may not shut down Iran's program. Only a series of ongoing attacks is likely to accomplish that goal.

- Yet an overt military operation could make Tehran even more determined to acquire a weapons capability as a deterrent to future attacks.

- The military consequences and political costs could, over time, mount for whichever nation attacked Iran. Retaliation could play out across the world's most volatile region and potentially far beyond.

- Clandestine action against Iranian facilities would be more effective and less risky politically. But a covert effort would also take time, and its success could also not be guaranteed.

Dov S. Zakheim is senior adviser at the Center for Strategic and International Studies and vice chairman of the Foreign Policy Research Institute.

People, Places, and Key Events

Iran's Power Structure

Mehrzad Boroujerdi and Kourosh Rahimkhani

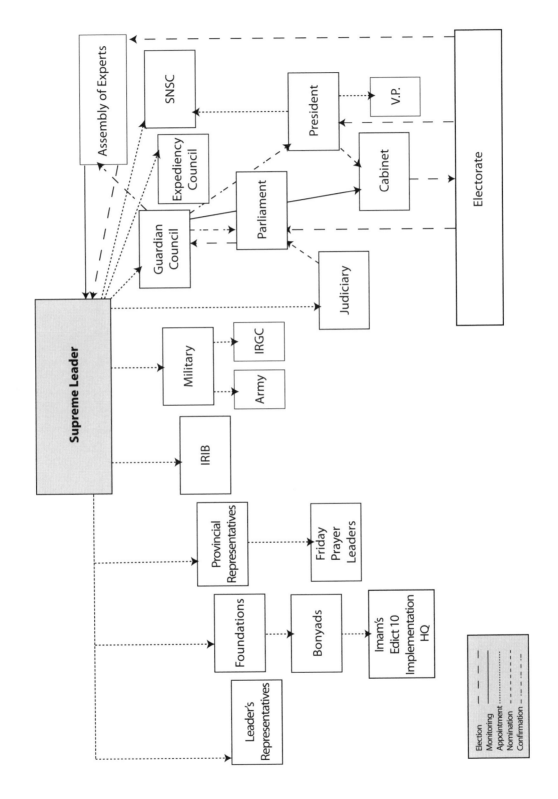

Iran's Political Elite

Mehrzad Boroujerdi and Kourosh Rahimkhani

Abdi, Abbas (1956–) A leading journalist and political analyst. He was one of the students who took over the American embassy on November 4, 1979, and in 1999, he took part in a debate with one of the former hostages at UNESCO headquarters in Paris. An engineer by training, he served after the revolution in the intelligence agencies, the judiciary and the Center for Strategic Studies, which is affiliated with the Office of the President. He was imprisoned for eight months in 1993 for writing critical columns in the *Salam* newspaper and later served a three-year jail term (2002–2005) for conducting a poll on behalf of Gallup that showed more than 74 percent of Iranians were interested in rapprochement with the United States.

Ahmadinejad, Mahmoud (1956–) A conservative populist politician who won 61 percent of the votes in a runoff presidential election against former president Rafsanjani in 2005. He was reelected in a disputed vote in 2009 that gave birth to the opposition Green Movement. Son of a blacksmith, he earned a doctorate in transport engineering and served with both the Basij and Revolutionary Guards (IRGC) during the Iran-Iraq War. In his website profile, he claims that during the war he worked as a Basiji volunteer in the engineering group in Kurdistan and West Azerbaijan. He reportedly became a member of the IRGC in 1986 when he joined the Special Forces division of IRGC. Afterwards, he served as governor general of Khoi and Mako, governor of Ardabil, mayor of Tehran (2003-2005), and then president. His acerbic comments about Israel and the United States and his messianic discourse have made him a controversial figure in international politics.

Asgaroladi, Habibollah (1932–) A heavyweight in the conservative political camp. There are rumors that his family was originally of Jewish descent and converted to Islam during the reign of Reza Shah Pahlavi. He served for many years as the secretary-general of the Islamic Coalition Party (Hezb-e Mo'talefeh-ye Eslami), the supreme leader's representative on the Imam Khomeini Relief Committee (the biggest governmental charity serving 10 million poor people), a member of Parliament, the commerce minister (1981–1983), and a member of the Expediency Council. He also twice (1981 and 1985) ran unsuccessfully as a candidate for the presidency.

Bahonar, Mohammad-Reza (1952–) A powerful conservative member of Parliament who has so far served six terms in the chamber (often in leadership posts) as well as three terms in the Expediency Council. He and like-minded colleagues founded the influential Islamic Society of Engineers (*Jame`eh-ye Eslami-ye Mohandesin*) in 1991. His older brother, Mohammad-Javad Bahonar, served only for 26 days as Iran's prime minister before a bomb claimed his life as well as that of President Mohammad-Ali Raja'i in 1981.

Bani-Sadr, Abolhassan (1933–) Iran's first post-revolutionary president. Son of an ayatollah, he studied economics before the revolution in France but did not finish his dissertation. In January 1980, he was elected to office with 75 percent of the popular vote, but he was forced by his opponents to flee the country some 16 months later and resettle back in Paris. Iraq's invasion of Iran happened on his watch and augmented his differences with the clerical establishment.

Bazargan, Mehdi (1907–1995) Iran's first post-revolutionary prime minister (1979). A French-educated mechanical engineer, he founded the Liberation Movement of Iran in 1961 and played a crucial role within Islamic intellectual circles before the revolution. He was a deputy minister under Premier Mohammad Mossadeq in the 1950s. He did not have a single cleric in his cabinet and resigned from the premiership after the U.S. Embassy takeover in 1979.

Beheshti, Ayatollah Mohammad (1928–1981) One of Khomeini's most trusted and powerful clerical allies during and immediately after the revolution. Son of an Isfahan cleric, he attended the Qom seminary and earned a doctorate in theology from Tehran University. He served as an Islamic missionary in Germany from 1965 to 1970. He was the secretary-general of the powerful Islamic Republican Party before being killed in a 1981 bombing. Beheshti also presided over the meetings of the Assembly of Experts that drafted the Islamic Republic's constitution and was chief of the judiciary until 1981.

Ebadi, Shirin (1947–) The only Iranian to have received a Nobel Prize. In 1975, she became the first female judge in Iran, but was forced to resign after the revolution. She subsequently opened her own law firm and became a tireless defender of women, children, human rights activists and political prisoners. She was awarded the 2003 Nobel Peace Prize. Her outspoken criticism of the regime after the contested 2009 presidential election forced her into exile.

Ebtekar, Masoumeh (1960–) Iran's first female vice president. Daughter of an engineer, the American-educated activist was known to American television audience as "Sister Mary," spokeswoman for the students who took over the U.S. Embassy. Her husband was also one of the hostage takers. After Ebtekar earned a Ph.D. in immunology, President Khatami appointed her vice president and head of the Environmental Protection Organization (1997–2005). She represented Iran at the World Women's Conferences in Nairobi and Beijing.

Ganji, Akbar (1960–) A prominent investigative journalist and dissident. An initial supporter of the Islamic Republic and former member of the Revolutionary Guards, he grew increasingly critical of the regime and played a leading role in exposing the serial killings of Iranian intellectuals. He spent six years in prison (2000–2006) for having attended a "counter-revolutionary" conference in Berlin. To protest his imprisonment, he staged a hunger strike in prison that galvanized public opinion. After his release he settled in the United States, where he writes and criticizes the Iranian regime.

Haddad-Adel, Gholamali (1945–) An influential conservative politician close to the supreme leader. Born into a business family, the former speaker of parliament has advanced degrees in physics and philosophy. After the revolution, he wrote many of the middle school and high school textbooks on religion and social studies. He is the father-in-law of Mojtaba Khamenei, the supreme leader's son and chief of staff.

Hejazi, Hojatoleslam Ali Asghar (19??–) A powerful yet shadowy cleric who is in charge of security for the office of the supreme leader. He was a deputy in the ministry of intelligence during Khamenei's presidency in the 1980s. During Khatami's presidency, he built what the Iranian media referred to as a structure of "parallel intelligence" (*Ettela`at Movazi*) to prosecute regime opponents. (Hojatoleslam is a clerical rank below ayatollah.)

Jafari, Mohammad-Ali [Aziz] (1957–) Supreme commander of the Revolutionary Guards (2007–). He was reportedly involved in the takeover of the U.S. Embassy and then joined the IRGC in 1981. After the end of the Iran-Iraq War, in which he was badly injured, he earned a master's degree in architecture. For 13 years (1992–2005), he was the commander of IRGC ground forces. His brother-in-law, Mohammad-Baqer Zulqadr, is also a top commander in the IRGC. Both are on the U.S. government sanctions list.

Jannati, Ayatollah Ahmad (1926–) An arch-conservative cleric who has spent 30 years on the Guardian Council, 28 years on the Assembly of Experts, and 22 years on the Expediency Council. Born into a clerical family from Isfahan known for producing good quality quince and pears, he lost a son who had joined the opposition Mujahedin-e Khalq Organization and was killed in a battle with the security forces in 1982. Jannati is a former head of the Iranian Islamic Propagation Organization and served for many years as one of the Friday Prayer Leaders of Tehran.

Kadivar, Hojatoleslam Mohsen (1959–) A dissident cleric who rejected the doctrine of clerical rule or *velayat-e faqih* (guardianship of the jurist) espoused by Ayatollah Khomeini. Son of a teacher, he abandoned his study of electrical engineering, which he had started at Shiraz University before the revolution, in favor of studying theology and jurisprudence at Qom seminary. He became one of the best students of Ayatollah Montazeri and, like his mentor, became critical of the regime. In 1999, the Special Court for the Clergy sentenced him to an 18-month prison term for his critical views. Now living in the United States, he remains a fierce critic of the Islamic Republic.

Karbaschi, Gholamhoseyn (1953–) Former mayor of Tehran and secretary-general of the Servants of Reconstruction Party (*Hezb-e Kargozaran-e Sazandegi-ye Iran*), which is close to former President Rafsanjani. The son of an ayatollah, he studied theology at Qom Seminary and mathematics at Tehran University. He traded in his clerical robe for civilian clothes and went on to have a successful political career, serving as governor of Isfahan and then mayor of Tehran. In 1998, as a reformist ally of President Khatami, he was arrested on corruption charges and his televised show trial captivated the Iranian public. The court first sentenced him to five years imprisonment for mismanagement of state funds but acquitted him on a bribery charge. The court of appeals later reduced his sentence from five years to two.

Karroubi, Hojatoleslam Mehdi (1937–) Former speaker of parliament and later opposition leader. Son of a clergyman from the Lorestan province, he was imprisoned under the shah and became a trusted lieutenant of Khomeini who put him in charge of the Martyrs Foundation (1979–1992) and Pilgrimage Affairs (1985–1990).

He was involved in the Iran-Contra negotiations that took place between Iranian and American officials. After serving for 16 years as a member of parliament, often as deputy-speaker or speaker, he ran for president in 2005 and 2009. Both times, he accused the regime of rigging the votes. Karroubi, who was one of the founders of the Assembly of Militant Clerics (*Majma`-e Ruhaniyyun-e Mobarez*), broke with his colleagues over his election protest and in 2005 founded The National Trust Party (*Hezb Etemad Melli*). In 2009, he and Mir-Hossein Mousavi emerged as the two most prominent leaders of the Green Movement.

Khamenei, Ayatollah Ali (1939–) Succeeded Khomeini as Iran's supreme leader. Son of a cleric, he was born in Mashhad and studied theology there and in Qom, where he was exposed to Khomeini's ideas. In the 1980s, he was elected president in 1981 and 1985 during the Iran-Iraq War. In 1989, after Ayatollah Khomeini's death, the Assembly of Experts selected him to be the supreme leader. Lacking Khomeini's charisma, he has emerged as a micromanager and has increasingly thrown his considerable weight behind the conservative camp. He survived an assassination attempt in 1981 but lost the use of one of his hands. He has six children.

Khamenei, Hojatoleslam Hadi (1947–) Younger brother of the supreme leader who opposes the concept of *velayat-e faqih*. He is a four-term member of parliament who also published two newspapers (*Jahan Islam* and *Hayat Nou*), both of which were banned by the Judiciary on the charge of castigating political leaders.

Khamenei, Hojatoleslam Mojtaba (1969–) Second son of the supreme leader. He is a cleric who both studies and teaches in the Qom seminary. Reputed to be a powerful behind-the-scenes player in his father's operations and an individual being primed to succeed him, he was the subject of harsh slogans after the 2009 disputed elections with the crowds shouting "Mojtaba, [we hope you] die and never get to be the leader."

Khatami, Hojatoleslam Mohammad (1943–) Reformist president. Son of an ayatollah, he was born in Yazd province, studied philosophy and theology in university and seminary settings, and married into Khomeini's family. After the revolution, he held a variety of posts such as administrator of an Islamic Center in Hamburg, head of a government publishing house, member of parliament, and three terms as minister of culture and Islamic guidance. In 1992, he was forced to resign as culture minister after protesting increasing censorship and headed the National Library before respectively winning 69 percent and 77 percent of the vote in the 1997 and 2001 presidential elections. He advocated the concept of "Dialogue of Civilizations" and pursued domestic and foreign policies that somewhat improved Iran's image during his term in office. He has three children.

Khoeiniha, Ayatollah Mohammad (1941–) Clerical guide of the students who took over the U.S. Embassy and father of left-wing activism in post-revolutionary Iran. Nicknamed the "Red Mullah" for reportedly having studied at Patrice Lumumba University in the Soviet Union, he has served in such posts as prosecutor general, member of parliament, and member of both the Assembly of Experts and the Expediency Council. In the 1990s, he was the publisher of the influential *Salam* newspaper, which was banned after releasing a secret governmental document that led to the student riots in July 1999.

Khomeini, Ayatollah Ruhollah (1902–1989) Charismatic leader of the Islamic Revolution and founder of the Islamic Republic. Born into a clerical family, he grew increasingly critical of the shah's regime, which then sent him into exile in Iraq. He continued his revolutionary activism during 16 years of exile in Najaf, where he articulated the doctrine of *velayat-e faqih* as a theory of statecraft. At the age of 73, he witnessed the realization of his dream and deposed one of America's strongest allies in the Middle East. His Shiite followers refer to him as "Imam," an honorific title previously reserved only for the "twelve infallible" descendents of the Prophet.

Khomeini, Hojatoleslam Hassan (1972–) The grandson of Ayatollah Khomeini. He was born in Najaf and presently teaches theology in Qom. He is in charge of the Khomeini mausoleum and has made it clear through his actions and speeches that he supports the reformist camp. Conservatives worry that the reformists may wish to tout him as a potential supreme leader.

Larijani, Ali (1957–) Speaker of parliament and former chief nuclear negotiator. He is the son of Ayatollah Mirza Hashem Amoli and son-in law of Ayatollah Morteza Motahhari. A student of mathematics and computer science, he also holds advanced degrees in philosophy. After serving in the Revolutionary Guards, he was a member of parliament, minister of culture, member of the Expediency Council, the supreme leader's representative to the Supreme National Security Council, and head of the Iran Broadcasting Corporation.

Larijani, Hojatoleslam Sadeq (1960–) Appointed judiciary chief in 2009. He is the younger clerical brother of Ali Larijani and son-in-law of Ayatollah Vahid Khorasani, a source of emulation in Qom. He earlier served in the Assembly of Experts and the Guardian Council. His reputation suffered due to the regime's harsh treatment of detainees from protests after the 2009 presidential election.

Mahdavi-Kani, Ayatollah Mohammad-Reza (1931–) Influential conservative politician who served briefly as a caretaker prime minister in the early years of the revolution. Born into a peasant family, he was sent into internal exile by the shah's regime. After the revolution, he became overseer of the revolutionary committees that mushroomed around the country. His resume includes posts such as minister of interior, secretary-general of the Association of the Militant Clergy (Jame`eh-ye Ruhaniyyat-e Mobarez), and chancellor of Imam Sadeq University, as well as member of the Expediency Council, the Guardian Council and Assembly of Experts.

Makarem-Shirazi, Ayatollah Naser (1926–) Powerful ayatollah and source of emulation. Son of a trader, he was born in Shiraz and attended seminary school in Qom. He was jailed and exiled in the pre-revolutionary period, and he defended more conservative Islamic positions against lay intellectuals like Ali Shariati. After the revolution, he served in the Assembly of Experts that drafted the constitution and then refused to hold other governmental posts. He issued a fatwa objecting to women attending stadiums to watch soccer matches.

Mashaei, Esfandyar Rahim (1960–) One of Ahmadinejad's closest confidants. Born in Ramsar, his career began with the Revolutionary Guards in that city and then in the Kurdistan region where he fought against Kurdish and Mojahedin-e Khalq forces as an intelligence officer. He subsequently served in both the intelligence and the interior ministries and then joined Ahmadinejad in the Tehran municipality. He served as vice president and head of the Cultural Heritage Organization in Ahmadinejad's first term and the chief of the Office of the President since 2009. It is rumored that Ahmadinejad would like to see him as his replacement in the 2013 presidential elections. Mashaei's daughter is married to Ahmadinejad's oldest son.

Mesbah-Yazdi, Ayatollah Mohammad-Taqi (1934–) An ultra-conservative senior ayatollah who serves as spiritual guide to many conservative clerics and politicians. Despite being from the same province (Yazd) as Khatami, he and his disciples created constant problems for the former president. Reputed as the only senior ayatollah who kisses the foot of the supreme leader, Mesbah-Yazdi is mentioned as a possible future supreme leader. He also heads the main opposition to Rafsanjani in the Assembly of Experts. Mesbah-Yazdi has been a member of the High Cultural Revolution Council and also heads the Imam Khomeini Educational and Research Institute. His son-in-law heads the Islamic Propaganda Organization.

Meshkini, Ayatollah Ali-Akbar (1921–2007) Served for 27 years (1980–2007) as the Chairman of the Assembly of Experts. Born into a clerical family from the province of Ardabil, he studied theology in the Qom seminary with Khomeini. He was heavily involved in drafting the land reform legislation after the revolution and served on the central committee of the Association of the Militant Clergy (Jame`eh-ye Ruhaniyyat-e Mobarez).

Mirdamadi, Mohsen (1955–) Former hostage-taker and secretary-general of the reformist Islamic Iran Participation Front (Jebhe-ye Mosharekat-e Iran-e Eslami). Born in Isfahan, he was one of the three masterminds of the U.S. Embassy takeover. He then joined the Revolutionary Guards and held other positions including governor of Khuzestan and member of the Sixth Parliament. In 2009, he was detained after the disputed presidential election and forced to take part in the show trials that were conducted on television.

Mohseni-Ezhehi, Hojatoleslam Gholamhoseyn (1957–) Prosecutor general. Son of a cleric from Isfahan, this hard-line and feared cleric has been intimately connected to the intelligence ministry and the judiciary. He was the prosecutor general of the Special Court for the Clergy (1998–2005) before becoming Ahmadinejad's intelligence minister. Ahmadinejad dismissed him a few months before his term was over, but the head of the judiciary rewarded him with the post of prosecutor general. He was heavily involved in the post-election related arrests and imprisonments in 2009.

Montazeri, Grand Ayatollah Ali (1922–2009) Clerical dissident and former designated heir to the supreme leader (1985–89). The son of a peasant from the Isfahan province, he studied theology in Qom, served time in prison under the shah, and became one of Khomeini's chief lieutenants. In the early days of the revolution, he was the target of jokes calling him a simpleton. In November 1985, a consultative council of experts in Islamic jurisprudence appointed him spiritual successor to Ayatollah Khomeini. But his opposition to the mass execution of dissidents in 1988 cost him his position. He spent the rest of his life in Qom under house arrest but continued to speak out against the regime and its human rights record.

Motahhari, Ayatollah Morteza (1920–1979) Leading theologian, political activist and cleric from Khorasan province who was beloved by Khomeini. A professor of Islamic philosophy at Tehran University before the revolution, he emerged as the head of the Council of the Islamic Revolution, a clandestine council appointed by Khomeini to oversee the consolidation of the revolution. His life was cut short a few months after the revolution when he was assassinated by a group of Islamic militants opposed to clerical rule. Khomeini provided his most famous eulogy on the occasion of Motahhari's death.

Mousavi, Mir Hossein (1942–) Former prime minister and leader of the Green Movement. Son of a tea merchant from East Azerbaijan, he became an architect by training before the revolution. After the revolution, he joined the Islamic Republic Party and became the chief editor of its newspaper (1979–1980). Because of Mousavi's left-wing reputation, President Khamenei did not want Mousavi as his prime minister, despite being distant relatives. He introduced Ali Akbar Velayati for the post, yet the parliament did not approve him. Mousavi was then offered the post of prime minister and served in that capacity from 1981 to 1989. He is generally credited with competent management of the country during the course of the Iran-Iraq War. From 1989 to 2009, he served as an advisor to Presidents Rafsanjani and Khatami. In 2009, he claimed to have won the presidential election and fiercely contested Ahmadinejad's official victory. His protest gave rise to the opposition Green Movement.

Qalibaf, Mohammad-Baqer (1961–) Mayor of Tehran. Son of a dried-fruit seller, he served in the Revolution-ary Guards (IRGC) and quickly moved up the ranks during and after the Iraq war. A pilot by training, he has held such posts as commander of IRGC's air force, chief of the Law Enforcement Force (2000–05), and since 2005, the mayor of Tehran. He has ambitions to become president and is not on good terms with Ahmadine-jad, who has prevented him from attending cabinet meetings.

Rafiqdoust, Mohsen (19?? –) Minister of Revolutionary Guards (1982–1988). He reportedly underwent training in PLO camps before the revolution and started his career as Khomeini's bodyguard. During the 1980s, he became the first and only minister of the IRGC, since the cabinet post was eliminated in 1989. He subsequently headed the Disenfranchised Foundation (*Bonyad Mostazafan*) from which he was dismissed in 1995 for corruption. Rafiqdoust refers to himself as the "father of Iran's missile program."

Rafsanjani, Hojatoleslam Akbar Hashemi (1934–) Former president and speaker of parliament. Born into a farming family from Kerman province, he emerged as one of the most powerful members of the political elite in post-revolutionary Iran. Nicknamed "the shark" since his smooth skinned face does not have a long beard, he has been a mover and shaker in Iranian politics. He served eight years (1989-1997) as president, but on his third try was soundly defeated by Ahmadinejad. He simultaneously heads the Guardian Council and the Expediency Council, despite his declining political fortunes. His family has received widespread criticism for their supposed ill-gotten wealth.

Rahnavard, Zahra (1945–) Writer and political activist. Born into a military family, she attended an art col-lege in the 1960s specializing in sculpture. In 1969, she married Mir Hossein Mousavi and gravitated toward the ideas of Ali Shariati. They spent a few years in the mid-1970s in the United States and went back to Iran at the time of the revolution. She later pursued a doctorate in political science and served as a high-level official at a women's university. She played an active role in her husband's 2009 presidential campaign and helped to galvanize his female supporters. Ahmadinejad's attacks on her personal integrity during the presidential debate with her husband violated a political and social taboo. She continues to be active in the Green Move-ment with her husband.

Rezaei, Mohsen (1954–) Supreme commander of the Revolutionary Guards (1981–1997). Born in Khuzestan province, he was reportedly involved in a number of assassinations before the revolution and became the IRGC supreme commander at the age of 27. He ran unsuccessfully for the sixth parliament in 1999, and for the presidency in 2005 and 2009. He presently serves as the secretary of the Expediency Council. INTERPOL issued a warrant for his arrest in 2007 for his involvement in the bombing of the Jewish center in Argentina.

Safavi, Yahya Rahim (1952–) Supreme commander of the Revolutionary Guards (1997–2007). Born into a peasant family in Isfahan province, he had military training in Syria before the revolution and served in the shah's army from 1975 to 1977. Two of his brothers were killed in the Iran-Iraq War. A war veteran himself, he replaced Rezaei as IRGC Commander in 1997. After his term ended, he was appointed by the supreme leader as his military advisor and senior aide for armed forces affairs. He is on the list of Iranian individuals sanctioned by the U.S. government.

Shariati, Ali (1933–1977) Ideologue of the Iranian revolution. Born into a religious family in Mashhad, he received a Ph.D. in hagiology from the University of Paris and subsequently taught Islamic history at Mashhad University. The essays of this prolific author were hugely influential in turning many of Iran's youth against the shah's regime. His sudden death from a heart attack significantly contributed to his popularity, as foul play by the shah's secret service was suspected. Shariati's anti-clerical views did not endear him to the class of clerical mandarins who came to power soon after he had passed away.

Shariatmadari, Ayatollah Kazem (1905–1986) A leading traditional Shiite cleric. Born in the Azerbaijan province, he was recognized as a leading ayatollah after the death of Ayatollah Boroujerdi (1875-1961). In

1963, Shariatmadari recognized Ayatollah Khomeini as a grand ayatollah. He played a key role in the Iranian revolution, but soon became a chief critic of the theory of *velayat-e faqih*. In December 1979, he opposed a referendum to centralize power in the hands of the supreme leader, a position that cost him his religious authority. The government accused him of being an accomplice in a plot to kill Khomeini, and they stripped him of his clerical robe. He lived the last six years of his life under house arrest until he passed away in 1986.

Soleymani, Qasem (19??–) Commander of Revolutionary Guard's Qods Forces, the elite unit that carries out foreign operations. A decorated veteran of the Iran-Iraq War whom Khamenei has referred to as a "living martyr," he was one of the 24 IRGC commanders who wrote a threatening letter to President Khatami in 1999. He is reportedly heavily involved in Iran's activities in Iraq.

Soroush, Abdolkarim (1945–) A leading Islamic thinker. Trained in pharmacy and the philosophy of science, he was a theoretician of the Islamic Republic in its early days and was appointed by Khomeini as a member of the Supreme Council for the Cultural Revolution. He increasingly grew critical of the regime and served as an intellectual mentor to young Islamic intellectuals disassociating themselves from the regime. In the 1990s, he was considered the father of the reform movement, which led to frequent attacks on his lectures. He presently resides in the United States.

Velayati, Ali-Akbar (1945–) Iran's foreign minister (1981–1997). A pediatrician who had advanced training at the Johns Hopkins Hospital in Baltimore, Velayati served as foreign minister under Khamenei and Rafsanjani. After leaving office, he became a foreign policy advisor to the supreme leader.

Yazdi, Ebrahim (1931–) Former foreign minister and secretary-general of the Liberation Movement of Iran (*Nehzat Azadi*). American-educated, he has a doctorate in pharmacy and was active in the overseas Iranian opposition movement against the shah. He served as one of Khomeini's closest confidants, spokesmen and translators during the ayatollah's stay in Paris (1978-1979). After serving briefly as Bazargan's foreign minister and then one term as a member of parliament, he was shunned politically. He remained active as an opposition politician; he has been jailed several times.

Yazdi, Ayatollah Mohammad (1921–) An arch-conservative cleric from Isfahan. He is one of the record holders in post-revolutionary Iran in terms of important positions occupied. Among his titles are head of Khomeini's Office in Qom, head of the Revolutionary Court in Qom, judiciary chief, and he spent many years in parliament, the Guardian Council, the Assembly of Experts, and Expediency Council.

Timeline of Iran's Political Events

Semira N. Nikou

1979

Jan. 16 – The shah and his family went into exile.

Feb. 1 – Ayatollah Ruhollah Khomeini returned to Iran after 14 years in exile in France and Iraq.

Feb. 11 – Mehdi Bazargan appointed interim prime minister.

March 30-31 – In a referendum, voters overwhelmingly approved the creation of an Islamic Republic. Khomeini declared April 1 the first day of "the government of God."

May-June – Five prominent clerics close to Ayatollah Khomeini established the Islamic Republican Party.

June 14 – First official draft of the constitution was published. It did not include the position of *velayat-e faqih* (guardianship of the jurist).

Oct. 24 - New constitution, with *velayat-e faqih,* is approved by referendum after months of debate over the role of Islam in the state. The new constitution went into effect in early December, and Khomeini became supreme leader.

Nov. 4 – Students seized the U.S. Embassy in Tehran. The hostage crisis dragged on for 444 days.

Nov. 5 – Interim Prime Minister Bazargan resigned along with his cabinet to protest the hostage seizure.

1980

Jan. 25 – Abolhassan Bani-Sadr was elected Iran's first president.

March-May – The first parliament was elected. The Islamic Republican Party had the most members, but other parties such as the Freedom Movement also had significant representation. Akbar Hashemi Rafsanjani was elected speaker.

March 21 – The Cultural Revolution began. In June, Khomeini ordered formation of the university Jihad and began the "Islamization" of universities. Around 20,000 teachers were fired.

Aug. 28 – Amnesty International appealed to Iran to end executions and imprisonments, after citing at least 1000 post-revolution executions.

Sept. 22 – Iraq invaded Iran. The war lasted until August 1988.

1981

Feb. 4 – Khomeini told squabbling politicians to stop "biting one another like scorpions," followed by a warning to clergy in government one week later that they "should by no means interfere in areas outside their competence."

June 21 – President Bani-Sadr was impeached; he fled the country in late July. Iran banned all political parties except the Islamic Republic Party.

June 28 – A bomb at the Islamic Republic Party headquarters killed 73 officials, including Chief Justice Ayatollah Mohammad Beheshti, four cabinet ministers and 27 members of parliament. The Mujahedin el-Khalq organization was believed responsible.

Aug. 15 – Mohammad Ali Raja'i became president, but was assassinated on Aug. 30 in a bombing that also killed Prime Minister Mohammad Javad Bahonar.

Oct. 2 – The third presidential election in 21 months—and the second in 10 weeks—was held. Ayatollah Ali Khamenei was elected president for the first of two four-year terms.

Oct. 31 - Mir Hossein Mousavi was appointed prime minister.

1982

April 10 – Former Foreign Minister Sadegh Ghotbzadeh and more than 1,000 others were arrested for plotting to assassinate Ayatollah Khomeini. He confessed on television. Grand Ayatollah Mohammad Shariatmadari, who advocated separating mosque and state, was implicated by Ghotbzadeh under torture and stripped of his religious rank. Ghotbzadeh was executed in September.

Dec. 15 – Ayatollah Khomeini outlined an eight-point human rights platform and warned the judiciary and Revolutionary Guards against abusing individual rights in arrests, searches and seizures. On Dec. 22, he said, "We should not engage in oppression. We should not investigate what is going on in people's homes." On Dec. 28, the Tehran and Qom prosecutors were dismissed. On Jan. 1, 1983, further purges of revolutionary tribunals were undertaken.

1983

May 11 – Ayatollah Khomeini appealed for an end to disagreements among government officials. On Aug. 23, Khomeini pledged that that the clergy would retreat from political life when the public "gets on the right track." In an Oct. 5 speech to clerics, he warned against "satans" fomenting discord.

Dec. 8 – Ayatollah Ali Montazeri, later to become Ayatollah Khomeini's heir apparent, urged government reforms, criticizing the revolution for lacking "a certain moral courage."

1984

April – In the second parliamentary elections, the Islamic Republican Party dominated, but divisions remained between the conservatives associated with President Ali Khamenei and leftists associated with Prime Minister Mousavi.

1986

Sept. 5 – In a clandestine broadcast, Reza II, son of the late shah, declared himself ruler of Iran and called for overthrow of Ayatollah Khomeini's regime.

1987

May – Ayatollah Khomeini disbanded the Islamic Republic Party because of internal conflicts.

1988

Feb. 6 – Khomeini established the Expediency Discernment Council to mediate conflicts between the Guardian Council and the parliament, and to advise the supreme leader.

March – A political split in the country's main clerical organization—the conservative Society of Combatant Clergy—led to the creation of a competing radical and populist clerical organization called the Association of Combatant Clerics.

April – In the third parliamentary elections, candidates identified with the leftist Society of Combatant Clerics and non-clerical Islamic Revolution Mujahedin won the majority of seats.

1989

March 28 – Khomeini fired heir apparent Ayatollah Montazeri, who later became the leading dissident cleric and was put under house arrest.

June 3 – Ayatollah Khomeini died.

June 4 - Ayatollah Ali Khamenei became the new supreme leader.

July 28 – A revised constitution eliminated the office of prime minister and made permanent the Expediency Discernment Council. The supreme leader's power was expanded.

Aug. 3 – Rafsanjani was elected president for the first of two four-year terms and launched the era of reconstruction.

1992

April-May – In the fourth parliamentary elections, the Guardian Council for the first time extensively vetted candidates and disqualified 30 incumbents. The conservative Society of Combatant Clergy won two-thirds of the seats. Ali Akbar Nateq Nouri was elected speaker.

1996

March-April – In the fifth parliamentary elections, the conservative Society of Combatant Clergy received the most seats. But candidates of the newly created Servants of Construction, which consisted of technocrats allied with President Rafsanjani, also did well. Nateq Nouri was reelected as speaker.

1997

May 23 – Mohammad Khatami won the presidency in an upset landslide with 70 percent of the vote. The reformist era began. A coalition of 18 organizations and parties identified as reformist formed a front called the Second Khordad Front, named for the Persian calendar date of Khatami's election.

1999

July 8 – Students demonstrated at Tehran University after reformist *Salaam* newspaper was closed by the judiciary. Protests continued for six days. More than 1,000 students were arrested.

2000

February-May – In the sixth parliamentary elections, the reformist Second Khordad Front won 65 percent of the 290 seats. Mehdi Karroubi was chosen as speaker.

April – Widening a crackdown on the burgeoning independent press, the judiciary banned 16 reformist newspapers.

2001

June 8 – Khatami was re-elected president by a landslide.

2003

June 10 – Students led protests against raising university fees and privatization of universities that grew into wider pro-democracy demands. They also condemned President Khatami for failing to support them.

Oct. 10 – Human rights activist and lawyer Shirin Ebadi won the Nobel Peace Prize.

2004

February – In the seventh parliamentary elections, the Guardian Council disqualified thousands of reformist candidates, including many incumbents. Conservatives took control of parliament. Gholamali Haddad Adel was elected speaker.

2005

June 24 – In presidential elections, conservative Mahmoud Ahmadinejad defeated Rafsanjani.

2007

June 27 – Protests erupted after the government imposed fuel rationing.

2008

March – In the eighth parliamentary elections, the Guardian Council's extensive disqualification of reformist candidates assured a conservative victory. But political rivalry among conservatives intensified. Ali Larijani replaced Haddad Adel as speaker.

2009

June 12 – Ahmadinejad won re-election, defeating former Prime Minister Mousavi, former parliamentary Karroubi and former Revolutionary Guard commander Mohsen Rezaie. The election featured the first televised debates. The defeated candidates and many others claimed massive voting fraud.

June 13 – The opposition Green Movement launched the most serious challenge to the theocracy since the revolution. Millions turned out on the streets of several Iranian cities for the next two weeks with banners declaring "Where is my vote?"

June 21 – The cell phone video capturing the shooting of Neda Agha Soltan, a 26-year-old student, was broadcast around the world. She became an international symbol of the Green Movement.

July 29 – Karroubi revealed incidents of death, torture and sexual abuse of protesters at Kahrizak Prison, which was followed by other first-hand accounts. Among the dead was the son of a senior Revolutionary Guards commander. The government closed the facility.

Aug. 1 – The judiciary launched televised trials of well-known reformers and former government officials such as former Vice-President Mohammad Ali Abtahi and Mohsen Mirdamadi, leader of the Islamic Iran Participation Front, the most popular reform party. They were accused of fomenting unrest and other anti-government activities. Five trials lasted into the fall.

Sept. 18 – On Qods Day (or Jerusalem Day), thousands demonstrated across Iran in support of opposition candidate Mousavi. A dominant slogan became, "No to Gaza and Lebanon. I will give my life for Iran," rejecting the government's support of Palestinian and Lebanese militancy. Qods Day marks the last Friday of the month of Ramadan, which Ayatollah Khamenei had dedicated as a day of solidarity with the Palestinian people

Nov. 4 – On the anniversary of the U.S. Embassy takeover, tens of thousands of protesters gathered across major cities. Instead of chanting "Death to America," protestors chanted, "Death to the dictator," a reference to Iran's supreme leader.

Dec. 19 – Leading dissident cleric Ayatollah Montazeri died, sparking widespread protests across Iran, including in the holy city of Qom.

Dec. 27 – Commemorations on Ashoura, the holiest day for Shiites, turned into violent anti-government protests.

Dec. 30 – Thousands of pro-government forces rallied in response to opposition protests on Ashoura.

2010

January – The parliament and the Guardian Council approved a plan for subsidy reform.

Feb. 11 – Both pro-government forces and members of the opposition movement turned out onto the streets on the anniversary of the revolution. But security forces prevented the opposition from mass protests, marking the success of a crackdown against the Green Movement.

July 21 – Ayatollah Khamenei issued a *fatwa* declaring that the supreme leader's rule is a direct succession to the Prophet Mohammed and the Shiite imams.

Timeline of Iran's Foreign Relations

Semira N. Nikou

1979

Feb. 12 – Syria was the first Arab country to recognize the revolutionary regime when President Bashar al-Assad sent a telegram of congratulations to Ayatollah Ruhollah Khomeini. The revolution transformed relations between Iran and Syria, which had often been hostile under the shah.

Feb. 14 – Students stormed the U.S. Embassy in Tehran, but were evicted by the deputy foreign minister and Iranian security forces.

Feb. 18 – Iran cut diplomatic relations with Israel.

Oct. 22 – The shah entered the United States for medical treatment. Iran demanded the shah's return to Tehran.

Nov. 4 – Students belonging to the Students Following the Imam's Line seized the U.S. Embassy in Tehran. The hostage crisis lasted 444 days. On Nov. 12, Washington cut off oil imports from Iran. On Nov. 14, President Carter issued Executive Order 12170 ordering a freeze on an estimated $6 billion of Iranian assets and official bank deposits in the United States.

March – Iran severed formal diplomatic ties with Egypt after it signed a peace deal with Israel. Three decades later, Egypt was still the only Arab country that did not have an embassy in Tehran.

1980

April 7 – The United States cut off diplomatic relations with Iran.

April 25 – The United States attempted a rescue mission of the American hostages during Operation Eagle Claw. The mission failed due to a sandstorm and eight American servicemen were killed. Ayatollah Khomeini credited the failure to divine intervention.

Sept. 22 – Iraq invaded Iran in a dispute over the Shatt al-Arab waterway. The war continued for eight years. Iran and Syria strengthened ties after Iraq's invasion, as Damascus provided Tehran with military and diplomatic support.

October – Iran cut all ties with Jordan after Amman declared support for Iraq. Relations did not resume until 1991.

1981

Jan. 20 – After weeks of mediation by Algeria, Washington and Tehran agreed to the Algiers Accord to end the hostage crisis. The United States agreed to release frozen Iranian assets and not to intervene in Iranian affairs, in exchange for the release of 52 American hostages. Both countries agreed to end lawsuits. All claims would be referred to international arbitration at a new Iran-U. S. Claims Tribunal in The Hague.

May 25 – The Gulf Cooperation Council was established in Riyadh, Saudi Arabia, in order to confront security challenges posed by the Iran-Iraq War and the percieved threat of Iran's Islamic revolution. The agreement was between Bahrain, Kuwait, Oman, Qatar, Saudi Arabia and the UAE.

1982

June – Iran dispatched more than 1,000 Revolutionary Guards to Lebanon after Israel's June 6 invasion. Iranian forces supported the formation of Hezbollah, a Shiite militia, but never directly confronted Israel. The invasion also strengthened ties between Iran and Syria.

July 19 – American University of Beirut President David Dodge became the first of several Americans to be taken hostage over the next nine years. He was the only one taken to Iran, where he spent one year in prison.

1983

Oct. 23 – The United States accused Iran of aiding the suicide bombing at the barracks of U.S. Marine peacekeepers in Lebanon, which killed 241 U.S. military personnel, the largest loss to the American military in a single incident since Iwo Jima in World War II.

1984

Jan. 23 – The Reagan administration put Iran on the State Department list of governments supporting terrorism.

March – An Iran-supported militia in Beirut again began abducting American hostages, including CIA station chief William Buckley, who died in captivity.

1985

Apr. 1 – Washington warned Iran it would be held responsible if American hostages were harmed. By midsummer, Washington had begun behind-the-scene diplomatic efforts that led to the arms-for-hostage swap.

June 2 – During a visit to Japan, Parliamentary Speaker Akbar Hashemi Rafsanjani called on the United States to restore relations with Iran. Later that month, he played a role in ending the hijacking of TWA 847, the 17-day hostage ordeal of 39 Americans in Beirut.

July 25 – Ayatollah Ali Montazeri, heir apparent to Ayatollah Khomeini, urged Iranian diplomats to improve relations with Western nations.

Aug. 14 – A shipment of U.S. TOW antitank missiles was sent to Tehran from Israel as part of the secret arms-for-hostage swap. The same day, Rev. Benjamin Weir became the first of three American hostages to be freed in Lebanon.

Nov. 22 – A shipment of HAWK antiaircraft missiles was sent to Tehran from Israel as the second phase of an arms-for-hostage swap, but the deal fell far short of what was promised and Iran ordered a refund of payment and a resupply.

1986

Jan. 17 – President Ronald Reagan signed a special finding to permit negotiations with Iran on hostages and to help promote "moderate" elements in Tehran. This was followed by a shipment of 1,000 TOW missiles to Iran at the end of February.

May 25-28 – Former national security adviser Robert McFarlane and Lt. Col. Oliver North made a secret trip to Iran to deliver arms. In July, American hostage Father Lawrence Jenco was freed in Lebanon. On Aug. 3, the United States delivered new HAWK missiles to Iran.

September – Two more Americans were taken hostage in Lebanon. On Sept. 19-20, an Iranian emissary related to Rafsanjani visited Washington for talks on arms, hostages and improved relations.

October – American writer Edward Tracy was taken hostage in Lebanon. A few days later, the United States provided 1,000 TOW missiles to Iran. On Nov. 2, American hostage David Jacobsen was freed in Beirut.

Nov. 3 – The Lebanese magazine *Ash-Shiraa* exposed secret dealings between Iran, Israel and the United States, which became known as the "Iran-Contra affair."

1987

April 7 – Parliamentary speaker Rafsanjani said that Iran would try to mediate the release of American hostages in Lebanon if the United States showed "good will" by unfreezing Iranian assets in the United States. On May 13, the United States returned $450 million in frozen assets.

July 31 – Saudi law enforcement agencies clashed with hundreds of demonstrators outside the Grand Mosque in Mecca. The dispute claimed the lives of around 400 pilgrims, two-thirds of whom were Iranian.

Saudi Arabia blamed Iran and banned all political activities during the annual Hajj pilgrimage. In retaliation, angry mobs in Tehran ransacked the Saudi embassy.

1988

April 27 – Saudi Arabia cut diplomatic relations with Iran. Official relations were restored in 1991.

June 19 – The *USS Vincennes* shot down an Iranian passenger plane, killing 290 passengers and crew on board.

1989

Nov. 3 – The United States returned $567 million of frozen Iranian assets, in accordance with the Algiers Accord of 1981. American officials denied the deal was linked to Iranian President Rafsanjani's offer to help in the release of hostages in Beirut. Iranian assets valued at $900 million remained frozen.

Jan. 4 – Ayatollah Khomeini wrote a letter to Soviet President Mikhail Gorbachev saying that communism was dead and that he should study Islam. Iran's relations with the Soviet Union soured after the Soviet support of Iraq during its eight-year war with Iran.

Jan. 20 – In his inaugural address, George H. W. Bush said, "good will begets good will," in reference to Iran and American hostages held by pro-Iranian Hezbollah in Lebanon.

Feb. 14 – Khomeini issued a fatwa calling for the death of British author Salman Rushdie for his book "The Satanic Verses." On March 7, Iran cut off diplomatic relations with Britain over Rushdie's book. In 1990, low-level diplomatic relations resumed.

1990

August-September – Iran and Iraq resumed diplomatic ties, although Iran condemned the Iraqi invasion of Kuwait.

1991

Dec. 4 – Terry Anderson, the last American hostage in Lebanon, was freed after Iranian intervention.

1992

March 17 – A suicide bombing at the Israeli Embassy in Buenos Aires killed around 30 and wounded more than 300 people. A group called the Islamic Jihad Organization, with alleged links to Iran and Hezbollah, claimed responsibility for the attack. Iran and Hezbollah denied involvement.

April – Iran took full control of Abu Musa, an oil-rich island claimed by both Iran and the United Arab Emirates. Rival claims over the island became a source of tension between the two countries.

Sept. 10 – China and Iran finalized an agreement on "nuclear energy" cooperation when Iranian President Rafsanjani visited Beijing, accompanied by senior military and atomic energy officials. The China Nuclear Energy Industry Corporation reportedly agreed to sell Iran a facility to convert uranium ore into uranium hexafluoride gas. This agreement was cancelled in 1996 after pressure from the Clinton administration.

December – The European Council announced the opening of a "critical dialogue" with Iran. The goal was to help end Iran's isolation while pressing it to improve its human rights record. The dialogue ended in 1997 when a German court found the Iranian government responsible for the murder of four Kurdish dissidents in Berlin.

1993

March – Iran and Algeria broke off ties after Algeria accused Iran of supporting the opposition Islamic Salvation Front. Tehran denied the charges. Diplomatic relations were restored in September.

1994

May 10 – Iran and South Africa reestablished diplomatic relations after the end of apartheid. The shah and South Africa had good relations, which ended after the 1979 revolution when the theocracy imposed a trade and oil boycott.

July 18 – The bombing of a Jewish community center in Buenos Aires, which killed 85 and wounded 300, was blamed on Iran and Hezbollah. The charges were denied by both parties. In 2006, Argentine prosecutors called for the arrest of former President Rafsanjani.

1995

Jan. 8 - Iran signed a contract with Russia to resume work on the partially complete Bushehr nuclear reactor.

March 15 – The Rafsanjani government offered a billion-dollar contract to U.S. oil giant Conoco to develop two offshore oil fields, which was blocked after President Clinton signed an executive order banning U.S. investment in the Iranian oil industry.

May 6 – President Clinton issued a total embargo of U.S.-Iran trade and investment over the country's alleged sponsorship of "terrorism," nuclear ambitions, and hostility to the Middle East peace process.

1996

April 6 - Belgian customs officials seized a large mortar from an Iranian shipment of pickles destined for Munich, Germany. Belgian officials speculated the military equipment was meant for attacks targeting Israeli interests in Europe.

June – Iran was suspected of masterminding the June 25 bombing of Khobar Towers, a U.S. Air Force housing complex in Saudi Arabia. Subsequently, the Clinton administration sent a letter to President Khatami, transmitted by the foreign minister of Oman. The letter indicated that Washington had direct evidence of the Revolutionary Guards' involvement in the attacks. The message also stated that the United States wanted to work toward better relations with Iran. Tehran's response was brusque, denying the allegations.

Aug. 4 – President Clinton signed into law the Iran-Libya Sanctions Act (ILSA), which penalized foreign companies doing business with the United States that also invested more than $20 million in the Iranian oil industry.

Aug. 10 - Turkish Prime Minister Necmettin Erbakan visited Tehran to negotiate a $20 billion natural gas agreement covering the delivery of 140 cubic feet of gas per year and the building of gas pipelines in both countries. Turkey said that the agreement involved trade, not investment, and therefore was not in violation of ILSA.

1997

January - Kazakhstan began shipping oil across the Caspian Sea to Iran, as part of an oil swap agreement negotiated in 1996.

April 10 - A German court ruled that Iran was behind the murders of four Kurdish dissidents in Berlin in 1992. The German government expelled four Iranian diplomats and recalled its ambassador from Tehran. Iran denied involvement. The European Union declared a mass recall of ambassadors from Tehran and joined Germany in suspending the "critical dialogue." New Zealand, Australia and Canada also recalled their ambassadors from Tehran.

August – In his inaugural address, President Mohammad Khatami said Iran was willing to have "relations with any state which respects our independence," and called for a "dialogue of civilizations" with all nations.

Dec. 9 – Iran hosted the eighth Islamic Summit Conference of all Muslim countries.

1998

Jan. 7 - In an interview with CNN, President Khatami said Iran had an "intellectual affinity with the essence of American civilization" because it was also trying to construct a system based on the pillars of "religiosity, liberty, and justice." He called for both countries to try to bring down the "wall of mistrust."

September – Iran deployed thousands of troops to its border with Afghanistan after the Taliban admitted killing eight Iranian diplomats and a journalist. But Iran ultimately did not go to war.

1999

March 9 - Iranian President Khatami arrived in Italy for the first visit to the West by an Iranian leader since 1979.

May 18 – Tehran restored full diplomatic relations with Britain after resolution of the dispute over Ayatollah Khomeini's fatwa against Salman Rushdie.

2000

March 17 – In a speech, Secretary of State Madeleine Albright apologized for America's role in the 1953 over-throw of democratically elected Prime Minister Mohammad Mossadegh. She admitted that the coup, which put the shah back on the throne after he fled into exile, "was clearly a setback for Iran's political development." The Clinton administration partially lifted sanctions on Iranian carpets and foodstuffs. But Iran denounced the goodwill gesture because Albright's speech ended by criticizing Iran's domestic policies.

May 19 – The World Bank approved its first loans to Iran in seven years, after the vote was postponed twice due to objections by Washington.

Sept. 30 – President Khatami paid an official visit to Cuba, where Cuban President Fidel Castro presented him with a medal of honor. Khatami said the visit symbolized solidarity between the two nations.

2001

March 12 – During a state visit to Moscow, Iranian President Khatami and Russian President Vladimir Putin signed the first cooperation and security agreement since the Iranian revolution.

Sept. 27 – Ayatollah Khamenei and President Khatami condemned the al Qaeda 9/11 attacks on New York and Washington D.C.

October-December - After the U.S. intervention in Afghanistan ousted the Taliban, Iran cooperated with the United States, Russia and India in providing support for the Northern Alliance opposition to bring down the Taliban. Iranian diplomats met with their U.S. and other Western counterparts in Bonn to form a new Afghan government. Iran also worked with the United Nations to repatriate nearly 1 million Afghan refugees.

2002

Jan. 29 – In his State of the Union address, President George W. Bush referred to Iran, Iraq and North Korea as an "axis of evil."

2003

March – Following the U.S.-led invasion and occupation of Iraq, Syria and Iran intensified their cooperation to ensure they would not become Washington's next targets. They expanded bilateral defense cooperation and support to insurgent groups to tie down U.S.-led forces in Iraq.

May – A Swiss diplomat relayed Iranian conditions for bilateral talks to the Bush administration shortly after the U.S. invasion of Iraq, but it was not taken seriously in Washington.

Dec. 26 – A devastating earthquake hit the southeastern city of Bam, killing more than 26,000 people. On Dec. 30, the United States flew in an emergency response team. The military aircraft were the first U.S. planes to land in Iran in 20 years.

2004

June 21 – Iran arrested six British sailors—part of the U.S.-led force in Iraq—for trespassing into Iran's territorial waters. As a blow to Britain, Tehran paraded the servicemen through the city and forced them to apologize. They were released three days later, after negotiations.

November – Iran's representative to the International Atomic Energy Agency heralded growing ties with China, noting "we mutually complement each other. They have industry and we have energy resources."

2005

March 27 – Newly elected Iranian President Mahmoud Ahmadinejad called for Israel to "vanish in the pages of time." The statement was widely interpreted as a call for Israel to be wiped off the face of the earth.

July 5 - Iran received observer status at the Shanghai Cooperation Organization Summit in Astana and applied for full membership in 2008. But Iran's membership was blocked because the organization stipulated that no country under U.N. sanctions could be admitted.

2006

May 8 – President Ahmadinejad sent President Bush an 18-page letter.

July 30 –Venezuelan President Hugo Chavez visited Iran, where President Ahmadinejad awarded him Iran's highest state medal for his support of Iran's nuclear energy program. The two presidents often referred to each other as brothers.

July 31 – The U.N. Security Council adopted Resolution 1696, demanding that Iran halt its nuclear enrichment program.

Dec. 15 – President Ahmadinejad said the Holocaust was exaggerated.

Dec. 23 – The U.N. Security Council passed Resolution 1737, which imposed sanctions against Iran for failing to stop its uranium enrichment.

2007

Feb. 8 – Ayatollah Khamenei warned that Iran would target U.S. interests around the world if it came under attack over its nuclear program.

March 24 - Iran detained 15 British sailors and Marines for trespassing into Iranian territorial waters. They were held almost two weeks.

March 24 – The U.N. Security Council adopted Resolution 1747. The resolution called for a tightening of sanctions on Iran's nuclear program.

Oct. 16 – Russian President Vladimir Putin met with Supreme Leader Khamenei on his first official visit to Iran, marking closer Russia-Iran ties. After the revolution, Washington had been called the "great satan," and Moscow labeled "the lesser Satan."

Oct. 25 – Washington imposed the most sweeping unilateral sanctions since the takeover of the U.S. Embassy in 1979. It sanctioned the Revolutionary Guards and a few Iranian banks, and individuals believed to have links to nuclear and terror-related activities.

Sept. 20 – New York City officials denied President Ahmadinejad's request to visit the site of Sept. 11 attacks during his visit to the United Nations.

December – A U.S. National Intelligence Estimate concluded that Iran halted its nuclear weapons program in 2003.

2008

March 4 – The U.N. Security Council adopted Resolution 1803, its fourth resolution against Iran for failing to suspend uranium enrichment.

Sept. 24 – President Ahmadinejad spoke at the United Nations and Columbia University, where he criticized U.S. policy and said there were no homosexuals in Iran.

Nov. 6 – President Ahmadinejad wrote President-elect Barack Obama congratulating him on his election and urging "real change."

2009

Feb. 10 – In a speech marking the 30th anniversary of the Islamic Revolution, President Ahmadinejad welcomed talks with the United States based on "mutual respect and in a fair atmosphere."

March 20 – President Barak Obama sent a *Nowruz* (Iranian New Year) message to the Iranian people and government that called for better relations. He also said that Iran's place in the international community "cannot be reached through terror or arms, but rather through peaceful actions."

March 20 – Ayatollah Khamenei referred to Obama's speech as deceptive. In light of recent sanctions, he said Iran would judge the United States by its actions and not by its words.

April 2 – At the G-20 London summit, President Chavez and President Ahmadinejad announced the formation of a joint Iranian-Venezuelan development bank.

May 1 – Iran rejected the April 2010 report by the U.S. State Department that designated Iran as the "most active state sponsor of terrorism." Tehran said that the United States could not accuse others of terrorism after its actions at Iraq's Abu Ghraib prison and Guantanamo Bay.

May – President Obama sent a letter to Ayatollah Khamenei before Iran's June presidential elections that called for improved relations through "co-operation and regional bilateral relations." Khamenei briefly mentioned the letter in his Friday sermon.

September – An Iranian news website reported a second letter sent by President Obama to Ayatollah Khamenei.

October – Iran blamed the United States and Britain for involvement in suicide bombings that killed 15 members of Iran's Revolutionary Guards in southeastern Iran. The attack was carried out by the Sunni Muslim rebel group Jundollah, which Iran claimed was funded by the United States. The group had carried out a similar attack, killing 40, around five months earlier.

Oct. 21 – Iran agreed to a U.S.- and U.N.-backed deal designed to provide fuel for Tehran's research reactor for medical needs and to remove a large part of Iran's enriched uranium from its control. The deal called for the transfer of 1,200 kg of low-enriched uranium to Russia for further enrichment and then to France to produce fuel for the Tehran Research Reactor. But Iran later backed off from the agreement.

Nov. 24 – President Ahmadinejad arrived in Brazil as part of a five-nation tour of Senegal, Gambia, Brazil, Bolivia and Venezuela. He was greeted by Brazilian President Luiz Inácio Lula da Silva, marking the first visit by an Iranian leader since 1965.

2010

June 9 – The U.N. Security Council adopted Resolution 1929, imposing additional sanctions on Iran.

March 20 – President Obama sent a second *Nowruz* message to the Iranian government and people. The message encouraged dialogue between the two countries and criticized Iran's human rights violations during post-election protests.

April 13 – President Ahmadinejad disclosed that he wrote a second letter to Obama. "Obama only has one way to tell the world that he has created change, and that is Iran," he said in a televised interview.

May 17 – Iran accepted a proposal from Turkey and Brazil for a nuclear fuel swap deal in which Iran would send 1200 kg of its Low Enriched Uranium (LEU) to Turkey, a modified version of the deal Iran accepted, then rejected, in October 2009. The United States rejected the proposal, in part because Iran had increased its stockpile of enriched uranium. Washington then pushed for tougher U.N. sanctions.

June 9 – The Security Council imposed a fourth round of sanctions on Iran in Resolution 1929.

June 12 – The president of the Iran-China Joint Chamber of Commerce predicted that the annual trade between Iran and China would reach $50 billion in the next five years.

June 26 – The U.S. Congress passed tough new sanctions against Iran's energy sector and IRGC affiliated companies. Congress also called for penalties against companies that export gasoline and other refined energy products to Iran.

July 26 – The 27 European foreign ministers agreed on a comprehensive package of sanctions against Iran in the areas of trade, financial services, energy and transport, as well as additional designations for visa bans and asset freezes. Measures focused on Iranian banks, the Islamic Revolutionary Guards Corps and the Islamic Republic of Iran Shipping Lines.

Sept. 29 – The United States imposed the first sanctions on Iran for human rights violations. President Obama signed an executive order that allowed financial and travel restrictions on senior government officials for "sustained and severe violation of human rights" during or after Iran's 2009 presidential election. The abuses included arrest, killing, torture, beating, blackmail and rape. The United States cited eight security and judicial officials but noted it would continue to add names as "credible evidence" became available.

Military and Security Timeline

Semira N. Nikou

1979

May 5 – The Revolutionary Guards were established by decree of Ayatollah Ruhollah Khomeini.

Aug. 10 – Iran canceled a $9 billion arms deal with the United States made during the shah's reign.

Aug. 18 – Khomeini appointed himself commander-in-chief and ordered a general mobilization against Iran's Kurdish nationalists. Fighting in northern Kurdistan continued until the fall of Kurdish strongholds on September 3.

1980

Feb. 19 – Ayatollah Khomeini appointed President Abolhassan Bani-Sadr commander-in-chief of the military. Bani-Sadr was deposed on June 10, 1981.

Sept. 22 – Iraqi troops invaded Iran, following weeks of clashes between their Iraqi forces along the border. Baghdad's conditions for peace included Iranian recognition of Iraqi claims to the entire Shatt al-Arab waterway and disputed territory, and the return of three Persian Gulf islands occupied by Iran in 1971. Iraq quickly penetrated deep into Iranian territory. Oil installations were targeted by both nations, leading to a suspension in oil shipments. PLO chairman Yasir Arafat began the first mediation effort on September 25, which was followed by a similar attempt by an Islamic Conference Organization delegation.

Sept. 28 – The U.N. Security Council passed a resolution calling on both nations to cease hostilities.

Oct. 1 – Iran said it would do its part to keep the Strait of Hormuz open to oil-tanker traffic in spite of regional hostility. Heavy bombardment was reported on cities in both nations, while fighting on the ground centered around the oil-rich southern cities of Khorramshahr and Abadan.

Nov. 12 – Kuwait charged Iran with an attack on its border post with Iraq. A second attack was reported on November 16.

Dec. 5 – As heavy fighting continued in Khuzistan, Iran hit the Iraqi oil terminal at Faw and Iraq struck an Iranian oil pipeline at Bandar Abbas. On December 16, OPEC appealed to the two nations to end the war.

1981

Jan. 14 – United Nations envoy Olof Palme began another round of peace talks to end the war, but he reported on January 18 that neither side would back down from their hard-line positions.

Jan. 28 – Iraqi President Saddam Hussein told the Islamic Conference Organization summit in Saudi Arabia that he was prepared to return captured Iranian territory in exchange for recovery of territorial and offshore rights usurped by Iran. Ayatollah Khomeini said troops would fight until final victory.

Feb. 3 – Foreign Minister Ali Akbar Velayati announced that Iran's preconditions for peace were, "withdrawal of Iraqi troops from all Iranian territory and compensation for damage inflicted." He added that Iran was not ready for diplomatic relations with the United States.

Sept. 27-29 – Iran claimed to have driven Iraq back across the Karun River from Abadan to Ahvaz on the southern front, capturing 3,000 Iraqi troops. The breaking of the Iraqi siege of Abadan was considered a turning point in the war.

Oct. 3 – The Supreme Defense Council was formed to coordinate the war effort, supervise a military reorganization, and begin an intense period of training.

Dec. 2 – Iran denied purchasing arms from Israel.

1982

Jan. 22 – Parliamentary Speaker Akbar Hashemi Rafsanjani said, "Iran does not want to attack the small countries of the Persian Gulf and does not want to interfere in their internal affairs." The next day, Bahrain's prime minister accused Iran of instigating Shiite communities throughout the Persian Gulf to overthrow their governments.

March 1 – Following weeks of heavy fighting around Susangerd, Shush and Bostan, Special U.N. Envoy Palme announced failure to mediate a truce between Iran and Iraq. Jordanian volunteers left to join Iraqi troops.

March 9 – Ayatollah Khomeini announced that President Saddam Hussein was "past salvation and we will not retreat even one step."

May 24 - Iran recaptured the City of Khorramshahr, an oil-rich area in southern Iran, taken by Iraq during its initial attacks in 1980.

June 12 – Iran dispatched a contingent of 1,000 Revolutionary Guards to Lebanon after Israel's invasion. Iranian forces supported the formation of Hezbollah, a Shiite militia, but never directly confronted Israel.

July 19 – American University of Beirut President David Dodge was taken hostage. He spent the next year in Iran, before being released after Syrian intervention.

June 20 – President Hussein announced that Iraq had begun to pull out of Iran. He announced completion of its withdrawal on June 29, which Iran said was "a lie."

July 12 – Iran rejected a U.N. ceasefire resolution. Iraq reported an Iranian attack that same day near the southern oil port of Basra.

Oct. 4 – The United Nations Security Council unanimously voted for an end to the Iran-Iraq War and a withdrawal of all forces from occupied territory. Tehran rejected the move, while Baghdad said it would accept a cease-fire.

1983

April – Washington suspected Iran was indirectly involved in a suicide bombing which killed 63 people at the U.S. Embassy in Lebanon. The Reagan administration blamed Hezbollah for the attack, which U.S. officials believed was being funded by Iran and Syria.

Aug. 23 – Reacting to internal squabbling, Ayatollah Khomeini urged unity between the military and the Revolutionary Guards

Sept. 17 – President Hussein said Baghdad wanted peace with Tehran based on mutual non-interference. The next day Iran repeated threats to block oil exports if its shipments were disrupted.

Oct. 23 – A suicide bomber attacked the barracks of U.S. Marine peacekeepers in Beirut, killing 241 Marines, the largest loss of U.S. military life in a single incident since Iwo Jima in World War II. The United States suspected Iran-backed Hezbollah.

Dec. 3 – The U.S. press reported the Reagan administration's policy shift toward Iraq was because of a belief that an Iraqi defeat would hurt U.S. interests.

1984

Jan. 23 – The Reagan administration put Iran on the State Department list of governments supporting terrorism.

Feb. 11 – Iraq attacked civilian targets in Dezful, triggering a new phase of the war. Iran responded on Feb. 12 by shelling seven Iraqi cities. After repeated incidents, Iran accepted an Iraqi ceasefire offer on Feb. 18. Both agreed to allow a U.N. mission to assess damage in civilian areas. But in late February, Iran announced new offensives on the northern and southern fronts.

March 3 – Iran charged Iraq with using chemical weapons, a practice which Iraq continued throughout the war.

March – Hezbollah abducted American hostages in Beirut, including CIA station chief William Buckley, who died in captivity.

May 13 – After a run of at least six Iraqi strikes on tankers doing business with Iran, Iran for the first time attacked a Persian Gulf ship, the Kuwaiti *Umm Casbah,* marking the outbreak of the "tanker war." Parliamentary Speaker Rafsanjani declared on May 15, "Either the Persian Gulf will be safe for all or for no one."

July – The CIA began giving Iraq intelligence that was reportedly used for subsequent mustard gas attacks against Iranian troops.

Sept. 20 – Hezbollah was once again suspected of being behind an attack against the new U.S. Embassy in Beirut, which killed 24 people.

1985

Feb. 21 - The United Nations reported that both Iran and Iraq were violating the Geneva Convention on prisoners of war treatment.

March 14 – Iraq began a bombing campaign against Iranian cities, particularly targeting Tehran. Iran responded with its own scud missile attacks. The "war of the cities" air strikes continued until 1988.

Aug. 14 – A shipment of U.S. TOW antitank missiles was shipped to Tehran from Israel as part of the Reagan administration's arms-for-hostage swap. The Reagan administration secretly facilitated the sale of Israeli arms to Iran (which was subject to an arms embargo), in exchange for Iran's help in the release of American hostages in Lebanon.

Nov. 22 – Another shipment of HAWK antiaircraft missiles was shipped to Tehran from Israel as the second phase of the arms-for-hostage swap. But the deal fell far short of what was promised, and Iran ordered a refund of payment and a resupply.

1986

Nov. 3 – The Lebanese magazine *Ash-Shiraa* exposed the secret arms-for-hostage dealings between Iran, Israel, and the United States.

July 20 – The U.N. Security Council unanimously passed Resolution 598, demanding an immediate ceasefire.

October – During Operation Nimble Archer, the United States attacked Iranian oil platforms in retaliation for an Iranian attack on the U.S.-flagged Kuwaiti tanker *Sea Isle City*.

1988

June 2 – Ayatollah Khomeini named Parliamentary Speaker Rafsanjani acting commander-in-chief of the Armed Forces of the Islamic Republic of Iran

April – The U.S. Department of Commerce reportedly approved the shipment to Iraq of chemicals for agricultural use that were later used to manufacture mustard gas. Four major battles were fought between April and August in which Iraqis used massive amounts of chemical weapons against Iran. By that time, the United States was aiding Saddam Hussein by gathering intelligence and assisting in battle plans.

Apr. 14 – The frigate *USS Samuel B. Roberts* was badly damaged by an Iranian mine. U.S. forces responded with Operation Praying Mantis on April 18, the U. S. Navy's largest engagement of surface warships since World War II. Two Iranian oil platforms, two Iranian ships and six Iranian gunboats were destroyed.

Aug. 20 – Iran and Iraq accepted U.N. Resolution 598, ending the eight-year war. Iran claimed to suffer over 1 million casualties.

1992

March 17 – A suicide bombing at the Israeli Embassy in Buenos Aires killed around 30 and wounded more than 300 individuals. A group called the Islamic Jihad Organization, with alleged links to Iran and Hezbollah, claimed responsibility for the attack. Iran and Hezbollah denied involvement.

1994

April – Iran expelled workers from the Island of Abu Musa. Tehran began to station Revolutionary Guards on the islands of Abu Musa and the Greater and Lesser Tunbs. The islands had been a source of tension between Iran and the United Arab Emirates (UAE) since Iran seized them in the early 1970s. Both countries claim rights to the islands.

April – President Clinton gave what Congress later termed a "green light" for Iran to transfer arms to the Muslim government of Bosnia fighting Serbian forces. The permission came despite a United Nations arms embargo against Iran. In 1996, the Senate Intelligence Committee and the House Select Subcommittee confirmed the U.S. role in the Iranian arms transfer.

July 18 – The bombing of a Jewish community center in Buenos Aires, which killed 85 and wounded 300, was blamed on Iran and Hezbollah. The charges were denied by both parties. In 2006, Argentine prosecutors called for the arrest of former President Rafsanjani.

1996

April 6 - Belgian customs officials seized a large mortar from an Iranian shipment of pickles destined for Munich, Germany. Belgian officials speculated the military equipment was meant for attacks targeting Israeli interests in Europe.

June – Iran was suspected of masterminding the June 25 bombing of Khobar Towers, a U.S. Air Force housing complex in Saudi Arabia. Iran denied the allegations.

1997

April 10 - A German court ruled that the Iranian government was behind the murders of four Kurdish dissidents in Berlin in 1992. Iran denied allegations.

1998

Aug. 8 – Nine diplomats were killed by the Taliban militia during an attack on the Iranian consulate in Mazar-e Sharif. At the time, more than 70,000 Iranian troops were deployed along the Afghan border. U.N. mediation defused the situation. Iran and the Taliban held talks in February 1999, but relations did not improve.

2001

April – Iran and Saudi Arabia signed a security agreement with particular emphasis on the fight against drug smuggling and terrorism.

October 2 – Russia signed a military accord with Tehran, six years after it halted arms sales to Iran under U.S. pressure. The agreement included the sale of jets, missiles and other weapons.

October 8 – Supreme Leader Khamenei condemned U.S. strikes on Afghanistan. At the same time, Iran agreed to perform search-and-rescue missions for U.S. pilots who crashed on Iranian soil during the war.

2002

January – Israel seized the *Karina A,* a ship carrying 50 tons of arms which Israeli officials claimed were supplied by Iran for the Palestinian authority.

2005

June – Former Revolutionary Guards commander and presidential candidate Mohsen Rezaei said Iran played a more significant part in the overthrow of the Taliban than given credit for by the United States. Washington consistently denied that Iranians made meaningful contributions.

June 16 – Iran and Syria signed an agreement for military cooperation against what they called the "common threats" presented by Israel and the United States. In a joint press conference, the defense ministers from the two countries said their talks had been aimed at consolidating their defense efforts and strengthening mutual support.

June 6 – Iran was given observer status in the Shanghai Cooperation Organization, a security organization including China, Kazakhstan, Kyrgyzstan, Russia, Tajikistan and Uzbekistan. It applied for full membership on March 24, 2008. But its admission was blocked because of ongoing sanctions levied by the United Nations.

2007

February – Iran denied accusations by the United States that it was stirring violence in Iraq.

May 28 – Iran and the United States held the first official high-level talks in 27 years. The meeting, which took place in Baghdad, came after Iraq hosted a security conference attended by regional states and the permanent members of the U.N. Security Council. The talks were on Iraq's security and were followed by two more rounds in July and November. The United States urged Tehran to stop supporting Shiite militias in Iraq. The talks ultimately did not lead anywhere and stopped after three meetings.

Sept. 6 – NATO forces in Afghanistan intercepted a large Iranian shipment of arms destined for the Taliban. The shipment included armor-piercing bombs. Washington said that the shipment's large quantity was a sign that Iranian officials were at least aware of the shipment, even if not directly involved. Tehran denied the charges.

October – U.S. military commander Gen. David Petraeus claimed Iran was triggering violence in Iraq. Petraeus also accused Iran's ambassador to Iraq of being a member of the elite Qods Force, a wing of the Revolutionary Guards responsible for foreign operations.

2008

April – The United States accused Iran of continuing its alleged support of Taliban insurgents.

July 9 – Iran test-fired a new version of the Shahab-3 long-range missile with a range of 1,240 miles, which Iran said was capable of hitting targets in Israel.

2009

Feb. 2 – President Mahmoud Ahmadinejad announced the launch of Iran's first domestically produced satellite, Omid, prompting fears in the West that it would enable Iran to launch long-range ballistic missiles.

May 1 –The State Department designated Iran as the "most active state sponsor of terrorism." Tehran countered that the United States could not accuse others of terrorism after its actions at Iraq's Abu Graib prison and Guantanamo Bay.

May 20 – Iran successfully tested the Sejjil-2 ballistic missile which has a range between 1,200 and 1,500 miles. The Obama administration said the missile was "a significant step," and indicated that Tehran was enhancing its weapons delivery capability.

Sept. 22 – Iran held a military parade showing off its Shahab-3 and Sejjil ballistic missiles and, for the first time, the Russian-built Tor-M1 air defense system. The medium-range ballistic missiles both have a range that can reach Israel.

Sept. 27-28 – Iran carried out a series of missile tests as part of a military exercise called Operation Great Prophet IV. Short-range missiles included the Shahab-1, Shahab-2, Fateh-110 and Tondar-69.

December – Gen. Petraeus accused Iran of backing Shiite militants in Iraq and giving a "modest level" of support to the Taliban in Afghanistan.

2010

March – Iran and Qatar signed a security agreement, underlying the need for security cooperation and a fight against terrorism.

August – Iran successfully test-fired a new generation of the Fateh-110, a medium-range ballistic missile with a 155-mile range.

Timeline of Iran's Nuclear Activities

Semira N. Nikou

1957

The United States and Iran signed a civil nuclear cooperation agreement as part of the United States Atoms for Peace program. The agreement provided for U.S. technical assistance and the lease of enriched uranium to Iran. It also called for research cooperation on peaceful nuclear energy uses.

1967

November – The Tehran Nuclear Research Center, supplied by the United States, opened. It was equipped with a 5-megawatt nuclear research reactor called the Tehran Research Reactor (TRR), fueled by highly enriched uranium.

1968

July 1 – Iran signed the Nuclear Non-Proliferation Treaty (NPT). Parliament ratified it in February 1970. Uranium enrichment was allowed under the treaty.

1974

May 15 – Iran signed the NPT's Safeguards Agreement with the International Atomic Energy Agency (IAEA). The safeguards allowed inspections for the purpose of verifying that nuclear enrichment for peaceful nuclear energy is not diverted to nuclear weapons or other nuclear explosive devices.

November – West German company Kraftwerk Union, a subsidiary of Siemens, agreed to construct two 1,200-megawatt light water reactors to produce nuclear energy at Bushehr. Construction began in August 1975, but the formal contract was not signed until mid-1976.

1975

The Ford administration expressed support in principle for the shah's plan to develop a full-fledged nuclear power program to diversify Iran's energy sources. The shah wanted the capacity to generate 23,000 megawatts of electricity with the ability to reprocess U.S.-supplied fuel.

1976

April 20 – President Gerald Ford issued National Security Decision Memorandum 324 supporting the shah's ambitions and helping Iran formulate a plan to build 23 nuclear power reactors. But the administration refused to allow Iran to have the independent reprocessing capabilities sought by the shah. Ford's memorandum instead approved a multinational reprocessing plant in Iran that would also enable the United States to participate in the project. Iran rejected the multinational option and pushed for a comprehensive national nuclear program.

1977

August - President Carter reopened negotiations on the shah's quest for a nuclear energy program.

1978

January – Iran and the United States initialed a nuclear agreement in which Iran agreed to safeguards beyond NPT requirements. In return, the United States granted Iran "most favored nation" status for reprocessing so that Iran would not be discriminated against when seeking permission to reprocess U.S.-supplied fuel.

1979

After the 1979 revolution, the United States stopped supplying highly enriched uranium for the Tehran Research Reactor.

July 31 – Kraftwerk Union terminated work on the Bushehr reactor when Iran failed to make payments.

1984

February – German engineers returned to Iran to do a feasibility study to complete the Bushehr reactor.

March 24 – Iraq's attack on the Bushehr nuclear power plant did serious damage.

December – Iran opened a nuclear research center at Isfahan with China's assistance. In 1985, China supplied the center with a "training reactor."

1987

May 5 – After 18 months of negotiations, Argentina concluded a $5.5 million deal with Tehran to supply a new core for the Tehran Research Reactor so it would operate with only 20 percent enriched uranium, instead of the previous 90 percent. In 1989, Argentina replaced the core. In 1993, Argentina delivered around 50 pounds of 20 percent enriched uranium to fuel the reactor.

1990

Oct. 9 – Iran decided to rebuild the damaged Bushehr nuclear power plant.

1992

Aug. 25 – Russia and Iran signed a cooperation agreement on the civil use of nuclear energy, including construction of a nuclear power plant.

1995

January – Iran signed a contract with the Russian Ministry of Atomic Energy to build a light water reactor at Bushehr under IAEA safeguards. Russia was under a contractual obligation to complete the plant within 55 months. The project's completion was delayed until August 2010.

1997

May – The IAEA expanded the Safeguards Agreement by adopting the Additional Protocol. Under the latter, inspectors would be allowed to conduct short notice inspections and be provided with multiple entry/exit visas. Iran signed the Additional Protocol in 2003, but had not ratified it as of 2010.

1998

Feb. 23 – The Clinton administration opposed Iran's nuclear energy program on grounds that Iran had sufficient oil and gas reserves for power and that work on the nuclear power reactor could indirectly contribute to a weapons program.

March 6 – Under U.S. pressure, Ukraine announced that it would not sell two turbines for use at the Bushehr reactor.

1999

May 7 – Russia said Iran wanted to expand nuclear cooperation, potentially including the building of a second nuclear power plant.

May 19 – President Mohammad Khatami paid a five-day state visit to Saudi Arabia, where Iran and Saudi Arabia issued a joint statement expressing support for turning the Middle East into a zone free of weapons of mass destruction. They said Israel's production and stockpiling of nuclear weapons, along with its non-compliance with international laws and treaties, posed a serious threat to peace and security in the region.

2000

March 14 – President Clinton signed the Iran Nonproliferation Act, which allowed the United States to sanction individuals and organizations providing material aid to Iran's nuclear, chemical, biological and ballistic missile weapons programs.

2001

March 12-15 – Russian President Vladimir Putin and Iranian President Khatami signed nuclear and military cooperation accords. Khatami said Iran wanted a second nuclear power plant after the completion of Bushehr.

2002

Jan. 8 – Former President Akbar Hashemi Rafsanjani said, "Iran is not seeking to arm itself with non-conventional weapons."

Aug. 15 – The National Council of Resistance of Iran, an exiled opposition group, revealed that Iran was building two secret nuclear sites – a uranium enrichment plant and research lab at Natanz and a heavy water production plant in Arak. President Khatami acknowledged the existence of Natanz and other facilities on Iran's state-run television and invited the International Atomic Energy Agency to visit them.

Sept. 1 – Russian technicians began to assemble heavy equipment in the Bushehr reactor, despite U.S. attempts to convince the Russians not to participate. But the plant faced frequent delays in construction.

2003

Feb. 9 – President Khatami said Iran had discovered and extracted uranium in the Savand area. He cited Iran's "legitimate right to obtain nuclear energy for peaceful aims" and expressed readiness to accept international inspections of its nuclear activities.

May 6 – Iran's Atomic Energy Organization presented the United Nations with a sketch of Iran's nuclear program, insisting that the program was peaceful.

May 17 – Tehran backed a proposal by Syria to rid the Middle East of weapons of mass destruction.

June 19 – An IAEA report did not find Iran in violation of the NPT but said Iran should have been more forthcoming about the Natanz uranium enrichment facility and the Arak heavy water production plant. The U.N. watchdog agency later urged Iran to sign and ratify the Additional Protocol to the Safeguards Agreement of the Nuclear Non-Proliferation Treaty, which would allow inspectors more access to nuclear sites and the right to sudden inspections.

Aug. 26 – IAEA inspectors found traces of highly enriched uranium at Iran's Natanz nuclear plant. Iran claimed the traces came from equipment imported from another country.

Sept. 19 – President Khatami said, "We don't need atomic bombs, and based on our religious teaching, we will not pursue them…but at the same time, we want to be strong, and being strong means having knowledge and technology."

Sept. 25 – U.N. weapons inspectors found traces of highly enriched weapons-grade uranium at a second site near the capital city of Tehran. The IAEA set a deadline of Oct. 31 for Iran to prove it was not making nuclear weapons.

Oct. 21 – In talks with Britain, France and Germany (EU-3), Iran agreed to suspend uranium enrichment and processing activities and to open nuclear sites to unannounced inspections by the U.N. watchdog agency. It also agreed to sign the Additional Protocols of the Non-Proliferation Treaty and its safeguards agreement with the IAEA.

Oct. 24 – 1,500 Iranian protesters gathered in Tehran to denounce the recently concluded agreement between Tehran and the EU-3.

Nov. 12 – The IAEA concluded there was no evidence of a secret nuclear weapons program in Iran but showed concern about its production of plutonium. President Khatami said that the plutonium was used for manufacturing pharmaceuticals and the small amount produced by Iran could not make a nuclear bomb.

Dec. 18 – Tehran signed the Additional Protocol to the Non-Proliferation Treaty's Safeguards Agreement. The Additional Protocol granted IAEA inspectors greater authority in their nuclear verification programs. Since then, Iran has at times voluntarily allowed more intrusive inspections, but the Iranian parliament has not yet ratified the Additional Protocol.

2004

Feb. 22 – Iran acknowledged having secretly bought nuclear parts from international sources, although Tehran continued to insist that its goal was electricity production and not nuclear weapons.

Apr. 7 – Iran declared its plans to construct a heavy water reactor to produce radioisotopes for medical research. Western envoys warned that the facility could reprocess the spent fuel rods to produce plutonium.

Aug. 28 – President Khatami said Iran had a right to enrich uranium and was willing to provide guarantees to the IAEA that it was not developing nuclear weapons.

Oct. 6 – Tehran announced that it had produced tons of the hexafluoride gas needed to enrich uranium by converting a few tons of yellowcake uranium.

Nov. 14 – In negotiations with Britain, France and Germany, Iran accepted the Paris accord, which recognized Tehran's rights to pursue nuclear technology for peaceful purposes and reaffirmed Iran's commitment not to acquire nuclear weapons. In exchange, Iran voluntarily agreed to temporarily suspend uranium enrichment activities and allow the IAEA to monitor the suspension.

Nov. 15 – The IAEA reported that it had not found any evidence that Iran had tried to develop nuclear weapons, although it could not rule out the existence of nuclear materials that had not been declared.

Nov. 22 – Iran invited the IAEA to monitor the suspension of all enrichment-related activities.

Nov. 30 – Iran said that it had not abandoned its right to enrich uranium and that the suspension was only temporary. European officials hoped to make the suspension permanent in return for trade deals and other incentives.

Dec. 22 – Iran's intelligence minister announced the arrest of more than 10 people on spying charges. Tehran charged the spies were passing sensitive information on Iran's nuclear program to the Israeli Mossad and the CIA.

2005

Jan. 13 – IAEA inspectors were only allowed partial access to the Parchin military base near Tehran. Under the NPT, Iran was not required to allow inspectors into its military bases. But the Bush administration consistently expressed concern that Iran's failure to allow full access to its suspected military bases and facilities was linked to a secret nuclear weapons program.

Jan. 17 – President Bush said military action against Iran remained an option, "if it continues to stonewall the international community about the existence of its nuclear weapons program."

Feb. 7 - Iran's Minister of Defense Ali Shamkhani said in an interview that it was not in Iran's national interest to acquire nuclear weapons.

Feb. 28 – Tehran and Moscow signed an agreement that stipulated that Russia would supply nuclear fuel for the Bushehr facility and that Iran would return all spent fuel rods to Russia to ensure the fuel was not diverted for other use.

May 15 – Iran's parliament approved a non-binding resolution urging the government to resume uranium enrichment for peaceful use.

Aug. 1 – Iran informed the IAEA that it had decided to resume activities at the Isfahan uranium conversion center. The U.N. nuclear watchdog agency urged Iran not to take any action that would prejudice negotiations with Britain, France and Germany (the EU-3) or undermine the IAEA inspection process.

Aug. 5 – Britain, France and Germany (the EU-3) proposed the "Framework for a Long-term Agreement" to Iran. The deal offered assistance in developing peaceful nuclear energy in exchange for a binding commitment that Iran would not to pursue fuel cycle activities other than for light water power and research reactors. It also called for a halt on construction of a heavy water research reactor at Arak. Iran rejected the proposal, as it required Tehran to abandon all nuclear fuel work.

Aug. 8 – Iran resumed uranium conversion at the Isfahan facility under surveillance of the IAEA.

Aug. 9 – Supreme Leader Ayatollah Ali Khamenei issued a fatwa forbidding the "production, stockpiling and use of nuclear weapons."

Aug. 11 – The IAEA urged Iran to suspend all enrichment activities and re-instate IAEA seals.

Sept. 24 – The IAEA found Iran in noncompliance with the NPT Safeguards Agreement and decided to refer Tehran to the U.N. Security Council for further action. The decision followed Iran's repeated failure to fully report its nuclear activities. Tehran countered that it might suspend its voluntary implementation of the Additional Protocol that allowed more intrusive and sudden inspections.

Nov. 20 – Iran's parliament approved a bill requiring the government to stop voluntary implementation of the Safeguards Agreement's separate Additional Protocol, which allowed more intrusive and surprise inspections, if Iran were referred to the Security Council. The parliament did not move to block normal inspections required under the Safeguards Agreement, which had been ratified by parliament in 1974.

2006

January – Iran broke open internationally monitored seals on the Natanz enrichment facility and at two related storage and testing locations, which cleared the way to resume nuclear fuel research under IAEA supervision.

Feb. 4 – The IAEA voted to report Iran to the U.N. Security Council for its non-compliance with its NPT Safeguards Agreement obligations.

July 31 – The U.N. Security Council passed Resolution 1696 demanding that Iran suspend its uranium enrichment activities within one month. No sanctions were imposed but the resolution warned that "appropriate measures" would be taken in the case of Iranian non-compliance. Tehran called the resolution illegal.

Aug. 26 – Iran's President Mahmoud Ahmadinejad inaugurated a heavy water production plant at Arak. The United States expressed concern that the heavy water would be used in the heavy water reactor at Arak to produce plutonium, an ingredient in making nuclear weapons.

Oct. 2 – President Bush signed into law the Iran Freedom Support Act, which imposed economic sanctions on nations and companies that aided Iran's nuclear program.

Dec. 23 – The U.N. Security Council adopted Resolution 1737, sanctioning Iran for its failure to comply with Resolution 1696 and halt uranium enrichment. The resolution banned the sale of nuclear-related technology to Iran and froze the assets of key individuals and companies related to the nuclear program.

2007

March 24 – The U.N. Security Council adopted Resolution 1747, which banned the sale of arms to Iran increased the freeze on assets.

Dec. 4 – A U.S. National Intelligence Estimate on Iran's nuclear activities said there was evidence that Tehran halted its nuclear weapons program in 2003. It assessed with "moderate confidence" that Iran had not re-started its nuclear weapons program as of mid-2007. The findings contradicted the 2005 U.S. intelligence assessment that Tehran was seeking nuclear weapons capability.

2008

Feb. 22 – An IAEA report concluded that Iran had not fully answered the international community's questions about its nuclear program and testing of new centrifuge technology for faster uranium enrichment. The report was based in part on intelligence acquired by the Bush administration that allegedly pointed to Iranian efforts to weaponize nuclear materials. The data was extracted from a laptop reportedly smuggled out of Iran in 2004.

March 3 – The U.N. Security Council approved Resolution 1803, imposing further economic sanctions on Iran.

July 18 – The Bush administration agreed to send U.S. Undersecretary of State William Burns to Geneva to participate with his European counterparts in talks with Iran about its nuclear program. But Iran again rejected the suspension or freeze of its enrichment activities.

Sept. 26 – The U.N. Security Council passed Resolution 1835 which reaffirmed three earlier rounds of sanctions against Iran. No new sanctions were imposed, largely because of objections by Russia and China.

2009

Sept. 25 – President Obama, French President Sarkozy and British Prime Minister Brown told a press conference that Iran had a covert fuel enrichment plant near Qom. Iran said it had already confirmed the construction of a new pilot enrichment plant to the IAEA in a letter four days earlier. Critics said Tehran disclosed the site once it discovered the facility was already under surveillance.

Oct. 1 – Iran met in Geneva with permanent members of the U.N. Security Council and Germany to discuss Iran's nuclear program. The parties outlined a proposal for Iran to ship 80 percent of its stockpile of low-enriched uranium from Natanz to Russia. The shipment would then go to France for further enrichment and fabrication of fuel rods for the Tehran Research Reactor, which produced isotopes for medical use.

Oct. 19-21 – The early October talks in Geneva were continued in Vienna with the presence of the IAEA, on the transfer of Iran's low-enriched uranium. A consensus was reached on a draft agreement. The United States, France and Russia approved the agreement, but Iran backed down due to domestic opposition.

2010

Feb. 12 – President Ahmadinejad announced that Iran had produced 20 percent enriched uranium, up from 3.5 percent, in a move that marked a major increase in its capabilities. He said Iran had the capability to enrich the fuel even further.

May 17 – Turkey, Brazil and Iran agreed to a nuclear deal similar to the agreement outlined in Geneva in 2009. The proposal called for the transfer of 1,200 kg of low-enriched uranium (3.5 percent) to Turkey, in exchange for 120 kg of 20 percent enriched uranium needed to run the Tehran Research Reactor. The United States and Europeans rejected the deal because Iran had increased its uranium stockpile. The 1,200 kg then represented only about half of Iran's stockpile, rather than the 80 percent it had in the October 2009 deal. Washington also believed the move was a delaying tactic to avert sanctions.

June 9 – The U.N. Security Council adopted Resolution 1929, imposing a fourth round of sanctions on Iran. They included tighter financial measures and an expanded arms embargo. President Ahmadinejad said the sanctions were a "used handkerchief that should be thrown in the dustbin," and that they were "not capable of harming Iranians."

June 24 – Congress approved the Comprehensive Iran Sanctions, Accountability, and Divestment Act of 2010. It passed unanimously in the Senate and overwhelmingly in the House. The bill expanded existing U.S. sanctions on Iran. It imposed extensive sanctions on foreign companies that export refined petroleum to Iran or invest in Iran's energy sector. The legislation went well beyond U.N. Resolution 1929.

July 6 – Iran announced that talks with U.N. Security Council and Germany could begin in September.

July 11 – Iran announced it had produced 20 kilograms of 20 percent enriched uranium and had begun work on fuel plates. The fuel was to be delivered to the Tehran Research Reactor by September 2011, for creating medical isotopes. Western powers have repeatedly expressed fear that Iran's capability to enrich 20 percent would help it produce nuclear weapon material, which is around 90 percent.

July 26 – The European Union passed sanctions, which banned technical assistance to Iran's oil and gas industry.

Aug. 13 – The Russian Federal Atomic Energy Agency (Rosatom) announced that the first reactor at the Bushehr would soon be loaded with nuclear fuel and become Iran's first operational nuclear power plant.

Aug. 21 – An official launch ceremony was held to mark completion of the Bushehr reactor, after years of delays. Iran began loading the plant with fuel, in hopes of making it fully operational within a few months. As part of the deal, Russia supplied the reactor with fuel and Iran is required to send back the spent fuel to Russia.

Iran's Key Nuclear-related Sites

Semira N. Nikou

Bushehr Nuclear Facility

The Bushehr facility contains Iran's first nuclear power plant. Its light-water reactor was loaded with nuclear fuel in August 2010. It has an operating capacity of 1,000 megawatts. Bushehr was originally launched in 1976 under contract with a Germany company, but after the 1979 revolution, Washington opposed it on the grounds that weapons grade plutonium could be extracted from the reactor's waste, allowing Iran to construct nuclear weapons. Iran says the plant is for power-generation purposes only and will be subject to International Atomic Energy Agency safeguards.

The theocracy halted construction of the Bushehr reactor after the 1979 revolution, and it was badly damaged during the 1980-1988 Iran-Iraq War. But Tehran decided to revive the project in 1990 to provide energy. The contract was awarded to Russia's Rosatom Corp. To address international concerns, Moscow agreed to supply the enriched uranium fuel for the power plant and take back its plutonium-bearing spent fuel. In February 2005, Tehran and Moscow signed an agreement designed to ensure Iran could not divert enriched uranium for a weapons program.

Natanz Fuel Enrichment Facility

This fuel enrichment facility is at the heart of Iran's dispute with the United Nations. The National Council of Resistance of Iran, an exiled opposition group, revealed the existence of the facility in 2002. It is located just outside the city of Natanz, approximately 130 miles south of Tehran.

The site consists of two facilities:

- An above-ground pilot fuel enrichment plant (PFEP)

- A larger, underground fuel enrichment plant with the capacity to hold up to 50,000 centrifuges (FEP).

Activities at Natanz were suspended in 2004 following an agreement negotiated by Britain, France and Germany. But Iran restarted its uranium enrichment at the FEP after President Mahmoud Ahmadinejad's election in 2005. By mid-2010, Iran had 3,936 P-1 centrifuges producing low enriched uranium up to 3.5 percent, and a total of 8,428 P-1 centrifuges installed. The PFEP is currently used for centrifuge research and development as well as re-feeding of LEU to produce 20 percent enriched uranium for the Tehran Research Reactor.

The international community is concerned that Iran may use the enrichment technology at Natanz for nuclear weapons. These activities were proscribed by U.N. Security Council Resolution 1696 in 2006. Iran rejects the legality of these resolutions.

Isfahan Uranium Conversion Facility

The historic city of Isfahan is home to several nuclear-related sites, but the most significant facility is the Isfahan Uranium Conversion Plant. Isfahan also has a fuel fabrication laboratory, a uranium chemistry laboratory and a zirconium production plant. The conversion plant has been operational since 2006, and converts uranium yellowcake into uranium hexafluoride (UF6) for Iran's uranium enrichment facilities. The facility can also produce uranium metal and oxides for fuel and other purposes.

Tehran Nuclear Research Center

The Tehran Nuclear Research Center is a complex of several laboratories, including the Tehran Research Reactor (TRR). The TRR produces radioisotopes for medical and research purposes. The United States supplied Iran with the 5-megawatt light-water reactor in 1967; it was fueled with highly enriched uranium (around 90 percent). In 1987, Argentina concluded a deal with Iran to change the core of the reactor so it could operate on low-enriched uranium (20 percent).

Arak Heavy–Water Plant and Reactor

The Arak nuclear facility includes a heavy water production plant, which has been operational since 2006, and a 40-megawatt heavy-water reactor still under construction. The National Council of Resistance of Iran, an exiled opposition group, also revealed the existence of this facility in 2002.

Heavy water production plants are not subject to traditional safeguards of the Nuclear Non-Proliferation Treaty, to which Iran is a signatory. Under the International Atomic Energy Agency's Additional Protocol, Tehran would be subject to declarations and complementary access for IAEA inspectors. Since Iran has signed but not yet ratified the Additional Protocol, the IAEA uses satellite imagery to monitor the facility. Iran's heavy-water-related activities are also proscribed by U.N. Resolution 1696, which Iran rejects.

Qom Uranium Enrichment Facility

This secret uranium enrichment facility was made public in 2009 after the United States shared intelligence about it with allies, and Iran confirmed its existence. Construction of the uranium enrichment plant near the holy city of Qom began around 2006, but Tehran maintained that it was not required to report its existence under the safeguard obligations until six months before it became operational. The plant has a few installed centrifuges, but Iran stopped all work once the site was publicized. The facility is located on a mountain on what was reportedly a former Iranian Revolutionary Guards' missile site.

The facility's revelation prompted concern that Iran intended to construct a potential breakout facility where it could make weapon-grade uranium for a nuclear bomb. Iran told the IAEA that the plant was intended to enrich uranium only to 5 percent, which is not enough for a nuclear weapon. The plant is believed to have room for 3,000 centrifuges for uranium enrichment.

In August 2010, Iran announced plans for the construction of 10 more uranium enrichment plants, with construction of the first site scheduled to start in March 2011.

Gchine Mine and Mill

The Gchine mine is located in southern Iran in Bandar Abbas. The associated mill is located at the same site. According to the IAEA, it began production in 2004 and has an estimated production capacity of 21 tons of uranium per year. The IAEA has questioned the mine's ownership and relationship to Iran's military.

With the assistance of John E. Pike of GlobalSecurity.org.

Timeline of U.S. Sanctions*

Jason Starr

Since 2005, the United States has designated Iranian individuals, companies and organizations for involvement in nuclear proliferation, ballistic missile development or support for terrorist groups. These designations have been made under two presidential executive orders:

- Executive Order 13224 was issued on Sept. 23, 2001. It applies to individuals or entities accused of supporting terrorism.
- Executive Order 13382 was issued on June 28, 2005. It applies to individuals or entities accused of supporting Iran's nuclear proliferation and missile-related activities.

June 28, 2005 (Executive Order 13382)

Military for involvement in Iran's ballistic missile development
- Aerospace Industries Organization (AIO)
- Shahid Hemmat Industrial Group
- Shahid Bakeri Industrial Group

Nuclear for operating Iran's nuclear facilities
- Atomic Energy Organization of Iran (AEOI)

January 4, 2006 (Executive Order 13382)

Nuclear
- Novin Energy Company: *Transferred millions of dollars on behalf the Atomic Energy Organization of Iran (AEOI) to entities associated with Iran's nuclear program.*
- Mesbah Energy Company: *AEOI Subordinate and procurer for Iran's heavy water project.*

July 18, 2006 (Executive Order 13382)

Construction, Engineering, and Technology
- Sanam Industrial Group: *Subordinate of Aerospace Industries Organization (AIO). Purchased millions of dollars worth of equipment from entities associated with missile proliferation.*
- Ya Mahdi Industries Group: *Subordinate of Iran's AIO. Made international purchases of missile-related technology and goods for Iran.*

January 9, 2007 (Executive Order 13382)

Banks
- Bank Sepah/Bank Sepah International Plc (UK): *State-owned bank. U.S. Treasury alleges Bank Sepah provides support to entities affiliated with Iran's nuclear program.*

Individuals
- Ahmad Derakhshandeh: *Chairman and Director of Bank Sepah.*

February 16, 2007 (Executive Order 13382)

Construction, Engineering, Industry and Technology
- Kalaye Electric Company: *Affiliated with centrifuge research and development through the Atomic Energy Organization of Iran (AEOI).*

*(As of September 1, 2010)

- Kavoshyar Company: *Wholly-owned by AEOI.*
- Pioneer Energy Industries Company: *Provides technical support services to AEOI.*

March 30, 2007 (Executive Order 13382)

Military
- Defense Industries Organization (DIO): *Controlled by Iran's Ministry of Defense Armed Forces Logistics. Involved in Iran's nuclear and missiles programs.*

June 8, 2007 (Executive Order 13382)

Construction, Engineering, Industry and Technology
- Pars Tarash (Pars Trash Co.): *Affiliated with the Atomic Energy Organization of Iran (AEOI).*
- Farayand Technique: *Affiliated with the AEOI.*
- Fajr Industries Group (Industrial Factories of Precision Machinery): *Affiliated with Aerospace Industries Organization (AIO).*
- Mizan Machine Manufacturing Group: *Affiliated with AIO.*

June 15, 2007 (Executive Order 13382)

Individuals
- Ali Hajinia Leilabadi: *Agent of Mesbah Energy Company. Involved in Iran's heavy water development.*
- Mohammad Qannadi: *Agent of the Atomic Energy Organization of Iran.*

October 25, 2007

Banks
- Bank Melli Iran (Executive Order 13382): *Iran's largest bank. Provides services to entities involved in nuclear and ballistic missile programs, Revolutionary Guards (IRGC) and Qods Force.*
- Bank Mellat (Executive Order 13382): *provides banking services to the Atomic Energy Organization of Iran (AEOI) and Novin Energy Company.*
- Bank Saderat Iran (Executive Order 13224): *Has approximately 3,200 branch offices. U.S. Treasury alleges Iranian Government uses the bank to channel funds to terrorist organizations.*

Petroleum and Petrochemicals (Executive Order 13382)
- Oriental Oil Kish: *Owned or controlled by the IRGC.*

Construction, Engineering, Industry and Technology (Executive Order 13382)
- Khatam al-Anbya Construction Headquarters: *Engineering arm of IRGC. Involved in construction of streets, highways, tunnels, water conveyance projects, agricultural restoration projects, and pipelines.*
- Ghorb Nooh: *Owned or controlled by the IRGC or its leaders. Affiliate of Khatam al-Anbya.*
- Sahel Consultant Engineering: *Owned or controlled by IRGC.*
- Ghorb-e Karbala: *Owned or controlled by IRGC.*
- Sepasad Engineering Co.: *Owned or controlled by IRGC. Specializes in earth and concrete dam construction, road construction, and tunneling.*
- Omran Sahel: *Owned or controlled by IRGC.*
- Hara Company: *Owned or controlled by IRGC. Reportedly building a tunnel facility in northeast Tehran for use in nuclear weapons research and development.*
- Gharargahe Sazandegi Ghaem: *Owned or controlled by IRGC.*

Military (Executive Order 13382)
- Islamic Revolutionary Guard Corps (IRGC): *Elite branch of Iran's military. Involved in nuclear and ballistic missiles programs.*
- Ministry of Defense and Armed Forces Logistics (MODAFL): *Iran's ministry of defense. It has ultimate authority over Aerospace Industries Organization (AIO). AIO was designated on June 28, 2005.*
- IRGC-Qods Force (Executive Order 13224): *Branch of IRGC. The United States alleges that Qods Force provides material support to terrorist organizations.*

Individuals (Executive Order 13382)
- Ahmad Vahid Dastjerdi, *Head of Aerospace Industries Organization (AIO)*.
- Bahmanyar Morteza Bahmanyar, *Head of Finance & Budget Department, AIO*
- Reza-Gholi Esmaeli, *Head of Trade and International Affairs Dept., AIO*
- General Hosein Salimi, *Commander of the Air Force, IRGC*
- Brigadier General Morteza Rezaie, *Deputy Commander of the IRGC*
- Vice Admiral Ali Akhbar Ahmadian, *then Chief of IRGC Joint Staff*
- Brigadier Gen. Mohammad Hejazi, *then Commander of Basij resistance force, IRGC*
- Brigadier General Qasem Soleimani, *Commander of the Qods Force, IRGC*

March 12, 2008 (Executive Order 13382)

Banks
- Future Bank, B.S.C.: *Investment bank operating in Iran and Persian Gulf States. Joint venture of Bank Saderat Iran, Bank Melli Iran, and Ahli United Bank (Bahrain) with branches and in Bahrain and a representative office in Tehran.*

July 8, 2008 (Executive Order 13382)

Construction, Engineering, Industry and Technology
- Parchin Chemical Industries: *Imports and exports chemical goods throughout the world as a subsidiary of Iran's Defense Industries Organization (DIO). DIO was designated on March 30, 2007.*
- 7th of Tir: *DIO subsidiary involved in Iran's nuclear centrifuge development program.*
- Ammunition and Metallurgy Industries Group: *DIO subsidiary and parent of 7th of Tir.*
- Shahid Sattari Industries: *Manufacturing and maintains ground support equipment for Shahid Bakeri Industries Group (SBIG). SBIG was designated on June 28, 2005 for its role in Iran's missile program.*
- TAMAS Company.

Individuals
- Dawood Agha-Jani: *Affiliated with the Atomic Energy Organization of Iran (AEOI). Head of Pilot Fuel Enrichment Plant at Natanz, Iran's main uranium enrichment facility.*
- Mohsen Fakhrizadeh-Mahabadi: *Director of nuclear program at Iran's Center for Readiness and New Defense Technology and former head of Iran's Physics Research Center.*
- Moshen Hojati: *Affiliated with Aerospace Industries Organization (AIO), the overall manager of Iran's missile program.*
- Mehrdada Akhlaghi Ketabachi: *Head of SBIG.*
- Naser Maleki: *Oversees work on the Shahab-3 ballistic missile program. Head of Shahid Hemmat Industrial Group (SHIG). SHIG was designated on June 28, 2005 for its role in Iran's ballistic missile program.*
- General Yahya Rahim-Safavi: *Armed forces advisor to Ayatollah Khamenei and former IRGC commander.*

August 12, 2008 (Executive Order 13382)

Nuclear
- Esfahan Nuclear Fuel Research and Production Center: *Uranium fuel conversion facility for the Atomic Energy Organization of Iran (AEOI).*
- Jabber Ibn Hayan: *Performs nuclear research, development, and laboratory services on the nuclear fuel cycle for the AEOI.*
- Nuclear Research Center for Agriculture and Medicine: *Research component of AEOI.*
- Joza Industrial Company: *Procurement front company for Shahid Hemmat Industrial Group (SHIG). SHIG was designated on June 28, 2005.*
- Safety Equipment Procurement Company (SEP Co.): *Procurement front company for Aerospace Industries Organization (AIO).*

September 10, 2008 (Executive Order 13382)

Shipping
- Islamic Republic of Iran Shipping Lines (IRISL): *State-owned shipping company. Transports sanctioned missile-related and proliferation-related military cargo for Iran's government.*

- Asia Marine Network PTE (IRISL Asia PTE) Ltd./CISCO Shipping Co. Ltd. (IRISL Korea Co. Ltd.)/ Iran o Hind Shipping Company/ Iran o Misr Shipping Company/Irinivestship, Ltd./IRISL Benelux NV/IRISL China Shipping Co., Ltd./IRISL Europe GMbH/IRISL (Malta) Limited/IRISL Marine Services & Engineering Company/IRISL Multimodal Transport Co./IRISL (UK) Ltd./IRITAL Shipping SRL Company/ Khazar Sea Shipping Lines/South Shipping Line Iran/ Shipping Computer Services Company/ Valfajr 8th Shipping Line Co. SSK: *Foreign and domestic subsidiaries of IRISL.*
- Oasis Freight Agencies: *Joint venture between IRISL and Sharaf Shipping Company (UAE).*

September 17, 2008 (Executive Order 13382)

Construction, Engineering, Industry and Technology

- Armament Industries Group: *Manufactures weapons and weapons systems. Subsidiary of Iran's Defense Industries Organization (DIO).*
- Iran Aircraft Manufacturing Industrial Company (HESA): *Aircraft manufacturing and assembly company. Provides support to IRGC. Owned or controlled by Iran's Ministry of Defense and Armed Forces Logistics (MODAFL). MODAFL was designated on October 25, 2007.*
- Farasakht Industries: *HESA subsidiary. Manufactures aerospace tools and designed aeronautical equipment.*
- Iran Electronics Industries (IEI): *Wholly-owned subsidiary of MODAFL. Largest manufacturer of electronic and communication equipment in Iran. Manufactures components for Iranian weapons systems.*
- Iran Communications Industries: *IEI subsidiary. Procurement company owned or controlled by MODAFL.*
- Shiraz Electronics Industries: *IEI subsidiary. Produces radars, electronic equipment for military.*

October 22, 2008 (Executive Order 13382)

Banks

- Export Development Bank of Iran (EDBI): *Provides financial services to Iran's Ministry of Defense and Armed Forces Logistics (MODAFL).*
- Banco Internacional de Desarrollo, C.A.: *Venezuela-based bank owned or controlled by EDBI.*
- EDBI Exchange Company/EDBI Stock Brokerage Company: *Owned or controlled by EDBI.*

December 17, 2008 (Executive Order 13382)

Banks

- ASSA Co. Ltd./ASSA Corporation: *Controlled by Bank Melli. Established as shell companies for Bank Melli to disguise the bank's 40 percent ownership interest in the 650 Fifth Avenue Company in New York City. ASSA Corp. the subsidiary of ASSA Co. Ltd.*

March 3, 2009 (Executive Order 13382)

Banks

- Bank Melli Iran Investment Company/BMIIC International General Trading Co.: *Owned or controlled by Bank Melli, designated October 25, 2007 for providing services to entities linked to Iran's nuclear program.*
- Bank Melli Printing and Publishing Co.: *Owned or controlled by Bank Melli. Responsible for printing for domestic branches of Bank Melli.*
- First Persian Equity Fund: *Owned or controlled by Melli Investment Holding International (MEHR) and Bank Melli Iran Investment Company (BMIIC).*
- MEHR Cayman Ltd.: *Cayman Islands-based. Owned or controlled by MEHR and BMIIC.*
- Melli Investment Holding International: *Dubai-based. Wholly-owned by BMIIC.*

Construction, Engineering, Industry and Technology (Executive Order 13382)

- Cement Investment and Development Co. (CIDCO): *Owned or controlled by BMIIC. Founded to manage BMIIC's holdings in cement industry in 2004.*
- Mazandaran Cement Company: *Owned or controlled by CIDCO.*
- Mazandaran Textile Company: *Owned or controlled by BMIIC.*
- Melli Agrochemical Company PJS: *Pesticide company established in 1986. Owned or controlled by BMIIC.*
- Shomal Cement Company: *Owned or controlled by CIDCO.*

April 7, 2009 (Executive Order 13382)

Construction, Engineering, Industry and Technology

- Amin Industrial Complex: *Owned or controlled by Defense Industries Organization (DIO). DIO was designated on March 30, 2007.*
- Kaveh Cutting Tools Company: *Owned or controlled by DIO. Produces centrifuge components for Iran's nuclear centrifuge program.*
- Khorasan Metallurgy Industries: *Owned or controlled by DIO. Subsidiary of Ammunition Industries Group. Produces centrifuge components.*
- Niru Battery Manufacturing Company: *DIO subsidiary. Manufactures power units for Iranian missile systems.*
- Shahid Sayyade Shirazi Industries: *Produces large caliber items and cartridge cases. Produces components for improvised explosive devices (IEDs).*
- Yazd Metallurgy Industries: *Ammunition Industries Group (AMIG) subsidiary owned or controlled by DIO.*

November 5, 2009 (Executive Order 13382)

Banks

- First East Export Bank, P.L.C.: *Malaysian subsidiary of Bank Mellat. Bank Mellat was designated on October 25, 2007 for providing financial services for Iran's nuclear program.*

Individuals

- Ali Divandari: *Chairman of Bank Mellat.*

February 10, 2010 (Executive Order 13382)

Construction, Engineering, Industry and Technology

- Fater Engineering Institute: *Subsidiary of Khatam al-Anbya Construction Headquarters, the engineering arm of the IRGC.*
- Imensazen Consultant Engineers Institute: *Subsidiary of Khatam al-Anbya. Supports IRGC mining and engineering projects.*
- Makin Institute: *Subsidiary of Khatam al-Anbya. Supports IRGC mining and engineering projects.*
- Rahab Institute: *Subsidiary of Khatam al-Anbya. Supports IRGC mining and engineering projects.*

Individuals

- General Rostam Qasemi: *IRGC General. Commander of Khatam al-Anbya Construction Headquarters.*

June 16, 2010 (Executive Order 13382)

Shipping

- Hafiz Darya Shipping Co.: *Islamic Republic of Iran Shipping Lines (IRISL) front company. Used for IRISL containerized shipping operations beginning in 2009.*
- Safiran Payan Darya Shipping: *IRISL front company. Used for IRISL bulk and cargo operations beginning in April 2009.*
- Soroush Sarzamin Asatir Ship Management Co.: *IRISL front company. Performs ship management for IRISL.*
- Seibow Limited/Seibow Logistics Limited: *Hong Kong-based IRISL front companies.*

Military

- IRGC Air Force: *In charge of deployment and operations of Iran's ballistic missile program.*
- IRGC Missile Command: *In charge of deployment and operations of Iran's ballistic missile program.*
- Naval Defense Missile Industry Group: *Owned or controlled by AIO.*

Individuals

- Mohammad Ali Jafari: *Commander-in-Chief, IRGC since September 2007.*
- Javedan Mehr Toos: *Procurement broker for Kalaye Electric Co. Kalaye was designated on February 16, 2007 for its affiliation with Iran's nuclear program.*
- Mohammad Reza Naqdi: *Head of IRGC Basij Resistance Force since October 2009.*
- Javad Karimi Sabet: *Affiliated with the AEOI as head of Novin Energy Company.*
- Ahmad Vahidi: *Iran's Minister of Defense and Armed Forces Logistics since September 2009.*

Banks
- Post Bank: *Provides financial services to Bank Sepah and acts on its behalf. Bank Sepah was designated on January 9, 2007 for providing services to Iran's nuclear program.*

Construction, Engineering, Industry and Technology
- Rah Sahel Institute: *Owned or controlled by Khatam al-Anbya. Khatam al-Anbya was designated on October 25, 2007 for its affiliation with the IRGC. Rah Sahel has served as a contractor for Iran's natural gas plant project in Tombak.*
- Sepanir Oil and Gas Engineering Co.: *Owned or controlled by Khatam al-Anbya. Sepanir is a major contractor for Iran's petroleum industry.*

August 3, 2010 (Executive Order 13224)

Organizations Supporting Terrorist Organizations
- Iranian Committee for the Reconstruction of Lebanon: *Channels Iranian material and financial support for Hezbollah.*
- Imam Khomeini Relief Committee (IKRC) Lebanon Branch: *Helped fund Hezbollah youth training camps to recruit future Hezbollah members and operatives. Hezbollah leaders acknowledge IKRC is funded by Iran.*

Individuals
- Hushang Allahdad: *IRGC-Qods Force financial officer. Oversees distribution of funds to Hezbollah, Hamas and Palestinian Islamic Jihad.*
- Hossein Musavi: *Qods Force General and Commander of Ansar Corps. Provides financial and material support to the Taliban.*
- Hasan Mortezavi: *Qods Force Colonel. Provides financial and material support to the Taliban.*
- Mohammad Reza Zahedi: *Qods Force commander in Lebanon. Acted as liaison to Hezbollah and Syrian intelligence services.*
- Hessam Khoshnevis: *Director of the Iranian Committee for the Reconstruction of Lebanon. Provides financial, material, and technological support to Hezbollah.*
- Ali Zuraik: *Director of the Imam Khomeini Relief Committee Lebanon branch. Provides financial and material support to Hezbollah.*
- Razi Musavi: *Syria-based Iranian official. Provides financial and material support to Hezbollah.*

U.S. Sanctions for Human Rights Abuses

Robin Wright

On Sept. 29, 2010, the United States imposed the first sanctions on Iran for human rights violations. President Obama signed an executive order that allowed financial and travel restrictions on senior government officials for "sustained and severe violation of human rights" during or after Iran's 2009 presidential election. The abuses included arrest, killing, torture, beating, blackmail and rape. The United States cited eight security and judicial officials but noted it would continue to add names as "credible evidence" became available.

The executive order introduced a new tool for the United States to address human rights issues in the Islamic Republic. The sanctions:

- Bar the eight officials from travel to the United States.
- Block any assets that might be in the United States or in U.S. institutions.
- Prohibit Americans from doing business with them.

The White House statement said, "The United States will always stand with those in Iran who aspire to have their voices heard. We will be a voice for those aspirations that are universal, and we continue to call upon the Iranian government to respect the rights of its people."

A U.S. fact sheet charged that the officials played a variety of roles:

Mohammad Ali Jafari, commander of the Islamic Revolutionary Guard Corps. "As commander of the IRGC, Jafari controlled the Basij Forces during the June 2009 election. Forces under his command participated in beatings, murder, and arbitrary arrests and detentions of peaceful protestors."

Sadeq Mahsouli, currently the minister of welfare and social security and former minister of the interior during the 2009 election. "Mahsouli had authority over all police forces and interior ministry security agents. His forces were responsible for attacks on the dormitories of Tehran University on June 15, 2009, during which students were severely beaten and detained. Detained students were tortured and ill-treated in the basement of the Interior Ministry building; other protestors were severely abused at the Kahrizak Detention Center, which was operated by police under Mahsouli's control."

Qolam-Hossein Mohseni-Ejei, current prosecutor general of Iran. As minister of intelligence during the 2009 election, Mohseni-Ejei "confirmed that he authorized confrontations with protesters and their arrests … Protesters were detained without formal charges brought against them and during this detention detainees were subjected to beatings, solitary confinement, and a denial of due process rights at the hands of intelligence officers under the direction of Mohseni-Ejei. In addition, political figures were coerced into making false confessions under unbearable interrogations, which included torture, abuse, blackmail, and the threatening of family members."

Saeed Mortazavi, former Tehran prosecutor general. "He issued a blanket order used for the detention of hundreds of activists, journalists, and students, and was responsible for sending detainees to the Kahrizak Detention Center, where they were tortured and abused, resulting in several deaths." He was suspended from office in August 2010 after an judicial investigation into role in the death of three detainees.

Heydar Moslehi, the minister of intelligence since August 2009. "Under his leadership, the Ministry of Intelligence has continued the practices of widespread arbitrary detention and persecution of protestors and dissidents. The Ministry of Intelligence continues to run Ward 209 of Evin Prison, where many activists are being held for their peaceful activities in opposition to the ruling government; interrogators from the Ministry of Intelligence have subjected prisoners in Ward 209 to beatings, mental abuse, and sexual abuse. In recent months, prisoners in Ward 209 have reported forced confessions and interference by the Ministry of Intelligence in the judicial process; one detainee from the ward was executed after a forced confession and another was executed when torture failed to yield a confession. As the Minister of Intelligence, Moslehi bears responsibility for the ongoing abuses."

Mostafa Mohammad Najjar, appointed deputy commander of Armed Forces in charge of police forces in November 2009. "He was in charge of the government response to protests on Ashoura, one of the holiest days in Shia Islam, which in 2009 coincided with December 27, 2009. State media reported 37 dead and hundreds arrested. He is currently the minister of interior and, as such, has authority over all police forces, Interior Ministry security agents, and plainsclothes agents."

Ahmad-Reza Radan, deputy chief of Iran's National Police. He "was responsible for beatings, murder, and arbitrary arrests and detentions against protestors that were committed by the police forces. In addition, several detainees taken to Kahrizak Detention Center, the detention center where at least three protestors lost their lives after being subject to abuses, have alleged that Radan was present in Kahrizak and personally participated in the beatings and ill-treatment of detainees."

Hossein Taeb, currently deputy Revolutionary Guards commander for intelligence. "As commander of the paramilitary Basij Forces during the 2009 election, forces under Taeb's command participated in beatings, extrajudicial killings, and arbitrary arrests and detentions of peaceful protestors and other political activists."

Timeline of U.N. Resolutions

Jason Starr

Security Council Resolution 1737, Vote: 15–0 (December 23, 2006)

Ballistic Missiles: Requires[1] states to prevent sale or transfer to Iran of items contributing to weapon delivery systems. Imposes asset freeze on eight individuals and companies for involvement in ballistic missile programs (see "Sanctioned" below).

Nuclear: Requires states to prevent sale or transfer of items to Iran contributing to nuclear proliferation. Calls on states to prevent nuclear proliferation-related training to Iranian nationals. Imposes asset freezes on 15 individuals and companies for involvement in Iran's nuclear programs (see "Sanctioned" below).

Travel: Calls on states to exercise vigilance regarding entry to their territories of individuals affiliated with Iran's nuclear program.

Sanctioned: Companies and individuals involved in ballistic missile programs (*Shahid Hemmat Industrial Group, Shahid Bagheri Industrial Group, Fajr Industrial Group, Gen. Hosein Salimi, Ahmad Vahid Dastjerdi, Reza-Gholi Esmaeli, Bahmanyar Morteza Bahhmanyar, Maj. Gen. Yahya Rahim Safavi*); companies and individuals involved in nuclear program (*Atomic Energy Organization of Iran, Mesbah Energy Company, Kala-Electric, Pars Trash Company, Farayand Technique, Defence Industries Organization, 7th of Tir, Mohammad Qannadi, Behman Asgarpour, Dawood Agha-Jani, Ehsan Monajemi, Jafar Mohammadi, Ali Hajinia Leilabadi, Lt. Gen.Mahammad Mehdi Nejad Nouri, Maj. Gen. Yahya Rahim Safavi*)

Security Council Resolution 1747, Vote: 15–0 (March 24, 2007)

Arms: Requires that states prohibit the procurement of arms and related material from Iran. Calls on states to restrict supply of specified arms and combat equipment to Iran.

Ballistic Missiles: Imposes asset freeze on individuals, companies, and banks involved in ballistic missile activities (see "Sanctioned," below). Calls on states to restrict such individuals from entry into their territories.

Nuclear: Imposes asset freeze on individuals, companies, and banks involved in Iran's nuclear activities (see "Sanctioned," below). Calls on states to restrict such individuals from entry into their territories.

Banking and Finance: Imposes asset freeze on three companies and seven individuals affiliated with the IRGC. Calls on states to restrict travel of aforementioned individuals.

IRGC/Military: Imposes asset freeze on three companies and seven individuals affiliated with the IRGC. Calls on states to restrict travel of aforementioned individuals.

Travel: Requires states to notify the Security Council Committee of entry into or transit through their territory of any person named in Resolutions 1737 or 1747 for involvement in Iran's nuclear or ballistic missile programs, or affiliated with the IRGC.

Sanctioned: Individuals and companies involved in nuclear or ballistic missile programs (*Ammunition and Metallurgy Industries Group, Esfahan Nuclear Fuel Research and Production Centre, Kavoshyar Company, Parchin Chemical Industries, Karaj Nuclear Research Centre, Novin Energy Company, Cruise Missile Industry Group, Bank Sepah and Bank Sepah International, Sanam Industrial Group, Ya Mahdi Industries Group, Fereidoun Abbasi-Danavi, Mohsen Fakhrizadeh-Mahabadi, Seyed Jaber Safdari, Amir Rahimi, Mohsen Hojati, Mehrdada Akhlaghi Ketabachi, Naser Maleki, Ahmad Derakhshandeh*); individuals and companies affiliated with the IRGC (*Qods Aeronautics Industries, Pars Aviation Services Company, Sho'a' Aviation, Brig. Gen. Morteza Rezaie, Vice Adm. Ali Akbar Ahmadian, Brig. Gen. Mohammad Reza Zahedi, Rear Adm. Morteza Safari, Brig. Gen. Mohammad Hejazi, Brig. Gen. Qasem Soleimani, Gen. Zolqadr*)

---

1. "Requires" indicates an obligatory action. "Calls on" indicates a recommended but voluntary action.

Security Council Resolution 1803, Vote: 14-0-1 (March 3, 2008)

Ballistic Missiles: Imposes asset freeze on individuals and companies involved in Iran's ballistic missile programs (see "Sanctioned" below). Calls on states to restrict travel of aforementioned individuals. Extends list of nuclear proliferation-related items banned from Iran.

Nuclear: Imposes asset freeze on individuals and companies involved in Iran's nuclear programs (see "Sanctioned" below). Calls on states to restrict travel of aforementioned individuals. Imposes mandatory travel ban on five individuals involved in nuclear programs, named in Resolutions 1737 and 1747. Extends list of nuclear proliferation-related items barred from Iran.

Banking and Finance: Calls on states to exercise vigilance in entering new public financial support commitments with Iran. Calls on states to exercise vigilance over Iranian bank transactions in their territories.

Sanctioned: Individuals and companies affiliated with nuclear and/or ballistic missile programs (*Amir Moayyed Alai, Mohammad Fedai Ashiani, Abbas Rezaee Ashtiani, Haleh Bakhtiar, Morteza Behzad, Dr. Mohammad Eslami, Seyyed Hussein Hosseini, M. Javad Karimi Sabet, Hamid-Reza Mohajerani, Brig.-Gen. Mohammad Reza Naqdi, Houshang Nobari, Abbas Rashidi, Ghasem Soleymani, Abzar Boresh Kaveh Co., Barzahani Tejarat Tavanmad Saccal companies, Electro Sanam Company, Ettehad Technical Group, Industrial Factories of Precision, Jabber Ibn Hayan, Joza Industrial Co., Khorasan Metallurgy Industries, Niru Battery Manufacturing Company, Pishgam (Pioneer) Energy Industries, Safety Equipment Procurement, TAMAS Company*)

Security Council Resolution 1929, Vote: 12-2-1(June 9, 2010)

Arms: Requires states to prevent supply of specified arms and combat equipment to Iran.

Ballistic Missiles: Prohibits Iran from developing ballistic missile capabilities. Requires states to prevent sale or transfer of missile systems. Imposes asset freeze and travel ban on persons, companies, and banks for involvement in ballistic missile programs (see "Sanctioned" below).

Nuclear: Prohibits Iran from acquiring interest in commercial activity in other states involving uranium mining, production or use of nuclear materials and weapons-related technologies. Imposes asset freeze and travel ban on persons, companies and banks for involvement in nuclear program (see "Sanctioned" below).

IRGC/Military: Imposes asset freeze on IRGC and 15 affiliated companies and organizations.

Sanctioned: Individuals and companies involved in nuclear or ballistic missile activities (*Amin Industrial Complex, Armament Industries Group, Defense Technology and Science Research Center, Doostan International Company, Farasakht Industries, First East Export Bank, P.L.C., Kaveh Cutting Tools Co., M. Babaie Industries, Malek Ashtar University, Ministry of Defense Logistics Export, Mizan Machinery Manufacturing, Modern Industries Technique Co., Nuclear Research Center for Agriculture and Medicine, Pejman Industrieal Services Corp., Sabalan Co., Sahand Aluminum Parts Industrial Co., Shahid Karrazi Industries, Special Industries Group, Tiz Pars, Yazd Metallurgy Industries, Javad Rahiqi*); IRGC entities (*Fater Institute, Gharagahe Sazandegi Ghaem, Ghorb Karbala, Ghorb Nooh, Hara Co., Imensazan Consultant Engineers Institute, Khatam al-Anbiya Construction Headquarters, Makin, Omran Sahel, Oriental Oil Kish, Rah Sahel, Rahab Engineering Institute, Sahel Consultant Engineers, Sepanir, Sepasad Engineering Co.*); IRISL front companies (*Irano Hind Shipping Co., IRISL Benelux NV, South Shipping Line Iran*)

Oil Price and Production Charts

Fareed Mohamedi

WTI Price

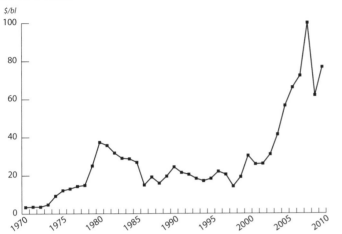

Key for labels:

WTI = West Texas Intermediate, also known as Texas light sweet, is a type of crude oil used as a benchmark in oil pricing.

Mb/d = million barrels per day

Mcf/d = million cubic feet per day

Iranian Crude Production

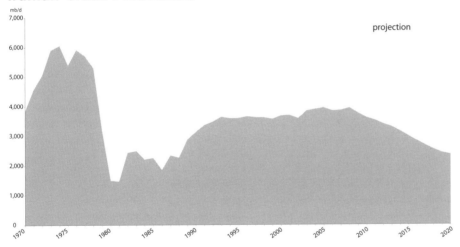

Iranian Natural Gas Production

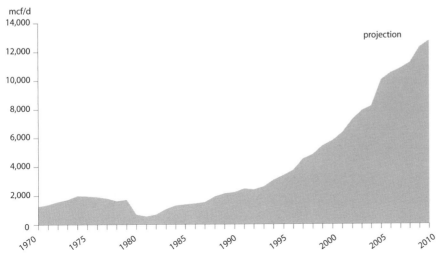

Production

Year	WTI ($/bl)	Crude (mb/d)	Natural Gas (mcf/d)
1970	3.39	3,848	1,246
1971	3.6	4,572	1,381
1972	3.6	5,059	1,577
1973	4.75	5,907	1,721
1974	9.35	6,060	1,999
1975	12.21	5,387	1,962
1976	13.1	5,918	1,929
1977	14.4	5,714	1,824
1978	14.95	5,302	1,640
1979	25.1	3,218	1,733
1980	37.42	1,505	689
1981	35.75	1,472	576
1982	31.83	2,446	697
1983	29.08	2,497	1,064
1984	28.75	2,215	1,303
1985	26.92	2,264	1,413
1986	15.05	1,854	1,471
1987	19.2	2,348	1,548
1988	15.97	2,271	1,930
1989	19.64	2,881	2,148
1990	24.45	3,140	2,240
1991	21.55	3,371	2,491
1992	20.56	3,487	2,412
1993	18.43	3,650	2,619
1994	17.2	3,604	3,077
1995	18.42	3,608	3,415
1996	22.13	3,666	3,763
1997	20.58	3,632	4,547
1998	14.38	3,625	4,838
1999	19.3	3,577	5,453
2000	30.37	3,686	5,812

Year	WTI ($/bl)	Crude (mb/d)	Natural Gas (mcf/d)
2001	25.96	3,703	6,386
2002	26.17	3,594	7,256
2003	31.06	3,854	7,885
2004	41.51	3,906	8,192
2005	56.59	3,948	10,014
2006	66.09	3,853	10,507
2007	72.23	3,863	10,827
2008	99.92	3,949	11,222
2009	61.99	3,770	12,289
2010	76.75	3,619	12,741
2011		3,531	13,473
2012		3,404	13,632
2013		3,307	13,924
2014		3,157	14,097
2015		2,993	14,528
2016		2,831	14,984
2017		2,682	15,447
2018		2,545	15,885
2019		2,431	16,308
2020		2,368	16,667
2021			16,984
2022			17,273
2023			17,585
2024			17,849
2025			18,123
2026			18,389
2027			18,631
2028			18,899
2029			19,185
2030			18,900

Websites for Additional Information

Semira N. Nikou

Official news sites

- Supreme Leader Ayatollah Ali Khamenei's website: http://english.khamenei.ir
- Office of the president's website: http://president.ir/en
- Permanent Mission of the Islamic Republic of Iran to the United Nations: http://www.iran-un.org
- Iranian Parliament's website: http://www.sepahnews.com
- Islamic Republic News Agency (IRNA): http://www.irna.ir/En
  - *State-run online news agency.*
- PressTV: http://www.presstv.ir
  - *State-run television network broadcast in English. Based in Tehran with several foreign bureaus, including Washington D.C.*
- *Tehran Times*: http://www.tehrantimes.com
  - *Government-run English daily.*

Iranian news

- Fars News Agency: http://english.farsnews.com
  - *Semi-official news agency.*
- Iranian Labor News Agency (ILNA): http://www.ilna.ir/indexen.aspx
  - *Reformist inclined news agency operated by the Worker's House, a labor union set up by the government.*
- Iranian Students News Agency (ISNA): http://isna.ir/Isna/Default.aspx?Lang=E
  - *Moderate media organization run by Tehran University students.*
- Khabar Online: http://www.khabaronline.ir/service/english
  - *Pro-Ali Larijani daily, published by the Khabar Publishing Group.*
- Mehr News Agency: http://mehrnews.com/en
  - *Private news agency. Affiliated with the* Tehran Times.

Non-governmental websites run outside Iran

- Inside Iran: http://www.insideiran.org
  - *Iran-focused project of the Century Foundation.*
- International Campaign for Human Rights in Iran: http://www.iranhumanrights.org
- Iran Labor Report: http://iranlaborreport.com
  - *Labor-focused news site.*
- Iran Times: http://www.iran-times.com
  - *Independent weekly established in Washington D.C.*
- Mianeh: http://mianeh.net
  - *Iran news site affiliated with the Institute for War and Peace Reporting.*
- Mir Hossein Mousavi Facebook page: http://www.facebook.com/mousavi

- Persian Letters: http://www.rferl.org/archive/Persian_Letters/latest/2098/2098.html
  - *Iran blog run by Radio Free Europe/ Radio Liberty.*
- Radio Zamaneh: http://www.radiozamaneh.com/enzam
  - *Non-profit media organization established by the Dutch government.*
- Rooz Online: http://www.roozonline.com/english.html
  - *Independent agency advocating human rights in Iran.*
- Tehran Bureau: http://www.pbs.org/wgbh/pages/frontline/tehranbureau
  - *Independent news organization in partnership with FRONTLINE, the PBS public affairs series.*
- Tehran Review: http://tehranreview.net
  - *Daily online magazine.*

News Aggregators

- Iran News Digest: http://www.irannewsdigest.com
- Persia house: http://persia-house.com

Select Persian language websites

- BBC Persian: http://www.bbc.co.uk/persian
  - *The BBC's Persian language news site.*
- JARAS: http://www.rahesabz.net (Persian)
  - *Green Movement site operated from outside Iran.*
- Kaleme: http://www.kaleme.com (Persian)
  - *Affiliated with opposition leader Mir Hossein Mousavi.*
- Official website of Ayatollah Hashemi Rafsanjani (Persian): http://rafsanjani.ir/index.php
- Saham News: http://www.sahamnews.org
  - *Affiliated with opposition leader Mehdi Karroubi*
- Sepah News: http://www.sepahnews.com (Persian)
  - *Official website of the Revolutionary Guards.*
- Tabnak: http://www.tabnak.ir (Persian)
  - *Affiliated with former Revolutionary Guard commander Mohsen Rezaie, and one of the most popular websites in Iran.*

About the Authors

Geneive Abdo is director of the Iran Program at The Century Foundation, a Washington and New York-based think tank. Her research focuses on contemporary Iran and political Islam. She is the creator and editor of www.insideIRAN.org and was liaison officer for the U.N. Alliance of Civilizations. Among her three books is *Answering Only to God: Faith and Freedom in Twenty-First Century Iran*. She is a former USIP grantee.

Michael Adler is a public policy scholar at the Woodrow Wilson International Center for Scholars, on sabbatical from Agence France-Presse news agency. From 2002-2007, he covered the Vienna-based International Atomic Energy Agency. He also did reporting in Tehran, Geneva, Brussels, Berlin, New York, Tripoli and elsewhere on the Iran's nuclear issue. He is a former USIP grantee working on a study of diplomacy, the Iranian nuclear issue and the IAEA.

David Albright, a physicist, is president and founder of the Institute for Science and International Security in Washington. Albright cooperated with the International Atomic Energy Agency Action Team to investigate Iraq's covert nuclear program from 1992 until 1997, and was the first non-governmental inspector of the Iraqi nuclear program in 1996. The author of many assessments on secret nuclear weapons programs world-wide, he is a former USIP grantee.

Ali Alfoneh is a resident fellow at the American Enterprise Institute (AEI). He is currently writing a book on civil-military relations in Iran. One of his most recent pieces is "The Revolutionary Guards' Looting of Iran's Economy."

Shaul Bakhash is the Clarence Robinson Professor of History at George Mason University. He is the author of "The Reign of the Ayatollahs: Iran and the Islamic Revolution" (1990). His articles on Iran have appeared in *The New York Review of Books, The New Republic, Foreign Policy, The New York Times, The Washington Post* and the *Los Angeles Times*. He is a former Woodrow Wilson Center scholar.

Henri J. Barkey is a professor of international relations at Lehigh University and a visiting scholar at the Carnegie Endowment for International Peace. He formerly served on the State Department's Policy Planning staff. His most recent publication is "Turkey's Moment of Inflection" in *Survival* (June-July 2010). He is a former Woodrow Wilson Center scholar and a former USIP grantee.

Mehrzad Boroujerdi is associate professor of political science and director of the Middle Eastern Studies Program at Syracuse University. He is the author of "Tarashidam, Parastidam, Shikastam: Guftarhay-i dar Siyasat va Huvyiyat-i Irani" (2010). As a USIP grantee, he is engaged in a study of political elite in post-revolutionary Iran and co-manages the Iran Data Portal at http://www.princeton.edu/irandataportal/.

Rachel Brandenburg was a Middle East program specialist at USIP and coordinator of the USIP Senior Working Group on Middle East Peace. She has travelled extensively in the Middle East, including to Iran. She was a Fulbright Scholar in Israel, and a State Department Critical Language Scholar in Jordan.

Daniel Brumberg is a senior adviser to the Center for Conflict Analysis and Prevention at USIP, where he also served as acting director of USIP's Muslim World Initiative. An associate professor of government at Georgetown University and co-director of its Democracy and Governance Program, he is also author of many articles and books on Islam and politics, including *Reinventing Khomeini: The Struggle for Reform in Iran* (2001).

Shahram Chubin is a Geneva-based specialist on Iranian politics and a non-resident senior associate of the Carnegie Endowment for International Peace. His latest book is, "Iran's Nuclear Ambitions" (2006). He is a former Woodrow Wilson Center scholar and received a USIP grant for a study of conflict and cooperation in the Persian Gulf.

Patrick Clawson is deputy director of research at The Washington Institute of Near Easy Policy, where he directs the Iran Security Initiative. He is the co-author of *Eternal Iran: Continuity and Chaos,* and is a former USIP grantee.

Juan Cole is professor of history at the University of Michigan and runs the Informed Comment weblog. He has authored many books on the Middle East. His latest is *Engaging the Muslim World* (2010).

Michael Connell is a member of the research staff at the Center for Naval Analyses, where he is director of the Iranian Studies Program. He has authored several studies that focus on political, military, and security issues related to Iran and the other Persian Gulf countries. He is a former intelligence officer in the U.S. Army.

Anthony H. Cordesman holds the Arleigh A. Burke Chair in Strategy at the Center for Strategic and International Studies and is a national security analyst for ABC News. He is a recipient of the Department of Defense Distinguished Service Medal. At CSIS, Cordesman is director of the Gulf Net Assessment Project, the Gulf in Transition study, and principal investigator of the Homeland Defense Project. He also directed the Middle East Net Assessment Project.

Suzanne DiMaggio is director of policy studies at the Asia Society, where she leads the Iran Initiative. From 2002-2007, she directed a U.S.-Iran track II dialogue, while she was vice president of Global Policy Programs at the United Nations Association-USA. She received a USIP grant for U.S.-Iran dialogue.

James Dobbins directs the RAND Corp.'s International Security and Defense Policy Center. He served as assistant secretary of state for Europe, special assistant to the president for the Western Hemisphere, special adviser to the president and secretary of state for the Balkans, and ambassador to the European Community. He was the Clinton administration's special envoy for Somalia, Haiti, Bosnia and Kosovo, and the Bush administration's special envoy for Afghanistan. He represented the United States at the 2001 Bonn Conference.

Michael Eisenstadt is senior fellow and director of the Military and Security Studies Program at The Washington Institute for Near East Policy. A specialist in Persian Gulf and Arab-Israeli security affairs, he is also a former Middle East Foreign Area Officer in the U.S. Army Reserve.

Michael Elleman is a senior fellow at the International Institute for Strategic Studies. He is the principal author of the IISS Strategic Dossier, "Iran's Ballistic Missile Capabilities: a net assessment." He spent 18 months at the U.N. Monitoring, Verification and Inspection Commission as a missile expert for weapons inspection missions in Iraq. Before the United Nations, he spent two decades as a scientist at Lockheed Martin's Research and Development Laboratory.

Haleh Esfandiari is director of the Middle East Program at the Woodrow Wilson International Center for Scholars. She is the author of *My Prison, My Home: One Woman's Story of Captivity in Iran* (2009), and her articles appear in essay collections, books, journals and national and international press, including blogs. A former journalist in Iran, she also taught Persian at Oxford University and Princeton University.

Farideh Farhi is affiliate graduate faculty and lecturer at the University of Hawai'i at Manoa. She writes extensively about Iranian domestic politics and nuclear policy. Her publications include, "Constitutionalism and Parliamentary Struggle for Relevance and Independence in Post-Khomeini Iran." Farhi is a Woodrow Wilson Center scholar and received a USIP grant to study evolving political discourse in Iran.

Hadi Ghaemi, a physicist, is an Iran analyst and human rights expert. He is the executive director of the International Campaign for Human Rights in Iran. He formerly worked for Human Rights Watch, where he focused on the repression of civil society in Iran and the plight of migrant workers in Dubai.

Jubin Goodarzi is a professor in the International Relations Program at Webster University Geneva, Switzerland. He is author of *Syria and Iran: Diplomatic Alliance and Power Politics in the Middle East* (2009) and numerous articles on the international relations of the Middle East. He has worked in the past for a number of U.S. and British research institutes and the United Nations.

Richard N. Haass is president of the Council on Foreign Relations. He served on the National Security Council during the George H.W. Bush administration and headed the State Department's Policy Planning staff under the George W. Bush administration. Haass is the author or editor of eleven books on American foreign policy, including *War of Necessity, War of Choice: A Memoir of Two Iraq Wars* (2009).

Stephen J. Hadley was national security adviser for the George W. Bush administration from 2005 to 2009. He previously served as assistant secretary of defense for international security policy during the George H.W. Bush administration. He was counsel to the Tower Commission in 1987, as it investigated U.S. arms sales to Iran, and served on the National Security Council under President Ford from 1974 to 1977. He is senior adviser on international affairs at USIP.

Kevan Harris is a Ph.D. candidate at Johns Hopkins University. He frequently travels to Iran and recently spent a year doing economic research in Iran. He writes a weblog called, "The Thirsty Fish."

Steven Heydemann is vice president of USIP's Grant and Fellowship Program and a specialist on the comparative politics and political economy of the Middle East. He is the author or editor of several books and numerous other publications on the Middle East, focusing on authoritarian governance, state formation and state-market relations.

Emile Hokayem is the senior fellow for regional security at the International Institute for Strategic Studies, based in Bahrain. Previously, he was the political editor of *The National,* the Abu Dhabi-based English-language newspaper. A native of Lebanon, he is a specialist in security affairs in the Levant and the Gulf.

Mark N. Katz is professor of government and politics at George Mason University and a senior fellow at the Middle East Policy Council in Washington in the fall of 2010. He has written numerous articles on Russian-Iranian relations, including "Russian-Iranian Relations in the Obama Era," *Middle East Policy* (2010). He is a former Woodrow Wilson Center scholar and received a USIP grant for a study of Islamic revolutions.

Geoffrey Kemp is director of Regional Strategic Programs at the Nixon Center. During the Reagan administration's first term, he was special assistant to the president for national security affairs, and senior director for Near East and South Asian affairs on the National Security Council Staff. His most recent book is, *The East Moves West: India, China, and Asia's Growing Presence in the Middle East* (2010). He is a former USIP grantee.

Mehdi Khalaji, a senior fellow at The Washington Institute for Near East Policy, studied Shiite theology in the Qom seminary of Iran. He is the author of *Last Marja, Sistani and the End of Traditional Religious Authority in Shiism,* and *Apocalyptic Politics: On the Rationality of Iranian Policy.* His forthcoming book is *The Political Biography of Ali Khamenei, Leader of Islamic Republic of Iran.*

Ellen Laipson is president and CEO of the Stimson Center. In her 25-year government career, she worked on Iran and other Middle East issues on the National Security Council, the National Intelligence Council, and at the Congressional Research Service. Her last position in government was vice chairman of the NIC from 1997 to 2002. She is on President Obama's Intelligence Advisory Board and is a former USIP grantee.

Matthew Levitt is director of The Washington Institute for Near East Policy's Stein Program on Counterterrorism and Intelligence and a lecturer at Johns Hopkins University's Paul H. Nitze School of Advanced International Studies. He is a former deputy assistant secretary for intelligence and analysis at the Department of the Treasury and a former counterterrorism intelligence analyst at the Federal Bureau of Investigation.

John Limbert is a former deputy assistant secretary for Iran in the State Department's Bureau of Near Eastern Affairs. He is the distinguished professor of international affairs at the U.S. Naval Academy. With funding from USIP, he is the author of *Negotiating with Iran: Wrestling the Ghosts of History* (2009). He was among the 52 Americans held hostage in Iran for 444 days.

Suzanne Maloney is a senior fellow at the Saban Center for Middle East Policy at the Brookings Institution. She is the author of *Iran's Long Reach: Iran as a Pivotal State in the Muslim World* (2008) and a forthcoming book on Iran's political economy since the revolution. She has previously worked for the U.S. government and in the private sector, and currently serves as an external advisor to the U.S. Department of State on long-range issues related to Iran.

Omid Memarian currently writes for IPS News Agency, the Daily Beast and the Huffington Post. He teaches journalism at the International Center for Journalists. He received the Human Rights Defender Award in 2005, the Human Rights Watch's highest honor. He has been published in *The New York Times, Los Angeles Times, The Wall Street Journal*, and *The San Francisco Chronicle.*

Abbas Milani is the Hamid and Christina Moghadam Director of Iranian Studies at Stanford University, where he is also a co-director of the Iran Democracy Project at Hoover Institution. His last book is *The Myth of the Great Satan* (2010). His biography of the shah is scheduled to be published in 2011.

Mohsen Milani is chairman of the Department of Government and International Affairs at the University of South Florida. He has served as a research fellow at Harvard University, Oxford University's St. Antony's College and the Foscari University in Venice, Italy. Milani authored *The Making of Iran's Islamic Revolution: From Monarchy to Islamic Republic* (1994).

Fareed Mohamedi is a partner at PFC Energy, a Washington-based consultancy specializing in the oil and gas industry. He manages PFC Energy's oil market analysis and country risk practice.

Afshin Molavi is a senior fellow at the New America Foundation. He has worked as a Dubai-based correspondent for Reuters news agency, a Riyadh-based correspondent for *The Arab News* of Saudi Arabia, and a Tehran-based correspondent for *The Washington Post.* He is the author of the *Soul of Iran: A Nation's Journey to Freedom* (2005).

Alireza Nader is an international policy analyst at the RAND Corp. His research has focused on Iran's political dynamics, elite decision making, and Iranian foreign policy. His current research focuses on the 2009 Iranian presidential election and the role of the supreme leader in Iran.

Tara Nesvaderani is a research assistant at the U.S. Institute of Peace.

Semira N. Nikou works for the Center for Conflict Analysis and Prevention at the U. S. Institute of Peace. She lived in and still travels to Iran. She was in Iran for the 2009 election and aftermath.

John S. Park is a senior research associate and director of Northeast Asia projects at USIP's Center for Conflict Analysis and Prevention. He is also co-director of the USIP Financial Sanctions Study Group.

Kenneth M. Pollack is director of the Saban Center for Middle East Policy at the Brookings Institution. He is the author of a half dozen books on the Middle East including *The Persian Puzzle: The Conflict Between Iran and America,* and *Which Path to Persia? Options for a New American Strategy Toward Iran.*

Walter Posch is a senior research fellow working on Iranian domestic, foreign and security policy at the German International and Foreign Policy Institute in Berlin. He previously worked at the European Union's Institute for Security Studies in Paris and at the National Defense Academy in Vienna. His most recent paper on the opposition movement in Iran is entitled: "A Last Chance for Iran's Reformists? The 'Green Struggle' Reconsidered."

Kourosh Rahimkhani is an independent scholar specializing in Iranian affairs. He worked as a journalist for a number of reformist newspapers in Iran before moving to the United States.

Bruce O. Riedel is a senior fellow at the Saban Center for Middle East Policy at the Brookings Institution. He served in the CIA for almost 30 years and has advised four presidents on Iran. He published "If Israel Attacks" in *The National Interest* in September 2010 about the consequences of an Israeli attack on Iran's nuclear facilities. He is also author of *In Search of al Qaeda* (2009).

Karim Sadjadpour is an associate at the Carnegie Endowment for International Peace. He spent four years as the chief Iran analyst at the International Crisis Group, based in Washington and Tehran. He is a regular contributor to BBC TV and radio, CNN, National Public Radio, PBS NewsHour as well as publications such as the *Economist, The Washington Post, The New York Times, The International Herald Tribune,* and *Foreign Policy.*

Gary Sick is adjunct professor of international affairs at Columbia University. He is executive director of Gulf/2000, an international online research project on political, economic and security developments in the Persian Gulf. He served on the National Security Council under Presidents Ford, Carter and Reagan and was the principal aide for Iran during the Iranian revolution and hostage crisis. A former captain in the U.S. Navy, he wrote two books on U.S.-Iran relations.

Steven Simon is adjunct senior fellow for Middle Eastern Studies at the Council on Foreign Relations, adjunct professor of security studies at Georgetown University, and senior advisor at Good Harbor Consulting, LLC. He is coauthor of *The Sixth Crisis: America, Israel, Iran and the Rumors of War* (2010). He served at the State Department, the National Security Council, the RAND Corp. and the International Institute for Strategic Studies.

Jason Starr is a former Research Assistant at USIP. He is currently a Presidential Management Fellow at the U.S. Department of State. Any views expressed herein are the author's own and not necessarily those of the Department of State or the U.S. government.

Andrea Stricker is a research analyst at the Institute for Science and International Security (ISIS). Stricker writes ISIS's country-specific and regional proliferation assessments and develops policy recommendations for U.S. and international nonproliferation efforts.

Robin Wright, a former *Washington Post* diplomatic correspondent, is a joint fellow at USIP and the Woodrow Wilson International Center for Scholars. She has covered Iran since 1973 and is the author of five books on Iran or the Middle East, including *Dreams and Shadows: The Future of the Middle East* (2008). She won the National Magazine Award for her coverage of Iran in *The New Yorker* and the U.N. Correspondents Gold Medal for international coverage.

Dov S. Zakheim is vice chairman of the Foreign policy Research Institute and a senior advisor at the Center for Strategic and International Studies. He was Under Secretary of Defense (Comptroller) and Chief Financial Officer (2001-2004). He has published numerous articles on Middle Eastern security issues.

United States Institute of Peace

Woodrow Wilson International Center for Scholars

The Woodrow Wilson International Center for Scholars is the national, living U.S. memorial honoring President Woodrow Wilson. In providing an essential link between the worlds of ideas and public policy, the Center addresses current and emerging challenges confronting the United States and the world. The Center promotes policy-relevant research and dialogue to increase understanding and enhance the capabilities and knowledge of leaders, citizens, and institutions worldwide. Created by an Act of Congress in 1968, the Center is a non-partisan institution headquartered in Washington, D.C. and supported by both public and private funds.

Conclusions or opinions expressed in Center publications and programs are those of the authors and speakers and do not necessarily reflect the views of the Center's staff, fellows, trustees, or advisory groups, or any individuals or organizations that provide financial support to the Center.

The Center is the publisher of *The Wilson Quarterly* and home of Woodrow Wilson Center Press and dialogue television and radio. For more information about the Center's activities and publications, including the monthly newsletter Centerpoint, please visit us on the web at www.wilsoncenter.org.

Lee H. Hamilton, President and Director